Cases on Emerging Market Responses to the COVID-19 Pandemic

Raj K. Kovid
Sharda University, India

Vikas Kumar
Central University of Haryana, India

A volume in the Advances in Business Strategy and Competitive Advantage (ABSCA) Book Series

IGI Global
PUBLISHER of TIMELY KNOWLEDGE

Published in the United States of America by
IGI Global
Business Science Reference (an imprint of IGI Global)
701 E. Chocolate Avenue
Hershey PA, USA 17033
Tel: 717-533-8845
Fax: 717-533-8661
E-mail: cust@igi-global.com
Web site: http://www.igi-global.com

Library of Congress Cataloging-in-Publication Data

Names: Kovid, Raj K., 1972- editor. | Kumar, Vikas, 1979- editor.
Title: Cases on emerging market responses to the COVID-19 pandemic / Raj K. Kovid, and Vikas Kumar, editors.
Description: Hershey, PA : Business Science Reference, 2022. | Includes bibliographical references and index. | Summary: "The present book highlights the organizational response to COVID- 19 pandemic with the case studies in different functional and integrated level of business management, presenting systematic case studies developed on the work done by the organizations with a strategic focus on unique initiatives taken for balancing the interest of different stakeholders, for example, taking care of employee with nil operations and business development and adopting technologies to minimize the decline in sales"-- Provided by publisher.
Identifiers: LCCN 2021048766 (print) | LCCN 2021048767 (ebook) | ISBN 9781668435045 (hardcover) | ISBN 9781668435052 (paperback) | ISBN 9781668435069 (ebook)
Subjects: LCSH: Crisis management--India. | Management--India. | COVID-19 (Disease)--Economic aspects--India. | Technological innovations--India.
Classification: LCC HV551.5.I4 C37 2022 (print) | LCC HV551.5.I4 (ebook) | DDC 363.34/80954--dc23/eng/20211117
LC record available at https://lccn.loc.gov/2021048766
LC ebook record available at https://lccn.loc.gov/2021048767

This book is published in the IGI Global book series Advances in Business Strategy and Competitive Advantage (ABSCA) (ISSN: 2327-3429; eISSN: 2327-3437)

British Cataloguing in Publication Data
A Cataloguing in Publication record for this book is available from the British Library.

All work contributed to this book is new, previously-unpublished material.
The views expressed in this book are those of the authors, but not necessarily of the publisher.

For electronic access to this publication, please contact: eresources@igi-global.com.

Advances in Business Strategy and Competitive Advantage (ABSCA) Book Series

ISSN:2327-3429
EISSN:2327-3437

Editor-in-Chief: Patricia Ordóñez de Pablos, Universidad de Oviedo, Spain

MISSION

Business entities are constantly seeking new ways through which to gain advantage over their competitors and strengthen their position within the business environment. With competition at an all-time high due to technological advancements allowing for competition on a global scale, firms continue to seek new ways through which to improve and strengthen their business processes, procedures, and profitability.

The **Advances in Business Strategy and Competitive Advantage (ABSCA) Book Series** is a timely series responding to the high demand for state-of-the-art research on how business strategies are created, implemented and re-designed to meet the demands of globalized competitive markets. With a focus on local and global challenges, business opportunities and the needs of society, the **ABSCA** encourages scientific discourse on doing business and managing information technologies for the creation of sustainable competitive advantage.

COVERAGE

- Innovation Strategy
- Joint Ventures
- Strategic Alliances
- Value Creation
- Globalization
- Entrepreneurship & Innovation
- International Business Strategy
- Strategic Management
- Customer-Orientation Strategy
- Business Models

IGI Global is currently accepting manuscripts for publication within this series. To submit a proposal for a volume in this series, please contact our Acquisition Editors at Acquisitions@igi-global.com or visit: http://www.igi-global.com/publish/.

The Advances in Business Strategy and Competitive Advantage (ABSCA) Book Series (ISSN 2327-3429) is published by IGI Global, 701 E. Chocolate Avenue, Hershey, PA 17033-1240, USA, www.igi-global.com. This series is composed of titles available for purchase individually; each title is edited to be contextually exclusive from any other title within the series. For pricing and ordering information please visit http://www.igi-global.com/book-series/advances-business-strategy-competitive-advantage/73672. Postmaster: Send all address changes to above address.

Titles in this Series

For a list of additional titles in this series, please visit:
http://www.igi-global.com/book-series/advances-business-strategy-competitive-advantage/73672

Analyzing International Business Operations in the Post-Pandemic Era
Bryan Christiansen (The Christiansen Foundation, USA) and John Branch (University of Michigan, USA)
Business Science Reference • © 2022 • 335pp • H/C (ISBN: 9781668437490) • US $225.00

Impact of Digital Transformation on the Development of New Business Models and Consumer Experience
Maria Antónia Rodrigues (Polytechnic of Porto, Portugal & CEOS.PP, Portugal & SIIS Porto, Portugal) and João F. Proença (Faculty of Economics, University of Porto, Portugal & Advance/CSG, University of Lisbon, Portugal & ISEG, University of Lisbon, Portugal)
Business Science Reference • © 2022 • 347pp • H/C (ISBN: 9781799891796) • US $215.00

Cases on Survival and Sustainability Strategies of Social Entrepreneurs
Charles Oham (University of Greenwich, UK)
Business Science Reference • © 2022 • 312pp • H/C (ISBN: 9781799877240) • US $195.00

Career Re-Invention in the Post-Pandemic Era
Shalin Hai-Jew (Kansas State University, USA)
Business Science Reference • © 2022 • 332pp • H/C (ISBN: 9781799886266) • US $205.00

Handbook of Research on Cross-Disciplinary Uses of Gamification in Organizations
Oscar Bernardes (ISCAP, ISEP, Polytechnic Institute of Porto, Portugal & University of Aveiro, Portugal) Vanessa Amorim (ISCAP, Polytechnic Institute of Porto, Portugal) and António Carrizo Moreira (University of Aveiro, Portugal)
Business Science Reference • © 2022 • 657pp • H/C (ISBN: 9781799892236) • US $295.00

Critical Analysis and Architecture for Strategic Business Planning
James McKee (Independent Researcher, Australia)
Business Science Reference • © 2022 • 289pp • H/C (ISBN: 9781799880738) • US $215.00

For an entire list of titles in this series, please visit:
http://www.igi-global.com/book-series/advances-business-strategy-competitive-advantage/73672

IGI Global
PUBLISHER of TIMELY KNOWLEDGE

701 East Chocolate Avenue, Hershey, PA 17033, USA
Tel: 717-533-8845 x100 • Fax: 717-533-8661
E-Mail: cust@igi-global.com • www.igi-global.com

Editorial Advisory Board

Table of Contents

Detailed Table of Contents

Although there are studies on COVID-19's impact on supply chains for essential goods, the authors agree that SMEs have been largely ignored in this context. National statistics indicate that micro, small, and medium enterprises represent 99.8% of total business units in Mexico and are therefore a relevant unit of analysis. Such companies had to deal with lack of materials and delayed delivery times combined with a slowed-down demand of products. The adoption of e-commerce as an alternative channel was finally embraced by small enterprises in the country in order to survive. Original research with data from interviews to five micro and small enterprises managers is used to write mini-case studies, showing that both omni-channel and vertical integration were the most commonly used strategies. Results indicate that both flexibility and control are at the center of the decision to vertically integrate and therefore disintermediate (reducing the level number of the channel structure). A model of distribution channel innovation is proposed together with theoretical and practical implications.

Though the company InnAccel Technologies Pvt. Ltd. started as an incubator in 2012, it combined its operations with Coeo Labs and Sattva Medtech, the former incubates, in 2019, thereby creating a single entity with a portfolio of innovative and life-saving products in the field of medical technology. It developed three innovative products, namely VapCare, Fetal Lite, and SAANS. With growing COVID-19 cases worldwide, there was a dire need for respiratory support, which could be in the form of invasive and non-invasive ventilation systems. Hence, InnAccel launched Saans Pro, which is a non-invasive ventilation system, an infrastructure independent technology for COVID-19 patients in ICU. It could be used to treat patients who are not stressed and have no other organ failure. The case presents the three main challenges faced by firms: commercialization, consumer acceptance of its products (Indian) in domestic and international markets, and dilemma of whether to venture into the international markets.

During COVID-19, several disruptions were reported, activities got halted, and the focus of marketing shifted towards social media due to engagements of the clients towards various available platforms. The use of the internet and social media increased during and after the pandemic. Digital communications attracted customers towards contactless access and the availability of required services. Interactions among various stakeholders including companies, suppliers, and customers increased during these times for hassle-free and uninterrupted services. A paradigm shift was observed in advertising patterns, customer relationship management, service management, and digital tools and media engagements during the pandemic. A strategic shift, observed during the pandemic, has been explored and covered in this chapter. A theoretical framework of hassle-free uses of digital tools in the pandemic has also been developed and included using various social media platforms.

This chapter aims to study operation mode of wine tourism and coping strategies of major wine producing regions in the context of COVID-19. This study uses Citespace to analyze the changes of research hotspots in wine tourism industry before and after COVID-19. Through the comparison between the global wine industry management strategy and the Chinese wine industry management strategy, the similarities and differences between the two are analyzed through specific cases. This chapter investigates the driving force and factors of sustainable development of tourism economy with wine tourism as the core sector. It also studies innovative strategies such as the promotional effects of digital tourism in response to COVID-19 on wine tourism, thereby extending the protection and utilization of intellectual property rights of each wine producer. Case studies of China will be used for discussion. Finally, this chapter provides suggestions for policymakers to build a sustainable wine tourism for enterprises.

This chapter discusses the impact of COVID-19 on the Chinese aviation industry. Specifically, China Southern Airlines (CSAIR) was chosen as a focal airline company, from which its approach and strategies in dealing with various challenges and difficulties brought by COVID-19 was investigated and analyzed. Challenges that airline companies faced during pandemic include a decline in traffic volume, operation funds shortage, and uncertain situations and difficulties in making predictions. The case starts with introducing general impact of COVID-19 on airline industry, followed by delineating regulations from the industry as prevention and control of the pandemic situation. It identifies several pathways to civil aviation industry recovery, namely group standard measures, fleet storage, domestic passengers flight operation, and transition to cargo flight.

The COVID-19 pandemic presented a challenging situation to the business organizations all over the world. This challenge was even more tough for the social enterprises as they function in resource constraints which increased due to the restrictions on physical movement. The case study discusses how a social entrepreneur repurposed her operations through adaptive resilience. The framework of adaptive resilience has been studied in the context of the social enterprise, Vyomini, a rural women entrepreneurs' network that used to manufacture sanitary napkins at affordable rates before the pandemic. During the pandemic, Vyomini showcased their adaptive resilience and started manufacturing essential items like masks, sanitizers, etc. The case study explores the various components of adaptive resilience with the various stages of adversity (i.e., immediate response, recovery, and renewal). It shows that the components of adaptive resilience (i.e., communication, collaboration, leadership, and learning) are necessary for creating as well as sustaining adaptive resilience.

The chapter examines how women-owned small businesses in Bangladesh responded to crisis episodes such as COVID-19 and discusses their resilience to shocking events. The study involved a qualitative exploration of three women-owned online small businesses conducted using the case study method. The cases included businesses that sold jewelry and fashion accessories, both imported and locally procured, and exclusively operated on social media platforms, including Facebook and Instagram. The findings suggest that the businesses adopted innovative social media strategies to survive the crisis episode, including page boosting and paid promotions, Facebook and Instagram Live coupled with sales and discount promotions, temporary closure, vendor switching, and product basket modification. The enterprises showed an overall moderate level of resilience, with a moderate level of adaptability, agility, and low flexibility with a high vulnerability to crisis events. Recommendations for policymakers and credit institutions are also discussed.

The WHO, in collaboration with national and international health authorities, set the standard for preparing global healthcare systems facing the pandemic which claimed more lives than any other single disease during the corona pandemic. The preparedness and management of the pandemic, being the subject of national priority, witnessed concrete measures taken by the Indian Government to fight the pandemic with executive support of the Ministry of Health and other nationwide Health Services. Ayurveda, an Indian indigenous wholistic healthcare approach, was widely adopted at large. Ayurvedic medicine producing companies saw exponential growth in their revenue during the period of pandemic. This chapter aims at exploring responses of certain constituents of the Ayurvedic treatment system in India—the leading Ayurvedic companies and AYUSH department—to the coronavirus pandemic. The Ayurvedic companies and the AYUSH department responded to the pandemic in a varied way including product diversification, digital marketing, and promotion of yogic exercises and herbal remedies.

The whole world was disturbed because of COVID-19. It brought several positive and negative effects on human, environment, and climate. During the lockdown period of COVID-19, all movements and activities slowed. All socio-economic activities, industrial workshops, and production units were completely closed. Due to restriction and slowdown of these activities, some environmental conditions improved including air quality and water pollution. But due to the increasing number of COVID-19 patients, rate of generation of medical waste increased (PPE kit, face mask, and hand gloves). Unplanned discarding and production of medical waste causes ill effects on the environment as well as human beings. These environmental and human consequences have long-lasting effects; therefore, they require proper and well-planned sustainable strategies for a better future and to overcome these consequences. The COVID-19 pandemic has obtained an overall global response to win this COVID-19 battle.

Foreword

The Covid 19 pandemic took the world by surprise by creating an unprecedented impact on all stakeholders. The crisis has unexpectedly lasted for a longer duration. Quick standard operational procedures and protocols became the major part of public communications. Governments, with support of many institutions, across the world worked relentlessly to take up the challenges thrown by the pandemic. Public and private institutions came up with tweaking policies and emergency plans, using limited pool of resources and capabilities, embarked on digital platform to combat the crisis. These organisations responded to the crisis in a varied forms and innovated to survive and sustain their performance. The world is still not out of danger of the pandemic crisis. However, intense vaccination drive has been helping people to withstand danger of the successive corona pandemic waves. Moreover, organisations are likely to continue with some new practices such as work from home or anywhere -at least partially. The pandemic has enforced the humanity to make the best use of digital platform without which the crisis would have worsened to unmanageable level.

The book volume *Cases on Emerging Markets Responses to the COVID-19 Pandemic* edited by Raj K. Kovid and Vikas Kumar presents chapters which captures the real-life insights on emerging markets' responses to the unprecedented crisis in the form of corona pandemic and suggests the strategies to deal with it.

I opine that the book further enriches the existing understanding of interplay among relevant factors. The case-based chapters of the book provide very interesting and meaningful insights into the responses of various businesses and social enterprises. This volume contributes to offering practical solutions to a number of problems, society has faced during the pandemic. The book's coverage includes thirteen chapters, which forms the body of this book. A group of practitioners and academicians from a number of emerging economies come together to contribute chapters on a variety of contexts such as healthcare, manufacturing, aviation, hospitality among others. The coverage and depth of the book chapters is very comprehensive to be considered as a reference book related to different dimensions of pandemic. This book has certainly potential to be a meaningful resource for policy makers, practitioner, students and academicians, who need insights for decision making to deal with the post pandemic challenging situations.

I congratulate the chapter contributors and editors of the book for compiling this piece of excellent work. I am very hopeful that the readers will certainly get a deep insights and knowledge from the chapters of this book which can be tailored and customized to suit the individual needs.

Chowdhury Mofizur Rahman
United International University, Dhaka, Bangladesh

Foreword

The Corona Pandemic is unprecedented in its own way of affecting lives of people adversely across the globe. It has affected different stakeholders disproportionately and hence was responded in varied forms such as digitalisation, flexible working hours, product diversification. Organisations, communities and individuals showed resilience and pivoted their approaches to withstand the pandemic crisis.

Governments and non-government organisations across the world have worked very hard to manage the challenges posed by the pandemic. However, organisations and individual, building on learning from consecutive COVID-19 waves, are looking forward for effective and sustainable solutions to live with evolving nature of this pandemic which is yet to lose its grip.

The book volume titled *Cases on Emerging Markets Responses to the COVID-19 Pandemic* edited by Raj K. Kovid and Vikas Kumar offers deep insights on responses and strategies organisations have used to withstand the challenges thrown by the pandemic crisis. The cases highlight the innovative and contextually appropriate integrated responses of managers and entrepreneurs at the different levels.

I firmly believe that this volume contributes to provide meaningful insights and practical solutions to the problems and challenges facing the society at large, during the pandemic. The chapters provide valuable insights into how individual and organisation have found opportunities in adversities, during and after the pandemic. The practitioners and academicians from many emerging markets and diverse disciplines have contributed thirteen chapters, thereby bringing a variety of thoughts and perspectives to the table. The book has come up well to be considered as a comprehensive resource to refer to a pool of knowledge on many dimensions of pandemic. I am very sure that this book would certainly be a valuable resource for managers, policy makers, academicians, students and other professionals, who are likely to use the knowledge and insights to successfully overcome post pandemic challenges across the walks of life.

I congratulate all chapter authors and editors of the book for bring out an excellent academic piece of work and hope this compilation of chapters would profoundly create an impact on the readers' perspective about pandemic induced issues.

Vaibhav Singh
MakeMyTrip India Pvt Ltd., India

Preface

The Covid-19 pandemic brought an unprecedented and exogenous shock to the normal life at large. It has a created adverse impact on all walks of life of people across the world, perhaps most significantly after the World War II. The impact of corona pandemic varied in view of geography, sector, economic groups, and socio-cultural settings. The regional and gendered inequalities became more prominently visible and intensified. Public services, logistics and supply chain systems were put to test during the pandemic. Many business and social organisations succumbed to the unparallel shock while some tweaked their business models to adjust with the new normal to survive. However, consistent with a common saying that adversity also brings opportunity, the pandemic also made people and organisations to innovate encashing opportunities, sometimes unrealising the same. The firms in number of sectors, for example in healthcare sector and online services sector, found a big opportunity to outperform all their past measures. However, these organisations also learnt many lessons and continued to respond during the successive waves of Corona pandemic.

Emerging markets have their unique set of problems and challenges and hence the way institutions responded to the pandemic in these markets becomes important and interesting to study. How they have leveraged their limited resource base to combat and survive the situation? How the learning of institutions in emerging markets add to the pool of overall knowledge and wisdom to deal effectively with Corona-type crisis in future? Present book volume explores these questions and elaborate on the emerging markets response during pandemic.

The book provides a set of illustrative cases on responses and strategies chosen by organisations irrespective of their industry, sector, ownership type, size, location, scope, and technology-embeddedness. It highlights organisations' innovative approaches of dealing with crises to sail through the crisis. The book consists of 13 chapters written on various dimensions of crisis management approaches in context of number of emerging markets including India.

The first chapter, 'Channel Structure Innovation as a Response to COVID-19 Pandemic: Cases From Mexico', elaborates on the adoption of e-commerce as an alternative channel by small enterprises in order to survive in context of Mexico, an emerging market. Medical technological innovations as a response to the pandemic has been captured by the second chapter. Staying connected with customer in view of 'social-distance' norms was a herculean task. How firms resorted to innovative forms of marketing communication during Covid-19 has well been captured in next chapter. If we look for severely hit industries, tourism would probable compete for first position. This is well discussed in fourth chapter on how wine tourism in China adopted innovative responses to Covid-19. The fifth chapter discusses the impact of COVID-19 on the aviation industry by taking a case of Chinese aviation industry, The chapter identifies several ways to recovery of civil aviation industry such as group standard measures, fleet storage, and conversion to cargo flight. Hospitality industry, in addition to tourism and aviation can be considered severely hit by the pandemic. Chapters six and seven illustrate the cases of select hotels' response to the crisis in Indian context. The crisis made hotels to recalibrate their cost structure and profitability

Adaptive resilience of a social enterprise, Vyomini, during adversity posed by the pandemic is well documented in the eight chapter which shows that the components of adaptive resilience i.e., communication, collaboration, leadership, and learning are necessary for creating as well as sustaining adaptive resilience. Next chapter, nine, presents insights about women-owned small enterprises response to the crisis in Bangladesh. To survive the crisis episode, these SMEs adopted innovative social media strategies, including page boosting and paid promotions.

At a time when work from home became imperative almost for all, engaging employees put an unparallel challenge before the managers. Tenth chapter addresses this issue of employee engagement by analysing the cases of select organisations in Indian context. Moreover, psychological health of employees and public at large have become very serious issue for public health. So, the eleventh chapter captures details on how various initiatives taken on part of government and NGOs contributed to upkeep psychological health of people.

Amidst all adverse impact of the pandemic crisis, some sectors and industry, for example, healthcare, acquired prominence. How ayurvedic healthcare sector followed an unprecedented approach to respond to Covid-19 in Indian market is elaborated in the next chapter. The last chapter explores the sustainability practices of hospitals in managing the waste which was a very challenging task during the pandemic.

We sincerely hope that the book volume will serve as a comprehensive resource to both the industry and academia and will be a guiding path to the business organisations. Learnings from the case studies will give rise to new business models to support the businesses during volatile environment.

Raj K. Kovid
Sharda University, India

Vikas Kumar
Central University of Haryana, India

Acknowledgment

Bringing out an edited book necessitates the sincere and timely efforts of a number of intellectuals, and we feel honoured to acknowledge this support. First of all, we are thankful to IGI Global for providing us this wonderful opportunity to come-up with this collection and invite the scholars to contribute to this volume.

Our sincere thanks to Prof. Tankeshwar Kumar (Vice Chancellor, Central University of Haryana) and Prof. Siba Ram Khara (Vice Chancellor, Sharda University) for their continued guidance and support towards the completion of this project. We are indebted to Prof. Raj Kumar Mittal (Vice-Chancellor, Chaudhary Bansi Lal University, Bhiwani), who has always been kind to support our endeavours.

We would like to acknowledge the support of our colleagues and friends: Dr Sudhir Rana (Gulf Medical University, UAE), Dr. Prashant Gupta (Indian Institute of Management Trichy), Dr. Sunita Bharatwal (Chaudhary Bansi Lal University), Dr. Mridul Dharwal and Dr Manisha Gupta (Sharda University), Dr. Gaurav Gupta (Christ University), Dr. Subagyo (Nusantara PGRI University), Dr. Surender Kumar (Jaipuria Institute of Management), Dr. Saurabh Mittal (Fortune Institute of International Business) among others from academia who cooperated to their full in order to complete this project in many ways.

We thank all authors who contributed by submitting their scholarly work and worked to respond to the review comments following the tight deadlines. We express our gratitude to all reviewers who volunteered to devout time to review the submissions and suggested improvements. We are also thankful to all members of the Editorial Advisory Board for their valuable inputs and critical observations on various dimensions of this book project. Without support of administrative and editorial staff from IGI -Global, it was not possible to bring this project to completion and launch stage.

Last but not least, we cannot afford to ignore silent and unabated support of family members who were source of our continuous motivation to work with full spirits, especially, during the corona pandemic period to complete this project.

Raj K. Kovid
Sharda University, India

Vikas Kumar
Central University of Haryana, India

Chapter 1
Channel Structure Innovation as a Response to the COVID-19 Pandemic:
Cases From Mexico

Manuela Gutiérrez-Leefmans
https://orcid.org/0000-0001-5755-6294
Universidad de las Américas Puebla, Mexico

EXECUTIVE SUMMARY

Although there are studies on COVID-19's impact on supply chains for essential goods, the authors agree that SMEs have been largely ignored in this context. National statistics indicate that micro, small, and medium enterprises represent 99.8% of total business units in Mexico and are therefore a relevant unit of analysis. Such companies had to deal with lack of materials and delayed delivery times combined with a slowed-down demand of products. The adoption of e-commerce as an alternative channel was finally embraced by small enterprises in the country in order to survive. Original research with data from interviews to five micro and small enterprises managers is used to write mini-case studies, showing that both omni-channel and vertical integration were the most commonly used strategies. Results indicate that both flexibility and control are at the center of the decision to vertically integrate and therefore disintermediate (reducing the level number of the channel structure). A model of distribution channel innovation is proposed together with theoretical and practical implications.

DOI: 10.4018/978-1-6684-3504-5.ch001

INTRODUCTION

The COVID-19 pandemic has caused small and medium enterprises (SMEs) to change some of their processes (Kumar & Gupta, 2021). Due to their nature, these are enterprises limited in resources that somehow managed to survive and even grown in the middle of the sanitary and economic crisis. Entrepreneurs experienced business closure and reduced income due to government restrictions (Subagyo et al., 2020). Small companies depending on them had to deal with lack of materials and delayed delivery times combined with a demand decrease for some of their products(Kumar et al, 2022).

Micro, small, and medium enterprises represent 99.8% of total business units in Mexico (INEGI, 2020). They are therefore very relevant to the country's economy and the strategies been used in this emerging market in the present situation are worth studying. In Mexico, an enterprise with 10 employees or less is considered as micro while one with less than 50 is considered as small.

SMEs responded to the crisis by searching for new suppliers, adopting e-commerce for the first time and changing their traditional roles in the distribution channel structure (Kumar & Malhotra, 2021). An example are SMEs who did not only look for economic ways to keep delivering their products but who found a way to do the delivery themselves. Discount coupons were also a way to attract and retain customers (Kumar & Ayodeji, 2020). SMEs also used social networks to communicate and some of them adopted social commerce (Nanda & Kumar, 2022).

Another strategy used by SMEs was digital transformation. Priyono et al. (2020) find that SMEs used this strategy, however, with degrees of transformation depending on each enterprises' capabilities. They find that SMEs with a high level of digital maturity responded to the challenges by accelerating the transition toward digitalized firms (Kumar & Vidhyalakshmi, 2012). That is different to SMEs that experience liquidity issues and have a low level of digital maturity who decided to digitalize the sales function only. Finally, there are SMEs that have very limited digital literacy but are supported by a high level of social capital (Mittal & Kumar,2019) . In the last case, collaboration seemed to be a key element for success (Sharma & Kumar, 2017).

Channel distribution innovation is regarded of benefit for small and medium enterprises in the current crisis (Meristö, 2020). However, although the adoption of e-commerce as an alternative channel has been present for a few decades in the country, it was until the sanitary crisis that very small enterprises finally embraced it. In 2019, the amount of online sales showed a growth of 24% compared to the previous year, according to data from the study of Online Shopping Habits of Internet Users in Mexico (IAB, 2020). There are estimates that predict e-commerce will be two years ahead of its expected level of growth (Hernández, 2020).

In addition to technology, other strategies were also adopted by small enterprises such as omni channeling (Song et al. 2020) and disintermediation/re-intermediation (Rosenbloom, 2013), which change a company's channel structure. Hence, this chapter proposes the following research questions: *What are the distribution channel strategies followed by Mexican micro and small enterprises to overcome the COVID-19 crisis? And, how do they affect their channel structures?*

The use of original research with data from interviews to five micro and small enterprise managers in the country is presented. A qualitative data analysis helps to detect patterns that show successful strategies used. As a result, a model of distribution channel innovation is proposed together with theoretical and practical implications.

INNOVATION IN DISTRIBUTIONS CHANNELS, E-COMMERCE AND VERTICAL INTEGRATION

Innovation in Distribution Channels

According to Musso (2010), globalization has brought a more complex concept of marketing channels, with disintermediation and re-intermediation, multi-channels and new roles/specializations that emerged as new issues. This author presents a structural perspective when referring to innovation in marketing channels, which comprises innovations that emerge in the retail sector such as multi-channeling. Innovation also occurs at the manufacturer level by using multi-channeling as well: e-commerce, franchising, pop-up stores and manufacturer-owned stores. Innovations in distribution channels are relevant as they are related to more efficiency in small and medium enterprises and improve company performance (Kuswantoro et al. 2012).

More recently, multichannel is differentiated from omni-channel. Omni-channel focuses on synergy and integration of available channels to streamline customer interactions and retailer control across channels (Li et al. 2018) while multichannel emphasizes retailers' intense presence in different channels. This is related to whether a company decides to use direct or indirect channels. Leenders and Chandra (2013) confirm the moderating effect of channel structures in a sustainable context. That is, the benefits of green innovation in terms of business performance are found to be larger when firms use more direct sales channels (selling directly to consumers and businesses).

According to Ketchen & Craighead (2020), as a result of the sanitary crisis, organizations experimented with new ideas and approaches, and some of these inventions can improve their transiliency regardless of what the future brings. This is related to the idea of flexibility. Chenarides et al. (2021) present a model of supply chain flexibility, after reviewing how the COVID-19 crisis affected the food industry logistics. They encourage the flexibility to switch between food service and retail distribution.

Finally, scope, spillover and shift, are important factors considered by Ketchen & Craighead (2020) when referring to the COVID-19 crisis. In terms of scope, the authors consider that a typical disruption is localized geographically and/or by sector. That is, while some industries may be suffering the disruption, others may be going ahead. This is why it is interesting to look at a variety of industries. The spillover refers to the torrent of waves' spills over from region to region and sector to sector. While governments set regulations such as closing down certain activities, effects can be seen in others (Ketchen & Craighead, 2020). Finally, the shift in a pandemic refers to the force of disruption, which is strong enough to force supply and demand to extreme highs and lows. Small and micro enterprises are very sensitive to such shifts. And in turn, bring changes to their channel structures.

COVID Pandemic and E-Commerce

Previous research has found that manufacturers or service providers whose channel strategy include the Internet may potentially gain channel control with respect to the retailer, by nature of the manufacturer or service provider's enhanced ability to control the marketing mix (Rohm, 2001). Although a business that sells to consumers via fewer sales intermediaries has the opportunity to yield greater profits, intermediaries also have information and knowledge relative to the producer (Bucklin et al. 1996) and provide contact efficiency (Rosenbloom, 2013; Rosenbloom, 2007). That is, the producer reduces the contact effort by using an intermediary.

With the adoption of e-commerce, disintermediation and re-intermediation processes take place. The use of technology in such processes has had important implications already highlighted by researchers (Kumar & Ayoeji, 2021a). For example, Stephen and Toubia (2010) refer to social commerce as a form of Internet-based social media, which enables individuals to engage in the selling and marketing of products and services in online communities and marketplaces. Social commerce is then, part of the online channel where the intermediary is the marketplace.

On the other side, third-party platforms as marketplaces have gained popularity in most countries (Kumar & Ayoeji, 2021b). They offer the platform and act as the intermediary that decreases transaction costs for a company. Research has shown that marketplaces (Gengatharen & Standing, 2005) are very useful for export activities. This, due to the global market that is opened for companies through the use of technology. Platforms also generate networks effects that increase a company's audience and the number of potential customers.

The effect is particularly significant in small and micro-enterprises, where entrepreneurs experience business cancellation or closure and reduced income due to the closure of several supporting sectors such as retail and transportation (Fabeil et al. 2020). The authors show the change in the channel structure after the strategy used by some companies, where the traditional five-level channel system (independent distribution approach) is replaced by a manufacturer that distributes to a main collector, which in turn, uses several distributors to arrive to retailers and consumers. An approach similar to the omni-channel one where several channels are used in distributing goods to the customer, for example through distributors, mobile apps, and physical stores.

Aldin and Stahre (2003) refer to the vertical perspective of multiple channels by considering the lengths of the different channels were e-commerce acts as a direct channel to the end customer and a dealer is an indirect channel. A two-level, three-level or four-level channel structure are common (e.g. e-commerce represents commonly a two-level one where producer and consumer are the two agents involved). These authors confirm that by coordinating and offering multiple channels in the horizontal dimensions, the vertical decomposition of logistical functions may arise.

Collaboration and Vertical Integration as Strategies

Vertical integration has two modalities. Upstream integration means the company starts to produce what it used to buy from the supplier. A vertical integration downstream means integrating the activity of intermediaries in order to eliminate them and to sell directly to the customer. In their study, Guan and Rehme (2012) find that vertical integration transforms the manufacturer into a supplier to product resellers, offering the firm a greater potential to provide integrated solutions and, therefore, become a strategic partner to its customers. This means the shift experienced by the integration provides important benefits for the producer.

Elimination of intermediaries or vertical disintermediation has been an appealing scenario for members of supply chains seeking the shortest way to end customers (Aldin and Stahre, 2003). For example manufacturers bypassing wholesalers, and wholesalers eliminating dealers or retailers. Such activity is not new and as digital platforms emerged, the idea of re-intermediation appeared. Early on, collaboration was viewed as a logistics and marketing strategy. An e-commerce portal can be used as a marketing channel in collaboration with existing intermediaries or through bypassing intermediaries (disintermediation) (Aldin and Stahre, 2003).

Li & Chen (2020) find that although backward or upstream integration hurts the unintegrated supplier, forward integration (downstream) can lead to a win-win outcome for the manufacturer and unintegrated retailer and, that its choice of integration strategy always leads to the best performance for the entire supply chain. Hence, vertical integration acts not only as a survival strategy for example in the middle of a crisis, but can be of benefit to the whole channel system.

Literature on collaboration is also important when faced with a crisis. Open innovation as defined by Chesbrough (2003) happens when a company uses assets, capabilities and knowledge that belong to another company. The same happens when a company lets its internal assets, capabilities and knowledge be used by another company. Both companies derive benefits from this and there are formal ways of doing open innovation. The idea that micro or small companies could adopt this practice is interesting and much less explored than open innovation practices in large companies. Other integration strategies for innovation include integration for product development with suppliers, in different degrees of formality. Suppliers have the knowledge of a product, and in many cases they have further knowledge as they work with other companies in the same industry. They are therefore a rich source of innovation.

METHODOLOGY

This study uses the case study method based on a total of five semi-structured interviews, which were conducted to micro and small enterprise founders or general managers. Yin (2011) considers case studies the preferred strategy when 'how and 'why' questions are being posed and when the focus is on a contemporary phenomenon within a real-life context. The case study method also allows uncovering aspects and inter-relationships of complex phenomena in an organizational setting (Yin, 2009). Multiple case studies are useful as the likelihood of valid theory is high because the theory-building process is so intimately tied with evidence that it is very likely that the resultant theory will be consistent with empirical observation (Eisenhardt, 1989).

Interviews

Table 1 shows the characteristics of the micro and small enterprises. According to Eisenhardt (1989) the ideal number of cases is between four and ten. Convenience sampling was used as small companies known in the local area were contacted. The selection was also based on the role of each enterprise as channel member (producer, wholesaler or retailer). The interviews took place during 2020 and the first semester of 2021. They were focused on analyzing and understanding the distribution channel structure of the enterprise and the use of technology to uncover the mechanisms of its channel structure during the COVID-19 pandemic. The interviews were first analyzed using a qualitative software where constructs for the proposed model were detected.

Table 1. Interview enterprises' profile

Enterprise Sector	Number of Employees
Clothing boutique	3
Industrial glasses	4
Traditional hats	6
Baby products	20
Traditional jewelry	50

Source: own elaboration of the author

Case Studies

Although a single case study provides detail and richness, multiple cases are effective because they enable the collection of comparative data, and so are likely to yield more accurate, generalizable theory than single cases (Eisenhardt, 1989). Therefore, five mini-case studies are presented below together with a cross-case analysis that helps to identify patterns across the cases for individual constructs (Eisenhardt 1989).

Case A - Baby Products

Company A produces baby products. The company designs and imports, outsources production, they then pack and distribute. It uses other marketplaces to commercialize its products. It has its own trucks to distribute to a department store and delivers directly using FEDEX or sends the products to Amazon's warehouse. If the item is returned, the customer must do this via DHL or FEDEX directly to them. In a physical store, this is different as the company has to collect the product and there is a loss for it. However, the owner considers that claims help the company grow.

Payment systems used by the company are Paypal, MercadoPago. The company considers it has a learning processes with Amazon, with online metrics that help to measure also its channel members. MercadoLibre also offers them reputation metrics. However, for the company, it is important to have its own platform and position the product. Although it considers that online shopping is still slow in the country.

When COVID-19 pandemic began, company A had to face scarcity of materials to produce and experienced a decrease in sales. It experienced a change from 3-level channel structure to a 2-level one. With the pandemic, there was a scarcity of materials from China, which made the company reflect on the issue of depending on a single supplier. Some products increased its prices and at the same time they experienced a decrease in sales. The company decided to increase product variety not to depend so much on some materials and not to stop production.

It developed its online platform and searched for vendors . It also increased the number of products on the platform. Both offline and online channels are an advantage against the company's competition. Understanding how Internet works limits some producers according the founder, and gives advantages to wholesalers like them.

Company A has connections with department stores. As a result of the pandemic, they increased the warehouse space for themselves and for other company's products.

The company plans to go hybrid between production and commercialization and become the wholesaler. Distributors to MercadoLibre are growing and it does not want to depend on the wholesaler. The founder also does not trust other channel members as they usually do not follow the same lines as the producer.

They plan to look for better distribution channels like Amazon, to study them and to have a proper sales forecast for physical sales. Amazon invests in advertising to position the product. The platform creates the promotional campaign with joint positioning.

They use category management and systems that only operate administrative matters, they do not have a customer relationship management (CRM) in place. In terms of social networks, the company is in Shopify through Instagram and Facebook. They plan to start with Whatsapp and hire a social media manager.

Global sales are contemplated with online platforms. In the future they plan to sell artisan products from a southern state online. However, there is no specific logistics staff.

Case B - Industrial Glasses

Company B is a brick and mortar company specialized on industrial glasses. It has a website and is present in Facebook however, the online channel is little used. It is a retailer that buys to the producer and in some cases due to volume they use a wholesaler who sells less quantity. It uses traditional point of sale technology.

Company B saw a dramatic decrease in sales due to the COVID-19 pandemic. When glasses sales went down as a result of the pandemic, it began selling googles, a product considered as essential and contacted a distributor. Many sales and questions arised in Facebook so the owner decided to migrate completely to their website. The company is now looking for organic traffic. It has now a shopping cart and offers more products. It began using Facebook Business recently, and uses social networks used for publicity, however the owner recognizes that they to be given maintenance.

Its online sales have arrived to 80% but due to the unstable current situation they can be 20-30% sometimes. A change the company experimented was the move from being a retailer to acting as a wholesaler by buying directly from the producer to resell later. For example, the company contacted directly googles producers, however due to the pandemic producers who were only beginning.

It looked at other platforms like Shopiffy and Wix but it was more convenient to do to e-commerce directly with their own website. It uses Paypal and now measures delivery times. Due to issues with COVID imports delaying too much, it started buying Mexican products or non-national ones but stored in a Mexican warehouse. It realized wholesalers started promotions as discounts for cash payments to receive cash that would help them continue operating. Accounting, customer relationship and distributor control is necessary via a system so the company is working on this.

In terms of deliveries, they experienced issues with the major international delivery companies, and the service became very expensive so the company started to use its own trucks and charged the consumer a small part of the delivery. They tried using Rappi Favores, however it finally started working with a company who used to sell materials and migrated to delivery. It also used buses to send products when people did not want home delivery.

The company has experienced a problem to forecast due to fluctuation in sales. Competition has also been an issue, as marketplaces such as Amazon and MercadoLibre sell the same product with no delivery charge. It worked for some time with Mercado Libre however, the platform charged them for delivery, which increased up to 30% (17-18% alone to be in the platform). The use of social networks, such as Facebook has brought demand from other states and cities.

A worry of the owner is that consumers are gaining attention from the producer and that is worrying for resellers like them. Company B is now buying from Alibaba and wants to be a wholesalers in the future. They have their own platforms to sell directly to the customer and could go back to MercadoLibre. It is experimenting with loyalty programs and keeps learning with online courses.

It recognizes that its channel system is faster than those of franchises, and it can react faster to changes. Multichannel helped them as being online (compared to other SMEs) gave them the first-mover advantage. They are currently the only ones in town selling googles.

Case C - Traditional Hats

Company C has less than 1 year and 7 months. Originally, the company works as manufacturer (outsourcing with local handcraftsmen) that sells to customer. Their buyer resells the products. It has only one intermediary, which are the delivery companies such as DHL. Its artisanal product begins to be exported through a distributor to the US. The company is very niche oriented and benefits from word of mouth.

It uses PayPal, offers deferred payments and accepts bank cards. It rewards with percentage of sales to the intermediary and provides training on the product. Only about 10% of its sales were originally online. The owner thinks this is due to a cultural and socio-economic aspect of Mexicans. It has mobile POS technology and money transfers too. The company considers it has a competitive advantage for being a personalized product, which is why the direct sell to the customer works well.

Company C could not pay the rent to keep its product stored anymore when the COVID-19 crisis hit them. It had to make sure there would be salaries for all its employees. When the pandemic began, the owner brought home his stock. The company also offered discount coupons for personalized hats. It realized people spend more time on their mobile phones, and therefore increased its presence on social networks and expanded its online catalog. Before the pandemic, 80% of the sale was physical and now it is only 20%. It uses Google Analytics to monitor its work.

They suffered the saturation of packers who did not deliver on time. For example, they experienced problems with RedPack, who seemed to have 50% staff only. This is when the company decided to change packaging to adapt to other modes of transport and packers.

The company is in Facebook, Instagram and now has its own e-commerce website. Since the crisis emerged, only items on stock can be purchased online, hats cannot be customized yet. The pandemic also brought a geographical market change, the majority of clients were local and now 50% of the clients come from the capital city. It uses category management and offers frequent customer discounts. As its suppliers are indigenous population with little education that does not allow the use of other types of technology, however it could be a possibility for large suppliers in the future.

As they grow in machinery and production, they will be able to sell better by volume and will perhaps increase the reseller intermediaries. Future plans are to open a store in Mexico City. It will also try to explore affiliate marketing strategies if it joins a platform with complementary products (is not interested in large platforms).

However, it does not contemplate the use of other platforms. The owner does not agree with that model because the product is not based on volume, a platform that groups products of the same type could be an option although it charges a commission.

Case D - Clothing Boutique

D is a clothing boutique. The company already had an online catalogue, which was set up five years ago and it was until last year that it started to sell online. It initially began with the sales platform Kichink but after trouble with payments it moved to its own platform. It set up payments with Paypal, credit cards and uses mobile point of sale technology (mPOS) for deferred payments.

It has two line products, one high range where the owner designs and outsources the production and another one with cheaper items that come directly from the producer. Its suppliers are both national and international. The national wholesalers in the capital city improve prices with volume.

Company D had to close its physical store when the COVID-19 pandemic urged non-essential businesses to close. Before the pandemic, only 1% of the sales came from the online channel, while now 100% of the sales are online. It is present in Facebook and Instagram among other social networks and is engaged in social commerce. For clients who still want to try on its products, the company has a showroom that can be visited via appointments. As some wholesalers were closed, the owner started sewing herself and producing clothes.

When the struggles with delivery and prices arised as a consequence of the pandemic, users wanted free delivery. The owner learnt about bike deliveries, however the official ones were too expensive, so she found an economic one for local sales and ended up doing an alliance with other companies for deliveries. She realized that clients would rather wait for products from other places than pay more for the products. Loyal clients who recognize the company's good customer service kept buying and moved to the online channel easily. A major change experimented by the company was a change of products, as the owner realized that accessories were not being sold but comfortable clothing and shoes were demanded. The company currently uses Shopify for payments and inventory and accepts clients payments through convenient stores. By using Instagram statistics, the company has managed to market other ages and geographical areas.

Company D is thinking of expanding to technology and home products, always trying to retain the customer by promotions and small gifts. It is also beginning to understand better the market by using Google Analytics. A mobile (truck type) store is an idea that the owner thinks will help no to depend on a single market again.

Case E- Traditional Jewelry

Company E does direct sales of traditional jewelry. It began online only 6 months ago. They are wholesalers who sell to retailers. It began with a physical store with orders in cash, and later began to give credit to small companies and other wholesalers. They import from the producer and then resell. The company has distribution points all over the country.

Company E was a pure brick and mortar company, which experienced an important delay on imported goods and a decrease in sales due to the COVID-19 pandemic. Nowadays, social networks are used for publicity only. Whatsapp business is used to plan appointments with clients. Online sales receive a payment upon delivery via post office. Such sales come from people who see the online catalog, however the company does not have an online shopping cart yet.

Company E uses videos to train retailers on the product. It has the advantage that their main competitor is not online. Its products are directed to 35-50 year old females who are now shopping more online. They offer retailers discounts and commissions to reseller. It has two lines in its catalogs, one for offline and the other one for online sell.

During the pandemic, goods took longer to arrive due to security (sanitary) filters and costed more. There were regulations as imported goods and that complicated the arrival of goods. This, together with a high decrease on demand (50-70%) created an equilibrium, where less demand, meant less purchases so less trouble with the lack of imports.

The company's online clients are known clients from the physical store. They realized that unemployed people wanted to get extra money by selling their product. Online orders are to be delivered regionally, for this they have a distribution center. They will use the delivery company but will try to do the delivery themselves too.

Its selection of suppliers is based on quality and it does promotions and discounts for retailers. It has loyalty programs through bonus. In online sales, it plans to do volume discounts. As this is a slight larger company, there is personnel in charge of logistics, however, not in all offices. The company uses internal software for credit management but haven't heard of other technologies. It may start using Facebook business for a product line. The e-commerce website they are working on will be directed directly to the consumer.

ANALYSIS AND RESULTS

Results of the cross-case analysis (Table 2) show that flexibility is at the center of innovation (see Figure 1). Such approach leads to a crisis management where micro and small enterprise owners look for other sources of supply. At the same time, it leads to changes in activities. Three of the enterprises decided to adapt and change roles increasing or decreasing the number of levels in their channel structure. In most of the cases, the owner decided to disintermediate by embracing e-commerce. Cases where the role of the enterprise as manufacturer changed to wholesaler, or vice versa, show the importance of vertical integration. This also relates to the view that changes in activity-systems lead to innovation (Gutiérrez-Leefmans and Holland, 2019).

An important factor related to the decision to integrate vertically is control. This was constantly mentioned by the enterprise owners together with words as "own platform", which some of them found more attractive than using third party platforms. This is similar to Gengatharen and Standing's (2005) idea on electronic markets' ownership structure and governance, which they find to engender trust and build critical mass by including SMEs in their development and management.

On the one side, as a result of adopting the online channel, more control is gained together with direct interaction with the customer. On the other side, vertical integration was chosen as a good strategy due to the control it gives to the channel member (manufacturer or retailer for example by moving to the wholesaler role). This is particularly interesting as faced with a crisis and realizing that the dependence on other channel members was no longer convenient, a change of roles was seen as an appropriate option.

Such flexibility also allowed to innovate in products and packaging as seen in two of the enterprises. Other companies changed their product line, while most of them extended their range of products, mainly due to the adoption of e-commerce. Hence, the use of multiple channels derives from such flexibility and triggers innovation. Another change seen in most enterprises is the market segment due to the global access of e-commerce.

Collaboration however, seems to have been little used as a strategy. Two enterprises mentioned changing to use other delivery companies due to the high costs and lack of service they had to face. However, although they adapted to work with other new and smaller companies, they did not form formal alliances with them. Reciprocity was not mentioned in any of the cases, which means they simply hired a different service. Formal collaboration strategies may be more used in larger companies and require a more robust setting.

The use of technology seems to be key in all cases as not only it enables the online channel, but it prompts the need to analyze data and encourages enterprise owners to use systems that help to monitor business metrics. However, the use of modern technologies for internal use (such as accounting, relationship with clients, e-sourcing, etc.) seems to be still limited as observed in most of the cases. The use of mobile point of sale technologies is the only one that was confirmed in two cases.

Changes in distribution channels, market segments and key activities derived from them, change costs and probably value propositions and revenue streams, transforming not only the channel structure but the company's business model.

Figure 1. Channel structure innovation model for micro and SMEs.
Source: own elaboration of the author

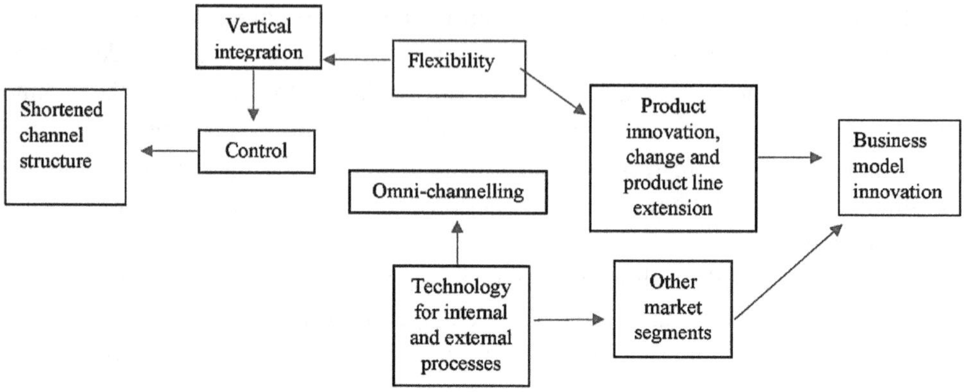

As described in Table 2, in all cases there are processes involving omni-channel by adopting the online channel and disintermediating (up and downstream vertical integration). Despite the view of some authors like Rosenbloom (2013) who defend intermediation due to the increase on contact efficiency, it seems that in the middle of a crisis, disintermediation is the most used strategy as it is translated into a decrease in costs.

Table 2. Cross-case analysis of mini-cases.

Company	Original Channel Distribution	COVID-19 Issues	Changes in Channel Distribution	Use of Technology	External Factors	Innovation Results
A – Baby products (PRODUCER)	3-level channel structure. Uses marketplaces. Direct distribution to department stores.	Scarcity of materials from China. Increased prices on some products to cope with low sales.	2-level channel structure. Increase of warehouse space. Plans to go hybrid between production and commercialization (become wholesaler).	PayPal MercadoPago. Amazon for promotion. Shopify, social networks and plans to use Whatsapp metrics.	Slow growth of online shopping in the country (cultural issues).	Increased product variety to stop material dependency. Increased number of suppliers to be more independent.
B - Industrial glasses (RETAILER)	3-level channel structure. Poor use of online channel.	Instability in sales. Bought national goods due to delayed imports. Issues with major delivery companies.	Acts as wholesaler. Tried to move to a 2-level channel structure by contacting directly the new product producer. Uses a new small company for deliveries.	E-commerce. PayPal. Social networks. Facebook Business. Traditional POS. Working on a system for customer control.	Regulations allowed to sell such essential item.	Social commerce. New product offering. Customers from other geographical areas.

Continued on following page

Table 2. Continued

Company	Original Channel Distribution	COVID-19 Issues	Changes in Channel Distribution	Use of Technology	External Factors	Innovation Results
C - Traditional hats (PRODUCER)	Level-1 channel structure. Uses delivery companies.	Delivery companies saturated.	Online sale of stock products Brought stock home. Discount coupons on personalized items. Stayed on level 1 as it is a personalized product.	Social networks. PayPal and banking cards. Google analytics. mPOS and Whatsapp for clients and internal systems.	Cultural issues. Direct contact with handcraft indigenous people. Almost no use of technology.	Increased online catalogue. Customers from other geographical areas. Package innovation.
D – Clothing boutique (PRODUCER/ RETAILER)	Level 2 channel structure for a product line and level 3 for another one. 2 lines.	Started sewing herself to keep production. Found an economic bike delivery for local sales.	Online channel after closing the physical store. Keeps emphasizing customer service.	Shopify. Social networks, social commerce. PayPal, mPOS. Google analytics.		Social commerce. Changed products, instead of accessories focuses on comfortable clothing.
E - Traditional jewelry (WHOLESALER)	Level 3 channel structure. Imports from producer and then resells. Distribution center and network.	Delays and cost increase on imported goods. High decrease on demand.	Online channel using delivery companies. Online orders to be delivered regionally. Promotions for retailers. Loyalty program.	E-commerce. Whatsapp Business. Videos to train retailers.	Online clients are known clients (physical purchase). Trust issues to get new online customers.	2 lines (catalogues): direct sell and online sell. Directed to 35-50 year old who are now shopping more online.

Source: author's elaboration

Different innovation practices emerged in search of survival and efficiency. Supply chain flexibility as suggested by Chenarides et al. (2021) seems to be a key capability in this process, where opportunities for innovation are salient. For example, company C created a different packaging for its product to make it easier to distribute. Short-term storage to guarantee supply was also a key strategy followed by this enterprise.

The interviewed enterprises had basic technology (a website with contact details) and as a response to the COVID-19 pandemic they developed an online product catalogue. Some have a full e-commerce platform now or use marketplaces to sell their products. Others use social commerce (product sales through social networks) as a strategy due to the lack of physical contact produced by the crisis. Hence, technology has been key in overcoming COVID-19 pandemic challenges.

Company A stands out with the idea to be "mobile". This is similar to the idea applied in the form of food trucks, which some service providers have rented to have the necessary equipment and then drive from place to place to serve customers, one by one (Meristö, 2020). A creative idea to reduce market dependency.

DISCUSSION AND CONCLUSION

As highlighted by Chowdhury et al. (2021), although there are studies on COVID-19 impact on supply chains for high-demand essential goods, low-demand items and SMEs have been largely ignored. The cross-case analysis uncovered high-level patterns via comparison of distribution channel structures and strategies used to overcome the crisis by micro and SMEs. Such analysis helped to build a theoretical model that aims to help educators, practitioners, policy makers and development agencies in their efforts to support micro and small enterprises in crisis.

Although faced with a transformation challenge, micro and small enterprises seem to gain more channel control through e-commerce as pointed out by previous researchers. Based on the results, a model of distribution channel innovation is proposed, which is aimed to advance theory on this field. This study contributes by showing how successful enterprises found a way to survive and grow by embracing technology and following certain strategies. The mini-cases here presented show how different channel members innovate via vertical integration and omni-channel. Independence was an important factor to consider when faced with the decision to disintermediate.

Managerial and policy implications include the necessary training for micro and small enterprises to embrace e-commerce faster and the formation and promotion of collaboration settings for joint strategies among channel members. Cultural and regulatory issues also emerge from this study, which would be worth exploring more in depth in further research studies. They relate to changes in regulations derived from the COVID-19 pandemic and socio-economic factors that are country-specific and affect the way and speed to which small producers and enterprises decide to embrace technology.

ACKNOWLEDGMENT

The author would like to thank the SME owners who kindly shared their experiences to complete this chapter, which aims to help other small companies as well as Marketing and Management students.

This research received no specific grant from any funding agency in the public, commercial, or not-for-profit sectors.

REFERENCES

Aldin, N., & Stahre, F. (2003). Electronic commerce, marketing channels and logistics platforms—a wholesaler perspective. *European Journal of Operational Research, 144*(2), 270–279. doi:10.1016/S0377-2217(02)00393-4

Bucklin, L. P., Ramaswamy, V., & Majumdar, S. K. (1996). Analyzing channel structures of business markets via the structure-output paradigm. *International Journal of Research in Marketing, 13*(1), 73–87. doi:10.1016/0167-8116(95)00035-6

Chenarides, L., Manfredo, M., & Richards, T. J. (2021). Covid-19 and food supply chains. *Applied Economic Perspectives and Policy, 43*(1), 270–279. doi:10.1002/aepp.13085

Chesbrough, H. W. (2003). *Open innovation: The new imperative for creating and profiting from technology*. Harvard Business Press.

Chowdhury, P., Paul, S. K., Kaisar, S., & Moktadir, M. A. (2021). COVID-19 pandemic related supply chain studies: A systematic review. *Transportation Research Part E, Logistics and Transportation Review, 148*, 102271. doi:10.1016/j.tre.2021.102271 PMID:33613082

Fabeil, N. F., Pazim, K. H., & Langgat, J. (2020). The impact of Covid-19 pandemic crisis on micro-enterprises: Entrepreneurs' perspective on business continuity and recovery strategy. *Journal of Economics and Business, 3*(2). Available at SSRN: https://ssrn.com/abstract=3612830

Gengatharen, D. E., & Standing, C. (2005). A framework to assess the factors affecting success or failure of the implementation of government-supported regional e-marketplaces for SMEs. *European Journal of Information Systems, 14*(4), 417–433. doi:10.1057/palgrave.ejis.3000551

Guan, W., & Rehme, J. (2012). Vertical integration in supply chains: Driving forces and consequences for a manufacturer's downstream integration. *Supply Chain Management, 2*(17), 187–201. doi:10.1108/13598541211212915

Gutiérrez-Leefmans, M., & Holland, C. P. (2019). SME Platforms as Business Models: A User-Centric Activity-System Approach. *Cuadernos Americanos, 35*(64), 51–76. doi:10.25100/cdea.v35i64.7248

Hernández, M. (2020). El coronavirus acelerará hasta dos años la adopción del e-commerce en México. *Forbes*. Available at:https://www.forbes.com.mx/tecnologia-ecommerce-coronavirus-adopcion-mexico/

IAB. (2020). *Estudio de consumo de medios y dispositivos entre internautas mexicanos*. Available at: https://www.iabmexico.com/estudios/estudio-de-consumo-de-medios-y-dispositivos-entre-internautas-mexicanos-2020/

INEGI. (2020, June 25). *Estadísticas a propósito del día de las Micros, Pequeñas y Medianas Empresas Comunicado de Prensa*. Available at https://www.inegi.org.mx/contenidos/saladeprensa/aproposito/2020/MYPIMES20.pdf

Ketchen, D. J. Jr, & Craighead, C. W. (2020). Research at the intersection of entrepreneurship, supply chain management, and strategic management: Opportunities highlighted by COVID-19. *Journal of Management*, *46*(8), 1330–1341. doi:10.1177/0149206320945028

Kumar, V., & Ayodeji, O. G. (2021). E-retail Factors for Customer Activation and Retention: An Empirical Study from Indian e-Commerce Customers. *Journal of Retailing and Consumer Services*, *59C*, 102399. doi:10.1016/j.jretconser.2020.102399

Kumar, V., & Ayodeji, O. G. (2021a). Determinants of the Success of Online Retail in India. *International Journal of Business Information Systems*, *37*(2), 246–262. doi:10.1504/IJBIS.2021.115373

Kumar, V., Ayodeji, O. G., & Kumar, S. (2020). Online Retail in India: A Comparative Analysis of top Business Players. *Int. J. Indian Culture and Business Management*, *20*(3), 359–384. doi:10.1504/IJICBM.2020.107672

Kumar, V., & Gupta, G. (Eds.). (2021). *Strategic Management During a Pandemic*. Routledge. doi:10.4324/9781003125648

Kumar, V., & Malhotra, G. (Eds.). (2021). *Stakeholder Strategies for Reducing the Impact of Global Health Crises*. IGI Global Publications. doi:10.4018/978-1-7998-7495-9

Kumar, V., Nanda, P., & Tawangar, S. (2022). Social Media in Business Decisions of MSMES: Practices and Challenges. *International Journal of Decision Support System Technology*, *14*(1), 1–12. doi:10.4018/IJDSST.286686

Kumar, V., & Vidhyalakshmi, P. (2012). Cloud computing for business sustainability. *Asia-Pacific Journal of Management Research and Innovation*, *8*(4), 461–474. doi:10.1177/2319510X13481905

Kuswantoro, F., Rosli, M. M., Abdul, R., & Ghorbani, H. (2012). Impact of distribution channel innovation on the performance of small and medium enterprises. *International Business Management*, *5*(1), 52–61.

Leenders, M. A., & Chandra, Y. (2013). Antecedents and consequences of green innovation in the wine industry: The role of channel structure. *Technology Analysis and Strategic Management*, *25*(2), 203–218. doi:10.1080/09537325.2012.759203

Li, W., & Chen, J. (2020). Manufacturer's vertical integration strategies in a three-tier supply chain. *Transportation Research Part E, Logistics and Transportation Review*, *135*, 101884. doi:10.1016/j.tre.2020.101884

Li, Y., Liu, H., Lim, E. T. K., Goh, J. M., Yang, F., & Lee, M. K. O. (2018). Customer's reaction to cross-channel integration in omnichannel retailing: The mediating roles of retailer uncertainty, identity attractiveness, and switching costs. *Decision Support Systems*, *109*, 50–60. doi:10.1016/j.dss.2017.12.010

Meristö, T. (2020). Scenarios will help SMEs out of corona crisis and beyond. In *Proceedings of the 2020 ISPIM Innovation Conference (Virtual) Event" Innovating in Times of Crisis" held on 7 to 10 June 2020*. LUT Scientific and Expertise Publications.

Mittal, S., & Kumar, V. (2019). Study of knowledge management models and their relevance in organisations. *Int. J. Knowledge Management Studies*, *10*(3), 322–335.

Musso, F. (2010). Innovation in marketing channels: Relationships, technology, channel structure. *Symphonya: Emerging Issues in Management*, (1), 23-42.

Nanda, P., & Kumar, V. (2022). Information Processing and Data Analytics for Decision Making: A Journey from Traditional to Modern Approaches. *Information Resources Management Journal*, *35*(2), 1–14.

Priyono, A., Moin, A., & Putri, V. N. A. O. (2020). Identifying digital transformation paths in the business model of SMEs during the COVID-19 pandemic. *Journal of Open Innovation*, *6*(4), 104.

Rohm, A. J. (2001). *Channel strategy transformation within an Internet-enabled channels environment: Findings and implications across five firms*. University of Massachusetts Amherst.

Rosenbloom, B. (2007). The wholesaler's role in the marketing channel: Disintermediation vs. reintermediation. *International Review of Retail, Distribution and Consumer Research*, *17*(4), 327–339.

Rosenbloom, B. (2013). Functions and institutions: The roots and the future of marketing channels. *Journal of Marketing Channels*, *20*(3-4), 191–203.

Song, P., Wang, Q., Liu, H., & Li, Q. (2020). The value of buy-online-and-pickup-in-store in omni-channel: Evidence from customer usage data. *Production and Operations Management*, *29*(4), 995–1010.

Stephen, A. T., & Toubia, O. (2010). Deriving value from social commerce networks. *JMR, Journal of Marketing Research*, (47), 215–228.

Subagyo, K. V., & Ernestivita, G. (2020). Entrepreneurial Parameters and Performance of MSMEs in East Java Province of Indonesia. *International Journal of Business Innovation and Research*, *23*(2), 267–282.

Yin, R. K. (2009). *Case study research: Design and methods* (4th ed.). Sage.

Yin, R. K. (2011). Applications of case study research. *Sage (Atlanta, Ga.)*.

Chapter 2
Responding to the COVID-19 Pandemic:
Medtech Innovations at Innaccel Technologies

Ameer Asra Ahmed
Dayananda Sagar College, India

Harold Andrew Patrick
Jain University (Deemed), India

EXECUTIVE SUMMARY

Though the company InnAccel Technologies Pvt. Ltd. started as an incubator in 2012, it combined its operations with Coeo Labs and Sattva Medtech, the former incubates, in 2019, thereby creating a single entity with a portfolio of innovative and life-saving products in the field of medical technology. It developed three innovative products, namely VapCare, Fetal Lite, and SAANS. With growing COVID-19 cases worldwide, there was a dire need for respiratory support, which could be in the form of invasive and non-invasive ventilation systems. Hence, InnAccel launched Saans Pro, which is a non-invasive ventilation system, an infrastructure independent technology for COVID-19 patients in ICU. It could be used to treat patients who are not stressed and have no other organ failure. The case presents the three main challenges faced by firms: commercialization, consumer acceptance of its products (Indian) in domestic and international markets, and dilemma of whether to venture into the international markets.

DOI: 10.4018/978-1-6684-3504-5.ch002

INTRODUCTION

Siraj Dhanani quoted "*While plastic was first used in roads in India, it was a British entrepreneur who patented the tech*" from an article he read in the *The Economist* about how a British entrepreneur once saw the road crews in India burning plastic in the potholes along with the tar in order to make the road stronger and pursued this innovation by converting it into a technology thereby resulting in a patented commercial product and enormous economic value creation (The Economist, n.d.). Though the innovation happened in the form of *"Jugaad"* in India, it was converted into a patented technology by Britisher by incorporating recycled plastic. The question that troubled Siraj Dhanani was why couldn't a road engineer in India who invented this *"Jugaad"* think of converting this innovation into a product? For several days Siraj Dhanani was deeply lost in his thoughts of how India could be transformed for the better by overcoming this inability of Indians to convert their own local inventions or innovations into a technology or a product. This led to the birth of a medical innovation based company called InnAccel Technologies Pvt. Ltd (Dhanani, 2019).

Thus, he was bitten by the entrepreneurial bug. Having studied and worked in the pharmaceutical industry, he decided to venture into it and started his first entrepreneurial venture called PharmARC in 2003, with his partner and co-founder, Amit Sadana. This was mainly a KPO that provided sales & marketing analytics and business consulting services across pharmaceutical and healthcare industry. Siraj successfully ran this venture with Amit, expanded to Basel (Switzerland) and New Jersey (USA), and then successfully sold PharmARC to IMS Health in 2012. Siraj now wished to focus on product innovation especially in the area of healthcare. His passion was to incubate innovative, life-saving products in the field of medical technologies (MedTech) which had a great societal impact (Dhanani, 2019). Siraj Dhanani realised that the biggest challenge in medical devices is that a lot of innovation happens mainly in the West. Work in India usually ended up with making cheaper versions or manufacturing of these advanced medical devices that were made by and for developed world requirements. There was hardly any innovation being done to develop products and solutions to solve the massive challenges facing developing countries such as India in the healthcare domain.

There were many challenges in India and other developing countries due to which they are not known for inventing or innovating medical equipment. The long gestation period from idea to commercialization, a poorly developed funding ecosystem for innovation, and a low perception among potential customers on the ability of local firms to produce world-class devices were just some such obstacles. Notwithstanding these, Siraj Dhanani realised that it was first necessary to identify the major healthcare problems that could be addressed through innovative medical equipment. He engaged with another veteran in the field of medical technology named A. Vijayarajan, who had spent more than thirty-five years in this space, and was the Head-Product development at GE Medical systems. They both decided to start an incubator to create a conducive platform for bright ideas and minds in this field to come together in one space. This led to the birth of InnAccel Technologies in 2012 as a medical technology accelerator with a purpose of supporting start-ups in the domain of medical technology and devices. Since then, the company has transformed to a medical device company having four innovative medical devices.

Over the period of the last 9 years, InnAccel has faced and overcome many issues and challenges. However, some of the main challenges being faced by InnAccel currently are:

1. **Commercialization** of InnAccel's portfolio of innovative medical devices – this requires access to patient capital and InnAccel is at the last stretch of the long cycle of product development. Further, there was the dilemma of whether to venture into the international markets given the duration and high costs involved in obtaining registrations, carrying out clinical validations and marketing in each geography.
2. **Consumer Acceptance** of InnAccel's products (Indian products) in the Domestic and International markets since hardly any Indian company has introduced first-in world technologies in the medical device market in India.
3. Inconsistencies in the Goods & Services **Taxation levels** and **Import Policies**
4. **Dilemma** of whether to venture into the international markets.

BACKGROUND OF THE INDUSTRY

"MedTech is a growing sector that comprises of everything from bandages to MRI machines and serves as a significant part of an effective healthcare system. It includes diagnostics, hospital equipment, consumables, surgical tools, implants, software, and various other kinds of lifesaving and life-enhancing technologies. The MedTech industry in India is estimated to be Rs.50-70,000 crore, growing briskly at 15 per cent annually, and is expected to reach Rs. 150,000 crores by 2025. Globally, the sector is also growing, from $500 billion today, to an expected $600 billion by 2025"(Biospectrumindia, n.d.).

The MedTech industry is dominated by the Western firms (mainly US based firms), which lead the world in product innovation. MedTech is a strong export sector for the US and a few other countries such as Israel, Switzerland, Japan and Ireland, while India still imports over 75 per cent of its medical technology. Indian companies have started treading into certain areas of MedTech, providing high-quality and affordable products in diagnostics, monitoring, implants, etc. China, though, has taken a lead in this area- having created global MedTech companies which compete on price and quality with global majors." Indian and Chinese companies on the other hand are limited to outsourced manufacturing from these global companies or do some incremental innovation on already existing technologies such X-rays, Ventilators, knee implants etc. and this innovation is mainly based on price and feature differentiation. There are limited number of Indian companies that are essentially manufacturing innovative products, as against the BioTech and Pharmaceutical space, where many Indian companies have traditionally done cutting edge work at a global level (Financialexpress, 2019).

"In the case of drugs, due to its strong reverse engineering skills, India is virtually self-sufficient. In contrast, 75% of the annual purchase of devices and diagnostics comes from imports. A WHO report (2017) on medical devices pointed out that: "almost all devices present in developing countries have been designed for use in industrialized countries". Consequently, they are often unaffordable and are maladapted to low resource settings. However, if one takes a closer look at the successes of Indian and Chinese companies, we find that these are restricted to incremental innovation on existing technologies (for price and feature differentiation). Very few companies are creating fundamentally new products, based on novel and patented, technologies, to address unmet healthcare needs, especially of the developing countries (Kumar & Bhardwaj, 2020)."

METAMORPHOSIS OF INNACCEL TECHNOLOGIES

Birth as an Incubator

InnAccel started in 2012 as a Medical Technology accelerator with a view to identify and support external healthcare start-ups in this field. With this approach, they thought that many budding entrepreneurs would come to them and they would help them to innovate novel medical equipment. However, they were disappointed as most of the ideas received focused on incremental activities such as cost reduction and adding features to the already existing products. Therefore, they decided that a different approach would be required to spur innovation. They decided to work together with a select group of young entrepreneurs who were willing to work on a new approach to identify problems through a structured process, and then to develop innovative medical technology products.

Innovation Using Stanford Biodesign Process

In 2015, they shifted their focus to identifying the key medical problems needing product / device based solutions and developing a portfolio of products based on these needs identified using Stanford's Biodesign process. They started working closely on this by themselves, and through two incubate companies, Coeo Labs and Sattva Medtech. This Biodesign innovation process adopts a multi-disciplinary and systematic approach in order to identify the unmet healthcare needs, development of new and prospective technologies to address these unmet needs following which is the development is of business and commercialization plans to bring them into patient care. Biodesign is well-suited for exploring prospective innovative solutions in the field of Healthcare and Medical technologies. Stanford Biodesign brings people from diverse backgrounds and forms multi-disciplinary teams consisting of doctors, engineers and designers to examine clinical needs within an Indian setting and identify opportunities for medical technology innovation. The Biodesign process is a 5-step design thinking process comprising of Empathize, Define, Ideate, Prototype and Test. Biodesign process invented by Thomas Krummel of the Stanford university is divided into three stages namely: Identify, Invent & Implement (SBCB, n.d.).

Siraj Dhanani and Vijayarajan onboarded an ENT surgeon Dr. Jagdish Chaturvedi, who had completed the Stanford India Biodesign fellowship and with his assistance, they led the clinical immersion efforts by undergoing training in this Biodesign process and then stepped into its initial stage to gain an insight into the unmet needs in the field of medical equipment. The InnAccel team, along with teams of their incubate companies, spent several months visiting various hospitals, engaging with doctors, spending hours observing the hospital environment and identifying why deaths are happening in hospitals in India, and further explore if there are any medical equipment that can help reduce or prevent such deaths taking place in these hospitals. This approach was further strengthened with detailed secondary research and analysis. This ground up innovation process that they followed was a big differentiator for them, it created a systematic approach in trying to derive solutions leading to a strong foundation to innovate in order to solve existing problems and challenges in the Indian hospitals, rather than the often used method of creating or importing a product and then trying to figure out where it works and push for sales.

Through 2015, the teams identified around 8 to 10 major reasons for deaths in hospitals. Some of these were high rate of deaths of ICU patients on ventilator's, high infant's or neonatal deaths, preventable perinatal and maternal deaths, lack of hygiene, unequal or limited distribution of skilled healthcare staff especially the ICU, high cost of medical treatment and drugs etc. The team then narrowed down their focus to 3 major reasons where death could be prevented in hospitals with the intervention of the appropriately designed medical devices. These are as below:

1. **Ventilator-Associated Pneumonia (VAP)** is one of the leading causes of mortality in the ICU, causing ~2.5 lakh deaths each year in India. While incidence of VAP in patients on invasive ventilators above 2 days has a high 30 to 40 per cent, the mortality rate once contracted is also very high.
2. Inadequate **foetal monitoring** and thus **undetected foetal asphyxia** leads to over ~3 lakh preventable perinatal and maternal deaths in India. The existing technology is cumbersome and constrained in low-resource settings as the infrastructure and skill requirements for operation and resulting usability challenges are high.
3. The teams found that more than 75% babies with **Respiratory Distress Syndrome** (breathing disorder) at birth did not have access to ambulance and had to be transported to the nearest Neonatal ICU (NICU) in auto rickshaws, private and public transport with a manually powered breathing support called an ambu-bag resulting in high infant mortality. Many neonatal deaths occur per annum due to lack of access to NICU and breathing support to just born babies (Yadavar, 2018).

Product Development and Merger

Over a period of four years, the teams of InnAccel, Coeo Labs and Sattva Medtech, worked on the above problems to create a portfolio of innovative life-saving products across specialty areas. This involved conceptualization and solution development for the problems identified. Solution validation and confirmation was done during the product design. Intellectual Property was developed and registered in the relevant geographies. A continuous cyclical effort at prototyping, pilot testing and validation has been done. Additionally, efforts on obtain international registration and certifications for the products developed were also initiated, as these are vital in establishing credibility in the medical device industry. In the year 2019, prior to the launch of the products, these two incubates -Coeo Labs and Sattva Medtech- merged with InnAccel. This was done to provide a strong base for the commercialization of the products. The InnAccel team of founders now comprises of five members namely Siraj Dhanani, (Founder & CEO), Vijayarajan (Founder & CTO), Nitesh Jangir (Director – Critical care), Vibhav Joshi (Director – Maternal & Child Health), Sumedh Kaulgad (Director – Maternal & Child Health). The list of some of the reputed national and international awards secured by InnAccel Technologies is as shown below:

- *Featured in Nasscom's Startup Konnect 2015*
- *Grant Award – The Affordable Inventions in MedTech Research Fellowship Lemelson Foundation, 2017*

- *Best MedTech Start-up, ASSOCHAM, 2018*
- *Biospectrum Feature, XIth Annual MedTech Summit of Biodesign Programme organised under The Indian Department of Biotechnology, 2018*
- *Millennium Alliance Grant 2018*
- *GCE India Award 2019*

PRODUCT INNOVATIONS AT INNACCEL TECHNOLOGIES

In 2019-20, InnAccel came out with innovative products in the form of first of kind medical equipment namely VapCare, Fetal Lite and SAANS. All these innovative medical devices were launched in 2019 – 2020. Subsequently in 2020-21, in response to COVID (Malhotra & Kumar, 2021), the company also developed a device named SAANS Pro.

VapCare medical device was launched to address the problem of lung infection in ventilated patients (Fig. 1). Research suggests that such infections result in high deaths in ICUs and is usually a result of poor nursing practices, high patient to nurse ratio particularly in developing country ICUs, high pathogen density environment and protocol non-compliance. In invasive ventilators, when the pipe is fitted into the throat, saliva and other secretions from the airway and the oral cavity gets passed on to the lungs resulting in acute bacterial infections. Such cases require manual suctioning of secretions from airway and oral cavities at regular intervals. The main drawback of this manual suctioning is that it is a blind procedure, it could induce trauma due to over-suctioning, it is heavily dependent on skill of ICU staff, and increases risk of cross-infections (Hindu Businessline Bureau, 2020)

Figure 1. VapCare medical equipment
Source: InnAccel presentation Brief Oct 2020

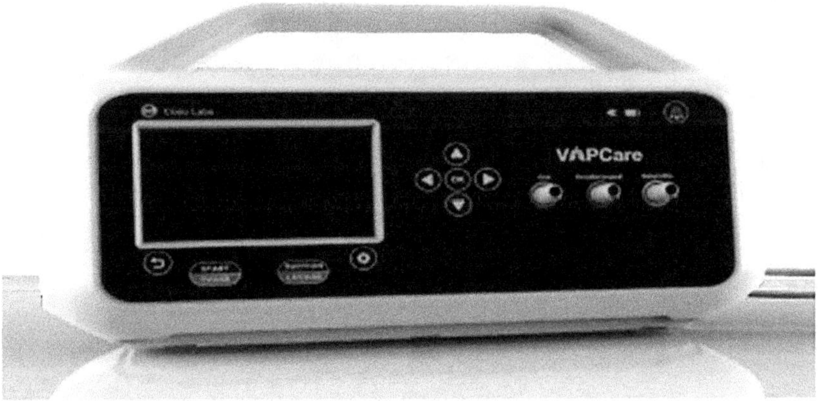

Further, manual oral suctioning especially during covid-19 like pandemic could result in infection to the nurses. VapCare is the world's first automated, intelligent, oral hygiene management system for ventilated patients in ICU which comprises of automated secretion clearance from the oral cavities, sensor-controlled suction duration, automated port block detection and is also compatible with most of the endotracheal and tracheostomy tubes. This result in improved patient safety, caregiver's safety, minimises cross-infections, reduces the workload of the ICU staff considerably and also ensures compliance with the safety protocols. VapCare is registered with US FDA and Indian CDSCO. InnAccel Technologies has received the following national and international awards for VapCare.

- *Winner of Top 16 healthcare technology global: American College of Cardiology, 2015*
- *Regional Winner of Challenge Cup: 1776 Washington DC, 2015*

Fetal Lite medical equipment (fig. 2) was developed to address the preventable perinatal and maternal deaths across India that occurs due to poor labour monitoring. As per the statistics, poor labour monitoring results in more than 3 lakh perinatal and maternal deaths in India. Contrary to the doppler-based ultrasound scanning devices that are normally used across hospitals in India, Fetal Lite is an fetal ECG-based labour monitor. The main highlight of this labour monitor is that it is portable in nature and can be used even in remote areas where it is difficult to install an ultrasound scanning machine. Fetal Lite has an intelligent probe localisation algorithm to make it easier for care providers to localise the foetal heart and has a single probe for doing so while the ultrasound scanning machines use multiple probes which constantly needs repositioning to locate the foetal heart. Also, movements can distort the signals, and the probes need to be frequently repositioned to get accurate readings. Further, the signal is digital and can be transmitted easily to other devices at the hospital or doctor.

Figure 2. Fetal Lite medical equipment
Source: InnAccel presentation Brief Oct 2020

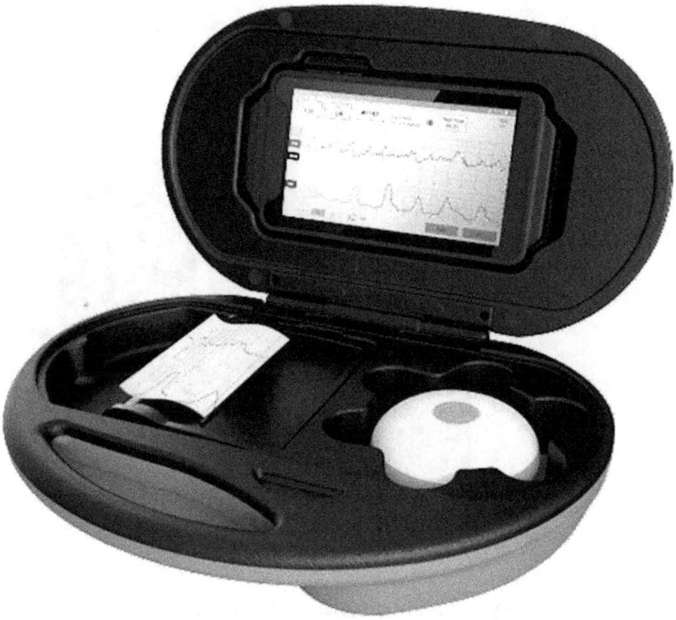

After GE and Fetal Lite InnAccel developed the second ECG-based labour monitoring device globally. Unlike the ultrasound based fetal heart rate (fHR) device and Uterine contraction monitoring (UC) this Fetal Lite device is AI enabled, does not require constant repositioning of probes as it uses just a single probe, has high accuracy in detecting fetal heart, provides consistent outputs and needs lower operating skill. Covid-19 pandemic has made all mothers-to-be reluctant to visit the hospitals for their routine scans and the current systems are not suited for monitoring at home, however Fetal Lite overcomes this drawback as well due to its portable nature and can also be used by smaller healthcare centres in India. It connects with InnAccel's cloud-based monitoring platform thereby allowing real-time monitoring, alerts and notifications for doctors, printable reports, patient scan history, patient record analytics. Fetal Lite is already European CE certified, also registered with Indian CDSCO as well as applying for US FDA registration.

Figure 3. SAANS medical device
Source: InnAccel presentation Brief Oct 2020

SAANS (fig. 3) is a truly one-of-a-kind medical technology innovation that has benefitted just born babies immensely. More than 1.5 lakh neonatal deaths occur in India every year due to lack of effective CPAP (Continuous Positive Airway Pressure) therapy at the point of birth, during transportation and in non-NICU settings. The current technology-based bubble CPAPs are highly resource intensive, has high skill dependency and is only available in NICUs which are few in developing countries and restricted to bigger cities and urban centres. The bag and mask technology that is an alternative, has high risk of Pneumothorax, has high skill dependency and there is no control over pressure while the Oxygen therapy technology has low efficacy due to no pressure regulation mechanism and is not clinically recommended. All these drawbacks of the existing technologies indicate a strong requirement for a neonatal CPAP system. SAANS is an effective specialized neonatal CPAP system that can operate in a variety of modes and has been made robust to work in difficult conditions.

Some of its unique features are in-built compressor, ability to work in all transport modes and power sources (AC, DC, vehicle battery charger), has a battery backup of 6 hours to operate in areas with no or intermittent electricity, light & portable, low skill requirement, compatible with all major humidifiers and interfaces. If all other modes fail, SAANS also has a patented manual mode whereby caregivers can manually pump the balloon, and the baby receives CPAP breathing support at safe levels. This device is in line for regulatory approval in 2021. InnAccel Technologies has received the following national and international awards for SAANS.

- *Commonwealth Innovation Award*
- *Winner, FICCI-Terumo Health Care Excellence Award (Innovation category), 2014*
- *Winner, Tata Social Enterprise Challenge: Tata Trust and IIMC, 2015*
- *Sixth position (4000$), Global Business Model Competition USA, 2015*
- *Winner, Millennium Alliance: FICCI USAID TBD, 2016*

Figure 4. SAANS Pro medical device
Source: InnAccel presentation Brief Oct 2020

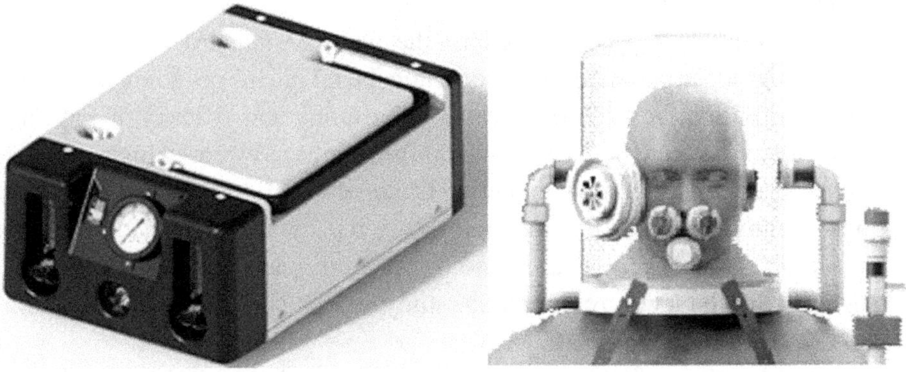

In a strategic response to COVID (Kumar & Gupta, 2021), InnAccel quickly mobilized and explored the options to utilise their expertise. Through intensive efforts and innovation, within a record period of 2-month (during the national lock-down), the InnAccel team was able to enhance the capabilities of their SAANS product to be used as a CPAP and HFNC (High Flow Nasal Cannula) device for adults. SAANS Pro (fig. 3) was tested and brought to market in a record time and is used to treat mild and moderate Covid-19 conditions. This non-invasive ventilation treatment of critical Covid-19 patients emerged as a first line respiratory support for mild to moderate covid-19 patients and prevented their conditions from worsening and needing invasive ventilation in ICUs. A further extension with a CPAP Helmet was launched in July 2020 which was invented for use by Covid-19 patients. This unique Helmet interface provided for safe ventilation for Covid-19 patients and also minimized the risk of cross-infection and enhanced safety for healthcare staff. Moreover, minimal skill was required for handling this equipment and it was compatible with other systems.

IPR AT INNACCEL TECHNOLOGIES

InnAccel has applied for and has been granted IPR in the following technologies:

1. Patent filed and granted for systems and methods for automatically removing fluid from multiple regions of a respiratory tract technology (used in VapCare) in USA, China, Europe, Japan, South Africa besides India. The clinical trial in India has been completed at Omni hospital, Hyderabad which comprised of a 30-patient study to assess the safety and performance of VapCare device. Another study at SL Raheja hospital, Mumbai wherein an observational study of secretion management and oral hygiene protocols for 6 intubated COVID patients comparing VapCare against the manual standard of care has been carried out and completed. Another clinical trial in still on-going at Narayana Health in Bangalore on 400 patients on the safety and efficacy of VapCare.
2. Provisional patent filed for Medical Electrode System which facilitates Impedance reduction and conductive Channel Creation between Sites of Gel Ingress and Conductive Part technology (used in Fetal Lite) in USA, EU, China and India. The clinical evaluation has been completed at DMH Hospital & BMC, Pune which was a comparative study between Fetal Lite and the standard NST-CTG system
3. Patent under process for Continuous Positive Airway Pressure Device technology (used in SAANS) in India, China & Nigeria. The clinical evaluation has been completed in MVJ hospital, Hoskote to study its safety and efficacy on 205 patients. SAANS Neonatal CPAP clinical trials have been completed in MVJ Hospital on 128 patients. The SAANS Helmet Interface clinical evaluation in still ongoing at Narayana Health, Bangalore for over a 100 SARI patients.

MARKET FOR MEDICAL DEVICES IN INDIA

The Medical Device market in India was estimated to be $6.3 billion in 2013 and was projected to grow to $42 billion by 2025 growing at a cumulative annual growth rate of over 17% but is accompanied by still-low levels of per capita spend (projected at $30/year in India, about 5% of the projected US per capita spend)- resulting in a growing need, and market, for affordable MedTech innovation. This need, and market, is not restricted to India but all emerging markets will have large MedTech spends at low per capita income levels, and India can become a global leader in MedTech innovation for these markets (www.innaccel.com, n.d.).

The Consumables segment is the only Indian device segment and is led by companies like Hindustan Syringes and Sutures India. The high-tech and high-quality medical products space, such as Diagnostic and Imaging equipment, is largely dominated by multinationals like GE Healthcare, Philips, and Siemens. The ecosystem to support medical technology innovation has been rapidly improving over the past few years, resulting in a growing number of entrepreneurs and start-ups in the ecosystem.

INDIAN GOVERNMENT'S ROLE IN STRENGTHENING THE HEALTHCARE ECOSYSTEM

There are quite a few government bodies in India which also provides grants to start-ups in the MedTech sector such as Department of Biotechnology (DBT), Start-up India schemes and Department of Science & Technology (DST). Some of the major granting agencies include Grand Challenges, Canada, the Wellcome Trust, Gates Foundation. DBT has a range of funding programs from early-stage research to manufacturing and commercialization, including Biotechnology Ignition Grant (BIG), which is the largest early-stage biotech funding programme in India, the Small Business Innovation Research Initiative (SBIRI) scheme, the Product Commercialization Program (PCP) fund and many more that are being administered by Biotechnology Industry Research Assistance Council (BIRAC) under DBT. DBT also sponsors a Fellowship called the Stanford India Biodesign (now rebranded School of International Biodesign) which trains Fellows in MedTech innovation and has resulted in some quality start-ups emerging in India (Jarosławski & Saberwal, 2013)..

The environment in India has become very conducive for innovation in the MedTech industry. India provides a very unique platform for nurturing medical innovations. To realise the full potential of Medtech sector, the government has taken several steps and policy initiatives including initiatives to facilitate ease of doing business, tax incentives to boost domestic manufacturing, 100 per cent FDI by MNCs, predictable regulatory regime to boost confidence of investors to develop quality medical devices and setting-up exclusive infrastructure facilities, etc. Both the BIG and SBIRI grant have been received by InnAccel which has been funded by BIRAC, the funding arm of DBT. Centre for Cellular and Molecular Platforms, or C-CAMP, was conceptualised by DBT in 2009 as an enabler or catalyst of cutting-edge research and innovation in the life sciences. World class infrastructure provided forms part of the Bangalore Life Sciences Cluster (BLiSC). C-CAMP facilitates Bioscience Research and Entrepreneurship by providing Research, Development, Training and Services in state-of-the-art Technology Platforms. **Coeo labs was one of the early incubates of C-CAMP** (Krishna, 2019)

At the state level as well, there have been various initiatives in boosting innovation and the start-up ecosystem in healthcare. The government of Karnataka set up the

Bangalore Bio innovation Centre (BBC), a Section 8 company through KBITS (Karnataka Biotechnology and Information Technology Services). The state has funded grants under the Idea2PoC (proof of concept) programme for many start-ups and provided strong infrastructure at the BBC for start-ups to set-up and operate companies, laboratories and access common infrastructure in the initial stages of the development of ideas (Krishnan, 2015). Another major leap for fostering indigenous medical device manufacturing at a state level in India has been the setting-up of an exclusive medical device park in Andhra Pradesh named as Andhra Pradesh MedTech Zone (AMTZ). It is Asia's first and largest medical technology park being set-up in Visakhapatnam in an area of 270 acres.

PRIVATE SECTOR INITIATIVES IN HEALTHCARE

The role of the private sector is very important in promoting and moving start-ups towards business success. Various players in the private ecosystem include Incubators and Accelerators, Angel and Seed funds, Venture Capital and Private Equity Funds, and the journey of a successful start-up usually ends up in a IPO where it gets listed in public markets. Incubators are often more focused on innovation and help building the business model around the idea whereas Accelerators focus on the scaling of the initial product/ service of the start-up. InnAccel attracted investments by numerous angel investors that helped fuel its early growth.

Once a start-up achieves product market fit and reasonable scale, and seeks to expand, it enters into the Venture Capital (VC) stage. VC firms provide assistance in terms of guidance, connections, and community to make start-ups successful. In the case of InnAccel, a funding of USD $1 million has been invested by a venture capitalist fund named Mount Judi Ventures. VC interest, and capital, in the sector, has been slowly increasing, and is likely to explode once a couple of successes are seen in this sector.

As India's public health prepared itself for the COVID-19 pandemic, creation of ICU capacity, oxygen and ventilators emerged as primary needs in India. To enable this, Action Covid-19 Team (ACT) was formed as a group of venture capital firms and start-up founders to help start-ups firms working on solutions to fight coronavirus in India. A Rs. 100 crore grant was set up by ACT. Among the start-ups selected, InnAccel Technologies was chosen by ACT to indigenously develop oxygen devices called HFNCs /CPAP devices vis-à-vis SAANS Pro with Helmet (www.indiacsr.in, 2020). InnAccel has also recently received grants from international agencies such as International Financial Corporation.

CHALLENGES OF INNACCEL TECHNOLOGIES AND MEDTECH SECTOR

Even though InnAccel Technologies has a promising future, it faced many challenges in its road to success and overcome them. One of the most significant problems addressed by InnAccel right at the beginning was to identify the problems of unmet healthcare needs using the Stanford Biodesign process. Through this, they focused on building solutions around existing problems, rather than the other way around.

The second area where InnAccel was able to overcome a significant challenge of converting a product idea into a workable Proof of Concept, where many companies falter. Coming out with an idea to solve the problem is a lot easier than converting this idea into a product that is completely safe, feasible, economical and functional. This is usually referred to as the "valley of death" for products as during this period, the company must operate without any existing revenue but invest significantly in product development, thereby relying on their initial invested capital. InnAccel survived this through constant infusion of funds by the Founders and Angel investors, who provided the necessary capital.

The third critical challenge overcome by InnAccel was that of finding and sustaining high calibre resources over a long gestation period that medical devices require. India being more of a services industry has the necessary availability of resources for software, but it is extremely difficult to find people having the necessary product development expertise particularly in a niche sector such as medical technology. InnAccel worked closely with the teams of Coeo Labs and Sattva MedTech, who had the necessary expertise, and eventually these teams merged and became part of the senior leadership at InnAccel itself. However, there remain many challenges still as InnAccel continues its journey. These are explained below along with a few possible approaches than can address them.

The founders of InnAccel have mentioned that the biggest challenge that they have faced and continue facing is the commercialization of products. When a consumer product comes out in the market, people would be readily willing to try it out even if it means paying a large price. However, whenever a new product or a device comes out in the market in the field of medical technology, there is significant reluctance to buy mainly because of validation issues, burden of proof, certification requirements and the risks involved. Companies from developed markets have already built the brand and credibility in this space. However, companies from emerging markets find it much harder to commercialize their products.

One of the macro challenges faced by Indian medical device manufacturers is that most of the innovations that have happened in the medical devices are in the developed countries like USA, Japan, Korea, Germany and other foreign countries therefore the consumer perception and acceptance about the Indian medical products could be a challenge in terms of their acceptability towards these Indian products because the consumers mainly rely on foreign machinery which they perceive to be more reliable.

Even though a lot has been told about how MedTech sector is a sunshine sector in the Government's Make in India initiative there still exist a lot many gaps to fill, in order to boost the growth of this important sector. Many challenges are faced by the medical equipment manufacturers that need to be addressed. To start with, there is significant room to address variances in GST on some of the diagnostics products. E.g., While Instruments usually attract 18%, consumables incur GST at 12%.

Another very big deterrent to the growth of this sector is India's dependency on imports. Currently many medical devices are importable at zero basic customs duty. On the other hand, the components required by domestic manufacturers to manufacture the same in India are charged 7.5% basic customs duty, thereby penalizing any efforts to make in India. Besides, lack of regulatory systems with global standards and lack of quality product testing are hampering this sector. At present most of the medical devices can be imported by anyone from anywhere without any regulatory checks. There are rampant imports of low-cost, poor-quality equipment. All these facts pose challenges for domestic manufacturers.

Validation of medical devices forms an integral part of the complete product development lifecycle. It is important that validation is performed throughout the design, manufacturing and release stages to ensure product quality and thereby, avoid costs associated with warranties and recalls (Www.ETHealthworld.com, 2019)."

As with many industries, one of the main challenges could be the growing number of competitors in the MedTech industry. In Bangalore alone there are a growing number of start-ups in this domain. Some of the growing companies in MedTech are XCyton Diagnostics (XCyton), Bigtec Labs (Bigtec), GEH, ReaMetrix India (ReaMetrix), Embrace Global (Embrace) and Achira Labs (Achira), Jana care, ReliaSystem Engineering Solutions, IfraEyes, MedPac systems, AxioBiosolutions, Niramai (Non-Invasive Risk Assessment with Machine Intelligence), Forus Health, SigTuple etc.

THE ROAD AHEAD

"The Medical Device market in India was estimated to be $6.3 billion in 2013, is estimated to be $11 billion in 202, and is projected to grow rapidly to $42 billion by 2025 The Indian MedTech industry looks promising and its future looks bright due to many reasons such as rising number of medical facilities boosting the demand for medical devices in the market, various government initiatives such as 'Production linked incentives (PLI) scheme for Medical Devices 2020' and establishing medical parks, the government planning to develop a manufacturing base for medical devices in India and encouraging exports, 100% FDI being allowed in the medical devices sector in India and categories such as equipment and instruments, consumables and implants attracting the most FDI. In addition to the above, as part of the invitation sent to Japanese investors to invest in medical device sector, India is targeting 1200 technical collaborations. The National Medical Devices Promotion Council has been formed to promote local manufacturing of high-end medical devices and attract investments in the sector. The government plans to invest significantly in establishing medical devices parks in four states of India – Andhra Pradesh, Telangana, Tamil Nadu and Kerala. A maximum grant-in-aid of Rs. 100 crore per park will be provided to each of the respective states (Sangwan, 2020)."

The founders of InnAccel Technologies three years ago put forward a vision for the company that is to impact more than 25 million lives using 20+ products that they wish to launch in the market in the field of medical technology. The entire team of InnAccel is very outcome focussed on this vision. In the words of Vijayarajan "*We are not only making money but we are making an impact on the society, we can impact lives and still make money*".

When Siraj and Vijayarajan were asked about the road ahead for their company they said that they would be following a three-pronged approach for their future.

1. Build towards commercial success of the existing product suite. This will enhance revenue and enable the company to focus on continuous product improvement based on customer feedback. This would also include development of adjacent products in the same therapeutic areas to strengthen the features, functionality and functioning of the products. Also InnAccel has launched their novel products in India, the promoters have plans to take it overseas in the near future.
2. Continue to explore, design, develop and launch need-based products based on the unmet healthcare needs of the patients and the hospitals. The exercise of visiting various hospitals from time to time and speaking to patients and engaging with doctors and hospital staff and trying to identify the problem areas and generating ideas and hence products to overcome those problem areas would be continued even in the future.
3. The team would also work consistently towards making InnAccel technologies more data-driven and bring about technology introduction into healthcare.
4. The team wishes to establish InnAccel technologies and its products in the International markets.

CONCLUSION

InnAccel Technologies, rather than copying existing technologies, tried to solve problems specific to emerging markets and developing countries like India, which are ignored so far by large multinational companies. Unlike other medical technology companies, which are typically working on a variant of an existing technology, InnAccel has focused on identifying existing problems and building a product to come up with completely novel solutions. All of these devices have been built from scratch following the Stanford Biodesign process. They are currently in the process of building towards the commercialization of its first suite of products in the Domestic as well as moving into International markets. InnAccel Technologies is one such company which not just believes in increasing their market share and revenues, but has focused on needs-based innovation in order to save lives.

REFERENCES

Biospectrumindia. (n.d.). *Medical device manufacturers are facing a lot of challenges.* Retrieved March 10, 2021, from https://www.biospectrumindia.com/features/17/11062/medical-device-manufacturers-are-facing-a-lot-of-challenges.html

Dhanani, S. (2019, April 24). *Making India a hub for product innovation.* Retrieved March 10, 2021, from https://bloncampus.thehindubusinessline.com/entrepreneurship/making-india-a-hub-for-product-innovation/article26933987.ece

Financialexpress. (2019). *InnAccel: The Medtech startup that is innovating to save lives.* Retrieved from https://www.financialexpress.com/industry/sme/innaccel-the-medtech-startup-that-is-innovating-to-save-lives/1651781/

Hindu Businessline Bureau. (2020, April 15). *InnAccel Technologies rolls out non-invasive ventilator.* Retrieved March 10, 2021, from https://www.thehindubusinessline.com/companies/innaccel-technologies-rolls-out-non-invasive-ventilator/article31348281.ece

Jarosławski, S., & Saberwal, G. (2013). Case studies of innovative medical device companies from India: Barriers and enablers to development. *BMC Health Services Research, 13*(1), 1–8. doi:10.1186/1472-6963-13-199 PMID:23721110

Krishna, V. (2019, April 22). *Watch: How incubator-turned-medtech company InnAccel is innovating for Indias needs.* Retrieved March 10, 2021, from https://yourstory.com/2019/04/innaccel-innovates-healthcare-india-emerging-markets

Krishnan, R. (2015, December 14). *Seven charts that show why India's healthcare system needs an overhaul*. Retrieved March 10, 2021, from https://www.livemint.com/Opinion/qXD81719wXXDQVpGyyARrO/Seven-charts-that-show-why-Indias-healthcare-system-needs-a.html

Kumar, V., & Bhardwaj, A. (2020). Deploying Cloud Based Healthcare Solutions: A Holistic Approach. *International Journal of Service Science, Management, Engineering, and Technology*, *11*(4), 87–100. doi:10.4018/IJSSMET.2020100106

Kumar, V., & Gupta, G. (Eds.). (2021). *Strategic Management During a Pandemic*. Routledge. doi:10.4324/9781003125648

Kumar, V., & Malhotra, G. (Eds.). (2021). *Stakeholder Strategies for Reducing the Impact of Global Health Crises*. IGI Global Publications. doi:10.4018/978-1-7998-7495-9

Sangwan, S. (2020, October 20). *Medtech startup InnAccel raises $1.5M in pre-Series A round led by Mount Judi Ventures*. Retrieved March 10, 2021, from https://yourstory.com/2020/10/funding-alert-medtech-startup-innaccel-mount-judi-ventures?utm_pageloadtype=scroll

SBCB. (n.d.). *Timeline & History, Stanford Byers Center for Biodesign*. Retrieved March 10, 2021, from https://biodesign.stanford.edu/about-us/timeline.html

The Economist. (n.d.). Biotechnology Saving Lives & Transforming Healthcare in the 21st Century. *The Economist Magazine*. Retrieved March 10, 2021, from https://archive.bio.org/TransformingHealthcare

Yadavar, S. (2018, September 6). *More Indians Die Of Poor Quality Care Than Due To Lack Of Access To Healthcare: 1.6 Million*. Retrieved March 10, 2021, from https://www.indiaspend.com/more-indians-die-of-poor-quality-care-than-due-to-lack-of-access-to-healthcare-1-6-million-64432/

Chapter 3
Strategic Shift in Marketing Communication During COVID-19

Rahul Gupta
https://orcid.org/0000-0002-2328-0119
Amity Business School, Amity University, Noida, India

Amit Kumar Pandey
Amity Business School, Amity University, Noida, India

Sanjeev Bansal
Amity Business School, Amity University, Noida, India

EXECUTIVE SUMMARY

During COVID-19, several disruptions were reported, activities got halted, and the focus of marketing shifted towards social media due to engagements of the clients towards various available platforms. The use of the internet and social media increased during and after the pandemic. Digital communications attracted customers towards contactless access and the availability of required services. Interactions among various stakeholders including companies, suppliers, and customers increased during these times for hassle-free and uninterrupted services. A paradigm shift was observed in advertising patterns, customer relationship management, service management, and digital tools and media engagements during the pandemic. A strategic shift, observed during the pandemic, has been explored and covered in this chapter. A theoretical framework of hassle-free uses of digital tools in the pandemic has also been developed and included using various social media platforms.

DOI: 10.4018/978-1-6684-3504-5.ch003

INTRODUCTION

Covid-19 stunned the world with an unprecedented crisis, stagnating numerous activities from daily chores to life-saving activities (Kumar & Malhotra, 2021). The catastrophic situation during the pandemic added a new meaning to remote working (Kumar & Gupta, 2021). Marketer did not pretend that every thig is normal and take this as head on. Internet became savior for performing various activities. The emergence of social media and digital marketing got an incomparable surge in their uses for communicating with their targeted segment. Mobiles phones, computers, tablets, and laptops were used as a medium to support social media platforms (Telegram, WhatsApp, MS Team, ZOOM, Wee box, YouTube, Linked In, and Edmodo, etc.), to work from home/remote working (Bhardwaj & Kumar, 2022). Millions of consumers made their e-commerce transaction for the first-time during Pandemic across the world. These platforms were extensively used by people of all ages, genders. Employees from private sector, self-employed and government employee used internet for their learning, entertainment, work-related assignments. Digital world attracted customers due to contact less access for availing required services. User's requirements are addressed with various features (free as primary and paid as advanced offerings) within their digital ecosystem. Managing their digital presence becomes an important aspect for not only start-ups but for established organizations. Digital platforms are likely to remain in due in large extent, as these e-commerce transactions are efficient, cost effective, and safe in comparison to visiting a physical store for shopping and other services (Saurabh & Kumar 2017). Uses of protective measures and social distancing is going to remain a norm in new normal. Before taking the final decision for purchase, customers search and rely on reviews through various digital platforms. Online transactions and use of social media come with its own challenges, like data breaches and site hacking, hence required strategies (encryptions and passwords) to secure the operations from external and internal threats. Strengthening the marketing strategies and achieve marketing goals, companies used various online tools of marketing communication to promote marketing activities and to check customer churnings. It helps to establish interactions among various stakeholders including companies, stakeholders, suppliers, and customers. A variety of business activities are supported by the various Information Technology tools in these times (Kumar et al., 2022). Digital marketing being an integral part of Integrated marketing communication helps to enhance the sales volume and strengthen the organization's competitive position during Covid -19 outbreaks. This chapter shall discuss about the rethinking for growth and support of digital marketing tools in various activities and hassle-free services during the pandemic.

DIGITAL TOOLS AND MARKETING COMMUNICATION

Emerging technologies make sales effort more convenient and helpful for the customers in 21st century (Nanda & Kumar, 2022). To effectively communicate the target audience and generate awareness about the products digital tools are extensively used. Managing customer integration with the organization has become convenient with the help of appropriate marketing communication tools. A successful marketer understands the uses of these tools to generate incremental business and to reach at the target audience across (Kusumawati et al., 2021).

One of the most prominent tools used for integrated marketing communication is advertising where a paradigm shift has been observed during the pandemic. For maximum reachability and awareness of products and services among the customers. Above the line (ATL) advertising is terminology used for the mass appeal, where different media like Television, Radio, Print media, Cinema and Outdoor media like billboard and commuter displays are extensively used for communication (Kumar & Saurabh, 2021).

DIGITAL TRANSFORMATION DURING PANDEMIC

For supply of raw materials (inclusive of essential services) to finished goods, digital tools have worked as a flickering light which gives strength from manufacturing to marketing organizations. Firms including small entrepreneurial ventures adopted digital strategy to survive during pandemic (Kovid et al., 2021). When world's major activities were put on hold, digital platform and online tools are only ray of hope for the same. Digital advertising offered unmatched reachability among customers when other media and modes of communication were non-functional/unavailable. Internet-based technologies and application platforms supported unlimited service. These services include ordering food, medicine, remote teaching, entertainment via OTT platforms and even personalized services like medical consultation, therapies all were available online.

According to McKinsey Global Survey for executives, "Companies have accelerated the digitization of their customer and supply-chain interactions and their internal operations from last few years. The share of digital or digitally enabled products in their portfolio has accelerated in the recent past. In a survey among many corporations, nearly all respondents confirmed that their companies have stood up with solutions to meet new demands, and much more quickly than they had thought, or it was possible before the crisis. Organizations have made considerable amounts of expenses in these technologies and expect to use them further even after the pandemic is over. Innovation in technology enabled platforms were the critical components to make strategy for speeding up services while pandemic.

Points for Effective Communication

During Pandemic, disseminating information across channels was a challenge for everyone. Sectors like medical to academia, revenue to brand building, networking to recruitment, logistics to supply chain, students to business fraternity, had to struggle for communication like the way they were communicating normally. Organization shifted their communication style during these times, they emphasized on the support and help received from others. Some issues are discussed in paras given below.

- **Shift in Messaging:** Pandemic forces marketing companies to indulge in karmic marketing. A Canadian car company changes their TV commercial and says "instead of showing you new models in normal time, we appreciate great work done by nurses and doctors. A new Budweiser advertisement also praises the nurses and doctors. Messages were supporting local communities in the vicinity. Offer hope, as customers will never forget how they were treated during their need and time of crisis, this creates positive energy. All our messages should make customers feel safe and not left alone during need, keep them informed with important messages for.
- **Search Data Review:** Pandemic impacted the drop in keyword searches and conversion rates, firms must keep a track on expressiveness on competitors' advertisement and grab on the opportunity to advertise.
- **Competitive Analysis and Auction Insights:** firms must seek an opportunity in case competitors have paused or scaled down communication, ramping up your communication will provide an opportunity.
- **Strategic Changes:** change is only constant and one must keep a pace with it. Firm must navigate employer strategies for effective communication. Firm shall indulge in trend analysis to view key words and test against search items. Key words may differ geographically and changed traffic shall be taken care.
- **Focus on Social and Top-of-Funnel Communication:** Trends suggest that customers can be communicated through social media, and other top-of-funnel approaches.
- **Review of Ad Copy:** critically review associated advertisement and advertisement copy before reactivating your communication. Offer a unique value proposition to the clients, by ensuring all relevant messages in the communication. Good results can be achieved by focusing on reactivating top twenty percent performances, this tempered and smart approach of reactivation will fetch promising results.

Business Environment and Social-Media

Millions of users are spending a good amount of time on social media sites like Twitter, Facebook, WhatsApp, Instagram, and LinkedIn as a daily routine (Ayodeji & Kumar, 2019). Hwang et al. (2020) studied that many conservative organizations are making their presence online due to pandemic. Omni channel retail formats are preferred by many retailers by adopting government guidelines and following Covid protocols. Crick & Crick, (2020) talked about sharing of technical knowhow in manufacturing, developing vaccines and sharing other relevant information. Firms used digital platforms for their marketing communication and analytics to increase their customer reach. Various innovative technologies like artificial intelligence, and block chain is used for better results. Habes et al., (2020) points out that Social media campaigns are extensively used to promote CSR activities by following Covid protocols as an attitudinal change in behavior. Keeping the technological features constant, users in varied cultures use these sites differently. Seetharaman (2020) emphasized on realignment of product development strategies, alliances, and value creation activities to overcome the situation.

Dhir et al. (2015), said that these web-based social networking sites enable users to develop their public profile and connect it with other users on these platforms. These social media sites are built on the idea of an interactive Web 2.o development. Malik et al. (2016) said users on these social platforms communicate within their extended networks, rather interact with new people. Social media allows users to share their live experience without boundaries. These interactive web services have been enhanced in the recent past. To remain relevant and competitive organizations use social media platforms to communicate with people. Technological advancements and information technologies have transformed the way social media platforms work and play a vital role in the success of business marketing. Social media strategies offer a platform to contribute, describe, find content, and build community. Among many available social media platforms, businesses choose which suits and are easy to use. When effective strategies are used efficiently, organizations offer better services and products (Susanto et al., 2020). Few opportunities are discussed below.

- **Revenue:** Better sales generate higher revenues, as social media generates leads which are inexpensive and effective.
- **Brand Building:** Social-media allows direct interaction among consumers and businesses and develops as a brand (Kumar & Nanda, 2019a) Enhanced customer engagements are practiced by organizing question answer sessions, with an instant feedback system remaining in place. Competitive advantages are achieved by reducing time gap in campaigns and projects.

- **Networking:** Valuable business connections are generated with professional social media sites like LinkedIn by connecting like minded people. Sites are used to maintain long term relations, exchange ideas and generate referrals. Social networking sites offer diverse learning, and exposure to multiple perspectives.
- **Recruitments:** Dhir et al. (2017) observed that Human resource departments search profiles of many prospective candidates and offer placements through social networking sites as specialists in the domain. Managers in the HR department create their own database as per their criteria. Social networking sites work beyond boundaries to generate better leads and select the right candidate.

Concern users connect with high response on a specific topic by eliminating barriers among media and participants, with openness to receive reviews as criticism/ suggestions for their services. (Kumar & Pradhan, 2015) Contents are password protected, information is exchanged effectively at a higher speed due to internet connectivity and various social media communities. Social media could easily connect users without breaching connectivity. Many scholars (Almunawar et al., 2013; Almunawar et al., 2018; Talwar et al., 2020) suggested the support of social media in business tactics to attract customers attention and acceptance of the firm's image. Using social media provides following benefits:

- Better communication among customer and organization is achieved
- Better customer service is achieved assisting their transactions.
- Better cost efficiency is achieved from marketing promotions.
- Better trends and interests can be analyzed to efficiently cater customers' demands.
- Better brand awareness is established with the help of social media.
- Brand sales traffic is steered towards the business by increasing market share through social media.

Almunawar (2013) studied and observed that Facebook is one of the best social media tools to enhance a business process, as businesses have shifted their focus on advertising through social media. Following features add their nominations as, ease of finding contact, access to notable personnel, construct better relationship, enrich exposure, niche marketing, better business positioning, and at a little cost.

Being operative continuously, control is lost while managing social media, as users utilize social media for exchanging information with high frequency. Social media contents are difficult to manage as dialogue handling among users and firms need different responses individually, the case where multiple employees work, identifying one person becomes difficult. Business operations have been transformed using social media; customer interactions are done with ease using social media platforms. Virtual communities of social media are managed by organizations.

Real word and virtual communities are somewhat similar with a difference of absence of real word restrictions available in online mode. Fine strategic advantages are achieved by firms by integrating public relations and social media. Talwar et al. (2020) said social media has the capability of innovation in processes and allows firms to gain a strategic advantage, like a blog which influences the public towards a certain opinion, generating potential followers/customers.

Social media acts as a fundamental business process for growth due to various benefits. Worldwide exposure is achieved by using social media platforms. It is a cost-efficient marketing tool to engage with a wider audience. For example, use of a content management system (CMS) to create the website and publish to the internet. Lot of useful information about products/services are available on site. Good contents acquire new customers, partners and even sponsors. Other benefits include customer satisfaction, as social media creates a voice for customers and company, both feel appreciated. Their personalized response becomes more effective in the process. Competitor's data is available on a click away, their websites are monitored, the way they interact with their customers, their blogs, contents, and designs are available. Firms can benchmark their performances with the best of their competitors.

Information Security and Social Media

Information breach is bound to happen when Businesses use social media applications. Firm must ensure to safeguard information from any unauthorized use. Susanto et al. (2016) and Susanto and Chen (2017) said security of information is characterized as data conservation and its support components inclusive of applications software, hardware for data management.

Firms are vulnerable for security breach from external and internal sources. Increased thread in social media crime demands better security. Organizations are using sophisticated tools to safeguard against malware. Many government and business organizations compulsorily use protection against malware attacks. Management at all levels must understand the complications and usability in adoption of information security. Organizations must communicate information security with training to employees as a policy and practice at all levels. Susanto et al. (2018) and Laato et al. (2020) studied and observed that security software implementation must be positively influenced by managers for developing strategy and training supports.

In this era of technology all business organizations rely on some of the other social media platforms and digital communications and services for their daily chores of activities like online banking, customer interaction through shopping, marketing etc. (Kumar & Ayodeji, 2020). Unauthorized access to confidential data is referred to as a security breach. An IBM survey with around 500 firms in 15 odd countries in 2018, revealed data breach costs around USD 3.86 million and increasing with 2.2 percent. Customer's data available at hotels, online shopping sites is prone to hacking. Failure to protect this personal data which is most conveniently used for payments leads to identity theft, due to vulnerability of network security at hotels and low technology computer systems, which are prone to attacks (Kumar & Bhardwaj, 2018). Firms brand reputation, and customers' trust and experience remain on stake in this scenario. Safeguard against these breaches is done with firewalls and antimalware software in place (Susanto, 2017; Dhir et al., 2017; Kang et al., 2019).

INTEGRATED MARKETING COMMUNICATION: THEORETICAL FRAMEWORK

Pandemic has changed the communication pattern across all the verticals including employee to employer. Essential services cannot be interrupted because of their nature of work and an alternative is essentially required. Invention often takes place in crisis time. Pandemic is a catastrophic situation for all the sectors and refocusing on the business activities are the prime objective for the corporate houses. Firms are responding to their customers as per their immediate needs like refund collections, services, delivery of the products or any kind of disposal services (Zenker, & Kock, 2020).

Brand communication is a social media tool which helps corporates to establish relationships across the channel. There are several challenges faced by the corporate houses like socially imbalance and commercial viability. Prediction about required social content is the prime objective of social media communication. Proposed strategic marketing communication model discusses the evolution of digital tools and how it is helping in various functions of sound communication. Digital tools help in creating awareness and specially to enhance the impact of advertising. It is also helpful in quantification of the effect of advertising so far. The purpose of every advertisement is to create a clear objective, to gain the knowledge about your customers and to make a funding plan for the campaigner.

Another aspect of marketing communication is to promote their contents and digital communication tools help in promoting their offers, as shoppers love to have specific discounts/offers for their purchase. Of late, consumers are using social media platforms to search the choice of their products and checking the customer review of the products to know the quality parameters (Kumar & Ayodeji, 2021).

Integrated strategic marketing communication is described by Professors Andreas Kaplan and Michael Heinlein of the ESCP. European Business School define social media as "A group of Internet-based applications that build on the ideological and technological foundations of Web 2.0, and that allow the creation and exchange of user-generated content." To create and exchange users generated content where information could be shared through technology such as blogs and social media. Social networking sites allow marketers to understand perfect segmentation of the market. It is possible with the help of the amount of information which is available in their database.

Figure 1. Strategic decision making in integrated marketing communication
(Source: Authors)

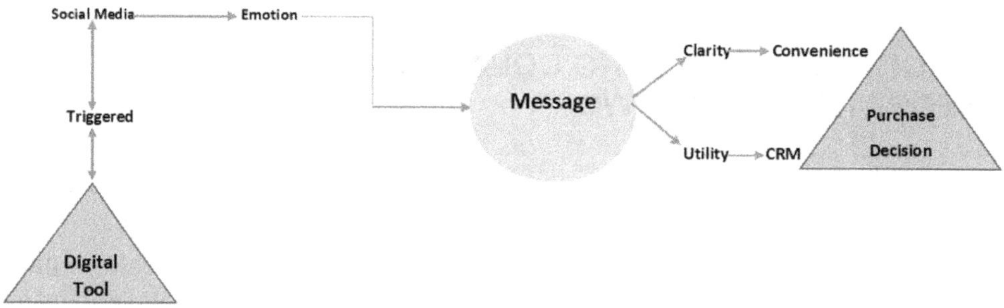

Digital tools like artificial intelligence and machine learning are also helping corporate houses to make their strategic decision making for brand promotion and also help in narrow target audience. This framework (see figure 1) represents the emergence of digital tools which triggered social media which aggravated the emotions of the customers. A repeated approached customer triggered by the advertisement aired on electronic media. Advertisement on Facebook, Instagram and twitter is also a form of promotion wherein clarity in messages is utterly required (Kumar & Nanda, 2019b). Creativity and further utility are the most important aspects of the digital media tools which maintain the customer relationship management activity, enhances the future purchase decision.

Strategic decision making in integrated marketing communication is to utilize the maximum benefits of the digital tools available in internal and external networks. Direct display has psychological impact on the mind-set of the customers wherein several digital applications are working on the advertising network. Monitoring the effort of the advertising implementing for the customer attraction is an integral part of digital platforms.

Changing Advertising Pattern While Pandemic

Advertising being a vital component of the promotion mix and during pandemic it was challenging to reach the prospective customers for new launches and building brand awareness. Statement by the Honorable Prime Minister 'Explore an opportunity in pandemic', motivated industry to focus on promotion of their products and services in a new avatar. Audience needs to be connected through advertisements and measuring the outcomes of advertisements is a tough task. Thanks to technologies like Artificial intelligence which helps advertising agencies to help in driving the real results. To target the niche populations, Artificial intelligence helps to get the right advertisements for the right segment.

Covid-19 has put the world on halt and urged the medical fraternity to rethink on the strategies to tackle such situations. The present scenario is different from the recession where sudden shrinking demands left people helpless, jobless, and clueless. Doctors are working in strenuous conditions where risk factors are high. Digital platform also helps health care workers to tackle the serious patients through available mediums. These digital platforms are still used in many hospitals to extend their services in remote locations.

Engage and Connect

Traditional media platforms with their limited capacity to expand became handy and extended their services in promotions during tough times like pandemic with the help of the emergence of digital platforms. Telemedicine and doctor on call for the consultation were available. Their consultancy charges were paid through e-wallets, changing the face of health care services during the pandemic.

New archetypal strategies were adopted to timely and effectively connect with consumers and enrich their engagements continuously. Wearing a creative hat and focusing on harnessing on the right media platform for meaningful engagement, to create brand awareness and inquisitiveness.

Influencing Marketing: Relationship building through influencing marketing in current situations with efficient use of social and digital platforms. Activities performed on these media significantly influence consumption patterns. Millennials being a huge audience depends largely on social media reviews, blog posts etc. before making their purchase choices. Influencer marketing tools can be a prodigious way for an organization to achieve its objectives with use of the right platform accompanied with the right content at appropriate time. Use of this tool is in a premature stage but slowly getting momentum due to its faster reach. A robust brand reputation can be built with the right marketing mix for the right audiences.

Understanding digital imminent: innovations are created through branding to strengthen competitive liveliness. Customer feedback serves as the best influencer in enlarging the customer base. Current pandemic has brought swift transformation into the digital epoch. Transparent message concepts create an eloquent impact on consumers.

Covid -19 Pandemic had an adverse impact on every part of our life, from places we visit to change our priorities, the way we spent our money widely changed. There was a surge in social and ecommerce advertisements during this time. India being the second fastest growing market among top 10 nations worldwide is the sixth largest advertisement expander.

With the pandemic getting deeper, media consumption habits get influenced across the channels. The web browsing saw a surge by 70 percent, with traditional Television viewing by 63% and engagement in social media grew by 61 per as compared to their normal usages. Use of WhatsApp saw the highest gain of approximately 40 percent among all applications to get connected with each other. This increased use of various messaging platforms was seen highest in the age group of 18 to 35 years. As per the research by WARC Data three firms Alphabet, Meta and Amazone accounted for half of the potential and one trillion market by 2025. Research firms observe a meteoric rise in the market, increasing 23.8% year on year to 771 billion. It is further advised that the market will grow approximately 10 percent year on year. Television advertisement is also expected to grow by 10 percent.

With the change in habits by viewer's marketers have changed the way their spending on advertising budgets. Spent on search advertising has seen a surge of 15 percent while online display by 12 percent. Their budget on cost-per-click online search advertising in telecom and internet as compared to previous when there was no impact of coronavirus. Whereas cost-per-click has increased in the sectors like pharmaceutical, skin/beauty care, online education, and insurance sector spending was highest during the same time. From now onwards for at least a few years things may not revert back to old normal but will transform to new normal. Hence marketer must build brand for future and beyond. We require redefined marketing during and after Covid-19.

Marketers must redefine rules with or without pandemic for moving forward. Instead of knowing your customers, marketing must begin with knowing your segment. Marketers should target very local and precise customers based on situations most relevant to them, meaning truly understand their need as per situation on the ground, and communicate with specific solutions. Influence customers with multiple dimensions to guide their purchase pattern from attitudinal to psychographic characteristics. Research on thousands of consumers across the countries have explored following cohorts of consumers.

- Affordability first- focusing more on functionality than brand, within their budget and means.
- Heath first- offer safe with minimum risk
- Planet first- mitigate environmental impact and enrich belief for safety
- Society first- buying from transparent and honest organizations
- Experience first- open for new experience, product, and brands.
- Compete with your buyer's best experience not with the competitors. They expect personalized experience across all their journeys.

After critical evaluation of the above statement, in spite of hope, your customers should be benefited with as per their expectations. Customers expect frictionless connection what they want when they go with no blocks. As a marketer, it is our prime responsibility to make available products as per the demand of the customers. In the present scenario, it was only possible virtually.

With robust technologies like artificial intelligence and machine learning in place, customers expect to enhance their experience across various dimensions. Make agility as an approach for marketing. Content wise like email/messages, trade like omni channel, community like virtual assistance/ home care, convenience like loyalty bonuses.

Customers must be at the center of the customer journey while connecting all the silos through which they are connected. Relationships not only matter now they are everything, built trust, develop relationships, and deliver customer experience. Organizations shall nurture their brands not behind great products but behind great values. These endeavors embodied the confluence of strategies, technologies and operation in pandemic recovery and success.

DIGITAL TOOLS IMPLICATION: A CASE STUDY OF EXACT INDIA

Exact India is an NCR based organization well known in solar module cleaning and manufacturing HDPE pipes used in various industrial applications. During the pandemic they faced the crisis of manpower to operate their machines and the number of orders were also drastically reduced due to strict lockdown imposed by authorities. It was one part of their problems but the major issue was to sustain their services with the existing customers. Mr. Safique Khan the CEO of Exact India utilized the digital media platforms to pamper their customers who were not keen to continue due to prevailing conditions. Safique discussed the issue with his core team and came out with an idea to develop a digital platform. The IT team at Exact India worked tirelessly and developed a website as "www.exactdealing.com"

to make their existing products lined up on the site. They promote solar module cleaning services and offer a discount for availing services during pandemics along with their other products like HDPF pipes and water purifiers. They were sure that their online presence and advertisement through social media would fetch him good orders. His confidence in their products, the service they offer and appreciation from their existing customers give them a confidence to further explore latest tools available for enhancing services. Safique ordered robotic machines from Ahmedabad to enhance the quality module cleaning with less manpower. Strategic team at Exact India was ready to provide the competitive services in the Indian solar market with new machines and methods. As Result of their online efforts Exact India started seeing a surge in getting orders for their products and services. With the reach of social media across the boundaries of the nation Exact India started receiving orders not only from India but from other parts of the word.

Another product HDPF pipes which has a wide use in numerous industrial applications were also displayed on digital platform. Buyers demands a virtual demonstration of products and services offered by Exact India. Mr. Shafiq prepared an excellent demonstration for their HDPE pipes and the way they offer their services to their current clients was real not virtual. Several companies from the South African continent approached for the supply of HDPE pipes after going through the product's presentation virtually available on various social media platforms. Shafiq started collecting all the required information from the various parties and demonstrated their products virtually.

Exact India upgraded their website with virtual visits on their website and started promoting their offerings at various social platforms, which gave a real sense of the opportunities for them. During the pandemic, his strategic team started lining up all those leads interested to associate with exact India. It was surprising to see that this virtual visit of customers provides a great scope of business. Apart from HDPE order from South Africa, solar module cleaning was another front where various Public Sector Undertakings dealing and working in solar energy, approached Exact India for module cleaning. Exact India witnessed a multiple surge in their business activities as compared to their business in pre pandemic times. Shafiq knew this credit goes to his virtual demonstrations and social media presence.

According to Safique "Digital platforms are a great tool to change the Sales and Marketing practices in India. There is great scope for business organizations to enhance their businesses through digital platforms". Exactdealing.com was an idea supported by the digital tools that was a revolution during the pandemic. Shafiq was thinking that before the pandemic their executives were visiting door to door for convincing and selling of the products. But during the pandemic the new problem was customer stigmatization, wherein they did not allow the executives to enter in their premises or even face to face contact became difficult due to strict Covid protocols prescribed by the authorities. Doing business and getting orders from the customers during a pandemic becomes a herculean task, but after using digital tools, it becomes handy for Exact India.

With online availability for their products and services there was a need for accepting online payments. Exact India developed a payment gateway integrated with online platforms so that their customers can make payments online through various online payment options against the product and services they buy. Exact India ensures that their executives who go to customer's premises for services are fully vaccinated and follow specified Covid guidelines. More than 700 products were available on their website exactdealing.com for the customers. As a result, Exact India recorded more than 20 percent incremental sales during the pandemic. Shafiq was happy and focused more on those products which were not available in the physical market so that online availability can further boost their sales. This pandemic taught Exact India to follow customer centric approaches and use digital platforms.

DISCUSSION

This chapter has explored various outcomes of Integrated marketing communication tools and its uses during the pandemic. A theoretical model (fig. 1) also shows the diverse impact of digital tools and social media which work as a torch bearer during the pandemic. Multiple aspects have been discussed which covered a throughout dimension of social media and digital tools. Case study of Exact India is also covering the way out of multiple hurdles in a positive way. During pandemic another challenge for marketing communication was consumer privacy wherein a small lag may lose the trust of loyal customers. As a marketer, knowledge about the legislation regarding data privacy was on priority and ensuring email campaigning under this compliance was must. Caring on the privacy of the consumers have also leveraged organization to generate business while maintaining the trust of the consumers. Repeated measures of communication for marketing activities may irritate the consumers' consequences in terms of losing customers have also seen in various places. Confidentiality, cybercrimes and breaching in security is being a challenge but with certain precautions it has been controlled by the business organizations. It doesn't mean that it has not happened. Handling of such issues are being the challenges (Pandey et al., 2020).

CONCLUSION

Shifting from online to virtual is not the solution to the problem. Since study is dealing with the uses of online promotional tools during pandemic and how to connect with the customers. Moreover, when subjects are exploratory in nature, it is difficult to conclude in a limited space. Pandemic has proved that connecting with customers and employees are easy online. Staying resilient and thriving could damage brand equity. Keep focus on those customers which you already have. Keep your customers on priority and use digital marketing strategy, online promotional tools to get back into your business on the track and in that way a head start against your competitors could be possible. Personalized emails are another tool of effective marketing communication while pandemic. Expectations of the consumers are high on a personal front, they really like to relate to not robotic or Chabot messages, rather they expect to receive personalized mails form the services providers wherein they spend money. Another aspect of communication was User Generated Content (UGC) where during online shopping, it was not possible to see and get a feel and experience of the products in person, it was only possible after purchasing and using the products. So, consumer's feedback and their reviews for the respective products fortify the purchase decision making. According to the data of Forbes, more than 93 percent of the consumers are influenced by other user's reviews.

Another challenge during the pandemic was, how to communicate with the new customers who were not aware about your product? Across the world, several manufacturers changed their track from existing facilities to manufacturing of the PPE kits, Mask and sanitizer. Entering a new field all of sudden, gave another scope cum challenge to them to communicate with their existing and new customers.

REFERENCES

Almunawar, M., Susanto, H., & Anshari, M. (2013). A cultural transferability on IT business application: IReservation system. *Journal of Hospitality and Tourism Technology*, *4*(2), 155–176. doi:10.1108/JHTT-05-2012-0015

Almunawar, M. N., Anshari, M., & Susanto, H. (2013). Crafting strategies for sustainability: How travel agents should react in facing a disintermediation. *Operations Research*, *13*(3), 317–342. doi:10.100712351-012-0129-7

Almunawar, M. N., Anshari, M., Susanto, H., & Chen, C. K. (2018). How People Choose and Use Their Smartphones. In *Management Strategies and Technology Fluidity in the Asian Business Sector* (pp. 235–252). IGI Global. doi:10.4018/978-1-5225-4056-4.ch014

Ayodeji, O. G., & Kumar, V. (2019). Social media analytics: A tool for the success of online retail industry. *Int. J. Services Operations and Informatics*, *10*(1), 79–95. doi:10.1504/IJSOI.2019.100630

Balis, J. (2020). Brand marketing through the coronavirus crisis. *Harvard Business Review*.

Bhardwaj, A., & Kumar, V. (2022). Privacy and Healthcare during COVID-19. In *Cybersecurity Crisis Management and Lessons Learned From the COVID-19 Pandemic* (pp. 82–96). IGI-Global. doi:10.4018/978-1-7998-9164-2.ch005

Cleveland, S. (2016). Social Media Systems in the Workplace: Toward Understanding Employee Knowledge Creation via Microblogging within Shared Knowledge Domains. *Informatics (MDPI)*, *3*(3), 11. doi:10.3390/informatics3030011

Crick, J. M., & Crick, D. (2020). *Coopetition and COVID-19: Collaborative business-to-business marketing strategies in a pandemic crisis*. Industrial Marketing Management.

Cummings, E., & Mather, C. (2017). Advancing Social Media and Mobile Technologies in Healthcare Education. *Informatics (MDPI)*, *4*(4), 35. doi:10.3390/informatics4040035

Dhir, A., Chen, G. M., & Chen, S. (2017). Why do we tag photographs on Facebook? Proposing a new gratifications scale. *New Media & Society*, *19*(4), 502–521. doi:10.1177/1461444815611062

Dhir, A., Chen, S., & Nieminen, M. (2015). Predicting adolescent Internet addiction: The roles of demographics, technology accessibility, unwillingness to communicate and sought Internet gratifications. *Computers in Human Behavior*, *51*, 24–33. doi:10.1016/j.chb.2015.04.056

Dhir, A., Khalil, A., Lonka, K., & Tsai, C. C. (2017). Do educational affordances and gratifications drive intensive Facebook use among adolescents? *Computers in Human Behavior*, *68*, 40–50. doi:10.1016/j.chb.2016.11.014

Dhir, A., & Tsai, C. C. (2017). Understanding the relationship between intensity and gratifications of Facebook use among adolescents and young adults. *Telematics and Informatics*, *34*(4), 350–364. doi:10.1016/j.tele.2016.08.017

Habes, M., Alghizzawi, M., Ali, S., Salih Alnaser, A., & Salloum, S. A. (2020). The Relation among Marketing ads, via Digital Media and mitigate (COVID-19) pandemic in Jordan. *International Journal of Advances Science and Technology*, *29*(7), 2326–12348.

HwangE. H.NageswaranL.ChoS. H. (2020). Impact of COVID-19 on Omnichannel Retail: Drivers of Online Sales during Pandemic. Available at SSRN 3657827. doi:10.2139/ssrn.3657827

Kang, X., Chen, W., & Kang, J. (2019). Art in the Age of Social Media: Interaction Behavior Analysis of Instagram Art Accounts. *Informatics (MDPI)*, *6*(4), 52. doi:10.3390/informatics6040052

Kovid, R. K., Kumari, D., & Pandey, S. (2021). Strategic Response to the Corona Pandemic Crisis: A Case of Indian Women Entrepreneurs. In V. Kumar & G. Malhotra (Eds.), *Stakeholder Strategies for Reducing the Impact of Global Health Crises* (pp. 68–84). doi:10.4018/978-1-7998-7495-9.ch005

Kumar, V., & Ayodeji, O. G. (2020). Web Analytics for Knowledge Creation: A Systematic Review of Tools, Techniques and Practices. *International Journal of Cyber Behavior, Psychology and Learning*, *10*(1), 1–14. doi:10.4018/IJCBPL.2020010101

Kumar, V., & Ayodeji, O. G. (2021). E-retail Factors for Customer Activation and Retention: An Empirical Study from Indian e-Commerce Customers. *Journal of Retailing and Consumer Services*, *59C*, 102399. doi:10.1016/j.jretconser.2020.102399

Kumar, V., & Bhardwaj, A. (2018). Identity Management Systems: A Comparative Analysis. *International Journal of Strategic Decision Sciences*, *9*(1), 63–78. doi:10.4018/IJSDS.2018010105

Kumar, V., & Gupta, G. (Eds.). (2021). *Strategic Management During a Pandemic*. Routledge. doi:10.4324/9781003125648

Kumar, V., & Malhotra, G. (Eds.). (2021). *Stakeholder Strategies for Reducing the Impact of Global Health Crises*. IGI Global Publications. doi:10.4018/978-1-7998-7495-9

Kumar, V., & Mittal, S. (2020). Mobile Marketing Campaigns: Practices, Challenges and Opportunities. *International Journal of Business Innovation and Research*, *21*(4), 523–539. doi:10.1504/IJBIR.2020.105996

Kumar, V., & Nanda, P. (2019a). Social Media to Social Media Analytics: Ethical Challenges. *International Journal of Technoethics*, *10*(2), 57–70. doi:10.4018/IJT.2019070104

Kumar, V., & Nanda, P. (2019b). Social Media in Higher Education: A Framework for Continuous Engagement. *International Journal of Information and Communication Technology Education*, *15*(1), 109–120. doi:10.4018/IJICTE.2019010107

Kumar, V., Nanda, P., & Tawangar, S. (2022). Social Media in Business Decisions of MSMES: Practices and Challenges. *International Journal of Decision Support System Technology*, *14*(1), 1–12. doi:10.4018/IJDSST.286686

Kumar, V., & Pradhan, P. (2015). Trust Management Issues in Social-Media Marketing. *International Journal of Online Marketing*, *5*(3), 47–64. doi:10.4018/IJOM.2015070104

Kusumawati, R. D., Oswari, T., Yusnitasari, T., Mittal, S., & Kumar, V. (2021). Impact of marketing-mix, culture and experience as moderator to purchase intention and purchase decision for online music product in Indonesia. *International Journal of Business Innovation and Research*, *25*(4), 475–495. doi:10.1504/IJBIR.2021.117089

Laato, S., Islam, A. N., Farooq, A., & Dhir, A. (2020). Unusual purchasing behavior during the early stages of the COVID-19 pandemic: The stimulus-organism-response approach. *Journal of Retailing and Consumer Services*, *2020*(57), 102224. doi:10.1016/j.jretconser.2020.102224

Malik, A., Dhir, A., & Nieminen, M. (2016). Uses and gratifications of digital photo sharing on Facebook. *Telematics and Informatics*, *33*(1), 129–138. doi:10.1016/j.tele.2015.06.009

Nanda, P., & Kumar, V. (2022). Information Processing and Data Analytics for Decision Making: A Journey from Traditional to Modern Approaches. *Information Resources Management Journal*, *35*(2), 1–14. doi:10.4018/IRMJ.291693

Pandey, A. K., Gupta, R., & Singh, A. (2020). Traditional remedies and COVID-19: A qualitative exploration of indigenous resources. *Plant Archives*, *§§§*, 2066–2069.

Saurabh & Kumar, V. (2017). Technology Integration for the Success of B2C M-Commerce in India: Opportunities and Challenges. *IUP Journal of Information Technology, 13*(1), 24-35.

Seetharaman, P. (2020). Business models shifts: Impact of COVID-19. *International Journal of Information Management*, *54*, 102–173. doi:10.1016/j.ijinfomgt.2020.102173 PMID:32834338

Susanto, H. (2017). Electronic Health System: Sensors Emerging and Intelligent Technology Approach. In *Smart Sensors Networks* (pp. 189–203). Elsevier. doi:10.1016/B978-0-12-809859-2.00012-7

Susanto, H., Almunawar, M. N., Leu, F. Y., & Chen, C. K. (2016). Android vs iOS or Others? SMD-OS Security Issues: Generation Y Perception. *International Journal of Technology Diffusion*, *7*(2), 1–18. doi:10.4018/IJTD.2016040101

Susanto, H., & Chen, C. K. (2017). Information and Communication Emerging Technology: Making Sense of Healthcare Innovation. In *Internet of Things and Big Data Technologies for Next Generation Healthcare* (pp. 229–250). Springer. doi:10.1007/978-3-319-49736-5_10

Susanto, H., Chen, C. K., & Almunawar, M. N. (2018). Revealing Big Data Emerging Technology as Enabler of LMS Technologies Transferability. In *Internet of Things and Big Data Analytics Toward Next-Generation Intelligence* (pp. 123–145). Springer. doi:10.1007/978-3-319-60435-0_5

Susanto, H., Leu, F.-Y., Caesarendra, W., Ibrahim, F., Haghi, P. K., Khusni, U., & Glowacz, A. (2020). Managing Cloud Intelligent Systems over Digital Ecosystems: Revealing Emerging App Technology in the Time of the COVID19 Pandemic. *Appl. Syst. Innov.*, *3*(3), 37. doi:10.3390/asi3030037

Talwar, M., Talwar, S., Kaur, P., Tripathy, N., & Dhir, A. (2020). Has financial attitude impacted the trading activity of retail investors during the COVID-19 pandemic? *Journal of Retailing and Consumer Services*, *58*, 102341. doi:10.1016/j.jretconser.2020.102341

Zenker, S., & Kock, F. (2020). The coronavirus pandemic–A critical discussion of a tourism research agenda. *Tourism Management*, *81*, 104164.

Chapter 4
Innovative Management Strategy of Wine Tourism in the COVID-19 Era:
A Case Study of China

Poshan Yu
https://orcid.org/0000-0003-1069-3675
Soochow University, China & Australian Studies Centre, Shanghai University, China

YuHan Wang
Independent Researcher, China

Emanuela Hanes
Independent Researcher, Austria

EXECUTIVE SUMMARY

This chapter aims to study operation mode of wine tourism and coping strategies of major wine producing regions in the context of COVID-19. This study uses Citespace to analyze the changes of research hotspots in wine tourism industry before and after COVID-19. Through the comparison between the global wine industry management strategy and the Chinese wine industry management strategy, the similarities and differences between the two are analyzed through specific cases. This chapter investigates the driving force and factors of sustainable development of tourism economy with wine tourism as the core sector. It also studies innovative strategies such as the promotional effects of digital tourism in response to COVID-19 on wine tourism, thereby extending the protection and utilization of intellectual property rights of each wine producer. Case studies of China will be used for discussion. Finally, this chapter provides suggestions for policymakers to build a sustainable wine tourism for enterprises.

DOI: 10.4018/978-1-6684-3504-5.ch004

INTRODUCTION

With the development of tourism in the past decade, wine culture tourism has also increasingly been a choice for tourists. Visitors visit wineries and wine-producing regions and get a wide range of experiences, including full-day or longer recreational activities such as wine tasting, wine viewing, food and sightseeing of the surrounding wineries, as well as a series of activities to learn about the culture and lifestyle of wine-producing regions. The development of wine culture tourism has improved and enriched the industry chain of the wine industry, from the planting areas of wine raw materials, to the production of wine estates and wine factories, and then to the sales channels. Every link in the wine industry chain can be used as a basis for wine culture tourism.

In the world-famous wine producing regions such as Bordeaux, Burgundy and Piedmont, wine culture tours and winery culture attract tens of thousands of tourists, wine lovers and investors every year. Each wine region has its own regional and climate advantages. These advantages have formed the unique soil conditions in this area, and also bred the local human conditions. All these laid a solid foundation for the development of wine culture tourism. As can be seen from the wine production data in 2020, the development of the wine culture tourism industry is based on the huge wine production and excellent quality. Tourists from countries such as Italy, France, Spain and Argentina have dominated the number of wine culture tourists until COVID-19.

The emergence of COVID-19 has cast a shadow on the tourism economy, with the rapid decrease of international movement and the decrease of the trade volume of the tourism industry (Kumar & Gupta, 2021). The liquor culture tourism industry has plummeted with the downturn of international trade. The travel industry has been directly affected by the stay-at-home requirements enacted during the COVID-19 pandemic (Kumar & Malhotra, 2019). This sudden public health event is a challenge to tourism economy, especially wine culture tourism, but also an opportunity for adjustment. The impact on the wine culture tourism puts forward the challenge of how to turn the crisis into an opportunity, how to quickly recover after the collapse of wine culture tourism, how to improve the efficiency by minimizing excess capacities, how to use digital online tourism promotion of wine culture tourism for its sustainable development, how to stimulate the wine culture tourism industry diversification, how to address questions of branding and personalization, how to establish an effective supply system for wine culture tourism in line with people's travel needs after the epidemic?

This study will start to summarize the research directions of wine culture tourism economy before the COVID-19 epidemic, make comparative analysis and study on the advantages and characteristics of the world's leading wine producing regions, and analyze which advantages and characteristics can provide suggestions for the establishment of wine culture tourism in other regions of the world. Comparing the development speed and trend of wine culture tourism before and after COVID-19 with big data, and providing post-COVID-19 recovery and innovation suggestions; the branding of wine culture tourism and the application and advantages of digital innovation in the context of COVID-19 can pave the way for the innovation of wine culture tourism. Whereas in the west, Wine and Liquor is treated separately with their own culture, China's Alcohol culture is mainly based around Liquor (*Baijiu*), with wine having entered the Chinese production and consumption only in the last 106 years. Chinese Liquor culture has an equal importance and development as Western Wine culture. Thus, we will analyze the Western Wine culture tourism and provide analogous Chinese Liquor culture examples. Through the example of Chinese liquor industry, the paper analyzes brand values and digital practices, and provides valuable experience for the world liquor culture tourism industry with Chinese cases. Finally, the whole paper will be summarized, and suggestions on innovative development of wine culture tourism provided by different parts will be summarized, so as to provide reference opinions for policy makers and investors of wine culture tourism.

LITERATURE REVIEW

This section first reviews the literature on the definition of wine tourism. Hall et al. (2000) describe wine tourism as a category of special interest tourism. Byrd, Canziani, Hsieh, Debbage, and Sonmez (2016) go further and place the visitor and the visitor experience at the core of their definition, presenting it in terms of someone "who travels to wineries" and "what the wine tourists are experiencing at these destinations".

In order to research the wine culture tourism, Gómez et al. (2015) showed the destinations for tourists of different countries for wine culture, defined the wine tourism destination branding, analyze the advantages and disadvantages of different countries in which wine can be experienced, and develop a priority map for wine tourism development strategies. Gómez et al. (2015) mentioned that the formation of brand equity is the key to the success of wine tourism. As not only the comparison between different countries in the world, but also between different regions in the same country are relevant, the success stories of wine tourism are also collected and analyzed. In the collection of literature, the earliest countries to develop wine culture tourism in the world are Italy, France and Spain with a set of complete wine culture tourism governance policies. Chile is the world's top wine production power; However, wine culture tourism accounts for a small percentage of the country's tourism economy, as wine culture tourism did not get the deserved attention and the economic policies have not been tilted toward promoting wine culture tourism.

Festa et al. (2020) stressed that wine culture tourism is a key opportunity for the diversity of the wine industry, and the world's top wine producing regions should include wine culture tourism when considering how to promote the development of the wine industry. Selecting the routes is an important driving force for the expansion and development of wine culture tourism. Public and private capital should be accepted in the operation process. The development and expansion of wine culture tourism gives a good example for this, involving the consideration of public-private partnership.

Festa et al. (2020) discuss the driving factors in wine culture tourism, and then study how they affect the level of tourists' active participation in wine culture tourism activities. The results show that experiencing co-creation enables tourists to get more interaction with local residents, and interaction with front-line wine production personnel is conducive to tourists' experience of the whole process of wine culture. The more activities available for physical operation, the higher the satisfaction and participation of tourists. The test model proposed by Festa et al. (2020) contributes to the knowledge system of wine culture tourism and has practical management significance.

As mentioned above, wine culture tourism is inseparable from physical tourist experience. However, faced with the sudden new situation of COVID-19, the tourism economy needs to adapt and go through three stages: response stage, recovery stage and reset stage (Sigala, 2020). During the response phase and recovery phase, the visitor experience will certainly not be as good as it was without the impact of COVID-19. With the background of not being able to travel abroad, digital tourism brings a new development model and opportunity for the wine tourism economy. In the available literature, there is a lack of research and sorting on the topic of digital innovation strategy application in wine culture tourism industry, and this paper will make up for this gap.

Innovative management strategies of wine culture tourism will be presented to wine business decision makers to provide new opportunities in responding to COVID-19 (Sigala, 2020). According to the objective phenomenon put forward by Gomez et al. (2015) that managers' perceptions are more favorable than visitors' in the development of wine culture tourism industry. Innovative management strategies of wine culture tourism are based on the difference between managers' perspective and visitors' perspective and it helps to better understand the needs of the tourists. Güzel et al. (2020) emphasize that attitudes and behaviors such as imagination, creativity, pioneering behavior, courage and risk taking are important for a wine tourism entrepreneur. These factors affect policy makers' decisions and investors' interests of wine culture tourism industry. Wine tourism entrepreneurs have to analyze and understand the dynamic wine regions and local conditions, make good use of local advantages for innovative decisions, the decision makers and shareholders also need to consider future trends in order to avoid repeating downturns due to emergent public health and safety problems around the world.

This paper will summarize the previous research experiences on wine culture tourism, make a comparative analysis of the development trend of wine culture tourism before and after the epidemic, make up for the vacancy in the research field of digital wine culture tourism, and propose innovative wine culture tourism development strategies based on the case of Chinese *Baijiu.*

METHODOLOGY

To fulfil the research objective, this paper adopted CiteSpace to visualize a field of research and create a systematic review of the literature. CiteSpace is a generic approach to detecting and visualizing emerging trends and transient patterns in scientific literature (Chen, 2006). It helps researchers learn to understand the whole picture of a study field and construct relationships between publications from different subareas. CiteSpace focuses on the interrelations between a cocitation clusters's members and their citers (Chen et al., 2010).

To study wine industry and wine tourism before and after COVID-19, this section uses subject terms in the "Web of Science Core Collection" database to search the key word research changes due to the outbreak of COVID-19. In this section, we retrieve papers from 1900 to 2022 which subject words are "tourism business". Based on these standards, we get 504 records in CiteSpace. We eliminated the duplicates of the text. In order to study the shift in research direction caused by COVID-19, we studied the research literature from 1990 to 2019 through time slice, and again used CiteSpace time slice to study the keywords of many relevant literature from 2019 to present. In the end, 318 pre-outbreak of COVID-19 records were selected, as were 270 post-outbreak records. This part of the research is based on CiteSpace keywords.

In order to find the strategies of managing the wine industry and the difference between Chinese wine business and international wine business, the Case study section uses subject terms in the " Web of Science Core Collection" database to search articles in the process of literature retrieval. In order to study the management strategies of the wine industry, we retrieve papers from 1900 to 2022 in this section by keyword "strategy" "wine business" and "management". Based on these standards, we get 290 records in CiteSpace. And to compare the similarities and differences between the global wine business model and the Chinese wine industry, we used the keyword "Chinese wine business" to retrieve papers and 105 records, whereas keyword "international wine business" was used to retrieve papers from "Web of science Core Collection" database.

This paper uses CiteSpace 5.8.R3 software to analyze the keywords co-occurrence and co-citation network, constructs the research atlas of the innovative management strategy of wine tourism and explores the research hotspots and frontiers in this field.

CHARACTERISTICS OF WORLD TOP WINE TOURISM

In order to promote the wine culture and tourism industry in a region, there inevitably needs to be a huge wine output. 2020 data show (Figure 1) the world's leading wine producing countries ranked as follows: Italy, France, Spain, the United States, Argentina, Australia, South Africa, Chile, Germany and China.

Figure 1. Leading countries in wine production worldwide 2020 (in million hectoliters)
Data source: International Organisation of Vine and Wine

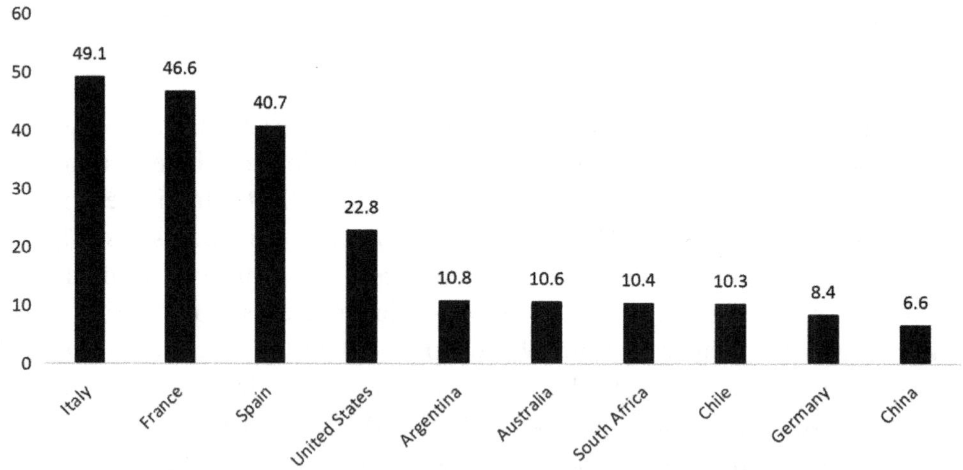

The development of a relatively perfect wine culture tourism industry can also be found in the leading wine production areas. The core characteristics of the top countries have been compiled in the table 1.

Table 1. Characteristics of world top wine tourism destinations

Country	Characteristics	References
Italy	• Customer loyalty • Political implications. Like political institutions aid • Historic and geographical attributes of the region	Santeramo et al. (2017), Festa et al. (2020)
France	• Natural environment • Daily data analysis • Well-known French vineyards	Song et al. (2019)
Spain	• Denominacion de Origen Calificada (DOCa) • Brand equity management • Native grape variety	Gómez et al. (2015)
United States	• Well-known tour operators • Growing interest towards food tourism • Higher world economic status • The vast territory creates a variety of local experiences	Garibaldi et al. (2017)
Argentina	• Public-private partnerships • Neoliberal policies • Amenity migration	Rainer (2016)
Australia	• Formulated development and planning strategies • Development of innovative tourism products	Gu and Huang (2019)
South Africa	• Wine route estates • Cultural heritage protection • Policy support • Active wine tourism market • Well-developed facilities and infrastructure	Bruwer (2003)
Chile	• Word-of-mouth recommendations • Product attractiveness • Tourism services • Tour operators' recommendations	Torres et al. (2021)
Germany	• Numerous wine regions • Regional unique culture • Sustainable development	Tafel and Szolnoki (2020)
China	• Brand culture • Policy support • Public-private partnerships • Destination loyalty	Duan et al. (2018)

As an investment focusing on quality and spending more money on products, tasting experience, catering and accommodation, wine tourism occupies a specific proportion in the tourism economy (Table 2).

Table 2. Share of Italians willing to travel abroad after the coronavirus outbreak 2020

Share of Italians Willing to Travel Abroad After the Coronavirus Outbreak 2020		
When the coronavirus (COVID-19) emergency will be over, where would you like to travel abroad?		
Art city	17	in %
Seaside	11	in %
Mountain	2	in %
Healthcare and wellness facilities	2	in %
Food and wine tourism facilities	1	in %
Lake	1	in %

Data source: Acqua Group

Wine has a strong social appeal (Lunardo et al., 2021). Wine culture tourism is an industry based on a complex of local land ownership systems, local land legends and myths and regional wine culture. Wine tourism is strongly based on local characteristics, from the wine itself up to the local conditions and customs: That is to say, wine culture tourism is ideal for meeting the curiosity for the local living environment and offering an increased participation of tourists. The trend is moving from only visiting to experiencing the whole wine production process. Wine itself is a product closely linked with local conditions and traditions, offering emotional and historical experience, thus enriching customers' horizons. Tourists interact with local residents to experience and create together. Increasing interaction and providing more operational tour modes can thus effectively increase tourists' satisfaction in wine culture tourism (Rachao et al., 2021). There is huge potential for communication between wine dealers and consumers (Hauck et al., 2021).

Torres et al. (2021) found five characteristics in the wine culture tourism industry in Chile, the world's leading wine producing region, which have become the key factors to promote the development of wine culture tourism industry: 1. Chilean wine culture tourism has a good reputation 2. Chilean wine products have product attraction 3. Chile has excellent tourism services 4. A lot of information about Chile's wine culture tourism can be found on the Internet 5. Tour operators invest in esthetics and packaging. Tour operators and tourism services are key factors in increasing the number of wine tourists, but the attractiveness of the product has a long-term impact. These five characteristics of Chile's wine culture tourism industry can also be extended to the world's other wine culture tourism industries. With time passing, the demand for wine culture tourism will only increase (Wilson, 2021).

As the world's largest wine-producing country, Italy has had stellar results in recent years. In Italy's wine culture tourism industry, cooperation between regions and brands is particularly frequent. Italy, as a country rich in cultural flavor, accounts for a large proportion of tourism economy and its wine consumption ranks third in the world's total consumption in 2020 (Figure 2 and Figure 3). Tourists in the wine tourism industry come from the surrounding scenic spots, and the percentage of this drainage accounts for 31.39% of the total wine tourism. Research shows that the frequent visits of tourists to wineries are not directly related to the properties of wineries themselves, such as establishment time, production capacity, scale, etc. Attractive tourism resources are more attractive to tourists. Wineries, the core of wine culture tourism, are close to famous scenic spots, create clusters with other wineries and are located close to important transportation hubs. All of these characteristics affect the attraction of winery tourism (Gu et al., 2021). It was determined that highly motivated long-distance wine tourists preferred to enjoy a wide range of cultural and outdoor attractions (Getz & Brown, 2006). On this basis, the cooperation of related industries has also become a feature of the world's leading wine culture tourism. It also confirms the challenges presented by Nicolosi et al. (2016) in their investigation of the development of wine culture tourism in specific regions. Regions that face challenges exhibit factors like lack of marketing and management capabilities of small enterprises as well as lack of trust and cooperation among stakeholders.

Figure 2. Leading countries in wine export worldwide in 2020, based on volume (in million hectoliters)
Data source: International Organisation of Vine and Wine

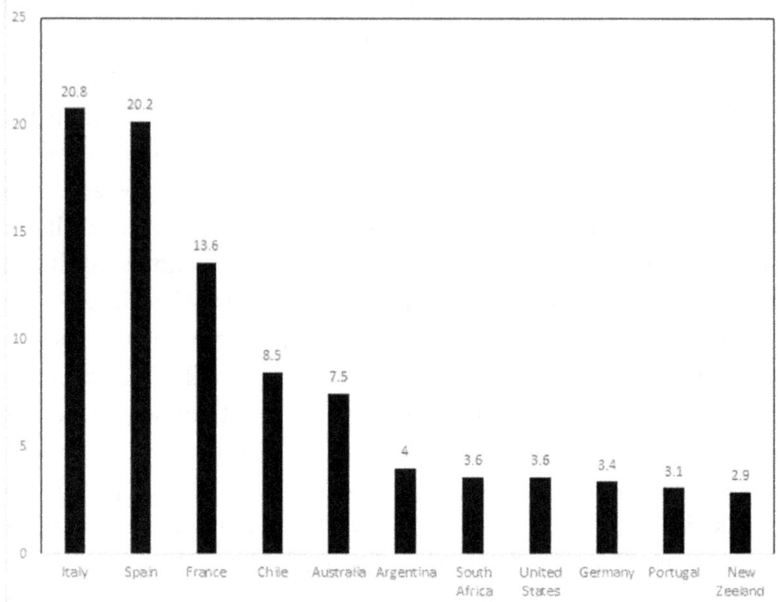

Figure 3. Wine consumption worldwide in 2020, by country (in million hectoliters)
Data source: International Organisation of Vine and Wine; Various sources (Trade Press); Food and Agriculture Organization of the United Nations

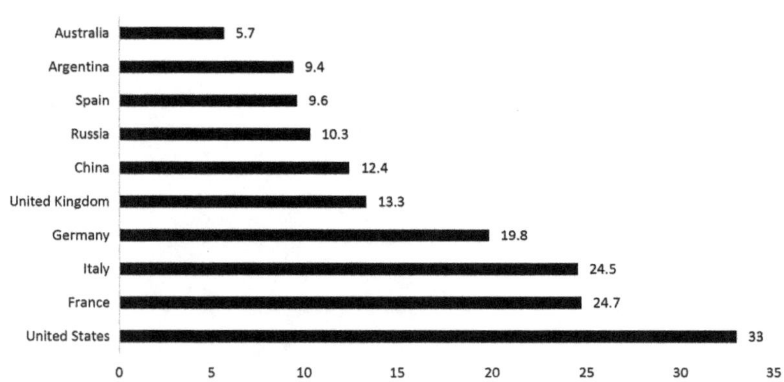

In the area of wine tourism, different institutional, regulatory and professional delays prevent Italy from fully developing as a wine tourism destination, most likely because the participation of all possible stakeholders is still unsatisfactory. In a recent advance, wine tourism was specifically revised in the 2018 Budget Law, which anticipated regulatory norms for the industry. In this context, the Italian wine route established by Law No. 268/1999 and consolidated by the Grape and Wine Act (Law No. 238/2016) should play a key role in the governance and management of local wine tourism (Festa et al., 2020).

Legislation, policy overall planning and coordination of wine production brand cooperation can improve the tourism service industry standards (Gu et al., 2021). Through policy formulation and proximity effect, the planning of wine culture tourism wineries around large scenic spots could be a fruitful next step, including cooperation between wineries and the use of aggregation effect for the design of tourism routes. The government could strategically plan the construction of transportation hubs and skillfully avoids the disadvantages of cultural tourism destinations being far away from big cities and passenger flow centers.

WINE INDUSTRY AND TOURISM BEFORE AND AFTER COVID19

This section uses subject terms in the "Web of Science Core Collection" database to search the key word research changes due to the outbreak of COVID-19. In this section, we retrieve papers from 1900 to 2022 which subject words are "tourism business". Based on these standards, 504 records in CiteSpace were retrieved. We eliminated the duplicates of the text. In order to study the shift in research direction caused by COVID-19, we studied the research literature from 1990 to 2019 through time slice, and again used CiteSpace time slice to study the keywords of a large number of relevant literatures from 2019 to present. In the end, 318 pre-outbreaks of COVID-19 records were selected, as were 270 post-outbreak records. This part of the research is based on CiteSpace keywords.

Using CiteSpace time slices, the changes in the wine industry before and after COVID-19 were studied. The visual view of CiteSpace keywords clearly shows that the wine business model before the outbreak of COVID-19 paid more attention to the quality and market performance of wine and reflected the success and failure of wine business through the response of consumers in the market. However, it can be found that the proposal and research of sustainable development is just in its infancy and has not become a hot topic in the wine industry. With the COVID-19 recession and the expanding global scope, the influence of wine business' sustainable development has become a new hot topic and research direction. In order to achieve sustainable development in the wine business, innovative management strategies have become the basis for decision making for wine businesses and thus also for the wine tourism industry. Visualization figures are listed in Figure 4 and Figure 5.

Figure 4. Wine business before 2019

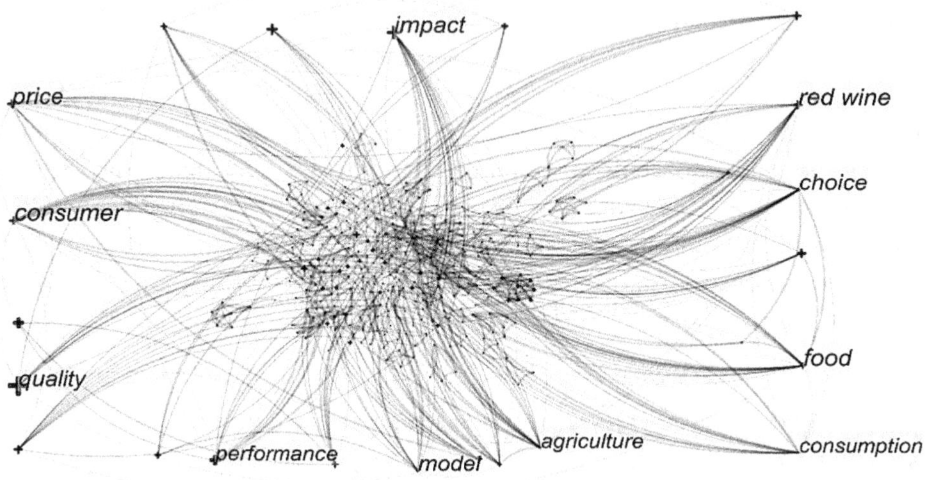

Figure 5. Wine business after 2019

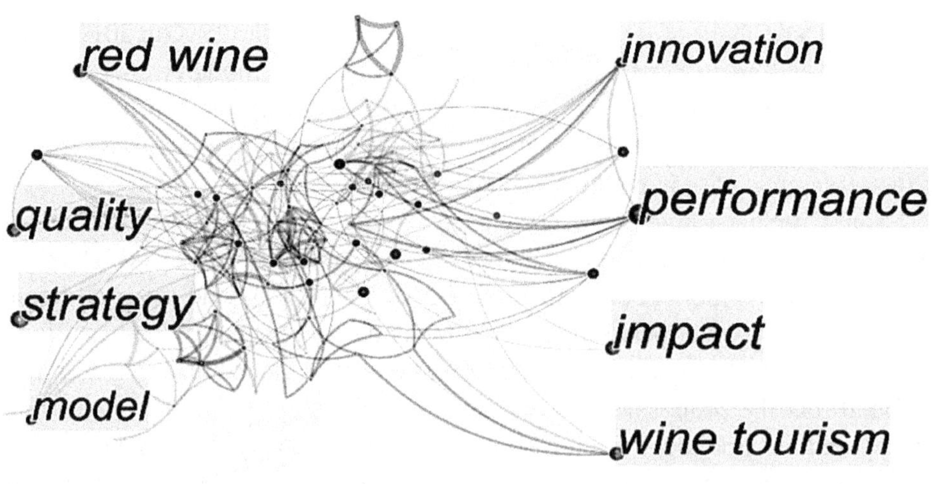

Asia dominates the projected growth in wine consumption and imports, with China being especially prominent (Anderson & Wittwer, 2021). Before the COVID-19 outbreak, the world's wine production stood at between 260 and 280 million liters and fluctuated periodically, peaking every five years before tapering off (Figure 6). The wine tourism economy follows the development cycle of wine output. Looking back from 1990 to 2020, the situation during the nearly 30 years of development has not been not plain sailing. The wine industry is affected by fundamental and cyclical internal and external economic factors, thus indirectly affecting the wine culture tourism industry. In the midst of twists and turns and fluctuations, the overall trend is positive, but attention needs to be paid to external pressure caused by cyclical fluctuations and uncertainties.

Figure 6. Wine production worldwide from 1990 to 2020 (in million hectoliters)
Data source: International Organisation of Vine and Wine

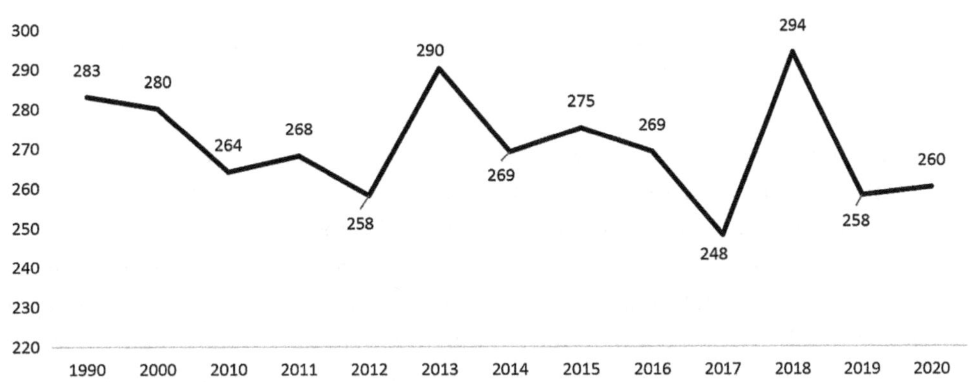

The wine industry involves the import and export of wine, the import and export of raw materials, and the import and export of wine products, which cannot be separated from the international economic environment. The import and export issues are related to globalization, and despite the signs of a global economic recession, the underlying factors in the data show a tendency toward optimism. For example, China's wine import showed a trend of continuous increase from 2015 to 2018, reaching 3914.64 million US dollars in 2018 (Figure 7). As can be seen from the data, China's demand for wine is increasing with the increasing consumption power and income expectation, and meanwhile, it also drives the consumption of wine culture tourism.

Figure 7. Volume of wine imports to China from 2012 to 2020
Data source: International Organisation of Vine and Wine; GTAP Data Base

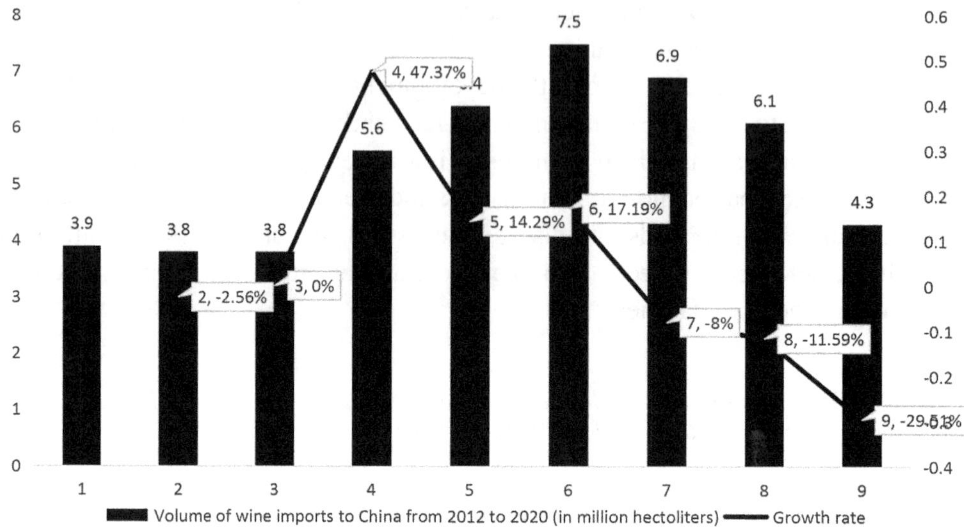

Before the COVID-19 outbreak, tourism was seen by many scholars as a powerful driver of economic growth since the 1990s. Tourism stimulates the consumption demand and improves the level of economic development.

In December 2019, the global news media began reporting on a new type of coronavirus infection in Wuhan, capital of central China's Hubei province (Bhardwaj & Kumar, 2022). The World Health Organization (WHO) has confirmed the spread of the virus, declaring that the new coronavirus strain poses a new international threat to public health by January 2020 (Yang et al. 2021; Singh & Kumar, 2022). The organization officially calls the virus Severe Acute Respiratory Syndrome Coronavirus 2 (SARS-CoV-2). At that time, blockade and quarantine measures were imposed in Wuhan, subsequently in the whole of China and later spread to the whole world. In March 2020, WHO declared the Coronary Virus Disease 2019, also known as COVID-19, a global pandemic. Two months later, more than 90 per cent of the world's population lived under travel restrictions (Asquith, 2020).

Under the development of COVID-19, production and operation of the wine industry have come to a standstill. The global decline in working hours due to the pandemic was 14 percent, equivalent to the loss of 400 million full-time 40-hour jobs. The wine industry has also been affected by the global epidemic, with a sharp decline in global wine production between 2019 and 2020. The import and export trade has become particularly difficult due to epidemic prevention and control. In China, a major wine demand country, wine imports fell by 9 percent between 2018 and 2019, and in the particularly severe COVID-19 outbreak window even by 19 percent. The global wine trade has entered an unprecedentedly difficult period. Travel restrictions and consumer concern about traveling during the pandemic significantly reduced the number of tourists and other visitors to wine regions, further eroding the winery's ability to use its tasting rooms to generate direct to consumer (DTC) sales (Lease and Conover, 2021).

The demand of wine culture tourism is positively correlated with residents' income expectation. The impact of the epidemic on the global economy has caused great uncertainty in people's income expectations and consumption attitudes. However, wine tourism consumption is a part of expenditure with strong selectivity and has great elasticity of income demand. The number of tourists choosing wine farms in Spain has fallen sharply since 2020, a reduction by 73% compared to 2019. As one of the world's top three countries in wine production, Spain has had an early start in wine culture tourism, boasting a rich wine culture tourism industry, perfect tourism service facilities and relatively stable tourist sources. However, it was also strongly affected by the outbreak of COVID-19, as the data in Figure 8 show.

Figure 8. Number of visitors to wineries and wine museums in Spain from 2008 to 2020 (in 1,000s)
Data source: Asociación Española de Ciudades del Vino (Rutas del Vino de España)

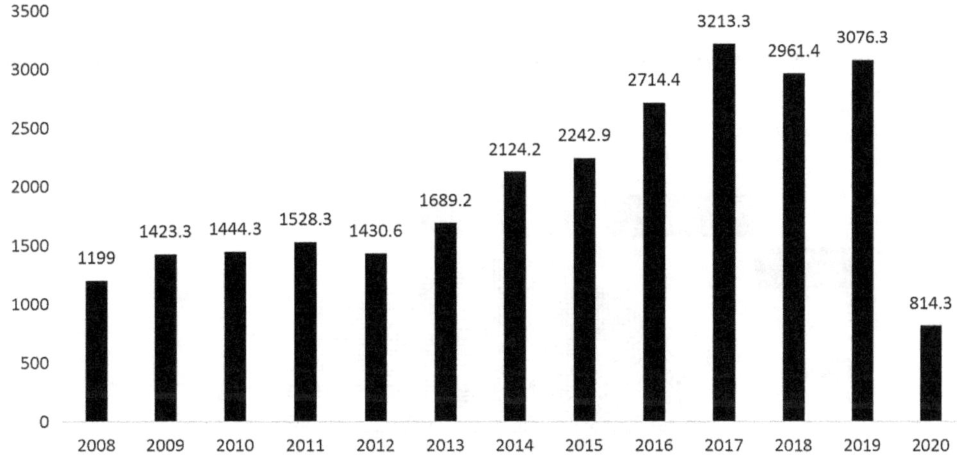

While the COVID-19 outbreak has not damaged tourist facilities per se, it has indirectly affected tourists' preference for food and wine culture tourism. Using Italy as an example to reflect global consumer trends, data collected from a questionnaire in Italy show that when the tourism industry will recover after the COVID-19 pandemic,

Italian tourists are more likely to choose the category of overseas travel. Only 1% of respondents chose wine culture tourism. Data are listed in Table 2 and the proportion is shown in Figure 9. The recovery of the tourism industry is not only the recovery of tourism facilities. Tourism industries dominated by hardware facilities and natural scenery are now better placed to attract tourists. Tourists in natural scenery tourism will pay less attention to the service experience of travel, and are more immersed in the enjoyment of landscape. However, the lack of tourist experience caused by COVID-19 is magnified in the wine culture tourism industry. Due to COVID-19 protection, local residents need to follow the medical and disease prevention rules. This includes a sense of distance when experiencing wine culture projects firsthand. Due to the lack of immersive sightseeing experiences and interaction, tourists are now naturally reluctant to choose wine culture tourism projects (Yang et al., 2021).

In the post-COVID-19 recovery stage, attention to the number of tourists is an indicator of recovery, but if not enough attention is paid to the experience and satisfaction degree of tourists during the tour, it will have a negative impact on the establishment of the reputation of the wine culture tourism industry after the COVID-19 pandemics (Yang et al., 2021).

COVID-19 has brought a disaster, a challenge and an opportunity to the wine culture tourism economy. At this critical historical juncture, due to the conditions of constraint, challenges are posed to the tourism economy, and require that the tourism economy gradually realize the normalization of COVID-19 prevention and control.

Figure 9. Share of Italians willing to travel abroad after the coronavirus outbreak 2020
Data source: Acqua Group

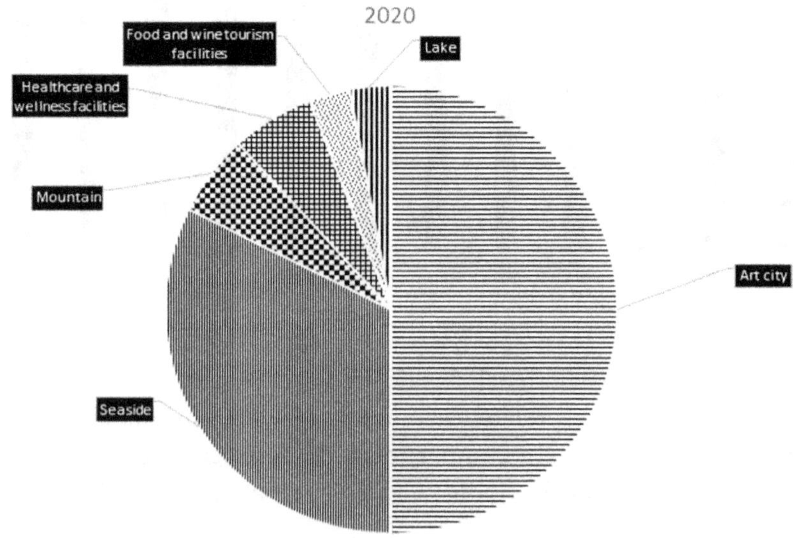

SUSTAINABLE WINE TOURISM THROUGH INTEGRATED INTELLECTUAL PROPERTY AND DIGITAL INNOVATION MANAGEMENT

Sustainable development is an enduring demand (Lata & Gupta, 2021). However, about 30% of wine estates are not economically sustainable and their profit does not sufficiently cover family wages and does not provide return on capital. The long-term survival of these businesses is at risk when investments are required and successors are sought (Loose et al. 2021).

Sustainability has become the key factor, not the exception, in the global wine industry. But sustainable development cannot be equated with environmental protection alone. It is defined as carrying out activities conducive to human activities within the limits of environmental bearing capacity. Sustainable development cannot ignore the interests of merchants and reduce consumers' expectations for services. Research shows that even under the pressure of external competition, businesses are more inclined to adopt sustainable development strategies (Nave et al., 2021).

Wine culture tourism as an extension of the wine industry. In a certain number of existing wineries, the wine industry creates additional value on the basis of increasing the utility of the wine industry. Through a better understanding of the co-creation activities between enterprises to create value, enterprises in the same wine industry can carry out a reasonable division of labor, cooperation in the same direction, help a single enterprise to increase sales, and drive economic growth. A variety of different types of enterprises can serve the same related field, forming a cluster effect and reducing operating costs, thereby achieving sustainable development of wine tourism. The competition of clusters within the same region and the complementation of clusters in different regions will be consistent with the sustainable development of the wine industry (Crick et al., 2020).

In the new round of global wine industry carbon emission assessment, the problem of carbon emission caused by the wine tourism economy is evaluated in an attempt to reduce carbon footprint and carbon emissions and to achieve sustainable development (Sun & Drakeman, 2020).

The original traditional model of wine culture tourism is to sell wine and visit the cellar tickets, provide wine knowledge education and entertainment, and promote the wine festival as a cultural starting point. However, during the prevention and control of COVID-19, all kinds of offline interaction modes cannot be carried out in a normal and orderly manner. In the era of digital economy, digitalization has given the wine culture industry new vitality against the backdrop of COVID-19. Embracing big data is what the wine industry needs to face.

The digital wine industry is no longer just about production, circulation and citation. The life cycle and value mission of the wine industry are extended with the advent of digitalization. The wine tourism industry is also closer to consumers with the help of digital technology, so that big data and digitalization can establish direct communication channels between consumers and distributors, and increase users' sense of experience and immersion. Through the analysis of consumers' age levels, wine cultural tourism projects in line with the different age target groups can be launched, ranging from the original unified tour to the online unique tour and wine culture tour route. This will not only provide deep experiences of the wine industry, but also create the possibility of field trips after the epidemic, and improve consumers' expectations of wine industry tourism.

Digitization not only meets the unique needs of individuals, but also expands its coverage to online channels, which has a high coverage rate in different age groups. Wine tourism digital and online sales combined can be the basis of a newly rebuilt business model. With the normalization of epidemic prevention and control, digitalization plays a key role in solving the problem of wine culture tourism consumption. COVID-19 can also be seen as a driving force for the overall digitalization of the wine tourism industry.

In the context of modern tourism, where communication devices and information are no longer scarce, wine tourism must be memorable and immersive, allowing visitors to fully immerse themselves in the existing environment. This leads to the concept of applying virtual reality technology to wine tourism development. The development of virtual reality technology in tourism is obvious to all (Martins et al., 2017).

With the digitization of major wine producers, the main body of wine tourism is no longer just a profitable industry, but takes on the mission of spreading the unique culture of the brand. It is the depth of brand culture that resonates with consumers. The goal of wine brand culture is to use intellectual property (IP) rights to protect brand creativity. In the era of digital economy, the success of brands often only needs more traffic and attention, and the value of traffic is the value of brand IP. Digitization has changed the needs of the wine tourism industry and the interactions visitors need. Big data provides users with rich information and the ability to better process information. Through data tracking, it provides tourists with better tour collaborative processing services. Through big data, decision makers are better aware of consumers' consumption tendencies even as they adjust resource allocation (Cuomo et al., 2021).

In the homogenization of serious branding and marketing, enterprises using innovative strategies will stand out in the market competition. It is for this reason that the IP rights of the brands are protected, and the corporate image and culture of the brand of the wine culture tourism industry are protected in the legislative stage, and the brand image of innovation is protected and publicized through social media and other platforms (Obermayer et al., 2021). Carrying out festivals related to wine culture tourism improve the intensity of publicity and participation. Combining the innovative image with the traditional wine industry, creates the image of wine culture tourism industry in line with the public aesthetic, and further expands its influence.

CASE STUDY – CURRENT IP AND DIGITAL PRACTICE IN CHINA: WINE TOURISM AND ITS IMPACT ON THE BUSINESS SECTOR IN THE REGION

In this case study section, we first need to use CiteSpace to find the strategies for managing the wine industry. This section uses subject terms in the "Web of Science Core Collection" database to search articles by literature retrieval. In order to study the management strategies of the wine industry, we retrieved papers from 1900 to 2022 in this section by keyword "strategy", "wine business" and "management". Based on these standards, we found 290 records in CiteSpace.

In order to study the Chinese case, the paper analyzes the hot spots and frontiers of Chinese wine business research in previous papers, builds a research map of Chinese wine business, and compares the similarities and differences with international research hotspots. This section uses subject terms in the "Web of Science Core Collection" database to search articles by literature retrieval. We retrieved "Chinese Wine Business" and "Chinese Wine Industry" in literature from 1900 to 2022 by keywords and obtained 523 records, excluding articles and articles unrelated to business. Finally, 125 records were obtained and the keyword view was visualized using CiteSpace. The effect is shown in Figure 10.

Several important nodes repeatedly appeared when dealing with the management strategy literature of the global wine industry through CiteSpace. The sustainability of the wine industry, innovative wine industry management strategy, the impact of wine market sales, and the quality of wine production are all the priorities of wine management strategy. It has a significant weight in all of the literature analyzed. The sustainable development of the wine industry has become a top priority amid the COVID-19 pandemic.

The similarities and differences between the global wine business model and the Chinese wine industry business model were compared and analyzed by CiteSpace. The research on wine business models in the world shows the development trend of the whole industry, while the research on the business model of Chinese wine industry tends to study the production process of Chinese specific alcoholic beverage, so as to improve the product quality by improving the production process of Chinese wine. Visualization Graphs are listed in Figure 10, Figure 11 and Figure 12.

Figure 10. Chinese wine business

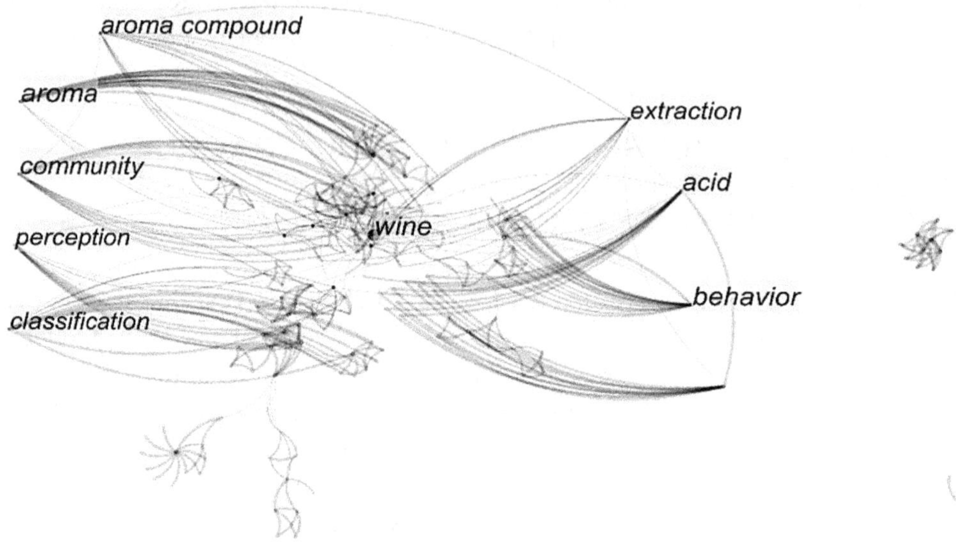

Figure 11. Management strategy of wine business

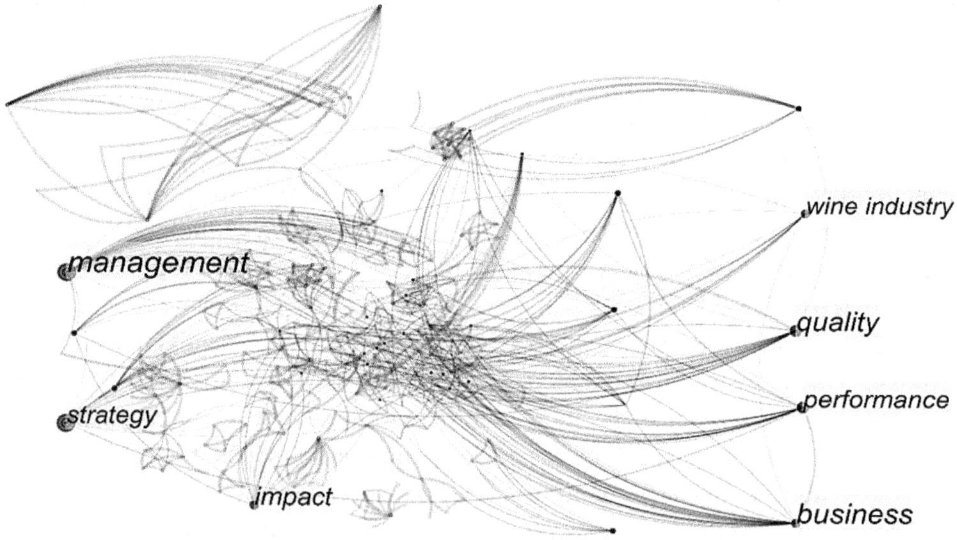

Figure 12. International wine business

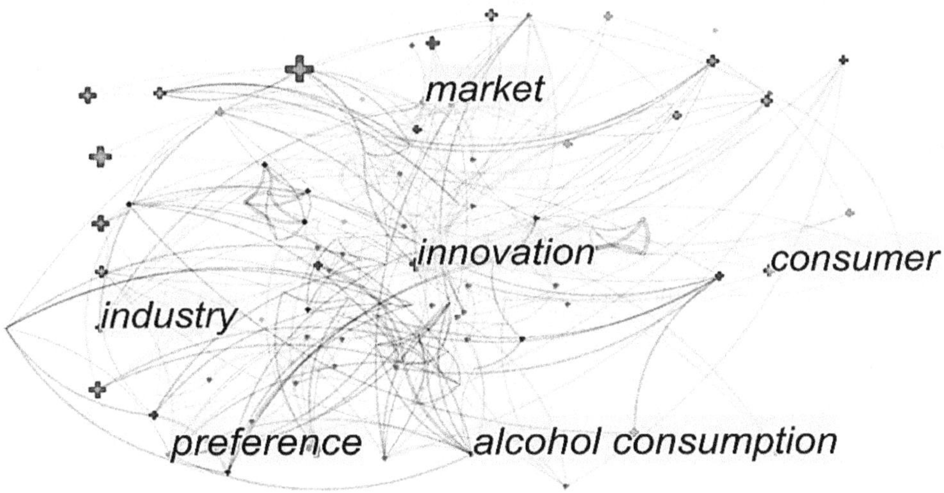

As the world's most populous country, China ranks only sixth in terms of wine consumption, because its large population does not consume as much wine per capita as other countries. As the largest developing country, wine consumption is mostly established in special economic regions, open coastal cities and economically developed regions of China. The main wine consumption provinces are Guangdong and Shanghai. China has its own unique wine-making industry. However, the type of wine produced is also different from wine and constitutes in mainly *baijiu* liquor. China's export sales of liquor products have exceeded imports for many years in a row, and the number of patent applications for Chinese liquor also hit a new high of 4,380 in 2016.

Chinese liquor has a history of nearly one thousand years (Jin et al., 2017). Because of its complex technology, profound culture and rich wisdom, it is not only a kind of liquor, but also a symbol for China abroad, forming a metaphysical culture and building a bridge between China and the West. China's *baijiu* producing regions are mainly distributed in Sichuan, Guizhou, northern Jiangsu and Shanxi province. These areas are based on the raw grain production, close to the Yangtze and Yellow Rivers and other water sources, and have a good ecological environment. After years of development, there is a large scale of different Chinese liquor brands. *Maotai* and *Wuliangye* have also become synonymous with Chinese *baijiu*. A specific liquor product will usually have a relatively fixed consumer group (Velikova et al., 2021).

Chinese liquor industry has formed a distinct brand culture according to regional characteristics and established brand IP on the basis of brand culture. Labels of different brands will bring result in different purchasing patterns (Dutton and

Normand-Marconnet, 2019). Now there are many well-known brands such as *Maotai* liquor. With mass consumption replacing the government consumption to become the backbone of liquor consumption, the liquor industry is facing new challenges. The traditional market model of stable input and output based on sales channels of Chinese liquor urgently needs to face the market and consumers. Value needs to be added to the product in the face of sales uncertainty. Drawing lessons from foreign high-quality wine culture tourism destinations, China's major wine-producing regions and provinces have also developed the liquor industry as a tourism project, resulting in the tourism project of Chinese liquor tourism.

The Chinese liquor industry is experiencing a serious market saturation. Small companies and small brands had to change their approach and change the focus of the enterprise from the sole liquor output to the additional value of tourism. With digital technology, even small companies can close the distance with the consumers, increase the degree of consumer satisfaction, and form a liquor industry tourism reputation.

Chinese liquor has an ancient and mysterious traditional cultural background based on the great tension between the background of traditional culture and the living environment and cultural identity of young people in the new era. China's liquor industry is also facing an age gap. *Baijiu* liquor culture was once equated with table culture, but is now being rejected by young people. With the help of digital big data processing, the consumption tendency of young people is tracked, and personalized online customized services are provided to young people. The liquor industry is expanded through digital and virtual technology and is thus no longer confined to the dining table, but closer to the ordinary life of young people.

Marketing and consumer behavior patterns still dominate the purchase of alcoholic products (Weatherbee et al., 2019). In order to conform to the pattern and trend of international research, this paper systematically analyzes the success and failure cases of Chinese alcohol industry in recent years from the perspective of innovative management strategies.

Improving consumer experience is a strategy that wine enterprises need to follow through the result of CiteSpace analysis in this paper.

The life cycle and value of liquor products in China has been expanded from production and circulation to drinking to cultural exchange. At the level of product digitization, active exploration of the "dynamic wine age" was carried out. *Shede* wine industry takes the lead in realizing visualization, dynamic and transparency of wine age through digital means in the industry. The identification of Chinese liquor is an important item for consumers (Qin et al., 2012). Consumers can scan the quick response (QR) code to observe the whole process of the wine from the brewing jar to the consumer's reference. This digital innovation strategy can make consumers better understand the cultural core of the wine industry, and increase the interaction of "*She de*" wine industry. It improves consumer satisfaction and greatly enriches consumer experience.

The market performance of the wine industry is not only reflected in the sales volume of the product, but also in the image of the brand of the wine enterprise. CiteSpace visual view shows that corporate brand image and external performance is also a core form of wine quality.

As the first liquor brand named after the Chinese traditional cultural word "*She de*" which refers to give up something to get something else in the liquor industry, *She de* Liquor itself has a value of brand cultural IP. With the song and dance drama "Fragrance of a Big Country", the first legendary poetry and dance drama with wine portraying the long-lasting flavor of the Chinese liquor industry is presented to consumers and the public. This drama is being performed in five countries on three continents.

As the above analysis shows, the sustainable development of the wine culture industry is the general trend and can enhance wine tourism projects. Wine culture tourism is also related to product performance and market influence.

The *She de* alcohol industry has established its own cultural tourism area for liquor industry, including a *She de* Wine Art Center, custom center, wine storage tour center, wine culture theme hotel, combining it with the national intangible cultural heritage brewing technology for tourists to visit. It integrates industrial production, tourism, liquor knowledge popularization, liquor culture experience and other functions. A new mode of developing liquor industry tourism and empowering liquor industry has been developed. In 2020, the *Shede* Wine Culture tourism area was rated as a national 4A level tourist attraction in China according to Classification and Evaluation of Quality Grades of Tourist Attractions (GB/T 17775-2003).

However, in the digitalization sphere, there are not only successful cases. The *"Qinchi"* wine industry is a typical failure case. The *"Qinchi"* wine industry has been the highest advertising bid enterprise for two consecutive years in China. But due to the deviation in management strategy and lack of the practice of wine tourism, the venture resulted in failure.

The *Qinchi* winery lacks core competitiveness. An enterprise is built with three competencies: innovation, marketing, and management. The *Qinchi* wine industry relies too much on marketing ability to make up for the other two. In the early stage of wine tourism development in China, *Qinchi* wine industry gave up the strategy of developing wine tourism. After tasting the dividend of advertising, the enterprise's innovation ability was greatly weakened and the physical construction of wine tourism is also not established. In addition, because the huge profits brought by the advertising industry the lack of management ability was covered up, whereas the, enterprise was unable to grow, find a sustainable development path, and eventually failed.

The *Qinchi* winery had difficulties to maximize the effectiveness of its marketing strategy. After the initial stage of brand IP, the marketing strategy was not adjusted. Not building a good wine tourism program through brand IP. Neither was the management strategy according to the environmental conditions and resource conditions. This resulted in unfocused advertising strategies and gambling psychology that ultimately ended in failure.

The *Qinchi* Wine industry has not clearly recognized the positioning of the enterprise. It has not grasped the fact that improving brand awareness is the only way for each brand to expand its influence. And wine tourism projects is an effective way to enhance brand awareness. Its famous brand IP was created through huge assets, but the product capacity and a single industrial structure were not able to match its popularity. As a result, the enterprise was tempted to reduce the production cycle and cost by reducing the quality of products, and finally fell into a crisis of bankruptcy due to quality problems and the collapse of consumer reputation.

The digital era has brought new vitality, but also brought challenges to the liquor industry. Digitization brings consumers more fragmented information and distracts their attention (Nanda & Kumar, 2022). It is particularly important for a liquor brand to catch consumers' eye amid the mass of readily available information by accurately reaching consumers' needs, and firmly establishing the brand in its consumers' hearts. Brands need to be clearer about their positioning, need to better address its consumer groups, and increase the brand loyalty of consumers. From the overall situation, digital tools can be used to empower the traditional wine industry, to provide an overall plan and to effectively combine the liquor industry tourism industry. The building of a brand strategy is in line with the needs of the Internet era to increase innovation and creativity.

Chinese liquor and wine brands and world wine brands need to seize the advantages brought by digitalization, shorten the distance with consumers, accurately reach the unique needs of their consumers, timely adjust the industrial structure according to big data analysis, and gradually get rid of the excessive dependence on the traditional sales industry.

CONCLUSION AND RECOMMENDATION

This chapter focuses on innovative management strategies of wine tourism in the era of COVID-19. This paper is the first to find the accepted definition of wine tourism from the previous research literature. Starting from the definition, the factors that make up wine tourism are analyzed: the wine industry, raw material cultivation, wine craft, tourist destination and the formation of wine brand equity. Reviewing the research on wine tourism in recent years, it is emphasized that wine tourism is the strategic deployment of wine industry diversity. Based on previous research literature, the driving force of wine tourism development was identified, and combined with the depression of global tourism economy brought by COVID-19, three stages of tourism economy after COVID-19 were summarized: response stage, recovery stage and reset stage. Combined with innovative management strategies, big data and brand IP are studied as innovative development strategies. When sorting out previous literature, we found that there was a lack of relevant articles and actual cases related to big data and brand IP in connection with wine tourism development. This paper will make up for the vacancy of actual case analysis.

To better understand the distribution of world grape and grain plantations, world wine production and world wine intake, we analyzed the data listed the world's top wine regions and the early development of wine tourism regions and compared the characteristics of wine culture tourism industry development. Based on regions with early, rapid development, we, analyzed the similarities and differences, and summed up the common experiences. The feasibility of the experience was then verified by an example.

In order to study the development speed of wine tourism industry in the context of COVID-19, the development status and development speed of wine before COVID-19 and the status quo of wine tourism after COVID-19 were studied through comparative data. The results show that the epidemic has greatly reduced the demand for wine tourism, and it is difficult to meet the consumption expectations of tourists in the recovery process. The world wine tourism landscape is reflected through countries with distinct characteristics.

Digital big data analysis and wine brand IP have brought new opportunities for wine industry upgrading in the context of COVID-19. The results show that digitization brings the wine industry closer to consumers, enabling consumers and tourists to have a deeper understanding of the wine industry and a more immersive experience. Brand IP can protect original and innovative strategies, increase the sense of belonging and loyalty of tourists and consumers, accumulate consumers and build brand reputation in the era of digitization.

Finally, the successful establishment and dissemination of brand culture was shown with the case study of *Shede* liquor industry with their industrial innovation strategy. Thus, Chinese experience can be shared by the world.

This paper also summarizes the experience and puts forward suggestions for the wine tourism industry. In order to avoid elimination by competition, wine industry investors should determine the brand positioning, combined with their own advantages, from the perspective of enabling the wine industry with wine tourism projects and cultural festival construction projects. Wine tourism investors should create a cultural core belonging to the brand characteristics and establish a global awareness, so that all investors reach a consensus on the direction of the project (Cusin et al., 2015). Another strategy is to strengthen cooperation between different wine tourism enterprises as well as small enterprises for cooperation and complementary, collaborative development (Güzel et al., 2021).

In the recovery stage of the global tourism economy, wine tourism strategy makers should avoid paying too much attention to the changes in the number of tourists. They should accurately meet the needs of consumers from the perspective of consumers, pay more attention to the experience and satisfaction of tourists in the process of wine tourism, and change the original mode of tourism economy from an export of wine culture to a tourist-centered interactive sightseeing experience, increasing the diversity of the wine industry.

Wine tourism promoters need to use a variety of media such as blogs, video delivery platforms, advertisement planning and other media to strengthen the cultural heritage of the brand. Authenticity is an important indicator of the wine tourism industry. Thus, the use of digital technology also needs to ensure the authenticity of the tour, in the face of internal and external competition (Frost et al., 2020). Decision makers should not be constrained by consistent industry, using digital technology to the construction of brand culture, creative brand unique IP, pay attention to the regulatory in industry and the whole chain.

The wine industry should prepare in advance for the normalization of COVID-19 prevention and control, and make good use of digital technology and virtual reality technology to open a new digital tourism route. A solid foundation for the subsequent return tour and on-the-spot wine tourism (Byrd et al., 2016) can be laid by making effective use of big data to analyze the individual, setting up a unique tour arrangement for each tourist, and actively collecting the state of tourist satisfaction in the tour arrangement.

ACKNOWLEDGMENT

The authors extend sincere gratitude to:

- Our colleagues from Soochow University, the Australian Studies Centre of Shanghai University and Krirk University as well as the independent research colleagues who provided insight and expertise that greatly assisted the research, although they may not agree with all of the interpretations/conclusions of this chapter.
- China Knowledge for supporting our research.
- The Editor and the International Editorial Advisory Board (IEAB) of this book who initially desk reviewed, arranged a rigorous double/triple blind review

process and conducted a thorough, minute and critical final review before accepting the chapter for publication.

- All anonymous reviewers who provided very constructive feedbacks for thorough revision, improvement, extension and fine tuning of the chapter.

REFERENCES

Anderson, K., & Wittwer, G. (2021). *Projecting Global Beverage Markets to 2025*. The International Wine Marketing & Wine Tourism Database.

Asquith, J. (2020). Coronavirus travel update—Over 90% of people live under travel restrictions. *Forbes*.

Bhardwaj, A., & Kumar, V. (2022). Privacy and Healthcare during COVID-19. In *Cybersecurity Crisis Management and Lessons Learned From the COVID-19 Pandemic* (pp. 82–96). IGI-Global. doi:10.4018/978-1-7998-9164-2.ch005

Bruwer, J. (2003). South African wine routes: Some perspectives on the wine tourism industry's structural dimensions and wine tourism product. *Tourism Management*, *24*(4), 423–435. doi:10.1016/S0261-5177(02)00105-X

Byrd, E., Canziani, B., Hsieh, Y. C., Debbage, K., & Sonmez, S. (2016). Wine tourism: Motivating visitors through core and supplementary services. *Tourism Management*, *52*, 19–29. doi:10.1016/j.tourman.2015.06.009

Chen, C. (2006). CiteSpace II: Detecting and Visualizing Emerging Trends and Transient Patterns in Scientific Literature. *JASIST*, *57*(3), 359–377. doi:10.1002/asi.20317

Chen, C., Ibekwe-Sanjuan, F., & Hou, J. (2010). The Structure and Dynamics of Cocitation Clusters: A Multiple-Perspective Cocitation Analysis. *JASIST*, *61*(7), 1386–1409. doi:10.1002/asi.21309

Crick, J. M., Crick, D., & Tebbett, N. (2020). Competitor orientation and value co-creation in sustaining rural New Zealand wine producers. *Journal of Rural Studies*, *73*, 122–134. doi:10.1016/j.jrurstud.2019.10.019

Cuomo, M. T., Tortora, D., Foroudi, P., Giordano, A., Festa, G., & Metallo, G. (2021). Digital transformation and tourist experience co-design: Big social data for planning cultural tourism. *Technological Forecasting and Social Change*, *162*, 120345. doi:10.1016/j.techfore.2020.120345

Cusin, J., & Passebois-Ducros, J. (2015). Appropriate persistence in a project: The case of the Wine Culture and Tourism Centre in Bordeaux. *European Management Journal, 33*(5), 341–353. doi:10.1016/j.emj.2015.04.001

Duan, B., Arcodia, C., Ma, E., & Hsiao, A. (2018). Understanding wine tourism in China using an integrated product-level and experience economy framework. *Asia Pacific Journal of Tourism Research, 23*(10), 949–960. doi:10.1080/10941665.2018.1512506

Dutton, J., & Normand-Marconnet, N. (2019). *Visual codes on French wine labels for cross-cultural marketing in China and Australia.* Academy of Wine Business Research.

Festa, G., Riad Shams, S. M., Metallo, G., & Cuomo, M. T. (2020). Opportunities and challenges in the contribution of wine routes to wine tourism in Italy – A stakeholders' perspective of development. *Tourism Management Perspectives, 33*, 100585. doi:10.1016/j.tmp.2019.100585

Frost, W., Frost, J., Strickland, P., & Maguire, J. S. (2020). Seeking a competitive advantage in wine tourism: Heritage and storytelling at the cellar-door. *International Journal of Hospitality Management, 87*, 102460. doi:10.1016/j.ijhm.2020.102460

Garibaldi, R., Stone, M. J., Wolf, E., & Pozzi, A. (2017). Wine travel in the United States: A profile of wine travellers and wine tours. *Tourism Management Perspectives, 23*, 53–57. doi:10.1016/j.tmp.2017.04.004

Getz, D., & Brown, G. (2006). Critical success factors for wine tourism regions: A demand analysis. *Tourism Management, 27*(1), 146–158. doi:10.1016/j.tourman.2004.08.002

Gómez, M., González-Díaz, M., & Molina, A. (2015). Priority maps at wine tourism destinations: An empirical approach in five Spanish wine regions. *Journal of Destination Marketing & Management, 4*(4), 258–267. doi:10.1016/j.jdmm.2015.09.003

Gomez, M., Lopez, C., & Molina, A. (2015). A model of tourism destination brand equity: The case of wine tourism destinations in Spain. *Tourism Management, 51*, 210–222. doi:10.1016/j.tourman.2015.05.019

Gu, Q. S., & Huang, S. S. (2019). Profiling Chinese wine tourists by wine tourism constraints: A comparison of Chinese Australians and long-haul Chinese tourists in Australia. *International Journal of Tourism Research, 21*(2), 206–220. doi:10.1002/jtr.2255

Gu, Q. S., Zhang, H., Huang, S., Zheng, F., & Chen, C. (2021). Tourists' spatiotemporal behaviors in an emerging wine region: A time-geography perspective. *Journal of Destination Marketing & Management, 19*, 100513. doi:10.1016/j.jdmm.2020.100513

Güzel, O., Ehtiyar, R., & Ryan, C. (2021). The Success Factors of wine tourism entrepreneurship for rural area: A thematic biographical narrative analysis in Turkey. *Journal of Rural Studies, 84*, 230–239. doi:10.1016/j.jrurstud.2021.04.021

Hall, C. M., Johnson, G., Cambourne, B., Macionis, N., Mitchell, R., & Sharples, L. (2000). Wine tourism: An introduction. In C. M. Hall, L. Sharples, B. Cambourne, & N. Macionis (Eds.), *Wine tourism around the world: Development, management and markets* (pp. 1–24). Butterworth-Heinemann.

Hauck, K., Fleuchaus, R., & Szolnoki, G. (2021). *Instagram & Wine – A Quantitative Analysis of the Usage Behaviour of Wine Consumers and Wineries on Instagram.* Academy of Wine Business Research.

Jin, G., Zhu, Y., & Xu, Y. (2017). Mystery behind Chinese liquor fermentation. *Trends in Food Science & Technology, 63*, 18–28. doi:10.1016/j.tifs.2017.02.016

Kumar, V., & Gupta, G. (Eds.). (2021). *Strategic Management During a Pandemic.* Routledge. doi:10.4324/9781003125648

Kumar, V., & Malhotra, G. (Eds.). (2021). *Stakeholder Strategies for Reducing the Impact of Global Health Crises.* IGI Global Publications. doi:10.4018/978-1-7998-7495-9

Lata, M., & Gupta, A. (2020). Role of Social Media in Environmental Democracy. In *Examining the Roles of IT and Social Media in Democratic Development and Social Change* (pp. 275–293). IGI Global. doi:10.4018/978-1-7998-1791-8.ch011

Lease, T., & Conover, T. (2021). *Characteristics of Successful Virtual Wine Tastings: The Participants' Perspective.* Academy of Wine Business Research.

Loose, S. M., Strub, L., & Kurth, A. (2021). *Economic Sustainability of Wine Estates: First Insights and a Roadmap for Future Research.* Academy of Wine Business Research.

Lunardo, R., Corsi, A. M., & Jaud, D. A. (2021). *Look at Me and My Glass of Wine! A Moderated Mediation Analysis of the Effect of Narcissism on (Over) Consumption of Wine.* Academy of Wine Business Research.

Martins, J., Gonçalves, R., Branco, F., Barbosa, L., Melo, M., & Bessa, M. (2017). A multisensory virtual experience model for thematic tourism: A Port wine tourism application proposal. *Journal of Destination Marketing & Management*, *6*(2), 103–109. doi:10.1016/j.jdmm.2017.02.002

Nanda, P., & Kumar, V. (2022). Information Processing and Data Analytics for Decision Making: A Journey from Traditional to Modern Approaches. *Information Resources Management Journal*, *35*(2), 1–14. doi:10.4018/IRMJ.291693

Nave, A., Laurett, R., & Paco, A. (2021). Relation between antecedents, barriers and consequences of sustainable practices in the wine tourism sector. *Journal of Destination Marketing & Management*, *20*, 100584. doi:10.1016/j.jdmm.2021.100584

Nicolosi, A., Cortese, L., Nesci, F. S., & Privitera, D. (2016). Combing Wine production and Tourism. The Aeolian Islands. *Social and Behavioral Sciences*, *223*, 662–667.

Obermayer, N., Kovari, E., Leinonen, J., Bak, G., & Valeri, M. (2021). How social media practices shape family business performance: The wine industry case study. *European Management Journal*. Advance online publication. doi:10.1016/j.emj.2021.08.003

Qin, H., Huo, D., Zhang, L., Yang, L., Zhang, S., Yang, M., Shen, C., & Hou, C. (2012). Colorimetric artificial nose for identification of Chinese liquor with different geographic origins. *Food Research International*, *45*(1), 45–51. doi:10.1016/j.foodres.2011.09.008

Rachao, S. A. S., Breda, Z. J., Fernandes, C. O., & Joukes, V. N. P. M. (2021). Drivers of experience co-creation in food-and-wine tourism: An exploratory quantitative analysis. *Tourism Management Perspectives*, *37*, 100783. doi:10.1016/j.tmp.2020.100783

Rainer, G. (2016). Constructing globalized spaces of tourism and leisure: Political ecologies of the Salta Wine Route (NW-Argentina). *Journal of Rural Studies*, *43*, 104–117. doi:10.1016/j.jrurstud.2015.11.007

Santeramo, F. G., Seccia, A., & Nardone, G. (2017). The synergies of the Italian wine and tourism sectors. *Wine Economics and Policy*, *6*(1), 71–74. doi:10.1016/j.wep.2016.11.004

Sigala, M. (2020). Tourism and COVID-19: Impacts and implications for advancing and resetting industry and research. *Journal of Business Research*, *117*, 312–321. doi:10.1016/j.jbusres.2020.06.015 PMID:32546875

Singh, J., & Kumar, V. (2022). Combating the Pandemic with ICT Based Learning tools and applications: A case of Indian Higher Education. *International Journal of Virtual and Personal Learning Environments Platforms, 12*(1), 1–21.

Song, H., Livat, F., & Ye, H. (2019). Effects of terrorist attacks on tourist flows to France: Is wine tourism a substitute for urban tourism? *Journal of Destination Marketing & Management, 14*, 100385. doi:10.1016/j.jdmm.2019.100385

Sun, Y. Y., & Drakeman, D. (2020). Measuring the carbon footprint of wine tourism and cellar door sales. *Journal of Cleaner Production, 266*, 121937. doi:10.1016/j.jclepro.2020.121937

Tafel, M., & Szolnoki, G. (2020). Estimating the economic impact of tourism in German wine regions. *International Journal of Tourism Research, 22*(6), 788–799. doi:10.1002/jtr.2380

Torres, J. P., Barrera, J. I., Kunc, M., & Charters, S. (2021). The dynamics of wine tourism adoption in Chile. *Journal of Business Research, 127*, 474–485. doi:10.1016/j.jbusres.2020.06.043

Velikova, N., Ghvanidze, S., & Mamardashvili, P. (2021). *Exploring the Role of Nostalgia in Wine Consumption: The Very Best of Georgia*. Academy of Wine Business Research.

Weatherbee, T., Sears, D., & MacNeil, R. (2019). *Mapping wine business studies: Part 1. International Journal of Wine Business Research*. Academy of Wine Business Research.

Wilson, D. (2021). *Navigating the Wine Involvement Continuum*. Academy of Wine Business Research.

Yang, Y., Ruan, Q., Huang, S., Lan, T., & Wang, Y. (2021). Impact of the COVID-19 outbreak on tourists' real-time on-site emotional experience in reopened tourism destinations. *Journal of Hospitality and Tourism Management, 48*, 390–394. doi:10.1016/j.jhtm.2021.07.014

Yang, Y., Zhang, C. X., & Rickly, J. M. (2021). A review of early COVID-19 research in tourism: Launching the Annals of Tourism Research's Curated Collection on coronavirus and tourism. *Annals of Tourism Research, 91*, 103313. Advance online publication. doi:10.1016/j.annals.2021.103313 PMID:34611371

Chapter 5
If Winter Comes, Can Spring Be Far Behind?
A Case Study on China Southern Airlines

Cheryl Qianru Zhang
Macau University of Science and Technology, Macao

Amy Yamei Wang
The Hang Seng University of Hong Kong, Hong Kong

Eko Yi Liao
The Hang Seng University of Hong Kong, Hong Kong

EXECUTIVE SUMMARY

This chapter discusses the impact of COVID-19 on the Chinese aviation industry. Specifically, China Southern Airlines (CSAIR) was chosen as a focal airline company, from which its approach and strategies in dealing with various challenges and difficulties brought by COVID-19 was investigated and analyzed. Challenges that airline companies faced during pandemic include a decline in traffic volume, operation funds shortage, and uncertain situations and difficulties in making predictions. The case starts with introducing general impact of COVID-19 on airline industry, followed by delineating regulations from the industry as prevention and control of the pandemic situation. It identifies several pathways to civil aviation industry recovery, namely group standard measures, fleet storage, domestic passengers flight operation, and transition to cargo flight.

DOI: 10.4018/978-1-6684-3504-5.ch005

BACKGROUND

Aviation Industry in China: Under Pandemic

According to the World Health Organization, as of August 2021, there have been more than 220 million confirmed cases of Covid-19 globally (Kumar & Gupta, 2021). The pandemic has had a profound impact on the global economy, particularly by limiting the movement of people across borders and geographical distances. Unsurprisingly, civil aviation has been one of the hardest hit industries due to the pandemic (Kumar & Malhotra, 2021). Statistics data issued by the International Air Transport Association (IATA), demonstrated that 2020 was the worst year for the airline industry on record (IATA, 2021) with 1.8 billion passengers flying in 2020 compared to 4.5 billion who flew in 2019 (60.2% decrease). Although some scholars have pointed out that Covid-19 may also have a positive impact on the aviation industry such as lower prices of aviation fuel which can help airline companies control operation costs (Mhalla, 2020) and increased opportunities in the cargo business (Li, 2020), Covid-19 has undoubtedly been devastating. Travel restrictions have contributed to the failure of 43 commercial airlines who completely ceased or suspended operations by October of 2020 (Ng, 2020). As the largest civil aviation industry in the world, China's aviation industry and the players within it were particularly hit hard by both the reluctance of customers to take flights and the governmental restrictions on transport services (Guo, 2021). These players include, but are not limited to, "airlines, airport authorities, air cargo providers, in-flight food caterers, aircraft or spare parts manufacturers and maintenance, repair and overhaul organizations" (Rahman, Rahim, Ahmad, & Hafizuddin-Syah, 2020). Although some gradual recovery has been noted, China's civil aviation industry still encounters challenges such as grounded aircrafts, declines in traffic volume, and a shortage of operational funds.

Grounded Aircrafts

Due to the withdrawal of services from aircraft operators, 44% of the total number of global commercial passenger fleets was grounded in storage in March 2020. Among these groundings, 10% of the passenger fleets came from Chinese operators. As shown in Figure 1, over 150 commercial passenger jets in China were grounded by the end of July 2020 (CIRIUM, 2021). With fleets grounded, Chinese airline operators are faced with wasted resources and inventory costs to compound their losses.

Figure 1. Aircraft in storage in China (end of July 2020)
Source: CIRIUM, 2021

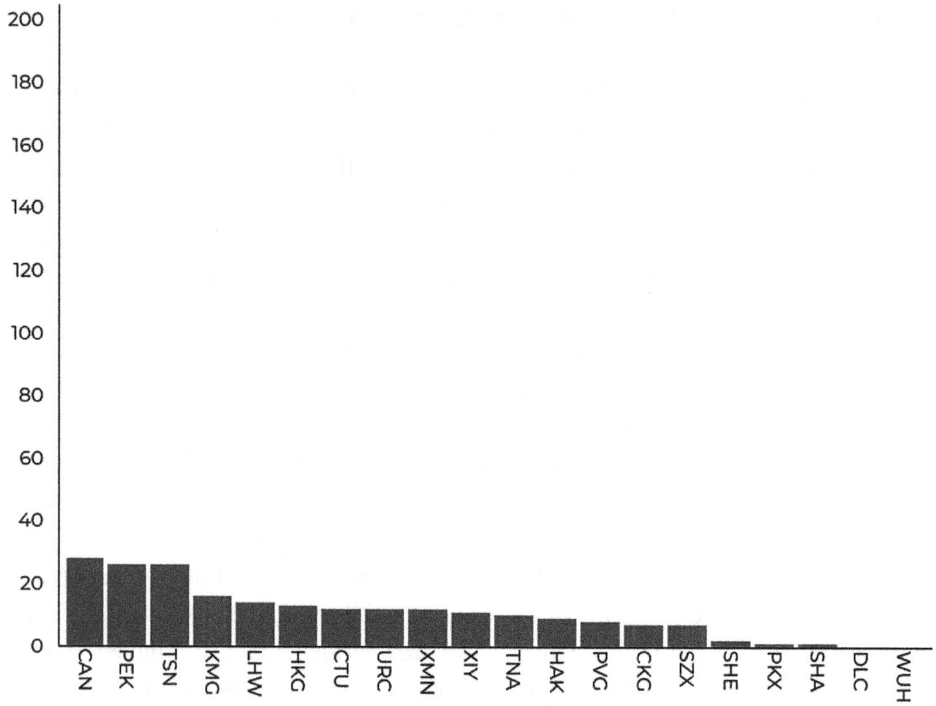

A Decline in Traffic Volume

Since January 2020, traffic volume in China declined drastically as a result of government-imposed travel restrictions which banned international as well as domestic air travel. Figure 2 shows that more than 6,000 scheduled domestic flights were cancelled due to the travel restrictions. The number of passengers in February 2020 fell by more than 80% as actual flights fell from approximately 16,000 to below 4,000 (CIRIUM, 2020).

Figure 2. Actual flights flown in China from September 2020 to July 2021
Source: CIRIUM, 2020

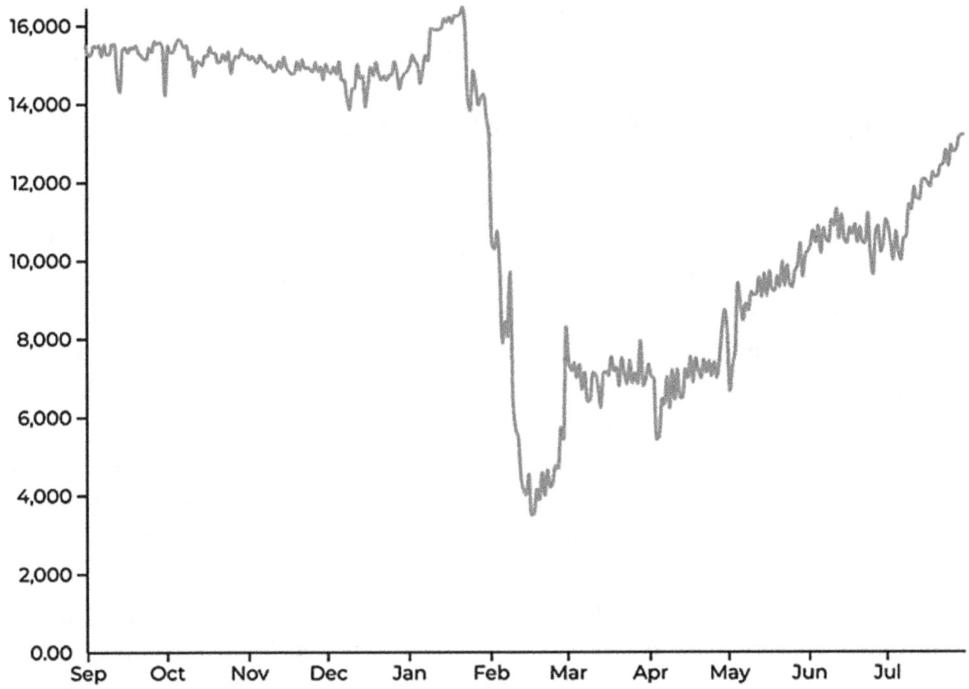

International passenger flight operations in China have also been depressed. As Covid-19 and its variants continue to affect countries all over the world, the prospects for the recovery of the international flight market depends heavily on the control of the pandemic. Only 879,900 international total flights hours were reported in 2020 (a YOY decrease of 63.3%) while the number of flights on international routes was only 137,900 (a YoY decrease of 71.8) (CAAC, 2020). To combat the transmission of Covid into China from other countries, 302 incoming international scheduled passenger flights from high-risk areas have been suspended. Until August 3, 2021, a total number of 621 inbound flights have been reduced (Hua, 2021).

Operation Funds Shortage

COVID-19 has caused 370 billion dollars in financial losses to airlines worldwide, with airports and air navigation service providers losing 115 billion dollars and 13 billion dollars respectively (Montréal, 2021). According to the Statistical Bulletin on the Development of China's Civil Aviation Industry, as of 2020, the aviation industry achieved a total revenue of 624.691 billion yuan (YoY decrease of 41%) and a total profit of 97.432 billion yuan (YoY decrease of 151.943 billion yuan). Operating revenues accounted for only 375.502 billion yuan (YoY decrease of 41.9%). The airline industry has called for the Chinese government to enact financially supportive policies as well as exploring self-rescue measures.

Industry Regulations for Control and Prevention

Due to the nature of the aviation industry which transports people across distance and facilitates the spread of the virus, the regulation of civil aviation has been necessary in the prevention and control of the epidemic. The absence of flights has not only naturally limited the movement of people, but also contributed to the fight against the virus by transporting important materials such as personal protective equipment (e.g., masks and gloves) and other healthcare items. Indeed, the Civil Aviation Administration of China (CAAC) has reduced the role of the civil aviation industry from regular services to emergency responses only and predicted that "the daily passenger traffic is expected to reach below 200,000, which is less than 1/10 of the traffic in the peak period, and the load factor will be less than 40%".

In the fight against the virus, every department of the civil aviation industry has made contributions. For example, airlines have transported front-line medical staff to hospitals, picked up hundreds of stranded passengers in Covid hotspots overseas, and aided in the delivery of medical equipment, medicines, vaccines and other basic daily necessities (CARNOC, 2020).

China's aviation industry played an irreplaceable role in preventing the spread of the disease. Public air transportation has been utilized at the frontline of pandemic prevention and control and is also a vital mechanism of China's public emergency response system. Additionally, in response to the outbreak of Covid-19, airlines cut down flights to prevent the spread of Covid-19. For example, in March 2020, China's "Five One" policy adopted by the Civil Aviation Administration of China (CAAC) limits airlines to just one international flight a week while foreign airlines also offer one flight to China a week (Czerny, Fu, Lei, & Oum, 2021).

PATHWAYS TO CIVIL AVIATION INDUSTRY RECOVERY IN CHINA

Based on the Statistical Bulletin of Civil Aviation Industry Development (CAAC, 2020; CAAC, 2021a), the aviation industry completed 417,778.200 passenger trips (a YoY decrease of 8.7%). Comprehensive measures have been implemented by the civil aviation industry to ensure the safety and stability of air transport during Covid-19. In the anti-epidemic fight, Chinese airlines are committed to providing passengers with high a standard of service, and the corresponding measures have been adopted.

Group Standard Measures

In face of public health emergencies, the China Air Transport Association issued – for the first time in the international aviation industry – several policies to ensure public transport safety (CAAC, 2021). For example, the Covid-19 Government Public Health Mitigation Measures was developed to closely monitor and oversee the hygiene procedures of airline catering companies. Furthermore, to implement the normalized disease prevention and control in the civil aviation industry, the *Guidelines for Regular Epidemic Prevention and Control of Covid-19 for Civil Airports in China* was developed to familiarize the industry with a new set of stringent and careful health measures (CCAA, 2020). In 2021, Guangzhou Baiyun International airport was the first airport in China to receive the highest 5-star Covid-19 airport safety rating (Skytrax, 2021) which recognizes good health, hygiene, and safety. This award signals the signs of gradual recovery for China's civil aviation industry.

In addition to the public policies in the civil aviation industry enacted by the government, airlines were also proactive in taking effective measures to ensure the safety of air transportation. In Air China's case for example, based on the 4C-based service including "credibility, convenience, comfort and choice" philosophy, the company voluntarily equipped themselves with medical evacuation equipment in each aircraft (Air China, n.d). Other aircrafts took additional care in maintain the hygiene of their aircrafts; for example, China Southern Airlines ensured thorough disinfection of its vehicles and a complete replacement of the air conditioning filter after each flight.

These positive measures contributed to the gradually normalizing civil aviation industry.

Fleet Storage

Due to the "Phase Five Plans" issued by CAAC stipulating one flight per week per airline per country from 8 June 2020, international flights were still heavily restricted (MFA, 2020) which meant that most of the wide-body fleets – which are better suited to long-haul flights – were kept in storage. However, the number of China's narrow-body aircrafts – which are better suited to short-haul flights – increased to accommodate the recovery of the domestic flight market. The increased travel of passengers within China allowed the number of narrow-body aircrafts to increase from less than 1000 in February 2020 to 2300 by the end of May 2020. At the same time, the fleet storage of narrow-body aircrafts decreased by 16% (CIRIUM, 2020) which suggests an increasing number of operating domestic flights.

Domestic Passengers Flight Operation

As lock downs were cancelled in February 2020, domestic flights within China began to recover and continued to increase in March 2020. Based on the statistical data between March 2020 and April 2020, the daily passenger traffic increased to 500,000 with an average of 50% loading of aircrafts (ACI, 2021). Another milestone to signal domestic air transport recovery was a national holiday in May 2020 which enabled workers to take up to a week off for holiday. As fewer confirmed cases were reported, travelers regained confidence. Domestic flights approached performance levels similar to those before the pandemic. The domestic market continued to recover until it reached normal levels in August 2020. Then, due to the annual 'Golden Week' holiday from Oct.1st to 7th, the daily domestic services flights reached more than 12,000. Concurrently, demand recovered to a degree that was higher than 9% daily, compared to September 2019 (CIRIUM, 2020).

Cargo Flight

The cancellation of scheduled passenger flights has also meant a shortage of capacity for cargo (located at the belly of passenger airlines). As a result, to meet demands for cargo services, some grounded aircrafts have been converted into special cabin cargo aircrafts. Cargo revenues have attracted airlines to convert their wide-body aircrafts into cargo freighters. This measure not only reduces the financial pressure on airline operations, but also increases aircraft utilization, which helps facilitate the recovery of the aviation industry.

COVID-19: CHINA SOUTHERN AIRLINES'S (CSAIR) APPROACH

China Southern Airlines

China Southern Airlines Company Limited, established on 1 July 1988, is a subsidiary of the state-owned enterprise China Southern Air Holding Company. The world headquarters of China Southern Airlines Co., Ltd. is located in Guangzhou, the capital of Guangdong Province, with a brilliant red kapok as the company's logo (Figure 3) and is delicately decorated with a blue vertical tail (CSAIR, 2021).

Figure 3. China Southern Airlines logo
Source: CSAIR website

中国南方航空
CHINA SOUTHERN AIRLINES

Being affected by the COVID-19 epidemic, China Southern Airlines experienced the most challenging period in history. Data illustrated that China Southern Airlines registered a loss of 10.8 billion yuan in 2020 (Global Times, 2021). The government has provided timely financial support, such as "*Notice on Implementing Financial Support Policy for Civil Air Transport Enterprises that Maintain and Increase International Air Cargo Transport Capacity*" (www.caac.gov.cn, 2020); however, it was only a temporary relief measure for airlines. Therefore, airlines were forced to come up with better crisis management strategies in response to the pandemic.

After being hit hard in the early 2020s, China Southern Airlines is now back to pre-epidemic capacity. As the largest airline in China, China Southern Airlines has been severely affected by Covid 19; however, through a series of proactive responses by the company, it has been evaluated better than most of the other airlines in the region (CAPA, 2021). How did China Southern Airlines break through the difficulties? How is it combatting the challenges of the new normal? How did China Southern Airlines thrive during Covid-19? The "Five Major Strategies" (Figure 4) of China Southern Airlines, which includes "Hub Network Strategy, Ecosystem Strategy, Innovation-driven Strategy, Lean and Control Strategy and Brand Management Strategy", guides China Southern to be one of the leading airlines in China, and contributes to the continued improvement of the quality in safety management.

Figure 4. Five strategies of CSAIR (Zhang, 2018)
Source: Corporate Social Responsibility Report of CSAIR

Vision, Mission and Company Value

As shown in Table 1, the vision and mission of CSAIR defines how the company describes its future position and long-term purpose. To facilitate the company's strategy, the corporate vision and mission of CSAIR is "Building a world-class air transport enterprise with global competitiveness" and "Connecting around the world for a prosperous life". These objectives promote management to continually identify opportunities and challenges as well as evaluate internal resources, especially in the fight against the epidemic.

The core values of CSAIR provide a moral compass and guide its corporate culture with respect to its stakeholders. The core values of CSAIR (Customer first, Salute talents, Achieve excellence, Innovate continuously, Return with kindness)" help CSAIR to define how it intends to maintain relationships with its stakeholders. To determine the proper strategies which are followed to fight the pandemic crisis, core value acts as a leading principle in the company's decisions.

Table 1. Corporate mission, vision and core value of CSAIR

Corporate Mission, Vision, and Core Value of CSAIR		
Corporate Vision *• Building a world-class air transport enterprise with global competitiveness*	*Corporate Mission* *• Connecting around the world for a prosperous life*	*Core Value* *• CSAIR (Customer first, Salute talents, Achieve excellence, Innovate continuously, Return with kindness)*

Source: CSAIR website

Strategic Decisions During COVID-19

To evaluate CSAIR's strategic decisions during Covid-19, three of the "Five Major Strategies" – **Hub Network Strategy (dual-hub), Innovation-driven Strategy**

(cabin cargo, promotions) and Brand Management Strategy (CSR) – are examined to understand how CSAIR took effective measures to mitigate risk and ensure sustainable development.

Dual-Hub

"Dual-hub" is a development strategy of CSAIR which aims to integrate its operations through a multi-airport system based in Guangzhou and Beijing – two of the largest airport hubs in China. To deal with slot constraints and insufficient capacity, CSAIR had been planning a "dual-hub for over a decade to create Beijing-Daxing airport as its second major hub. With the opening of the Daxing Airport in 2019, CSAIR'S Beijing hub can share the capacity with Guangzhou and increase the number of flights. CSAIR takes sustainability as one of its main corporate goals, and the "dual-hub" strategy effectively helps it achieve its goal. Especially during the epidemic, "dual hubs" made outstanding contributions to traffic dispatch and epidemic prevention and control.

"Dual-hub" plays an important role both in the company's development, utilization of resources, and improvement of transport capacity allocation.

- Development and utilization of resources
- Improvement of transport capacity allocation

Although Guangzhou Baiyun International Airport had served as the main hub of CSAIR (before the operation of "dual-hub"), there was a relative lack of access to operational resources in northern China. To better achieve corporate vision and mission, the transferring of all the flights of CSAIR in Beijing to Daxing airport facilitates the development and utilization of resources.

Moreover, the goal of hub operation control is to achieve the unified deployment of the company's three major resources - flights, aircrafts, and crews, to achieve rational and optimal allocation and to maximize the economic benefits of the hub. When external factors – such as the pandemic – affect the normal operation of airlines, transport capacity allocation could be deployed in a timely and decisive manner. For example, during the outbreak of the Delta variant in May 2021 in Guangzhou, affecting flight departures from Guangzhou, CSAIR was able to reallocate transport capacity based on "dual-hub" to Beijing.

Cabin Cargo Promotions

Since the start of the pandemic, the borders of most countries remain closed or has various restrictions. The passenger load of international flights has gradually decreased, leading to airlines having to reduce flights accordingly. The pandemic has had a different impact on passenger and cargo traffic of airlines in China. As the quarantine measures in the aviation industry are mainly aimed at air passengers, the impact of the epidemic on cargo aircrafts was less pronounced than passenger aircrafts (Li, 2020). Cargo flights increased compared to passenger flights, owing to the demand of medical equipment during the fight against the epidemic (Nižetić, 2020). What's more, the demand for personal protective equipment made in China has increased that distribution channels to other countries.

Figure 5. Cabin cargo of CSAIR
Source: CSAIR website

In March 2020, the CAAC officially approved a new program which permitted cargo to be placed in the passenger area of passenger planes by removing passenger seats entirely to enlarge the air cargo capabilities of each aircraft. This is referred to as cabin cargo, as Figure 5 shows.

In April 2020, the first cabin cargo flight of China Southern Airlines landed safely in Kuala Lumpur, Malaysia, carrying 18 tons of PPE cargo. China Southern Airlines cabin cargo flights are mainly wide-body passenger aircrafts, composed of two A330 passenger aircraft that had undergone a special cabin modification. In response to the specific aircraft type and cargo loading requirements, airlines communicated with customers regarding cargo packaging to maximize the payload of the flights. As of April 23, 2020, China Southern Airlines has completed 255 cabin cargo flights, transporting 2,930 tons of cargo to 22 countries and regions, including Italy, France, Canada, Australia, Turkey, Malaysia, Kenya, Japan, and South Korea.

The remarkable advantages of cabin cargo of CSAIR are as follows: first, China Southern Airlines has five wide-body aircrafts (generally with two aisles) transformed from passenger planes into cargo carriers which accounts for 5% of the global wide-body aircraft fleet (Chinairport, 2021). This reduced the operational costs by making efficient use of wide-body aircraft capacity during the epidemic; second, a bigger fuselage means more carrying capacity, which contributed to the diversified types of anti-epidemic materials taken by wide-body aircrafts of CSAIR.

Promotions

During COVID-19, airlines have had to rethink how their companies can engage with customers. Airlines launched certain service products based on various travel needs of passengers, such as multi-seater for one person and chartered flights for resumption of work. From mid-2020 onwards, a large number of "ALL YOU CAN FLY" services appeared in the market to encourage domestic travel. The service products of each company are different, with restricted and unrestricted schedules, destinations, and times. All of these products belong to the category of pre-sale products of travel rights for civil aviation passengers.

On July 28, 2020, China Southern Airlines launched "Fly Happily" as a promotional package that allow passengers to book unlimited flights, use passes for as many flights as they wish for destinations across China from August 26, 2020 to January 6, 2021 for the price of 3,699 yuan that is US $529 (REUTERS, 2020). This deal is suitable for people who are expected to have more free time and more flight plans, such as freelancers, long-distance lovers, and those who have plans to fly around for fun. Each flight is limited to 20 seats. The pass holder shall book the seat 5 days in advance and cancel the booking 4 days in advance. The advantages of the "Fly Happily" promotion are first, direct cash flows which are prepaid upfront by the customer for future flights; second, to take advantage of the low marginal cost of each incremental passenger; and third, to increase the number of seats sold and indirectly increase the average fare paid for flights.

China Southern Airlines has the most transported aircrafts and the most developed route network to attract customers and optimize its marketing strategy. Compared with other airlines' plans, its products are more diverse and have thus become increasingly popular.

Corporate Social Responsibility (CSR)

Business is more than just making profits – it is also engaging in its social responsibility (Pillay, 2015). For CSAIR, the company actively fulfills social responsibility during the pandemic. One of the main honors that China Southern Airlines Group has earned in 2020 was the "National Advanced Unit of Transportation System to Fight the Covid-19 Pandemic" by the Ministry of Transport of China (CSR-CSAIR, 2021). Additionally, the company was awarded the highest grade of "Good" in the assessment of China's Central State-Owned Enterprises in poverty alleviation in 2019. These awards recognized CSAIR for making a positive impact on society.

Covid-19 made all organizations reconsider who should be deemed as the most "essential stakeholders of business" (Crane & Matten, 2020). Concerning stakeholder identification, CSAIR's CSR widely includes (CSR-CSAIR, 2021):

- Making Profits
- Rewarding Shareholders
- Creating Value
- Rewarding Society
- Creating Services
- Rewarding Customers
- Creating Chances
- Rewarding Employees
- Caring for the Earth
- Green Flights

CSR applies to the civil aviation industry where it has promoted airlines engaging in positive activities (De Mestral et al., 2018). Specifically, CSAIR focused on Green Flights and Poverty Alleviation. Due to a decrease in revenues and passenger volume, CSAIR promoted green development to propose low-carbon and simple travel. Intelligent facilities such as self-service baggage checks, electronic boarding passes, ordering food online, luggage weight reduction, have been promoted and initiated. For example, over 2 million passengers have opted for the Green Flight service, saving 2 million meals and over 945 tons of food. This is beneficial for both the company and the customers as it reduces the economic pressure on airlines while benefitting a greener and cleaner earth. Due to the positive behaviors of CSAIR, the general achievements include but are not limited to "zero infections, anti-epidemic transport, material donation and momentum for the resumption of work".

Table 2. Positive behaviors of CSAIR from 2020 to 2021

Year	Events in Brief	Positive Behaviors
2020	1) B777 fleet – security guards of "lifeline in the air";	The B777 of the CSAIR fleet completed 36 important flights, picking up more than 4,500 passengers, in which five important flights to Wuhan for medical rescue, 1,294 medical personnel, and more than 100 tons of anti-pandemic masteries were transported to Wuhan.
	2) Flight to Wuhan to transport rescue medical team from Guangdong Province	On New Year's Eve 2020, Flight CZ5241, carrying 128 members of the rescue medical team, 3415kg luggage, and medical supplies, rushed from Guangdong Province to Wuhan.
	3) Free charter flight	CSAIR promised to open a green channel for the qualified anti-pandemic masteries with a free charter flight.
	4) Overseas transport of epidemic prevention materials	On February 4, 2020, 972,000 masks donated by the Macau Red Cross and Macau Federation of Returned Overseas Chinese were shipped from Indonesia back to China free of charge by Flight CZ388 and CZ3038.
	5) Flights of masks	Seven "masks (donated by Chinese in Kenya) flights" were made, providing valuable supplies for the front line, from the onset of the epidemic to the suspension of flights to Kenya.
	6) Bringing overseas students home	On May 8, 2020, 110 international students who were going to return to China from Amsterdam by CZ308, were stranded and could not return, due to the delay of the previous US flight. The Amsterdam business department of China Southern Airlines coordinated with the operation command center and customer service department, to transport the overseas students' return.
	7) Transporting the anti-epidemic medical team to Cambodia	The first anti-epidemic medical team from China went to the Association of Southeast Asian Nations (ASEAN), at 8:41 a.m. on March 23, 2020, with a chartered plane of China Southern Airlines escorted the anti-epidemic medical team to Phnom Penh International Airport of Cambodia.
	8) The most beautiful volunteer - Zhai Chenfei	Zhai, an excellent pilot of CSAIR, during the epidemic, joined the volunteer team and drove through the streets of Wuhan every day, helping to centralize and distribute large quantities of donated supplies.
2021	1) Escorting vaccines to Tajikistan	On June 20, 2021, CZ8069 departed from Daxing, Beijing, loaded with 300,000 doses of COVID-19 vaccine and more than 100 passengers flew to Dushanbe, the capital of Tajikistan.
	2) Launching China Southern Airlines' exclusive anti-epidemic packages	At the end of August 2021, China Southern Airlines cooperated with the New Zealand Trade and Enterprise (NZTE) to launch an international passenger care cooperation project with the theme of "China Southern Airlines Caring for the 'New' Heart Accompanying", which was the first time in the industry to present hotel quarantine and epidemic prevention kits to international tourists.
	3) Co-organizing the "Fun of China Southern Airline Studying Camp"	On August 14, 2021, "Fun of China Southern Airline Studying Camp" was officially launched by Guangdong CTS (China Travel Service) and China Southern Airlines Training Center, organizing public welfare activities for the children of anti-epidemic personnel by means of "integration of study and research".

Source: data collected from CSAIR news and CSR report

Strategies with a focus on making positive changes are particularly important in challenging times and can help lift a company to survive. China Southern Airlines kept in the top of five airlines ranked by total scheduled passenger kilometers (China daily, 2020). The above multicable measures adopted by CSAIR have helped make remarkable achievements in business recovery and are devoted to comprehensively promoting a high-quality aviation industry.

Adapting to the New Normal

What's next for CSAIR? As the world is recovering from Covid-19, the civil aviation industry is cautiously going back to normal. To support the capacities and revenues, CSAIR is eagerly looking forward to maintaining its strategic competitiveness post Covid-19. To remain on top of their game, CSAIR needs to not only respond to current crises, but also be forward thinking in planning for the new normal. To accomplish this, we suggest CSAIR to focus on Diversified Target Customers, Domestic Market Demand, Cargo Development, and Industry Restructuring Opportunities.

Diversified Target Customers

Before Covid-19, business travelers contributed more than 50% of airlines ticket revenue. However, the epidemic not only has suppressed the demand for traditional sources of travel, a shift into digital workplaces (e.g., remote collaboration, video conferencing, digital platforms) has minimized the necessity for business travel. To address this issue, CSAIR should grapple with the new realities to seek more operational opportunities and diversified target customers. Some examples include attracting travelers to reunite with family or friends, discounting packages to students, promoting an appreciation for outdoor experiences, etc.

Domestic Market Demand

Since international flights were affected by the epidemic, airlines were encouraged to launch products based on domestic market demand. For instance, Covid-19 probably influenced Chinese travelers' consumption patterns, in which "free and independent travel, luxury trips, health and wellness tourism, as well as slow and smart tourism" have changed business plans and resources allocation paths (Wen, Kozak, Yang & Liu, 2020). It is important to make sure that airlines should comply with business environmental changes. From mid-2020 onwards, most of the service products were in the form of pre-sale to airlines passengers, which might bring benefits for the companies and customers. Focusing on domestic market demand has been proven to be a highly effective measure. To maintain recovery, CSAIR will continue to rely on domestic markets and consumer confidence to offset reduced international flights.

Cargo Development Opportunities

It is important to sustain air fleets of cargo in the post Covid-19 age. The impact of the epidemic on the international supply chain of China's industry has caused a greater impact on air cargo, especially international air cargo development ushered in an important window of opportunity. Thus, with the seats removed, the "Cabin Cargo" fleet will continue to maximize the cargo-carrying capabilities of aircrafts.

Industry Restructuring Opportunities

In recent years, due to the operational pressure, privately-owned airlines are at risk of dissolution. Especially, under the impact of the epidemic, airlines with low operational capacity might face higher cost pressure. Relatively, it offered a better development opportunity for those airlines with greater adaptability. Thus, CSAIR should seize the opportunity to reshape the organizations and implement business accordingly.

CONCLUSION

Commercial airlines have been severely hit by COVID-19 (Ng, 2020) as more than 40 airlines ceased or suspended operations in 2020. To avoid a collapse of the aviation industry, air transport needs to be supported and improved in due course (Nižetić, 2020). In terms of the global aviation industry, major unknowns still bring concerns regarding the future development of air freight and future ticket prices (Suau-Sanchez, Voltes-Dorta, & Cugueró-Escofet, 2020).

Some of the key factors that will boost business travelers' confidence in restoring travel include mandatory mask requirements, crowding restrictions, maintaining social distance/blocking off middle seats on flights, and widespread COVID-19 testing. Vaccination programs are also crucial to airlines' recovery hopes, as they are widely considered a vital protection while travelling. When countries reach herd immunity vaccination levels of 70% or higher, governments will have more options for removing restrictions.

To conclude, airlines are fighting for the travel market during the Covid-19 pandemic. As demonstrated by CSAIR, airlines need to grapple with the new normal realities and do the best they can.

First, global passenger travel dropped by an estimated two-thirds in 2020 versus 2019 and was reduced to pre-pandemic levels. Airlines face little choice in having to adapt quickly to challenges. One of the most critical choices for airlines is determining whether to offer flights. On the one hand, flights with not enough customers will increase operational costs; however, on the other hand, not offering flight options may lose loyal customers in the long run. Airlines face the difficult decision of making the right balance of how many flights to offer.

Second, travel restrictions forced airlines to cut flights by half in 2020. Only narrow-body aircrafts were still in service compared to wide-body aircraft which remain mostly grounded. After the golden week of October 2020 in China, it was a good sign showing narrow-body aircrafts leading the recovery and domestic travel normalizing. With China's zero Covid-19 policy and more than a 80% vaccinated rate, the confidence in the flying of Chinese travelers has been increasing dramatically.

Third, to improve the financial health of airlines, companies may reconsider modifications of existing aircrafts to save costs. For example, high-fuel consumption aircrafts such as the Boeing 747 and the Airbus A380 are more costly while new generation aircrafts such as the Boeing 787 and Airbus A350 are more fuel-efficient.

ACKNOWLEDGEMENT

The work described in this paper was supported by a grant from the Research Grants Council of the Hong Kong Special Administrative Region, China (Project No. UGC/FDS14/B05/19).

REFERENCES

ACI. (2021). *The impact of COVID-19 on the airport business and the path to recovery*. Airports Council International. https://aci.aero/2021/03/25/the-impact-of-Covid-19-on-the-airport-business-and-the-path-to-recovery/

CAAC. (2021). *Group Standard of China Air Transport Association Promoted in International Aviation Industry for the First Time*. http://www.caac.gov.cn/XWZX/MHYW/202103/t20210324_206897.html

CAAC. (2020). *CAAC to Further Intensify and Refine Prevention and Control Measures to Win the Battle against the Novel Coronavirus Epidemic*. Civil Aviation Administration of China. http://www.caac.gov.cn/en/XWZX/202002/t20200221_201090.html

CAAC. (2021a). *2020 Statistical bulletin on the development of the civil aviation industry in 2020*. Civil Aviation Administration of China. http://www.caac.gov.cn/XXGK/XXGK/TJSJ/202106/P020210610582600192012.pdf

CAPA. (2021). *Domestic advantages boost China Southern's post-COVID prospects*. https://centreforaviation.com/analysis/reports/domestic-advantages-boost-china-southerns-post-covid-prospects-558104

CARNC. (2020). *The most beautiful retrograde: Several civil aviation-chartered planes pick up hundreds of overseas stranded passengers in Hubei*. Civil Aviation Resource Net of China. http://news.carnoc.com/newsList/index.html?date=2020-02-01

CCAA. (2020). *Guideline for regular epidemic prevention and control of COVID-19 for civil airports in China*. China Civil Airport Association. https://www.aci-asiapac.aero/f/blog/1798/4468/CCAA%20Guideline%20for%20regular%20epidemic%20prevention%20and%20control%20of%20COVID-19%20for%20civil%20airports%20in%20China%2020200828.pdf

China, A. (n.d.). *Information on Response to the COVID-19 Epidemic*. Retrieved August 19, 2021. https://www.airchina.us/US/GB/promotion/epidemicp?pid=TP_epidemicp:20200909:KV:KYQF:US:EN

China Daily. (2021). *China world's largest domestic air travel market in 2020*. https://www.chinadaily.com.cn/a/202108/10/WS6112254aa310efa1bd667ebd.html

Chinairport. (2021). *Operational status of domestic airlines' wide-body aircrafts*. Chinairport. https://www.chinairport.net/news/2630.html

CIRIUM. (2020). *Cirium weekly Covid-19 update – A golden week for Chinese operators*. https://www.cirium.com/thoughtcloud/cirium-weekly-Covid-19-update-a-golden-week-for-chinese-operators/

CIRIUM. (2021). *Impact of COVID-19 on China*. https://discover.cirium.com/discover/ideas/Covid-19-impact?intcmp=discover-idea-impact-china

Crane, A., & Matten, D. (2020). COVID-19 and the future of CSR research. *Journal of Management Studies*, *58*(1), 280–284. https://doi.org/10.1111/joms.12642

CSAIR. (2020). *Deploying the "cabin cargo" market, China Southern Airlines helps the world "carrying cargo"*. https://www.csair.com/cn/about/news/news/2020/1edqrf7pgjv24.shtml

CSR-CSAIR. (2021). *2020 Corporate Social Responsibility Report of China Southern Airlines Company Limited*. https://www.csair.com/au/en/about/shehuizerenbaogao/resource/f9d8ea27e25f5a475282e461d1067a57.pdf

Czerny, A. I., Fu, X., Lei, Z., & Oum, T. H. (2021). Post pandemic aviation market recovery: Experience and lessons from China. *Journal of Air Transport Management, 90*, 101971. https://doi.org/10.1016/j.jairtraman.2020.101971

De Mestral, A. L., Fitzgerald, P. P., & Ahmad, M. T. (Eds.). (2018). *Sustainable Development, International Aviation, and Treaty Implementation* (1st ed.). Cambridge University Press.

Global Times. (2021). *Grounded by Covid-19, Chinese airlines search for new opportunities.* https://www.globaltimes.cn/page/202108/1230665.shtml

Guo, C. S. (2021, January 12). *The impact of Covid-19 on the macro economy, civil aviation and aircraft manufacturing industry*. CCAonline. http://www.ccaonline.cn/yunshu/629516.html

Hua, X. (2021). *Lax Management Leads to COVID-19 Infections at Nanjing Airport.* XinHua Net. http://www.xinhuanet.com/english/2021-08/03/c_1310105566.htm

IATA. (2021). *Airline Industry Statistics Confirm 2020 Was Worst Year on Record.* https://www.iata.org/en/pressroom/pr/2021-08-03-01/

Kumar, V., & Gupta, G. (Eds.). (2021). *Strategic Management During a Pandemic*. Routledge.

Kumar, V., & Malhotra, G. (Eds.). (2021). *Stakeholder Strategies for Reducing the Impact of Global Health Crises*. IGI Global Publications.

Li, T. (2020). A SWOT analysis of China's air cargo sector in the context of COVID-19 pandemic. *Journal of Air Transport Management*, *88*, 101875. https://doi.org/10.1016/j.jairtraman.2020.101875

MFA. (2020). *CAAC Adjusts Rules on International Passenger Flights Introduces Incentives and Circuit Breaker*. Ministry of Foreign Affairs of the People's Republic of China. https://www.fmprc.gov.cn/mfa_eng/topics_665678/kjgzbdfyyq/t1786310.shtml

Mhalla, M. (2020). The impact of novel coronavirus (COVID-19) on the global oil and aviation markets. *Journal of Asian Scientific Research*, *10*(2), 96. https://doi.org/10.18488/journal.2.2020.102.96.104

Montréal. (2021, Jan 15). *2020 passenger totals drop 60 percent as COVID-19 assault on international mobility continues.* International Civil Aviation Organization (ICAO). https://www.icao.int/Newsroom/Pages/2020-passenger-totals-drop-60-percent-as-COVID19-assault-on-international-mobility-continues.aspx

Ng, A. (2020). *Over 40 airlines have failed so far this year- and more are set to come.* CNBC. https://www.cnbc.com/2020/10/08/over-40-airlines-have-failed-in-2020-so-far-and-more-are-set-to-come.html

Nižetić, S. (2020). Impact of coronavirus (COVID-19) pandemic on air transport mobility, energy, and environment: A case study. *International Journal of Energy Research, 44*(13), 10953–10961. https://doi.org/10.1002/er.5706

Pillay, R. (2015). *The changing nature of corporate social responsibility: CSR and development–the case of Mauritius* (1st ed.). Routledge.

Rahman, N. A. A., Rahim, S. A., Ahmad, M. F., & Hafizuddin-Syah, B. A. M. (2020). Exploring COVID-19 pandemic: Its impact to global aviation industry and the key strategy. *International Journal of Advanced Science and Technology*, 1829-1836. http://sersc.org/journals/index.php/IJAST/article/view/9344

Reuters. (2020). *In China, airlines plug 'all you can fly' deals to pierce coronavirus clouds*. https://www.reuters.com/article/us-health-coronavirus-china-airlines-idUSKCN24T0H9

Skytrax. (2021). *Guangzhou BaiYun International Airport Receives the Highest 5-Star COVID-19 Airport Safety Rating.* https://skytraxratings.com/guangzhou-baiyun-international-airport-receives-the-highest-5-star-Covid-19-airport-safety-rating

Suau-Sanchez, P., Voltes-Dorta, A., & Cugueró-Escofet, N. (2020). An early assessment of the impact of COVID-19 on air transport: Just another crisis or the end of aviation as we know it? *Journal of Transport Geography, 86*, 102749. https://doi.org/10.1016/j.jtrangeo.2020.102749

Wen, J., Kozak, M., Yang, S., & Liu, F. (2021). COVID-19: Potential effects on Chinese citizens' lifestyle and travel. *Tourism Review, 76*(1), 74–87. https://doi.org/10.1108/TR-03-2020-0110

Zhang. (2020, August 18). *Five strategies - A Perspective on China's civil aviation industry relief policy and proposed measures from airlines during COVID-19.* Aviation Think Tank. http://att.caacnews.com.cn/zkzj/Z/zy/202008/t20200818_56229.html

Chapter 6
Crisis Management: From a Stage of Shock to Reassurance in the Hospitality Industry

Puja Roshani
KIET Group of Institutions, India

Shivani Agarwal
https://orcid.org/0000-0002-3205-552X
KIET Group of Institutions, India

EXECUTIVE SUMMARY

The chapter discusses the adverse impinging of COVID-19 on Indian hotel business in general and on Hyatt Regency in particular. Large hospitality firms have major difficulties obtaining finances from financial institutions as the banks continued to have a poor lookout for the hospitality sector. In early phases of the pandemic, the measures which industry adopted in pandemics were related to prevention, pricing strategies, and maintenance efforts. The aid provided by government and human resources approaches also needs to be looked into. The hospitality and tourism industry needs to focus on their pricing schemes, which needs to be lower as compared to previous times. During the outbreak of the pandemic, a few of the hotels appeared to be forcing their workforce to go on non-paid leave and postpone business office and instrumentation upkeep. Seeking government aid or resources, the hotel industry appeared only be used as a last resort. The study confirms the bad shape of the hotels and their slow recovery after incorporating the various techniques of crisis management.

DOI: 10.4018/978-1-6684-3504-5.ch006

INTRODUCTION

Crisis management is a significant school of philosophy of management that works with businesses, institutions, or the country at large in periods of major catastrophes (Pardeep & Clark, 2009). Research on this topic has been a popular issue since the start of COVID-19 (Zhao and Xu, 2020). The importance of tourism, particularly the hospitality industry, has really been plunged into a whirl as a consequence of this unexpected crisis. 150 Hilton hotels in China had been forced to close due to the COVID-19 pandemic (HNN, 2020; Walters et al., 2019). In the hotel and tourism industry, there seems to be paucity of studies conducted, particularly on how to cope in such a pandemic.

According to the World Health Organization (WHO) preliminary report on January 21, 2020 (WHO, 2020a), the WHO had to review its outbreak as an international health problem on January 31, 2020 (WHO, 2020b), to be declared an pandemic worldwide on March 11, 2020 (WHO, 2020c). In fair 2 calendar months, the main centre of the COVID-19 eruption heavily traveled from China to Italy, Spain and the United States and gradually covered the entire globe (Kumar & Gupta, 2021). During the first stages of COVID-19 which led to the pandemic that started in the month of January to the end of February, numerous holidaymaker place in Continent, where the Chinese appear to be prominent tourists, established disaster management systems in the tourism sector in response to the pandemic. The road to hospitality corporation towards planning has grown significantly over time as the pandemic spreads around the world, and difficulty administration plan of action need to be developed and concluded in certain time period. Preceding research on problem management strategies (Israel, 2007; Israel and Reichel, 2003; Israel et al., 2011) and pandemic problems (Lee, 2009; Wan, 2013) focused on a specific period (Israel, 2007; Israel and Reichel, 2003; Israel et al., 2011). As a result, the research space should be filled by conducting consistent research during a crisis situation in order to address the research challenge of what problem-solving procedures should be used from time to time during a crisis. An unexpected emergency situation. Although several surveys have identified them as business enterprise problems (Backer and Ritchie, 2017; Ritchie and Jiang, 2019), to the highest degree former studies have focused on disaster risk management, preparation (Hilliard et al., 2011; Novelli et al., 2018).

Disaster management refers to something like the hotel's ability to cope with a disaster when it happens (Israel et al., 2011). At the same time, it often provides businesses with tools to prevent local and global catastrophe (Benaben et al., 2016). Tse et al. (2006) created a list that classifies problems into multiple clauses. They believe that external problems are caused by the environment and the environment, rather than by the internal factory. Disasters can occur as a result of natural disasters or by man-made actions-for example - bacteria, tsunamis, floods, and other natural disasters. Depending on the level of organizational responsibility, natural disasters, technological error risks, and human error risks, there are three types of potential disasters (Kumar & Malhotra, 2021).

According to reports, by mid of year 2021 more than five million people have died as a result of COVID-19 (Worldometers, 2021), and there have been various measures. Lockdown had a major economic impact on the global economy (Bhardwaj & Kumar, 2022). According to the Organization for Economic Co-operation and Development (OECD), the global economy fell by 2.4 percent to 2.9 percent, leading to a sharp rise in unemployment rising to levels similar to those seen during the 2008 financial crisis. To prevent this situation, governments around the world imposed forced closures, curfews etc. Tourist and tourism businesses had to bear the brunt of this damage. All over the world small and medium-sized hotels and tourism sectors due to their small size, limited resources, and complexity of cash flow, have been hit hard by the pandemic. Social and economic boundaries around the world affected hotels, food service, shops, entertainment and industry. The impact of COVID-19 on the global economy has been strongly felt more severely in developing economies compared to developed countries. COVID has unintended consequences for human survival, economic growth, and trade. Due to the sudden arrival of the coronavirus, an invisible enemy, the world did not know with certainty, how things would turn out at the time of the outbreak (Singh & Kumar, 2022). To combat this pandemic the activities had been partially or completely closed, for short or long periods of time in nature just to protect human lives. Various economists and forecasters expect the world economy to return to normal in the coming years, but the exact timing will not be known until the virus is wiped out worldwide.

COVID-19 had a devastating effect on the Indian hotel industry and with very little demand and a few reservations, with the exception of some hotels that the government had allowed for foreign tourists returning to India. COVID-19 came so quickly that the world did not have time to prepare, and although this problem was unlike any other society ever experienced. The Indian hotel business may be able to recover from this catastrophe, by changing temporary plans and planning for the future. The tourism and leisure industry can be revived by sharing good habits, keeping employees motivated, and trying to get business back on track. Industry participants need to come together and work through difficult times to get back on track. The global outbreak of corona virus undoubtedly affected the world and species and people began to adjust to new normal in view of second, and third wave.

So, this chapter seeks to identify and link how the hospitality business was affected by the COVID-19 crisis and how it was dealt with. The remaining sections of the chapter provides details about effects of COVID-19 on global and Indian economy by exploring a case of hospitality company – Hyatt Regency.

THE EFFECT OF COVID-19 ON GLOBAL ECONOMY

The outbreak of COVID-19 and its impact connected to economy has been severe. The real damage, according to most economists, will only become apparent as soon as the pandemic has been entirely contained. The GDP growth also had a hit globally (see Table 1).

Table 1. COVID-19 and GDP growth percentage across world (%)

Gross Domestic Product	2019	2020	2021
World	2.9	1.6	3.2
US	2.3	0.7	0.9
Eurozone:	1.2	-0.1	1.2
Germany	0.6	-0.3	1.1
France	1.3	0.3	1.4
Italy	0.2	-1.6	0.7
Spain	2	0.7	1.1
United Kingdom	1.4	0.3	-0.3
China	6.1	2.4	5.9
Japan	0.8	-0.4	1.3
Brazil	1.2	1.8	2.4
India	5.3	5.3	6.4
Australia	1.8	1.2	2.3

Source: Macrobond, IMF, RaboResearch

Economic experts are of the view that unlike the financial crisis of 2008 witnessed by the world this pandemic would take more time for recovery. The increasing figure of cases and deaths emerging rapidly on a day-to-day basis, in the current scenario even if the pandemic is quickly going to stop, it may result into recession in the economies. The adverse effect can only be calculated in absolute terms after the pandemic is completely eradicated.

The COVID-19 outbreak had certainly seemed to have the worst impact on the travel and tourism industries around the world. Various nations have issued travelling promulgation and gone into lockdown way since February 2020, cancelling all leading worldwide economic, social, and sporting events. According to the International Air Transport Association (IATA), international airlines will need to have an crisis monetary fund of up to US $ 200 billion or more in order to continue operating. The World Travel and Tourism Council estimates that the COVID-19 pandemic will result in the loss of 50 million jobs in the global tourism and touristry business, a decline of 12-14 percent. Travel abroad may be affected by up to 25% or more during the year, resulting in the loss of three months' vacation. It can take months for the condition to recover after the outbreak.

Hotels require liquidity and cash flows to support their running costs, which will rise as health regulations are followed. Due to the lack of liquidity, hoteliers feel that the State should have granted a payment delay on their tax obligations. The most crucial move a hotel may take to manage the crisis is to apply for an easy long term capital financing with overall low-interest rates. Earlier studies in the hospitality crisis management field show that when a crisis is extraneous, such as the COVID-19 pandemic, rather than interior owing to management non-achievement, hotel administrator look for Government assistance to stay open (e.g., Israeli, 2007; Israeli et al., 2011; Israeli & Reichel, 2003; Tse et al., 2006).

At first, hotel officials thought that the pandemic would soon be over. As a result, they proposed lowering prices to boost demand. However, once the pandemic spread, they realized that marketing strategies would not succeed in increasing sales, so they decided to completely stop marketing. Managers expect that marketing strategies will be reviewed at the end of the project, according to the following discussion. COVID-19 is in its early stages. Kim et al. (2005) observed the same in a case study, in which several hotels at the end of the SARS outbreak, Korea provided reduced rooms and successfully increased the number of guests. The length from the oblique line, according to Rial et al. (2008), can be used to measure the importance of performing tasks. Reduction in the number of working hours or working days was a priority for both levels of human resource management. In the pandemic phase, however, reducing staff with unpaid leave becomes a very important task. Because labor costs amount to about half of all operating costs (Mandelbaum, 2017), using these two methods can significantly reduce operating costs during a disaster. Other labor practices, such as shifting staff to new appointments and job vacancies, will not be effective in dealing with this situation.

Although Del Mar Alonso-Almeida and Bremser (2013) disagree on cost reductions by reducing the number of customers, hotel managers limited the institutional care to save money in times of crisis. Hotels were slowing down labor costs and the cost of health care vigorously, according to officials, as the pandemic lasts longer. Despite the fact that the pandemic survey did not support the voluntary provision of early retirement or cancellation programs, general hotel managers predicted a cancellation tsunami in the near future. Government responses became the subject of previous research on problem management strategies. This study shifts the perceptions of hotel managers from active to pandemic prevention, human resource management, care, and marketing. For example, in the beginning, respondents thought that "checking the body temperature in customers" should be given priority.

During the pandemic, however, managers were very concerned about educating "staff on pandemic protection technology." This shows that management attitudes changed from being busy to moving forward. Hotel staff members indicated that they were no longer in a position to deal with the pandemic. Staff who will be preventing pandemics should receive appropriate training. Outbreaks appear to be exacerbated during pregnancy and in some cases as well as hygiene measures and procedures. Training staff and guests reduce the risk of contracting the virus while improving the hotel image. Reduced working hours or working days were originally used as a strategy. Hotels can manage their operations to ensure efficiency by limiting important work hours such as security and reducing less important work hours such as laundry service. If the outbreak persists, taking voluntary leave may be a viable option. The two plans were confirmed in a series of interviews, which also revealed that a number of colleagues were looking for work. As a result, in the most recent stages of disaster, predicting "eradication programs" is essential. In addition, in order to show support for employees, senior management should consider a 10% –30% voluntary reduction. At each stage, maintenance costs should be reduced. Respondents considered closing down areas that were less commonly used in the first place.

As the outbreak escalated, hotels reduced costs by performing maintenance services without "purchasing low-cost office equipment". Hotels would stop repairs without sacrificing service quality. Hotels would take care of certain areas that needed security considerations, such as elevators, as usual. In times of crisis, government assistance to increase internal use might not work.

In the early stages of the pandemic, hotel stays in Macao dropped to 11 percent, while five-star hotels averaged 6.6%. Because the hotel business had to continue to deal with the negative effects of COVID-19, the government may consider alternatives to tax relief. However, because the bonus from gambling earns a large percentage of the hotel staff's salary, these measures may not immediately help them. Some workers will not be able to pay for housing loans and child care costs without such bonuses. As a result, the government may consider holding small professional gatherings in Macao to attract tourists. In the coming months, the government should implement a step-by-step plan to help hotels return to normalcy (Sio-Chong and Yuk-Chow, 2020). Although marketing strategies were not emphasized in the early stages or pandemics, there was a tendency for the recovery phase to emphasize marketing strategies. Once the travel ban has been lifted, hotel advertisers should make promotional plans.

To improve cash flow and speed up post-disaster recovery, hotels may create and sell special room packages that include discounts for future visits. Hotels take it importantly and decide to use marketing strategies (both in the domestic and foreign markets) that aim to convince potential customers that the hotel offers high security to its guests and adheres strictly to all health standards set by the State and the world health facilities to regulate new reality in the industry (e.g., World Health Organization). These activities aimed at giving future buyers assurance that hotels were "ready for COVID-19" to deal with the event being considered, which is why they were increasing hotel reservations. That is supported by recent findings in guest management literature that the most effective way to deal with "environmental" disasters, such as the COVID-19 pandemic, is to focus on people.

In addition to the adjustments authorized by health standards, hotels decided to improve their performance to protect the cleanliness and safety of their employees and guests, according to their supervisors. They want to focus on day-to-day communication and information, build a COVID-19 potential team with ongoing training, and invest in new technologies (e.g., computer input / exit, infrared technology). The goal of these procedures was to improve security without changing the hotel's behavior or making it a "health clinic." The first three types of practices were programs aimed at improving the efficiency of hotel management and contributing to increased revenue (Israel et al., 2011).

Hotels evaluated and decided to reduce pay and other personnel costs, as well as to keep the cost of facility care low, in order to effectively manage this problem. They would improve their efficiency and prosperity through cost-cutting measures (Israel, 2007). The most recent approach to this series is price tags. Hotel staff believe that discounts on service costs provided during COVID-19 are insignificant and decide not to offer them. They believe that the most important way for hotels to fix a problem is to change their pricing policy. One of the important findings of the study by Israel (2007) is that there are significant statistical changes in the value and application of hotel management strategies depending on the characteristics of the hotel. Five-star hotels feel that by making the necessary changes in their operations, they can continue to provide quality services while maintaining greater security. They also choose to invest in new technologies that will reduce the risks of COVID-19 risks, by focusing on daily health and safety information and customer engagement. Cost-cutting and price-cutting strategies are not the most important decisions five-star hotels may take to tackle the problem, as they may impact on the quality of their services.

Compared to low-bed hotels, multi-bed hotels need to be fully stocked to meet their high operating costs, which is why they will use marketing tools and pricing strategies to increase revenue. Hotels that are part of the national or international series would follow the chain's performance standards and marketing strategies. These hotels would receive ready-made problem management plans. These findings also indicate that hotel resorts are more important than city hotels and have opted for more government assistance. Resorts are highly resourceful and have a relatively stable cost (Pavlatos & Paggios, 2009b).

COVID-19 AND INDIAN HOSPITALITY INDUSTRY

As demand declined, India's hospitality industry became one of the communities hit the hardest by the COVID-19 pandemic. International tourist warnings, Visa denials, and Article 144 (ban on regular meetings) have put India, like the rest of the world, in crisis, with unprecedented consequences.

Foreign tourism is stagnant, there is no hope of a speedy recovery. Arrivals for overseas travelers to India began to decline in February, and the spread of COVID continued to grow rapidly in neighboring countries. The Indian government began suspending tourist visas. The spread of COVID has led to the suspension of all tourism industry business activities to protect people from this deadly disease. The effects of COVID-19 have been explored with the help of a case study of Hyatt Regency with details given in subsequent section.

COVID-19 and Hospitality Industry: A Case of Hyatt Regency

Due to the pandemic, the hospitality industry witnessed enormous downside effect, The Asian Hotels had to temporarily close its Hyatt Regency, Mumbai. According to BSE filing, Yes Bank, the lender to the company refused to release payments after the company defaulted on loans. The company's stock dropped more than 13% when the date of its closure was announced due to concerns about its business operations. The development revealed the hospitality industry's significant setback across numerous areas. Asian Hotel failed to settle the principal and interest which they had borrowed as term loans from Yes Bank, according to stock exchange records. The corporation owes a total of 262.54 crore in debt.

It was stated in BSE filing by Asian Hotels (West) that due to the tremendous influence of the pandemic on the company, the company defaulted on Yes Bank's instalment for the first time in its history. Yes Bank had already held all funds in the escrow account ever since, including daily hotel collections, and the company was not empowered to make any payments from the account, including taxes, vendor payments, on-roll over 300 hotel and corporate employee salaries and other critical hotel services. According to the corporation, Yes Bank made some payments from the escrow account to the hotel's essentials like power, water, and gas expenses etc.

More than 100 employees of the five-star hotel lodged a complaint with the industrial court, fearing they will be fired. The company was among large hospitality firms that had major difficulties obtaining finances from financial institutions as the banks continued to have a poor viewpoint for the hospitality sector. Banks have been criticized of being uncooperative with borrowers in the hotel industry, pressuring them to acquire funds from other sources. In India, every hotel business is in debt in some way. Because business relies primarily on tourist arrival, which was halted for more than a year and a half, most major chains struggle to earn money. As a consequence of the outbreak, these chains' revenues have decreased by 80%, creating serious cash-flow issues.

Across metros, big hotels were registering only a 5% occupancy rate. The essential costs such as water, power, and property taxes, including upkeep and salaries, depleted hospitality firms' cash reserves after more than a year without revenue. The Hyatt Regency in Mumbai, for example, is indeed a resource hotel that requires the whole amount of money to be invested up front. The 400-room hotel reportedly employs 800 to 1,000 people to operate it. Mostly through the Emergency Line of Credit Assistance Programme has the government provided some help to the hospitality industry. The Reserve Bank of India extended the loan restructuring limits for distressed small enterprises to Rs. 50 crore and announced a Rs. 15,000 crore liquidity windows. The hotel industry urgently requires a stimulus that will put money in the hands of hotel owners of all types. Non-performing assets will be created as a result of bank non-compliance, a lack of direct stimulus, and ongoing pandemic-related disruptions.

The Indian hotel industry generated 1.822 trillion rupees in revenue in the financial year 2020. In the financial year 2021, the industry lost over 75% of its revenue, which was anticipated to be more than 1.3 trillion dollars. The sector got in debt for more than 60,000 crores. The Indian hotel industry sailed into January 2020 after a record year in 2019, with 2020 projected to be "far greater." The country began to feel the ripple effects of the global COVID-19 turmoil towards the end of February 2020, which increased in the beginning of March. According to industry projections, hotel occupancy in major cities plunged by 45 percentage points over the previous year. In the history of the industry, there had never been such a dramatic reduction in such a short period of time.

The most challenging period of the year was the second quarter where hotels were unable to manage rates and were forced to give massive discounts in order to attract customers. In year 2020, the Indian hotel industry was estimated to lose between US$ 8.85 billion and US$ 10 billion in revenue, down 39 percent to 45 percent from last year. Apart from the actual firm loss, hotel owners would lose money due to fixed operating expenditures, debt repayments, interest payments, and a variety of other industry regulations. While the pandemic crippled India's hotel industry, experts are confident that it will rebound sooner rather than later.

SOLUTIONS AND SUGGESTIONS

At Government Level

The Indian government took a step in the right direction by announcing plans to build a COVID-19 Task Force to take appropriate action to address the financial crisis of the pandemic. We have highlighted some of the industry-specific measures which might be helpful for exploring the many scenarios to help the Indian hotel industry withstand the pandemic storm.

The government's disaster recovery plan in the short term can be implemented. This plan could include establishing a staff support fund to provide job security for employees. The government may impose a 6- to 12-month deficit on all debts including principal and interest, as well as effective capital payments and overdraft, this would ensure that no reduction in business debt rates is the result of the expected corporate instability. Further, the Government might provide any annual license renewals paid without any additional costs or taxes.

The government can set up a research centre to investigate the matter and make recommendations for the revitalization of the sector. The initiative can bring new ideas for coping effectively. Moreover, the shock of COVID-19 has had a profound effect on the tourism industry as a whole, as demand worldwide is at an all-time low. the consequences of the disaster.

In order for hotels to return to normalcy after COVID-19, government support should come in the form of a reduction or reduction of Cost, Incentive Fees, which can also be made in Distribution, Technology, and reimbursement costs. Specific product requirements may be delayed as all standard product offers that do not have a direct impact on hotel revenues but have high-cost budget should be postponed until operations return to normal. The fund established for the hotel to be replaced and periodically repaired, must be removed immediately and reused, depending on the conditions to meet the working capital requirements of any other costs.

At Industry Level

To address the immediate impact, the hotel industry has implemented a number of preventive measures. The steps taken by the hotels were never taken as this kind of disaster has never been seen in centuries. Now hotels are expected to maintain their efforts to quickly adapt to the rapidly changing business environment through technological innovation in crisis management (Ardito et al., 2021). To help with this, here is a list of a few strategies below that will help hotels deal with current attacks.

Development Steps

Hotels should develop and implement a development approach to ensure that when demand starts to rise they are not well suited to use the same again. The development rate should include the following features: A minimum of blank steps should be performed, which allows for a quick reboot when the opportunity arises. The marketing plan should include the use of a social media platform or digital media to revitalize the industry. Providers and vendors should be contacted to determine their ability to re-engage with the hotel once operations have resumed. Establish and maintain important customer relationships with team members.

Plan Ahead of Reopening

The re-opening strategy of the hotel should be evaluated in terms of the previous reopening strategies used in the hotel prior to its initial launch. The only obvious difference in the current situation is that the hotel will now reopen after a major catastrophe that threatens to devastate global industries. When demand arises again, the client will be more powerful and more demanding. Hotels should strive to use their reopening strategy as soon as possible. The following are some of the key commitments that hotels should consider as part of their reopening strategy.

Re-Engagement and Support of Returning Team Members

Employees who resume their professional life should be provided with adequate assistance, including issues such as housing, salary etc. Employees can be trained in re-engagement techniques that are specific to their role in departments. The hotel can restart with a team re-opening team. The re-opening team should analyze and recruit additional active team if necessary to fill any vacancies.

Sales and Marketing

A concerted effort must be made to revitalize all customer service through all available channels. Effective digital and communication strategies should be used as part of the communication strategy (Kumar & Pradhan, 2015). Hotels should respect any bookings previously canceled or postponed due to integrity. The industry should focus on Local rather than Global.The need for foreign passengers will be smaller by 2020, so it is wise to focus on local demand. Packages for specialized experiences and sales aimed at 'local people' should be a driving mantra.

Track Price Charts

Hotels should focus on long-term strategies and provide value-added services and flexible booking times. As a strategy to promote discounts can also be added and if promised a flexible booking and booking policy, it can provide a sense of security for current and potential visitors.

Increase Non-Traditional Income and Cautious Budgeting

Hotels can focus on non-core revenue producers such as gymnasiums, resorts, and other sources of additional revenue. Hotels can provide services that are rarely included in the usual hotel offerings, such as online food delivery or kitchen rental for cloud kitchen needs. Hotels should budget carefully, where non-profit spending should be avoided. To compensate for the continued loss during the disaster, hotels can continue with cost-cutting activities even after the need has returned to normal.

House Services and Resources

Due to the need for hotels, they should start opening additional front-door facilities such as restaurants, leisure centres, and gyms etc. Hotels should gradually reopen previously closed areas due to shortages as demand increases. Hotels should ensure that before opening any important equipment, a complete service plan is developed. It should also ensure that the equipment is fully functional, secure enough, and capable of producing the desired results.

Vendor Management

Vendor management refers to the management of retailers, hotels should verify and evaluate supplier capacity and categorization of all working assets, especially perishable, in essence, the procurement team should ensure proper stockpile.

Compliance

Hotels should check with any new government or product guidelines that may apply to the hotel. The hotel must adhere to the rules of health and hygiene, to reassure guests and staff, and to ensure regular care and thorough cleaning steps. Hotels should try to dry run, so that they can detect any remaining errors before full hotel delivery.

CONCLUSION

The chapter discussed a few remedies and steps that will help the hospitality industry to recover and revert from the Shock to Reassurance phase. As mentioned above the conditions of the Hotel Hyatt proposals can bring about a change in the same situation. As more and more people are vaccinated, the Indian subcontinent is slowly relaxing these restricted laws. This means that traveling between regions will be much easier and that people will be able to move around freely. Although India is making significant progress in terms of hotel operations, probably due to domestic demand, the sector still has a long way to go before the need for corporations and businesses can return. After the second wave, the hotel industry recovered faster than most other markets in the country, with living standards rising by almost 15% in May 2021 - the highest number of second waves - approaching 70% in November 2021, compared to pre pandemic levels. Since the outbreak of the second wave, Chandigarh, along with Goa, has had the highest number of monthly stays in the country. Thus, this indicates the hospitality industry, gradually, is going to revive back and re-cope with the declining demand.

REFERENCES

Ardito, L., Coccia, M., & Messeni Petruzzelli, A. (2021). Technological exaptation and crisis management: Evidence from COVID-19 outbreaks. *R & D Management*, *51*(4), 381–392. doi:10.1111/radm.12455

Backer, E., & Ritchie, B. W. (2017). VFR travel: A viable market for tourism crisis and disaster recovery? *International Journal of Tourism Research*, *19*(4), 400–411. doi:10.1002/jtr.2102

Benaben, F., Lauras, M., Trupil, S., & Salatage, N. (2016, January). *A metamodel for Knowledge Management in Crisis Management* [Paper presentation]. The 49th Hawaii International Conference De on System Sciences (HICSS 2016), Koloa, HI.

Bhardwaj, A., & Kumar, V. (2022). Privacy and Healthcare during COVID-19. In *Cybersecurity Crisis Management and Lessons Learned From the COVID-19 Pandemic*. IGI-Global. doi:10.4018/978-1-7998-9164-2.ch005

Del Mar Alonso-Almeida, M., & Bremser, K. (2013). Strategic responses of the Spanish hospitality sector to the financial crisis. *International Journal of Hospitality Management*, *32*(1), 141–148. doi:10.1016/j.ijhm.2012.05.004

Hilliard, T. W., Scott-Halsell, S., & Palakurthi, R. (2011). Core crisis preparedness measures implemented by meeting planners. *Journal of Hospitality Marketing & Management*, *20*(6), 638–660. doi:10.1080/19368623.2011.536077

HNN. (2020). *Coronavirus effects color Hilton's 2020 outlook*. Hotel News Now. Available at: www. hotelnewsnow.com/Articles/300258/Coronavirus-effects-color-Hiltons-2020-outlook

Israeli, A. A. (2007). Crisis-management practices in the restaurant industry. *International Journal of Hospitality Management*, *26*(4), 807–823. doi:10.1016/j.ijhm.2006.07.005

Israeli, A. A., Mohsin, A., & Kumar, B. (2011). Hospitality crisis management practices: The case of Indian luxury hotels. *International Journal of Hospitality Management*, *30*(2), 367–374. doi:10.1016/j.ijhm.2010.06.009

Israeli, A. A., & Reichel, A. (2003). Hospitality crisis management practices: The Israeli case. *International Journal of Hospitality Management*, *22*(4), 353–372. doi:10.1016/S0278-4319(03)00070-7

Kim, S. S., Chun, H., & Lee, H. (2005). The effects of SARS on the Korean hotel industry and measures to overcome the crisis: A case study of six Korean five-star hotels. *Asia Pacific Journal of Tourism Research*, *10*(4), 369–377. doi:10.1080/10941660500363694

Kumar, V., & Gupta, G. (Eds.). (2021). *Strategic Management During a Pandemic*. Routledge. doi:10.4324/9781003125648

Kumar, V., & Malhotra, G. (Eds.). (2021). *Stakeholder Strategies for Reducing the Impact of Global Health Crises*. IGI Global Publications. doi:10.4018/978-1-7998-7495-9

Kumar, V., & Pradhan, P. (2015). Trust Management Issues in Social-Media Marketing. *International Journal of Online Marketing*, *5*(3), 47–64. doi:10.4018/IJOM.2015070104

Lee, K. (2009). How the Hong Kong Government lost the public trust in SARS: Insights for government communication in a health crisis. *Public Relations Review*, *35*(1), 74–76. doi:10.1016/j.pubrev.2008.06.003 PMID:32288049

Mandelbaum, R. (2017). *How hotel managers are coping with rising wages*. Available at: https://www.hotelmanagement.net/operate/how-increases-compensation-labor-costs-are-leading-to-cost-savings

Novelli, M., Burgess, L. G., Jones, A., & Ritchie, B. W. (2018). 'No Ebola... still doomed' – the Ebolainduced tourism crisis. *Annals of Tourism Research, 70*, 76–87. doi:10.1016/j.annals.2018.03.006 PMID:32572288

Pardeep, R., & Clark, H. (2009). A framework for knowledge-based crisis management in hospitality and tourism industry. *Cornell Hospitality Quarterly, 50*(4), 561–577. doi:10.1177/1938965509341633

Pavlatos, O., & Paggios, I. (2009b). Activity-based costing in the hospitality industry: Evidence from Greece. *Journal of Hospitality & Tourism Research (Washington, D.C.), 33*(4), 511–527. doi:10.1177/1096348009344221

Rial, A., Rial, J., Varela, J., & Real, E. (2008). An application of importance-performance analysis (IPA) to the management of sport centres. *Managing Leisure, 13*(3/4), 179–188. doi:10.1080/13606710802200878

Ritchie, B. W., & Jiang, Y. (2019). A review of research on tourism risk, crisis and disaster management: Launching the annals of tourism research curated collection on tourism risk, crisis and disaster management. *Annals of Tourism Research, 79*, 1–15. doi:10.1016/j.annals.2019.102812

Singh, J., & Kumar, V. (2022). Combating the Pandemic with ICT Based Learning tools and applications: A case of Indian Higher Education. *International Journal of Virtual and Personal Learning Environments Platforms, 12*(1), 1–21.

Tse, A. C. B., So, S., & Sin, L. (2006). Crisis management and recovery: How restaurants in Hong Kong responded to SARS. *International Journal of Hospitality Management, 25*(1), 3–11. doi:10.1016/j.ijhm.2004.12.001 PMID:32287848

U, S.-C., & So, Y.-C. (2020). The impacts of financial and non-financial crises on tourism: Evidence from Macao and Hong Kong. *Tourism Management Perspectives, 33*, 100628. Advance online publication. doi:10.1016/j.tmp.2019.100628

Walters, G., Wallin, A., & Hartley, N. (2019). The threat of terrorism and tourist choice behavior. *Journal of Travel Research, 58*(3), 370–382. doi:10.1177/0047287518755503

Wan, Y. K. P. (2013). A comparison of the governance of tourism planning in the two special administrative regions (SARs) of China–Hong Kong and Macao. *Tourism Management, 36*, 164–177. doi:10.1016/j.tourman.2012.12.005 PMID:32287740

WHO. (2020a). *Novel coronavirus (2019-nCoV) situation report – 1*. Available at: www.who.int/docs/defaultsource/coronaviruse/situation-reports/20200121-sitrep-1-2019-ncov.pdf?sfvrsn=20a99c10_4

WHO. (2020b). *Novel coronavirus (2019-nCoV) situation report – 11*. Available at: www.who.int/docs/ default-source/coronaviruse/situation-reports/20200131-sitrep-11-ncov.pdf?sfvrsn=de7c0f7_4

WHO. (2020c). *WHO characterizes COVID-19 as a pandemic*. WHO.

Worldometers. (2021). https://www.worldometers.info/

Wut, T. M., Xu, J. B., & Wong, S. M. (2021). Crisis management research (1985–2020) in the hospitality and tourism industry: A review and research agenda. *Tourism Management, 85*, 104307. doi:10.1016/j.tourman.2021.104307

Zhao, Y., & Xu, H. (2020). *Chinese public attention to COVID-19 pandemic: based on social media*. doi:10.1101/2020.03.18.20038026

KEY TERMS AND DEFINITIONS

Financial Year: A financial year (FY) is the accounting year in which you make money, which runs from April 1 to March 31 in India.

Gross Booking Value: Gross booking value is defined as the full amount of payments (including host payments, service, and cleaning fees, but excluding cancellations) processed on the platform.

Hospitality Industry: A set of companies offering service related to stay, food and other care of travelers.

Online Travel Agency: Companies with websites that allow customers to order a variety of travel-related services directly over the Internet. They are third-party agencies who resell other people's excursions, hotels, automobiles, flights, vacation packages, and so on.

Pandemic: It refers to the Corona Virus Disease which commence its spread in 2019, globally.

Rupee: Indian currency.

Vendor Management: It refers to the management of retailers, hotels should verify and evaluate supplier capacity and categorization of all working assets, especially perishable, in essence, the procurement team should ensure proper stockpile.

Chapter 7
Responding to the Pandemic: A Case of the Indian Hotel Industry

Bhavna Sharma
JIMS Engineering Management Technical Campus, India

Ankur Budhiraja
JIMS Engineering Management Technical Campus, India

Shalini Singh
https://orcid.org/0000-0003-1580-2295
Christ University, India

Renu Bala
Mukhtiar Singh Memorial Degree College, Fatehabad, India

EXECUTIVE SUMMARY

The chapter presents a case study on how Indian hotel industry was affected by COVID-19. Three hotels—Lemon Tree, Oyo Rooms, and Taj Hotels—were selected to elaborate. The study found that the hotel industry developed various policies to keep running their hotels during the pandemic. Lemon Tree joined various hospitals to provide rooms to COVID patients, provided free food and face masks to individuals. Oyo Rooms gave employee stock ownership plans of Rs 130 crore to its COVID-hit employees. Taj Hotels did not cut down the salaries of their employees and reduced its seating capacity by 50%. The study concluded that as the hospitality sector battled hard to continue during the pandemic, modernization would become an imperative tool in the post-COVID period to beat obstructions and spotlight advancement. So, the companies should minimize fixed costs and maximize variable costs. They should preferably have liquid cash available that could enable them to mitigate the risk.

DOI: 10.4018/978-1-6684-3504-5.ch007

INTRODUCTION

The world has witnessed unprecedented challenges during and after the Covid-19 pandemic. The economies across the globe were shut down almost overnight (UNWTO, 2020). The authorities were completely shaken and went clueless as how to manage businesses during this worldwide spread contingency (Kumar & Gupta, 2021). There has been multi-sectoral impact of COVID-19 and it has had several adverse consequences which have been unique in themselves. Small and entrepreneurial ventures including owned and run by women responded to the pandemic challenges by adopting innovative approaches to survive (Kovid et al., 2021). Populations have experienced crises of resources, aggravated susceptible circumstances and paucity of basic survival elements which forced the health, infrastructure and other public service authorities to stretch themselves beyond capacities (Mullafiroze and Cha 2020). The tourism industry's contact-intensive nature makes it vulnerable to the spread of infectious diseases (Sobaih et al., 2021). Such diseases are increasing rapidly due to population, tourist and transportation increase (Kumar & Malhotra, 2021). Furthermore, open-air activities, nature, rural tourism and road trips are preferred by the tourists. The main worries of travellers are health and safety precautions, as well as cancellation rules, with last-minute bookings on the rise as a result of the volatile and unpredictable epidemic. COVID-19 has influenced lodging preferences, according to Pappas and Glyptou (2021), with tourists preferring to rent a house rather than reserve a hotel room. Zhang et al. (2021) make a similar point. The current literature is a discussion on the impact of COVID-19 on the very dynamic and ever demanded hospitality sector. There has been a direct impact on the working of this sector. Moreover, a lot of expectations were connected to the hospitality sector related to making incremental changes in the way they have been running their operations to adapt to the dynamics brought in the COVID-19 business environment. They were expected to look deeper into the safety protocols concerns, employees' safety, and customers' health and to make efforts to enhance the agreeableness of the customers to support their business (Gössling et al., 2020).

At the macro level, the economies have tried their best to establish approaches to curb the ill consequences brought in by COVID-19. Strict guidelines like community lockdowns, social distancing, orders to stay-at-home, restrictions on travel and mobility and many more have had ghastly impact on the existence of many hospitality businesses (Bhardwaj & Kumar, 2022). The demand for such businesses has fallen to an extent to which it became almost impossible for such ventures to even operate (Bartik et al., 2020). Amidst restrictions placed on travel, stays and dine-in functions, all the hotels and restaurants were struggling to survive and sustain. The novel coronavirus pandemic has brought significant disturbances in the way hotel industry has been working affecting customers' demand for hotel services, their behaviour and attitude towards hotel stays as well as the financial performance of the hotel companies across the globe.

A hotel is interconnected with various channel members in the supply chain. Because of their deep interdependence, each channel member has got affected directly or indirectly. This further resulted in a sharp decline in hotel occupancies and revenues; and the whole travel ecosystem got disrupted leading to adverse impact on worldwide tourism. The reports of the World Tourism Organization showed a whopping decline of around 74% in the movement of tourists internationally in 2020 which brought the international tourism to as low as it was some 30 years ago. Therefore, COVID-19 has specifically impacted the hotel industry which faced a fierce drop in business and sales arising due to travel restrictions, bans on events and gatherings and the psychological fear of getting affected by the infection. However, there is a gradual attempt to revamp the business through reopening of hotels with great deals being offered to the customers for stays. Along with this, the authorities have lifted the restrictions partially, facilitating the hospitality sector to survive somehow. Even when the things seem to be little normal, the customers have been feeling uncomfortable and have been showing a reluctance to dine in at restaurants and staying in at hotels out of the fear of COVID infection spread. The preliminary findings of a longitudinal study conducted by a team of the Journal of Hospitality Marketing & Management, there won't be an immediate willingness and comeback of the customers even when the hotels adopt a reopening strategy and the authorities ease the travel restrictions (Gursoy et al., 2020). Majority of customers, more than 50% showed resistance to travel to a destination and stay at any outside accommodation anytime soon. A minority of around one-third showed willingness to travel to any destination and stay at any hotel in the next few months (Gursoy et al., 2020). These findings suggest that customers in general still do not feel comfortable to dine in at a sit-down restaurant, travel to a destination and stay at a hotel. All this reinforce the fact that even when the hospitality industry is gradually recovering, the COVID-19 catastrophe continues to exert weighty impacts on how the hospitality businesses operate. COVID-19, they claim, has had a significant impact on the shared housing sector, where contacts between hosts and guests are more intense than in the traditional hotel industry. It was also discovered that, whereas demand-driven scarcity cues had a beneficial influence on visitors' purchasing inclinations in normal circumstances, they had the reverse effect during the present pandemic (Li et al., 2021).

Scarcity signals indicate a hotel's popularity and high quality, which encourages guests to stay there. Guests, on the other hand, currently regard such a location as less safe and prefer not to visit it. This suggests that the pandemic has shifted people's perceptions and influenced their purchasing decisions, with overly crowded areas being avoided. The current research is also an attempt to devise effective ways to manage business in hospitality somehow. These may include sanitizing efforts such as use of hand sanitizers at the entry, staff wearing masks and gloves, adhering to social distancing norms, putting a ceiling on the number of customers or guests, disinfecting the common area surfaces, educating the employees about safety protocols and health at the hotels and many more (Gursoy et al., 2020). While customers anticipate more robust safety and hygiene mechanisms to be adopted by hospitality businesses, a certain population is willing to shell extra amounts for those additional safety measures (Gursoy et al., 2020). In the middle of all the darkness, there lies a lot of scope of opportunities to arise so as to allow the hospitality sector transform their operations in positive and service-oriented ways. The hotel operators, employees and other members have shown a lot of maturity and have been constantly trying to help the society and the government by offering their accommodation capacity as isolation centres for the ones who needed to quarantine, promoting staycation or holistay concept, offering work from hotel long duration stays, etc.

The aim of this study is to introspect into the impact of COVID-19 on the hotel business and the ways and means adopted to cope up with the dynamics and commotion resulted from the spread of the virus. It will also throw light on the provisions including safety measures, technology application, quality enhancement measures and ways to manage human resources and supply chains across the hospitality sector. Further, using cases of some prominent hotels, the chapter will try to bring to surface the major challenges and crises faced by them and how they all strategized to overcome and combat the challenges that will be discussed. Each of the cases will individually deal with hotel specific problems and the approach that each one of the hotels taken for the chapter has implemented to tackle them. An attempt has also been made through the discussions to address the ongoing issues that the COVID-19 has posed for the hospitality industry as a whole.

Objectives

The chapter has explored the cases of some specific hotels so as to address and accomplish the following objectives through research and conceptual discussions:

- To understand the impact of COVID-19 on the hospitality industry
- To ascertain the effect of COVID-19 on specific hotels take up as cases for discussion
- To introspect into the ways and means through which the impact of COVID-19 and the challenges have been dealt with or addressed by the specific hotels under discussion

CASE METHOD APPROACH

The current chapter uses a case-based analysis to build discussions around responses of renowned hotel chains including Lemon Tree Hotels, OYO Rooms and Taj Hotels to the corona pandemic. Moreover, the discussion draws insights from three different star level hotel brands - the Taj Hotels, a premium high-end chain of hotels; Lemon Tree hotels, a level of three-to-four-star hotels; and OYO rooms, the ones lying in the economical stratum of hotel brands. Each of these had their own share of problems and challenges during and after the spread of COVID-19 and hence, the approach to deal with them is somewhat varying. The chapter is an attempt to understand the same.

Case-1: Lemon Tree Hotels

Lemon Tree hotel (LTH), started in 2002 by Mr. Patu Keswani in India. The company has 87 hotels across India with 8500 rooms. LTH is the largest hotel in mid-priced segment. In 2004, LTH started its first hotel with 49 rooms then in 2018 it went public and was listed on the NSE. LTH is operating in 54 cities like Ahmedabad, Bengaluru, Chennai, Delhi, Kerala, etc. (www.lemontreehotels.com, 2021).

The company functions under seven brands: Aurika Hotels and Resorts which is an expensive segment, Lemon Tree Premier and Keys Prima for superior midscale section, LTH and Keys Select (midscale), Red Fox and Keys Lite (Economical range). They also launched their hotel in foreign countries like Dubai in 2019 and Bhutan in 2020. Their management team consists of professionals from banking sector, fast moving consumer goods (FMCG), telecom sectors, etc. They have executed a comprehensive plan for learning and also developed tailored content and training methods for their employees. It has been ranked as one of the best companies to work in India from 2011 to 2017. They also provide job opportunities for underprivileged Indians like acid survivors, people with disability, economically weaker section, widow women etc. They started this initiative in 2007 and around 16 percent of their employees consist of this section (www.lemontreehotels.com, 2021).

Aurika Hotels & Resorts, which is in an expensive segment, gives an astonishing experience in a spectacular environment and provides new-age dining and advance entertainment choices, along with fitness and health facilities. Lemon Tree Premier and Keys Prima is for superior midscale section which focuses on the style conscious travellers and provides tailored services, premium rooms and fun experiences to their customers. LTH and Keys Select focuses on midscale section and offers comfort to the travellers while providing smart in-room facilities, vivacious cafe, bar, gym, pool, etc. Red Fox and Keys Lite which is an economical segment offers audacious interiors, lively environment, meeting room, gym, café, etc. (www.lemontreehotels.com. 2021).

They developed various policies to keep running their hotels during the pandemic. They took various initiatives for the people of the country. The Managing Director (MD) of the company said that their prices are flexible, when demand is less then prices are also kept less but when demand increases then the price also rises (Shenoy et al. 2021). In first quarter of 2020, around 80 percent of the hotel rooms were functional and there were around 2,500 staff staying in the hotel. Only 20 of 100 rooms were opened and they ran it with reduced cost. He also mentioned that during pandemic, the staff and visitors required maximum support (Sharma, 2021). During April 2020, the company deducted the salaries of their employees in order to safeguard their jobs. The Vice president's and manager's salary was deducted by 66 percent and 50 percent respectively from April to June 2020. LTH also tried to reduce their fixed cost including salaries, electricity, interest on loans etc. (Chaturvedi, 2020). During financial year 2019-20, the income of the company was Rs. 67,522 lakhs which was reduced to Rs. 25,172 lakhs in the financial year 2020-21 (www.lemontreehotels.com. 2021).

Initiatives Taken by Lemon Tree Hotels

- It joined various hospitals and started a programme named ''Support by Lemon Tree'' in which they offered hotels to various hospitals across the country for the early care to symptomless COVID patients only. Till May 17th, 2021, the hotel gave 1039 rooms (Business World, 2021).
- In another initiative, LTH united with Diversey and started ''Rest Assured initiative'' exhibiting their obligation to establishing a climate zeroed in on wellbeing, cleanliness, security and prosperity as a feature of the new tidiness and cleanliness norms. Diversey furnishes the lodgings with safe synthetics, working agendas, preparing backing, recordings and backing supplies to add to their own collection of strategies and will be conducting regular evaluations in all hotels (Business World, 2021).
- In March 2020, the hotel joined with state government to change over some of their hotels to isolation communities for Indians getting back from foreign country (Business World, 2021).
- They also worked with the neighbourhood organization to give free food to individuals who required them during the most troublesome time in the lockdown like Lemon Tree Premier in Dwarka, Delhi gave free meals to the patients suffering from Covid at the Civil Hospital and Lemon Tree Premier at Mumbai gave free food to BMC laborers etc. (Business World, 2021)

- The hotel chain also announced program for their employees named ''Lemon Tree Cares- Employee care program'' where they are covering the jab expenses for their staff and their family members. LTH also compensated all the medical expenses of employees who were in isolation and in case of critical cases, the company also paid for all other expenses in addition to the assured amount covered under insurance policy. The employees who were tested covid positive were given three weeks paid leave. They also allowed their staff to stay in the hotel to limit the contact to the virus (Business World, 2021).
- LTH distributed the face masks free of cost to the deprived people. They also conducted social awareness drive at public places related to covid (Kumar, 2021).
- They also teamed up with Apollo Hospitals on "Project Stay I'' to provide clean, comfortable isolation facilities for asymptomatic guests who have been in contact with potentially infected people (www.cntraveller.in, 2020).
- They also offered their rooms at limited rates for medical services laborers, police staff and fundamentally anyone who is at the cutting edge of battling this pandemic (Ameen, 2020).

Learning From Pandemic

The MD said in an interview that all hotel companies to an extent will have their costs permanently reduced and so will become much more profitable. "We will save over ₹100 crore a year with our optimized cost structures" (Khosla, 2022). Removing the touchpoints like holding up at the front work area is the easiest method for causing wary explorers to have a real sense of reassurance now and after the COVID period (Mukherjee, 2021).

Case-2: OYO Rooms

OYO Rooms, originally OYO Hotels & Homes, is a global Indian online travel agency that specialises on homes and living spaces. Ritesh Agarwal established OYO in 2012, and it consisted mostly of low-cost motels at the time. Over 80 nations, including India, Malaysia, the United Arab Emirates, Nepal, China, Brazil, Mexico, the United Kingdom, the Philippines, Japan, Saudi Arabia, Sri Lanka, Indonesia, Vietnam, and the United States, have added thousands of hotels, vacation homes, and millions of rooms. OYO Rooms has a multi-brand approach (wikipedia, n.d.). The details on OYO's gross booking value is given in table 1. OYO has a range of product offerings as given below.

- The OYO Townhouse is a midscale hotel aimed at millennials that touts itself as a neighbourhood hotel.
- OYO Vacation Homes claims to be the world's third-largest vacation house brand, with vacation rental management brands Belvilla, Danland, and DanCenter, as well as Germany-based Traum-Ferienwohnungen.
- OYO Home, which claims to be India's first home management system, provides individual homes in various locations that are completely maintained by OYO.
- Hotel reservations are available through Capital O, and Silver Key is designed to satisfy the needs of corporate travellers on short or long-term business trips.
- Palette, an upper-end leisure resorts category, provides the ideal staycation for those seeking a simple experience at a reasonable price; business travellers can use Collection O's booking and rental services.
- OYO LIFE is aimed towards millennials and young professionals looking for low-cost, fully managed long-term rentals.
- YO! can handle check-ins, check-outs, and payments. HELP is a self-help programme.
- Oyo 360 is a self-registration tool for listing your property on Oyo. This was made particularly to help small hotel and housing owners with the onboarding process.

Table 1. Gross booking value (in crores)

F.Y	Hotels	Homes	Listing	Others
2019	7355	100	447.5	148
2020	11591	16851.6	152.8	613.5
2021	3880	2393	170	196

Source: (Tyagi, 2021)

Challenges Faced by OYO

Covid-19, an unexpected entry on the planet earth, which impacted not only the health and life of people; in fact, every such segment which produces services for the livelihood of the people was also extremely impacted. The situation OYO's office in Gurugram, Haryana, was tight on March (Fortune India, 2020). It was time when Shri Narendra Modi, Honourable Prime Minister of India, proclaimed a lockdown of 21-day countrywide, in India to prevent the Pandemic spread (Ghosh,

2020). OYO operates over with a big figure approximately million rooms hotel in over 80 countries. Despite the commotion, the founder and CEO of OYO Hotels & Homes, Ritesh Agarwal, made an appearance to be reasonably quiet. Customers may easily cancel their orders because the company has made it simple for them to do so. On April 8, Agarwal had to inform his employees via video message that OYO was seeing a nearly 50%-60% drop-in rates of revenue and occupancy. He needed to assemble a large group of individuals on temporary leave or furloughs for at least 60-90 days all over the world. "The company's balance sheet runway has been severely strained; we must look at every controllable cost and decrease it swiftly," he stated. For a year, he would forsake his personal salary, while the leadership team would cheerfully accept pay cuts of up to 50%. Agarwal, like many of his contemporaries, company's seven-year history, is facing the most difficult and unusual endeavour. To begin with, he must prepare for OYO's survival in unusual circumstances. On the other hand, he must guarantee that the company maintains its reputation with key stakeholders, the most important of which is Japan's SoftBank. Numerous risks existed for OYO Rooms and Hotels or Oravel Stays Limited (its actual name), the pandemic-stricken internet travel business that filed for a public offering with SEBI in September 2021 for Rs 8,430 crore ($1.1 billion). Despite the fact that the tourism industry just recovered from repeated lockdowns, OYO's debt was one of the company's main concerns during COVID (Guha, 2021). OYO, a Softbank-backed accommodation company, has given all of its salaried employees affected by the coronavirus epidemic a total of Rs 130 crore has been invested in employee stock ownership plans (Business Today, 2020).

According to an inside e-mail from the company's founder Ritesh Agarwal, the action was part of the company's efforts to reduce employee economic disruption as a result of the COVID-19 outbreak. (Fortune India, 2020). After the company suspended operations globally due to the COVID-19 pandemic on 8th April 2020, Ritesh Agarwal, the founder and CEO of OYO, has announced that the company will take a certain number of employees on layoffs or temporary leaves.

The hotel chain operator, on the other hand, did not provide any information on the number of workers affected. According to a PTI report, the number of detained employees worldwide could reach in the thousands. The business, led by Ritesh Agarwal, generates revenue from a variety of sources, including the selling of accommodation services, commissions from the holiday home and property bookings, cancellation revenues, and the tours, packages, and events are available for purchase. It also makes money through leasing commercial space, selling refreshments, and charging clients for access to its platform (Tyagi, 2021). By the second part of 2020, COVID lockdowns had been relaxed around the world, and the business had although it had taken up again, it had lost the impetus that Oyo had enjoyed from FY17 to FY20. Operating income increased to almost Rs 13,500 crores in FY19, from pre-covid highs of around Rs 13,500 crores. fell by 70% to Rs 3,961.6 crore in the fiscal year that ended in March 2021. Prior to receiving at the start of FY21, Softbank and Agarwal's RA Holdings invested $807 million. the company implemented extreme reform measures to reduce increasing losses (Majumdar, 2021).

Table 2 provided details on expenditure breakdown of OYO. Marketing and promotion spending fell by 83 percent to Rs 542.7 crore in FY21 from Rs 1,880 crore in FY20 as the company aimed to increase the share of bookings from its own D2C channels rather than third-party OTAs. Employee benefit spending plummeted by 63.4 percent to Rs 1742 crore in FY21 as a result of mass furloughs and wage cuts across the board. In addition, legal and professional fees were cut by 48% to Rs 323 crore in FY21, while outsourced personnel costs were cut by 99 percent to Rs 2 crore. Oyo's annual costs were reduced by 69.6% to Rs 6,936 crore. due to a revamping of the business strategy and a lack of demand for substantial portions of FY21. Cost-cutting measures were seen across the company's expenditures sheet, and annual losses fell in pace with revenues, falling by 70% to Rs 3943.8 crore in FY21. At the end of March 2021, Oyo's financial statement showed outstanding losses of approximately Rs 16,792 crore, despite profitability margins improving to -29.3% in FY21 from -46.5% in FY20 (Money Control, n.d.).

Table 2. OYO expenditure

OYO Expense Breakdown	2019	2020	2021
Lease Rentals	2469	7975	1189
Employee Benefit Expense	1490	4765.3	17421
IT & Communication	40.6	191.3	111
Service Expense	2376	3718	1110.6
Marketing and Promotion Expenses	447.5	1880	543.7
Legal and Professional Fees	226.2	618.6	323
Hotel Transformation expense	148	624.4	230
Other Operating & Admin Cost	1612	7975	1687

Source: (Tyagi, 2021)

Case-3: Taj Hotels

Taj hotels which are popularly known for their luxurious standards are subsidiary of Indian Hotels Company Limited and headquartered in Mumbai. The first Taj hotel was founded in 1903 by Jamsetji Tata. Indian Hotels Company Limited is one of the oldest Tata group's companies, and also the largest business conglomerates in

Indian history. Such company has opened its large chain of resorts and 100 plus hotels in India. Even not only in India, but in other foreign countries there are various reputed hotels of this company. The founding father of Tata Group opened first hotel in Mumbai with named 'Taj Mahal Hotel' in 1903, which was the first property of Taj (Sharma and Kochher, 2018). Jamsetji Nusserwanji Tata opened this hotel due to racial discrimination, which he faced at Watson's Hotel of Mumbai. In that hotel only European people were allowed to take entry. The Tata group started to convert its royal palaces in luxurious hotels in India from 1970s. In 1971, the first palace of India was transformed into Taj luxury hotel named 'Lake Palace' of Udaipur. Various other palaces were transformed over a series of time such as Falaknuma palace of Hyderabad, Rambagh Palace of Jaipur, Nadesar Palace of Varanasi and Umaid Bhawan Palace of Jodhpur etc. During the year 1980, the first hotel of Taj group was opened from outside India (Wikipedia, n.d.). Taj group was the first group which opened its hotel chain in various metropolitan cities of India, named Mumbai, Bengaluru, Hyderabad, Chennai and Delhi. Till now 10 hotels of Taj group comes under the top chief hotels of world. The Taj hotels, resorts and palaces offered a new brand of itself with its standardized and luxurious facilities to customers (Deshpande and Sinha, 2011).

Taj Hotels Business Lines

Taj group comes under the umbrella of IHCL, after that under Taj hotel various Taj resorts, hotels and palaces take place. Vivanta by Taj, The Gateway hotel and Ginger are very popular and luxurious hotels of Taj. The ambience of Vivanta by Taj has been designed especially for upper class people and The Gateway hotel focus on the living standard of middle-class people. Third new brand of Taj, *i.e.* Ginger offers two-star economy stay as a separate subsidiary which is not related with Taj name. The amenities of Vivanta by Taj include airport pickup of guest, soothing music and massage chairs etc. Gallup surveys presented that Vivanta has the highest customer engagement services among its competitive hotels. Taj Group creation, Gateway hotel is a three-star national brand and comes under the corporate umbrella. The Gateway brands concentrate on hassle-free services with contemporary environments, cleanliness and perfection. Ginger is a two-star economy brand, centred on tertiary and secondary cities of India. The report of South Asian Travel Tourism Expo reported Ginger as the best budget hotel chain of India. The analysis of 'Credit Suisse' considered Taj as one of only 27 great brands of tomorrow' India in the coming three to five years. Taj group has created a roadmap for its future time period: under which it has been decided that Taj brand will be reserved only for the luxurious segment only and for future the Taj name will be used with limits (www.landor.com, n.d.).

Taj Hotels and COVID-19

The chief executive of Taj hotel gave a statement to the press conference that our industry does not face such financial decline over o period of last 100 years. A huge financial loss has been faced by Taj due to pandemic period. But by considering the welfare of employees, Taj did not cut down the salaries of their employees. IHCL Company, under which Taj group works reported that earnings of company were Rs 83 crore in 4th quarter of financial year 21. But the pandemic caused a serious decline of 720 crore rupees during the year 2020-21. During quarter of January-March, the decline was 91 crore rupees as opposite to profit of 74 crore rupees. But despite that harsh situation, to fulfil the quarantine purpose, 1400 rooms were offered to various partner hospitals by The Taj as well as IHCL's culinary provided home delivery services under the brand name of Qmin for serving humanity.

Response to COVID-19

To avoid the spread of Coronavirus by touch points, Taj hotel has taken several measures, under which the main measure is that such hotel decided to away with its lavish buffets. Taj hotel provided PPE kits to each staff member and guest as well as concentrated on sanitization of each and every place of hotel. During the pandemic period, Taj hotel reduced its seating capacity by 50 percent and gave training to the employees to deal with customers by avoiding the touch. The management of Taj hotel felt that to transport the staff from home to hotel and from hotel to home is also a major risk factor. To reduce that risk factor, Taj maintained living arrangements in the hotel for its 70 to 80 percent staff. When the situation started to be normal, hotel's management also started to reduce the number of staff members to stay at hotel. To be sure that every person who enters in the premises of hotel, is not covid positive; various check points have been settled at different locations of hotels. At those points, sanitisers are offered to guest and their check-up is done with the help of handheld thermometers. As well as each and every item of bag is sanitized and PPE kits are provided to guest. During the pandemic period, IHCL announced a mobile app with named Qmin. This app provided the services of food delivery from restaurants to the homes of customers. With the services of that app, guests can order food from eight iconic restaurants of Mumbai such as Taj hotel, Thai Pavilion, Golden Dragon and Ming Yang etc. IHCL gave a statement that Qmin will cover up top ten markets of India, by including Bengaluru, Delhi and Chennai over a period of some weeks.

The management of Taj hotel pays high concentration on the guest comfort and offer good services to them for their comfort. Various steps have been taken to maintain those good relations between customers and hotel' image. As to improve the loyalty, profitability and guest satisfaction there is a need of implementation of healthy CRM strategies in the hotel; Taj hotel update its CRM strategies from time to time by considering its advantages (Chadha, 2015).

DISCUSSION AND IMPLICATIONS

It is critical to safeguard the security of workforce in the organization. Individuals search for ways from their bosses, leaders and government officers. Talking their matters in an open and clear manner would go a long way towards enlisting their contribution and assuring continuation of business. The companies should minimize fixed costs and maximize variable costs. They need to have liquid cash available that can enable them to mitigate risk. Technology has turned into a need in daily life for everybody, from schooling to moving around a city.

As the hospitality sector battles hard to continue during pandemic, modernization will become imperative tool in the post-COVID period to beat obstructions and spotlight on advancement. Individuals depend on cell phones, rather than carrying actual wallets. At the post-COVID times, putting resources into more intelligent innovation choices is the best way to keep up with the track and development of this sector. Removing the touchpoints like holding up at the front work area is the easiest method for causing wary explorers to have a real sense of reassurance now and after the COVID period (Chadee et al., 2021). This is the place where the requirement for portable registration and look at instruments have risen. On the off chance that a lodging is running brilliant with sensors and voice-actuated gadgets, it would bring about less actual contact. Moving up to innovation is the most favoured choice to escape from the pandemic apprehensions and gain clients. This will draw more extensive crowd and elevate the business to a more significant level (Breier et al., 2021; Mukherjee, 2021). Staycations are an emerging trend in which individuals stay at opulent hotels to de-stress in a relaxing environment. Some of the major hotel chains such as Oberoi, Marriott International, etc. are launching staycation deals that allow visitors to select from a variety of personalised experience within the hotel to meet these needs.

As discussed in the chapter, the impact of sudden crisis resulting from any pandemic, disease spread or calamity would have varying degrees of consequences on business, economy and the nation as a whole. In this direction, there is a need to establish a robust and effective means to address the subsequent problems and issues. A structured model based on some authentic research or theory can be used to understand the crisis management amidst any of the above-mentioned emergencies. A widely accepted Crisis Management Model proposed by Gonzalez-Herrero and Pratt identifies three different stages of managing crisis of different kinds (www.

managementstudyguide.com, n.d.). These include the Diagnosis of Crisis that involves detection of early indicators of crisis and understanding and identifying the warning signals. The different sectors of the economy worldwide initially tried doing the same when COVID-19 started spreading its wings across the globe. The hospitality sector was no different and the concerned authorities immediately tried to identify the indicators of the problems that were about to disturb their functioning. Further, the second stage of the model is Planning, wherein the concerned start developing the measures to respond to the emergency or crisis immediately. In the hospitality sector too, quick decisions were taken to lay down measures so as to decide what needs to be done. And finally, the stage of adjusting is included in the model in which the stakeholders and managers need to develop a new system to accommodate the new set of circumstances. Similarly, the hotel industry too started adjusting their functions according to the new equilibrium that is set after the crisis created by COVID-19 gradually.

Another model on Crisis Management, the learnings from which can be used in any kind of crisis is the model by Can Alpaslan and colleagues that defines maturity with which crisis is dealt with over a maturity continuum involving Proactive Crisis Management, Accommodative Crisis Management, Defensive Crisis Management and Reactive Crisis Management. The levels of maturity with which crisis was dealt with and was managed varied a lot during and after COVID-19 situation. Many businesses including the hotel business responded to the crisis differently as per their strength, resources and understanding of the situation. As discussed in the model, some hotels responded to the problems with a high degree of maturity and the others lost themselves to the problem conditions (Marker, 2020).

CONCLUSION

The study took stock of how hospitality sector, using three cases, responded to the corona pandemic. It concluded that hotel industry worked at humanity level during the pandemic period. A lot of combined efforts have been made by different hotels to serve infected people such as free food delivery, distribution of PPE kits and sanitizers etc. Different kinds of measures have been taken by hotel industry by considering the safety of staff members also. The impact of pandemic was very harsh but it presented a picture of humanity level that exists in the mind of people, and combined society as a whole. The hospitality industry in India has various growth potential. Tourism industry is anticipating the expansion of e-Visa scheme, which is hoped to treble the number of tourists in India. The hotel operators, employees and other members have shown a lot of maturity and have been constantly trying to help the society and the government by offering their accommodation capacity as isolation centres for the ones who needed to quarantine, promoting staycation or holistay concept, offering work from hotel long duration stays, etc.

REFERENCES

Ameen, A. (2020, April 20). *TnlSalutes: This Is How Lemon Tree Hotels Is Helping In The Fight Against COVID-19*. Retrieved on November on 6, 2021, from https://www.travelandleisureindia.in/featured/lemon-tree-hotels-covid-19

Bartik, A. W., Bertrand, M., Cullen, Z. B., Glaeser, E. L., Luca, M., & Stanton, C. T. (2020). *How are small businesses adjusting to COVID-19? Early evidence from a survey (No. w26989)*. National Bureau of Economic Research. doi:10.3386/w26989

Bhardwaj, A., & Kumar, V. (2022). Privacy and Healthcare during COVID-19. In *Cybersecurity Crisis Management and Lessons Learned From the COVID-19 Pandemic*. IGI-Global. doi:10.4018/978-1-7998-9164-2.ch005

Breier, M., Kallmuenzer, A., Clauss, T., Gast, J., Kraus, S., & Tiberius, V. (2021). The role of business model innovation in the hospitality industry during the COVID-19 crisis. *International Journal of Hospitality Management*, *92*, 102723. doi:10.1016/j.ijhm.2020.102723

Business Today. (2020). Coronavirus impact: Oyo allots ESOPs worth Rs 130 crore to furloughed employees. *Business Today*. Retrieved from https://www.businesstoday.in/latest/corporate /story/oyo-allots-esops-worth-rs-130-crore-to-former-existing-staff-impacted-by-covid-19-259837-2020-06-01

Business World. (2021). *Lemon Tree Hotels introduces various initiatives amidst the COVID-19 pandemic.* Retrieved on November 4, 2021, from http://bwhotelier.businessworld.in/article/Lemon-Tree-Hotels-introduces-various-initiatives-amidst-the-COVID-19-pandemic-/05-06-2021-392063/

Chadee, D., Ren, S., & Tang, G. (2021). Is digital technology the magic bullet for performing work at home? Lessons learned for post COVID-19 recovery in hospitality management. *International Journal of Hospitality Management*, *92*, 102718. doi:10.1016/j.ijhm.2020.102718 PMID:33071425

Chadha, A. (2015). Hotel Taj in The Context Of CRM and Customer Retention. *Arabian Journal of Business and Management Review, 4*(7). Retrieved on October 24, 2021, from https://www.arabianjbmr.com/pdfs/KD_VOL_4_7/1.pdf

Chaturvedi, A. (2020, April 8). *COVID-19: Lemon Tree Hotels undertakes pay cuts for senior leadership*. Retrieved on December 2, 2021, from https://economictimes.indiatimes.com/ industry/services/hotels-/-restaurants/covid-19-lemon-tree-hotels-undertakes-pay-cuts-for-senior-leadership/articleshow/75050051.cms

Deshpande, R., & Sinha, M. (2011). *Taj Hotels, Resorts and Palaces*. Retrieved November 18, 2021, from www.researchgate.net

Ghosh, A. T. (2020, April). A host of troubles for OYO. *Fortune India*. Retrieved from https://www.fortuneindia.com/enterprise/a-host-of-troubles-for-oyo/104512

Gössling, S., Scott, D., & Hall, C. M. (2020). Pandemics, tourism and global change: A rapid assessment of COVID-19. *Journal of Sustainable Tourism, 29*(1), 1–20. doi:10.1080/09669582.2020.1758708

Guha, D. (2021). The great promise and dangers of being OYO. *Fortune India*. Retrieved from https://www.fortuneindia.com/enterprise/the-great-promise-and-dangers-of-being-oyo/106035

Gursoy, D., Chi, C. G., & Chi, O. H. (2020). *COVID-19 Study 2 Report: Restaurant and Hotel Industry: Restaurant and hotel customers' sentiment analysis. Would they come back? If they would, WHEN?* (Report No. 2), Carson College of Business, Washington State University.

Khosla, V. (2022, January 18). *Hotel industry would bounce back by Oct*. Retrieved on January 31, 2022, from https://www.livemint.com/companies/news/indians-have-got-used-to-the-idea-of-taking-holidays-lemon-tree-s-keswani-11642403374673.html

Kovid, R. K., Kumari, D., & Pandey, S. (2021). Strategic Response to the Corona Pandemic Crisis: A Case of Indian Women Entrepreneurs. In V. Kumar & G. Malhotra (Eds.), *Stakeholder Strategies for Reducing the Impact of Global Health Crises* (pp. 68–84). IGI. doi:10.4018/978-1-7998-7495-9.ch005

Kumar, A. (2021, June 15). *Hotel Chains Collaborates With Governments To Fight Second Wave*. Retrieved on December 22, 2021, from https://www.traveltrendstoday.in/news/ hotel-and-resorts/item/9789-hotel-chains-collaborates-with-governments-to-fight-second-wave

Kumar, V., & Gupta, G. (Eds.). (2021). *Strategic Management During a Pandemic*. Routledge. doi:10.4324/9781003125648

Kumar, V., & Malhotra, G. (Eds.). (2021). *Stakeholder Strategies for Reducing the Impact of Global Health Crises*. IGI Global Publications. doi:10.4018/978-1-7998-7495-9

Majumdar, S. (2021). Care, cash, evolution: How OYO navigated Covid-19. *Fortune India*. Retrieved from https://www.fortuneindia.com/people/care-cash-evolution-how-oyo-navigated-covid-19/105593

Marker, A. (2020). *Models and Theories to Improve Crisis Management*. Retrieved on February 24, 2022, from https://www.smartsheet.com/content/crisis-management-model-theories

Money Control. (n.d.). Oyo shedding loss-making assets and ventures: Report. *MoneyControl News*. Retrieved from https://www.moneycontrol.com/news/business/oyo-shedding-loss-making-assets-and-ventures-report-6641581.html Accessed on February 8, 2022

Mukherjee, A. (2021, June 13). *Why Has It Become Necessary For Hotels To Invest In Technology In A Post-COVID Era*. Retrieved on January 2, 2022, from https://www.travelbizmonitor.com/why-has-it-become-necessary-for-hotels-to-invest-in-technology-in-a-post-covid-era/

Mullafiroze, R., & Cha, J. (2020). *Evaluating the impact of COVID-19on multi sectoral humanitarian needs*. https://www.elrha.org/project/evaluating-the-impact-of-covid-19-on-multi-sectoral-humanitarian-needs/

Pappas, N., & Glyptou, K. (2021). Risk-induced Competitive Productivity in Times of Recession: a Chaordic Tourism Decision-making Perspective. *International Journal of Contemporary Hospitality Management*.

Sharma, A., & Kochher, P. (2018). Taj hotels, Palaces and Resorts: The Road Ahead. *Emerald Emerging Markets Case Studies, 8*(3), 1-21. Retrieved on October 28, 2021, from https://www.emerald.com/insight/content/doi/10.1108/EEMCS-01-2018-0001/full/html

Sharma, M. (2021, January 23). *MindRush 2021: How companies 'rebuilt' businesses amid Covid-19 crisis*. Retrieved on December 5, 2021, from https://www.businesstoday.in/mindrush/mindrush-2021/story/mindrush-2021-how-companies-rebuilt-businesses-amid-covid-19-crisis-285284-2021-01-23

Shenoy, S., Upadhyay, S., & Nair, P. (2021, October 18). *Lemon Tree Hotels expects pre-COVID level occupancies by Q4; says consumers preferring branded hotels*. Retrieved on October 31, 2021, from https://www.cnbctv18.com/hospitality/lemon-tree-hotels-expects-pre-covid-level-occupancies-by-q4-says-consumers-preferring-branded-hotels-11136032.htm

Sobaih, A. E., Hasanein, A. M., Elshaer, I. A., & Abdelaziz, A. S. (2021). Responses to COVID-19: The role of performance in the relationship between small hospitality enterprises' resilience and sustainable tourism development. *International Journal of Hospitality Management, 94*(1), 102824. doi:10.1016/j.ijhm.2020.102824 PMID:34785841

Tyagi, G. (2021). How Oyo's revenue contracted from $1.8 Bn in FY20 to $850 Mn in FY21. *Fintrackr*. Retrieved from https://entrackr.com/2021/10/how-oyos-revenue-contracted-from-1-8-bn-in-fy20-to-850-mn-in-fy21/

UNWTO. (2020). *UNWTO world tourism barometer*. UNWTO.

KEY TERMS AND DEFINITIONS

Direct to Customers: When a company sells directly to the consumer, it is known as direct-to-consumer marketing. In the past, brands relied heavily on retail partners to distribute their products. Tennis rackets, for example, were sold through a sporting goods store.

Earnings Before Interest, Taxes, Depreciation, and Amortization (EBITDA): It is a financial performance indicator that can be used instead of net income in some situations. EBITDA is also considered deceptive because it excludes the cost of capital investments like as property, plant, and equipment. By adding back interest expenditure and taxes to earnings, this statistic also removes debt-related expenses.

Employee Stock Option Plan (ESOP): It is an employee benefit plan offered to employees by the corporation to foster employee ownership of the company. Employees are given reduced shares in the companies they work for.

Financial Year: A financial year (FY) is the accounting year in which you make money, which runs from April 1 to March 31 in India.

Gross Booking Value: Gross booking value is defined as the full amount of payments (including host payments, service, and cleaning fees, but excluding cancellations) processed on the platform.

Online Travel Agency: Companies with websites that allow customers to order a variety of travel-related services directly over the Internet. They are third-party agencies who resell other people's excursions, hotels, automobiles, flights, vacation packages, and so on.

Rupee: Indian currency.

Chapter 8
Adaptive Resilience of a Social Enterprise During Adversity

Oly Mishra
GITAM (Deemed) University, Visakhapatnam, India

EXECUTIVE SUMMARY

The COVID-19 pandemic presented a challenging situation to the business organizations all over the world. This challenge was even more tough for the social enterprises as they function in resource constraints which increased due to the restrictions on physical movement. The case study discusses how a social entrepreneur repurposed her operations through adaptive resilience. The framework of adaptive resilience has been studied in the context of the social enterprise, Vyomini, a rural women entrepreneurs' network that used to manufacture sanitary napkins at affordable rates before the pandemic. During the pandemic, Vyomini showcased their adaptive resilience and started manufacturing essential items like masks, sanitizers, etc. The case study explores the various components of adaptive resilience with the various stages of adversity (i.e., immediate response, recovery, and renewal). It shows that the components of adaptive resilience (i.e., communication, collaboration, leadership, and learning) are necessary for creating as well as sustaining adaptive resilience.

ORGANIZATION BACKGROUND

Prachi Kaushik, a Delhi-based social entrepreneur quit her job with the Delhi government to pursue her desire to work for the rural women. She set up a social enterprise, Vyomini which is a manufacturing unit of biodegradable sanitary napkins. It aims to provide with affordable sanitary napkins to the unprivileged women from rural backgrounds of North India while using an innovative and adaptive business

DOI: 10.4018/978-1-6684-3504-5.ch008

model. It involved and encouraged the rural women to not only make sanitary napkins but also market the product that they made. In this regard, Prachi started working along with many rural women to improve the level of awareness about menstrual health and hygiene, and then educated them how to manufacture sanitary napkins followed up by scaling up the production.

In the rural parts of India, public usage of terms like 'menstruation' and 'sanitary napkins' were still considered as taboo. But she decided to bring a change in the mindset by making women independent. The idea is to encourage women to start an enterprise single-handedly. To do this, she conducted Entrepreneurship Development Programme (EDP) where she trained and changed the lives of thousands of women by giving them the knowledge and support to become women entrepreneurs by manufacturing Vyomini's biodegradable sanitary napkins.

Vyomini, a social enterprise, was started in the year 2016 with the aim of manufacturing affordable, low-cost, and biodegradable sanitary napkins. The aim was two-fold i.e., to make the low-cost sanitary napkins easily available to the rural women and make them independent by giving them adequate support to manufacture the product. Apart from this, Prachi and her team worked for using natural fibers as well as locally available raw materials which could be used for making the sanitary napkins. This required a lot of research and after almost two years of struggle, Vyomini launched its first low-cost, biodegradable sanitary napkin at a price of $0.03 per napkin. The manufacturing units of Vyomini were set up in the rural areas of Haryana, Rajasthan, Uttar Pradesh, and Delhi. The goal was to develop a manufacturing technique that would utilize the locally and easily available raw materials to make the best quality biodegradable sanitary napkin. The manufacturing system was also kept decentralized as well as localized so that the rural women could plan and arrange the materials required by themselves. The manufacturing process was explained to them in a simple manner so that it could be easily followed and scaled up effortlessly.

As on late 2021, Vyomini had around 50 full-time employees along with a large network of rural women entrepreneurs. This network had only been increasing in size along with time. This happens as the rural women interact among themselves and spread a positive word-of-mouth about the product. This led to a greater number of women using Rakshak, Vyomini's sanitary napkin. Since this is a recurring need, there are plenty of repeat purchases that happen as a result, more rural women join in the network. This way not only the network of rural women entrepreneurs increased but it also led to making them self-dependent and addressing a basic need. Towards the end of year 2021, a few lakhs of women were a part of the network, and this number was constantly growing. The network has been able to bring together women from the remote corners of the country and make them manufacture an essential product that is sold online i.e., through Vyomini's website as well as on e-commerce platforms like Amazon, Flipkart, and Government's e-marketplace. The product range has also been widened from basic products to premium products. The quality of the product has been taken care of by consulting with gynecologist and getting the quality approved according to International Standards Organization (ISO) and Bureau of India Standards (BIS). This business model has empowered rural women and it stands true to its vision that is, 'Women first—Prosperity for all'. It created an ecosystem for rural women's socio-economic welfare through awareness and training programs, followed by financial inclusion facilities, entrepreneurship development programs, marketing, trading, and manufacturing activities. The case of Vyomini social enterprise is about manufacturing sanitary napkins with an aim to remove 'period poverty' by using locally available fibers (Mishra, 2020). In the process of doing so, the rural women become financially independent. It also triggers further change in the way other women in their network become financially independent as well.

SETTING THE STAGE

When the COVID-19 pandemic started in early 2020, almost all countries' governments announced lockdown which affected the operations of almost all businesses (Kumar & Gupta, 2021). However, the social entrepreneur in this case study, tried to connect with her women entrepreneurs' network in the rural areas of north India to explore about their well-being and other socio-economic conditions. The social enterprise was only manufacturing sanitary napkins, which was continued as it was categorized under essential products by the government. The women entrepreneurs' network communicated with all network members to continue making sanitary napkins while following the government's safety protocols. Prachi, the social entrepreneur, was vigilant enough about the various sanitization and hygiene products required during the corona pandemic. When enquired about the women who were a part of their women entrepreneurs' network, they informed that they were worried about their income as the lockdown had led to the slowdown of their income from agricultural and other activities.

This led the social entrepreneur to realize that there was a need to make quick changes as a response to the rapidly changing determinants of the external business environment. In this regard, Prachi tried to connect with the relevant people in the government bodies, other women self-help groups and her own rural women entrepreneurs' network. The effort to promptly contact others in her network was well-received in the form of prompt responses. The women entrepreneurs' network members were reached through the Project officers and trainers dedicated to each state, for example - Uttar Pradesh, Delhi, Haryana, and Bihar. While the primary motive of contacting them was to inform them to continue manufacturing sanitary napkins, it was also felt that there was a need to provide them with masks. To do this, the entrepreneur had to communicate with the rural women entrepreneurs quickly and effectively. The aim was to emphasize the importance of following the COVID safety protocols like wearing masks, maintaining social distancing, etc. (Kumar & Malhotra, 2021). This was done through video calls on computers, laptops, or mobile phones. Since India's rural parts are not well-versed with technology, the existing infrastructure facilities that the government of India set up were utilized (Singh & Kumar, 2022). For example, Common Service Centres have been set up in almost every village of India. The government set these up in 2006 to digitally empower rural entrepreneurs at the village level. The trainers and Project managers used these at centers to carry out training sessions for rural women. The training session aimed to explain to the women entrepreneurs about re-purposing their activities and manufacturing items in high demand during the crisis. They were also briefed about World Health Organization's (WHO's) quality standards and medical lab specifications that needed to be followed. The production of masks was then started following social distancing norms and other protocols as set by the regulatory authorities.

The social entrepreneur was successfully able to handle the crisis by managing the production of essential items, i.e., masks and sanitary napkins. This was possible because of adaptive resilience of the entrepreneur and the ability to engage in frugal innovation through bricolage (Mishra, 2021). This could be understood from the findings of each step followed by the social entrepreneur while carrying out this process.

CASE DESCRIPTION

Every crisis is unique which prompts businesses to handle a different set of constraints and opportunities. In such situations, entrepreneurs and their enterprises are found to implement bricolage based on their locally available resources (Dahles and Susilowati, 2015; Laskovaia *et al.*, 2019). Resilience is an entrepreneur's ability to adapt to change (Salisu *et al.*, 2020). The term 'resilience' is derived from the Latin word 'resiliere', which means to bounce back (Sabatino, 2016). The concept has originated from ecology, which defines resilience as the ability of a system to return to balance after a big disturbance (Holling, 1973). It is also defined as 'the ability to continue living a purposeful life after hardship or adversity' (Tedeschi and Calhoun, 2004). In other words, resilience is a dynamic process that includes a positive adaptation to a significant adversity (Luthar *et al.*, 2000).

Entrepreneurs are supposed to possess the capacity to bear risks when they start a business of their own (Subagyo et al., 2020). They can deal with uncertainty and take risks (McMullen and Shepherd, 2006; York and Venkataraman, 2010) but when the risk is on a greater scale like a pandemic then it will have an impact on various facets of the entrepreneurs' business operations. The risk is of handling external shock as well as carrying on the business properly (Kumar & Vidhyalakshmi, 2012). The risk is more for social entrepreneurs as they do not have proper access to resources at par with that by commercial entrepreneurs. To overcome such risk, the social entrepreneurs integrate their arrangements (Santos *et al.*, 2015) and use resource mobilization strategies (Battilana, 2018; Siegner *et al.*, 2018). Social entrepreneurs have been handling critical situations time and again because of which they have a better understanding of addressing a problem (World Health Organization, 2020). They can design an effective solution as a response to the problem by incorporating community goals.

Resilience helps social entrepreneurs to withstand crisis and is one of the drivers of social entrepreneurial performance as well as success. The resilience of the social enterprises can be realized by its ability to survive the crisis by re-orienting their business (Branicki *et al.*, 2018). In the context of crisis and entrepreneurship, the concept of crisis and resilience are considered as two sides of the same coin (Doern *et al.*, 2019). Some of the other terms that are also used in place of resilience are persistence and self-efficacy (Korber and McNaughton, 2018). Resilience was exhibited at both level - the individual i.e., the social entrepreneur, and also by the organization i.e., the social enterprise.

Previous empirical studies on entrepreneurial resilience show that resilience can be categorized into two ways - planned resilience and adaptive resilience. Planned resilience is also known as first-order capacity which involves the usage of plans and capabilities to overcome the problem even before the problem occurs. On the other side, adaptive resilience is known as second-order capacity as it is found after the disaster has already occurred and the enterprise must respond and emerge out of it (Lee, Vargo, and Seville, 2013). For planned resilience, the entrepreneur has time as well as other resources to prepare, whereas in case of adaptive resilience, the entrepreneur must handle the situation suddenly. Previous studies show that the resilience of social entrepreneurs is a factor responsible for the success of business. This is because resilient social entrepreneurs demonstrate a high degree of tolerance to ambiguity, can adapt to change quickly (Ayala and

Manzano, 2014). According to Castro and Zermeño (2020), the resilience of a social enterprise depends on the relationship of the social enterprise with other institutions as well as stakeholders.

In the given case study, the social entrepreneur depicted adaptive resilience as the pandemic was an unexpected crisis. Moreover, such crises have led social entrepreneurs to confront various challenges and threats. Adaptive resilience provides a useful framework for studying how social entrepreneurs recover from the impact of the crisis suffered (Kitsos and Bishop, 2018). Adaptive resilience helps the organization to keep functioning reliably during the crisis period (Doern *et al.* 2019; Williams *et al.*, 2017). The challenge becomes even tougher for social enterprises as they aim at working for the welfare of the society despite the resource constraints.

The present case-based research is guided by the three broad questions:

1. How did the social entrepreneur in the case study react to the crisis?
2. How did the social enterprise positively adapt to the crisis?
3. What factors helped them in developing adaptive resilience to handle the crisis?

CURRENT CHALLENGES FACING THE ORGANIZATION

Social entrepreneurs in emerging economies already face many difficulties due to constraints in resource availability including institutional voids which are considered boosting entrepreneurship as a phenomenon (Khanna and Palepu, 2011; Kovid, Bhati and Sharma, 2021). The difficulty has become more challenging during the pandemic as businesses were forced to move online (Liguori and Winkler, 2020) due to the restrictions on people's physical movement. This forced the social entrepreneurs to adapt themselves to the existing situation and find a solution. The frequency of organizational crises and unpredictable situations which are faced by the social enterprises are more than commercial enterprises. They are therefore more resilient in nature than the commercial enterprises. Previous literature reveals that social enterprises have become more resilient as they have emerged from extreme events of crisis and uncertainty (Torres *et al.*, 2019; Kwong et al., 2019; DesJardine *et al.*, 2019; Salisu *et al.*, 2020).

The social entrepreneurs and their network of women entrepreneurs worked closely with the local people and solved their problem in resource constraints. Social entrepreneurs have overcome several socio-economic and institutional constraints to provide value through adaptive resilience. As the current crisis and demand for critical supplies was unprecedented, adaptive resilience was the only way to meet the demand. The social enterprise, Vyomini, also depicted adaptive resilience in handling the situation. The social entrepreneur had to face many challenges while responding to the crisis effectively. The different phases that the social entrepreneur handled during the crisis could be identified as:

- Immediate response
- Recovery and

- Long-term renewal

The 1st stage in handling the crisis is *Immediate response*. In this stage, the social entrepreneur takes the initiative to quickly connect with the stakeholders of the enterprise. A social entrepreneur's response to crisis depends on several factors like experience of the social entrepreneur, the stage of the crisis, risks faced by the social entrepreneur etc. Prachi actively connected with people from different walks of life to re-purpose and re-orient the business process of the social enterprise. The aim was to manufacture essential items whose supply was necessary for the people. The social enterprise was anyhow manufacturing sanitary napkins, which was listed as an essential item. Since they had the experience in manufacturing hygiene products, they decided to respond quickly to the changing business environment. The team at Vyomini had already gained the experience of making good quality sanitary napkins from naturally available fibers from the nearby areas. This experience enabled them in repurposing their business towards making face masks from the available resources. The social enterprise was relatively new in the market and the crisis was also in its early stages. This helped the social entrepreneur, the leader of the team, to take quick measures, design immediate response and communicate the same to all concerned stakeholders.

In the 2nd stage i.e., *Recovery*, the social entrepreneur took steps to collaborate with the other stakeholders of the social enterprise. There was need to learn new things and make use of the presence of mind so that the constraint of resources problem could be resolved quickly. Since the crisis was sudden, there was paucity of time and resource that could be used for quick preparation. The social entrepreneur along with her rural women entrepreneur network started making various designs of masks on a trial-and-error basis. The suppliers of the raw materials were contacted so that they could provide more raw materials and more prototypes of masks were created. These prototypes were then tested for their acceptability and ease of use among the rural women entrepreneurs. Based on the feedback received, the design of the masks was changed, and new prototypes were created. Once an acceptable prototype was obtained, the masks were sent for quality testing in view of the standards set by the government. This ensured that the masks were suitable for protecting the users from the COVID-19 virus.

The 3rd stage is the *Long-term renewal* stage. In this stage, the social entrepreneur decided that they would continue to keep manufacturing masks as the pandemic was here to stay for some more years. Moreover, masks were also used as a safety equipment in many sectors. Later, the designs of the masks were improved, and they were made available in several colors as well as designs without compromising with the quality of the mask. The social enterprise had now become experts in making masks and continues to manufacture it. They also started making other protective equipment like PPE kits, shields, sanitizers etc from the experience that they had gained from making masks.

In all the three stages mentioned above, the social entrepreneur along with the rural women entrepreneur network had to come across several challenges. The primary challenge was to get all the stakeholders to a common understanding of the issues involved that the business process would be re-purposed. Secondly, getting the required materials as well as the permissions and licenses necessary for making protective equipment was another challenging task. Thirdly, the manufactured items had to be tested for their quality and then distributed among the people. While these challenges seemed to be humongous in the beginning, the social entrepreneur had faith that they would be able to overcome all of them one by one. The adaptive resilience of the social entrepreneur as well as of the social enterprise led to overcoming the crisis. As observed by earlier researchers, the adaptive resilience of an enterprise in crisis is like the process of an entrepreneur starting their own enterprise (Davidsson *et al.*, 2007; Penrose, 2009).

SOLUTIONS AND RECOMMENDATIONS

While each social enterprise may face its own separate set of challenges, there are certain problems which were common across all the social enterprises. Figure 1 presents the components of adaptive resilience. The components of adaptive resilience that were observed in the social entrepreneur and the enterprise throughout the pandemic includes Communication, Collaboration, Leadership, and Learning. Figure 1 presents the framework of adaptive resilience. Table 1 provides the details of the components of Adaptive Resilience in the context of the social entrepreneur and her social enterprise considered in this case study.

Figure 1.

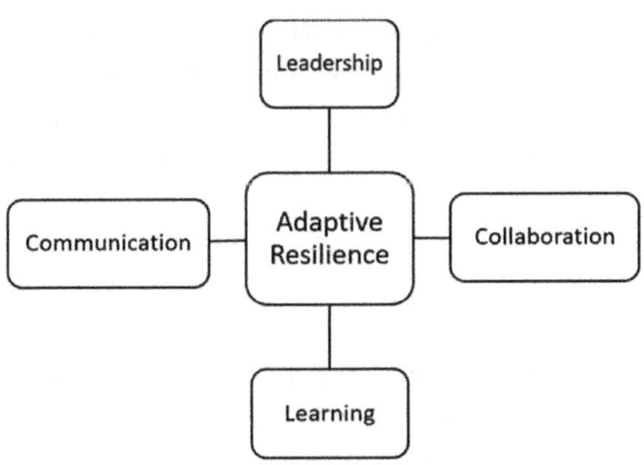

Table 1. Components of adaptive resilience

	Communication	Collaboration	Leadership	Learning
What?	• Discussing the problem. • Getting acquainted with the challenges faced by the people.	• Reflecting on the problem. • Working together with risk and uncertainty.	• Planning the way ahead. • Taking initiative to address the problems	• Gaining knowledge • Acquiring new skills
Why?	• Helps in understanding the problem. • Gives different perspectives on the problem. • Obtaining different solutions for the problem.	• Strengths of different stakeholders can be used for the welfare of the company. • Overcoming the weakness due to the diversity in the ecosystem.	• Identifies opportunity in adversity. • Being proactive • Taking risk • Being an active listener	• Discover new ways. • Obtain new perspectives.
How?	• Video calling • Online conferencing • Telephonic conversations.	• E-mails • Webinars • Debates and deliberation • Remote communication	• Being present in difficult situations • Encouraging different groups of people • Setting an example for others	• Discussions • Practical application • Trial and error

Source: Prepared by Author

Communication

Communication is an important component of adaptive resilience for the social entrepreneur. The pandemic had closed all ways of physically meeting with other members of the social enterprise. The only way to communicate was through the online platforms like Zoom and other communication applications like WhatsApp etc. (Bhardwaj & Kumar, 2022). There was a dire need to communicate about the problems that the social entrepreneur as well as the women working in the social enterprise were facing. The imposition of lockdown had limited the movement of vehicles which led to problems in supplying materials for production. The need for communication was more for motivating the women entrepreneurs. The process of communication includes active listening to monitor the changing needs which boosted the organizational resilience. The social entrepreneur's communication provided flexibility to the staff in dealing with the issues faced during the production. This also helped in developing a more comprehensive plan by taking inputs from the other workers. This also led to better implementation of the plan also. The social entrepreneur communicated not only with the people involved within the social enterprise but also with the other stakeholders. This helped in getting clarity about the execution of the plan.

Collaboration

Collaboration proved to be a second vital element of resilience (Sharma & Kumar, 2017). During the pandemic, the social entrepreneur had to respond to a new environment. The social entrepreneur had hardly any experience of handling such a situation. Moreover, there was lack of availability of resources during the pandemic. The only way forward for the social enterprise was through collaboration with others. The social entrepreneur worked in close co-ordination with the suppliers of materials to ensure that the essential items were made available to the frontline workers as well as others in the society. They continued with the manufacture the sanitary napkins as it was categorized under the essential items list of the government. However, there was also need for manufacturing covid related protective equipment. This was made possible by the collaboration between the social entrepreneur and the team of rural women entrepreneurs. They also collaborated with their suppliers of materials which were used for making sanitary napkins and used the same material for making masks. The suppliers were asked to provide more materials so that the rural women entrepreneurs would have sufficient material to carry out their production activity. According to Roundy *et al.*, (2017), the diversity of an entrepreneurial ecosystem is an important characteristic that influences the enterprise's resilience towards internal and external disturbances. This was found to be true in the case of the social entrepreneur referred to in the case study. The rural women entrepreneur network was diverse in nature as women from various backgrounds collaborated, which helped in gaining more resilience. They learned how to respond to a crisis by exhibiting greater-than-ordinary collaboration.

Leadership

In a crisis, an organization is forced to respond to a new context, often with only limited experience and resources. Social enterprises are used to working with minimal resources. They can therefore gain adaptive resilience quickly in a crisis. Adaptive resilience is boosted when social enterprises can bring out internal changes, like breaking down silos to combine resources and introduce synergy among the different groups of people involved. Likewise, when social enterprises use their established networks to link and collaborate with others, it also improves their ability to learn, and their capacity to respond to the situation. Such social enterprises can adapt themselves quickly to the changing environment due to the leadership. The social entrepreneur depicts her leadership skills by being proactive, innovative, able to identify opportunity in adversity and taking risks. Their leadership allows the social enterprises to be resilient by showing their adaptability, flexibility, and responsiveness to external crises.

Learning

Learning was observed as the fourth essential feature. Since the pandemic was an unexpected change, initial response of the social enterprise was that of shock. The social entrepreneur and her rural women entrepreneur network quickly came out of their standard daily routines and worked together to focus directly on the demanding issues associated with the crisis. The social entrepreneur was open to learning and mindful of the future. They also created a caring, learning, and collaborative culture. The culture of learning in the social enterprise led to promoting better response, faster recovery, and positive renewal. Post-crisis, it was observed that the learning led to creating new and enhanced ways of functioning. The effect of the learning was observed in the other areas of the social enterprise. The social enterprises developed processes and procedures to systematically learn from the past experiences.

Table 2 pressents the relevance of the components of adaptive resilience during the various stages of the crisis faced by the social enterprise. It is based on the observation of the social entrepreneur and its employees during the various stages of adversity. When the adversity strikes, the initial stage is Response. In this stage, communication and leadership are most relevant. In this context, the leader is the social entrepreneur and communication with the employees is the key to responding to the situation. In the second stage, i.e., recovery, the collaboration within and outside the social enterprise and learning from the collaboration plays a crucial role. In the third stage, i.e., long term renewal, all the four components of adaptive resilience are important.

Table 2. Components of adaptive resilience and stages of adversity

Stages of Adversity	Communication	Collaboration	Leadership	Learning
Immediate Response	ü		ü	
Recovery		ü		ü
Long term Renewal	ü	ü	ü	ü

Source: Prepared by Author

Therefore, it can be said that leadership and communication are essential for creating adaptive resilience whereas collaboration and learning are needed to sustain it. Our findings suggest that crisis like the COVID-19 pandemic will impact all businesses sooner or later. Every business organization, irrespective of their size will have to adapt themselves to the changed business environment through their adaptive resilience. Thus, the components and framework of adaptive resilience will be applicable to social enterprises as well as other enterprises.

CONCLUSION

The current case study explored the adaptive resilience of Vyomini, a social enterprise involving women of rural areas in North India. The approach of its founder, a woman entrepreneur, to deal with crisis was quite adaptive. The study contributes to the existing literature on women entrepreneurial resilience and innovation during the pandemic crisis in line with earlier studies in various context (Kovid, Kumari and Pandey, 2021). The findings in the given case study are in sync with the previous studies (Martin, 2011; Dahles and Susilowati, 2015; Korber and McNaughton's, 2018; Ratten, 2020) which state that resilience is a process that helps businesses to overcome the evolving restraints in the business environment. The adaptive resilience of a social enterprise makes it undergo a transformation process. Thus, adaptive resilience of a social enterprise is layered and must be explored across various stages especially in times of a crisis.

REFERENCES

Ayala, J.-C., & Manzano, G. (2014). The resilience of the entrepreneur. Influence on the success of the business: A longitudinal analysis. *Journal of Economic Psychology*, *42*, 126–135. doi:10.1016/j.joep.2014.02.004

Battilana, J. (2018). Cracking the organizational challenge of pursuing joint social and financial goals: social enterprise as a laboratory to understand hybrid organizing. *M@n@gement, 21*(4), 1278-1305.

Bhardwaj, A., & Kumar, V. (2022). Privacy and Healthcare during COVID-19. In *Cybersecurity Crisis Management and Lessons Learned From the COVID-19 Pandemic* (pp. 82–96). IGI-Global. doi:10.4018/978-1-7998-9164-2.ch005

Branicki, L. J., Sullivan-Taylor, B., & Livschitz, S. R. (2018). How entrepreneurial resilience generates resilient SMEs. *International Journal of Entrepreneurial Behaviour & Research, 24*(7), 1244–1263. doi:10.1108/IJEBR-11-2016-0396

Castro, M.P., & Zermeño, M.G.G. (2020). Being an entrepreneur post-COVID-19– resilience in times of crisis: a systematic literature review. *Journal of Entrepreneurship in Emerging Economies.*

Dahles, H., & Susilowati, T. P. (2015). Business resilience in times of growth and crisis. *Annals of Tourism Research*, *51*, 34–50. doi:10.1016/j.annals.2015.01.002

Davidsson, P., Achtenhagen, L., & Naldi, L. (2007). What Do We Know about Small Firm Growth? *Springer*.

DesJardine, M., Bansal, P., & Yang, Y. (2019). Bouncing back: Building resilience through social and environmental practices in the context of the 2008 global financial crisis. *Journal of Management*, *45*(4), 1434–1460. doi:10.1177/0149206317708854

Doern, R., Williams, N., & Vorley, T. (2019). Special issue on entrepreneurship and crises: Business as usual? An introduction and review of the literature. *Entrepreneurship and Regional Development*, *31*(5/6), 400–412. doi:10.1080/08985626.2018.1541590

Holling, C. S. (1973). Resilience and stability of ecological systems. *Annual Review of Ecology and Systematics*, *4*(1), 1–23. doi:10.1146/annurev.es.04.110173.000245

Khanna, T., & Palepu, K. G. (2011). Winning in emerging markets: Spotting and responding to institutional voids. *World Financial Review*, 18–20.

Kitsos, A., & Bishop, P. (2018). Economic resilience in Great Britain: The crisis impact and its determining factors for local authority districts. *The Annals of Regional Science*, *60*(2), 329–347. doi:10.100700168-016-0797-y

Korber, S., & McNaughton, R. B. (2018). Resilience and entrepreneurship: A systematic literature review. *International Journal of Entrepreneurial Behaviour & Research*, *24*(7), 1129–1154. doi:10.1108/IJEBR-10-2016-0356

Kovid, R. K., Bhati, B., & Sharma, G. M. (2021). Entrepreneurial competencies, institutional voids and performance of small and medium enterprises: Evidence from an emerging economy. *Vision: Journal of Business Perspective.* Advance online publication.

Kovid, R. K., Kumari, D., & Pandey, S. (2021). Strategic response to the corona pandemic crisis: A case of Indian women entrepreneurs. In V. Kumar & G. Malhotra (Eds.), *Stakeholder strategies for reducing the impact of global health crises* (pp. 68–84). IGI Global. doi:10.4018/978-1-7998-7495-9.ch005

Kumar, V., & Gupta, G. (Eds.). (2021). *Strategic Management During a Pandemic.* Routledge. doi:10.4324/9781003125648

Kumar, V., & Malhotra, G. (Eds.). (2021). *Stakeholder Strategies for Reducing the Impact of Global Health Crises*. IGI Global Publications. doi:10.4018/978-1-7998-7495-9

Kumar, V., & Vidhyalakshmi, P. (2012). Cloud computing for business sustainability. *Asia-Pacific Journal of Management Research and Innovation*, *8*(4), 461–474. doi:10.1177/2319510X13481905

Kwong, C. C. Y., Cheung, C. W. M., Manzoor, H., & Rashid, M. U. (2019). Entrepreneurship through bricolage: A study of displaced entrepreneurs at times of war and conflict. *Entrepreneurship and Regional Development*, *31*(5/6), 435–455. doi:10.1080/08985626.2018.1541592

Laskovaia, A., Marino, L., Shirokova, G., & Wales, W. (2019). Expect the unexpected: Examining the shaping role of entrepreneurial orientation on causal and effectual decision-making logic during economic crisis. *Entrepreneurship and Regional Development*, *31*(5/6), 456–475. doi:10.1080/08985626.2018.1541593

Lee, A. V., Vargo, J., & Seville, E. (2013). Developing a tool to measure and compare organizations' resilience. *Natural Hazards Review*, *14*(1), 29–41. doi:10.1061/(ASCE)NH.1527-6996.0000075

Liguori, E., & Winkler, C. (2020). *From Offline to Online: Challenges and Opportunities for Entrepreneurship Education Following the COVID-19 Pandemic*. Academic Press.

Luthar, S. S., Cicchetti, D., & Becker, B. (2000). The construct of resilience: A critical evaluation and guidelines for future work. *Child Development*, *71*(3), 543–562. doi:10.1111/1467-8624.00164 PMID:10953923

Martin, R. (2011). Regional economic resilience, hysteresis and recessionary shocks. *Journal of Economic Geography*, *12*(1), 1–32. doi:10.1093/jeg/lbr019

McMullen, J. S., & Shepherd, D. A. (2006). Entrepreneurial action and the role of uncertainty in the theory of the entrepreneur. *Academy of Management Review*, *31*(1), 132–152. doi:10.5465/amr.2006.19379628

Mishra, O. (2021). Principles of frugal innovation and its application by social entrepreneurs in times of adversity : An inductive single-case approach. *Journal of Entrepreneurship in Emerging Economies.*, *13*(4), 547–574. doi:10.1108/JEEE-07-2020-0247

Mishra, O., Sharma, R., & Agrawal, B. (2020). Facilitating Women Prosperity with Higher Purpose at Vyomini. *South Asian Journal of Business and Management Cases*, *9*(2), 198–207. doi:10.1177/2277977920905820

Penrose, E. (2009). *The Theory of the Growth of the Firm* (4th ed.). Oxford University Press.

Ratten, V. (2020). Coronavirus disease (COVID-19) and sport entrepreneurship. *International Journal of Entrepreneurial Behaviour & Research*, *26*(6), 1379–1388. doi:10.1108/IJEBR-06-2020-0387

Roundy, P. T., Holzhauer, H., & Dai, Y. (2017). Finance or philanthropy? Understanding the motivations and criteria of impact investors. *Social Responsibility Journal*, *13*(3), 419–512. doi:10.1108/SRJ-08-2016-0135

Sabatino, M. (2016). Economic crisis and resilience: Resilient capacity and competitiveness of the enterprises. *Journal of Business Research*, *69*(5), 1924–1927. doi:10.1016/j.jbusres.2015.10.081

Salisu, I., Hashim, N., Mashi, M. S., & Aliyu, H. G. (2020). Perseverance of effort and consistency of interest for entrepreneurial career success: Does resilience matter? *Journal of Entrepreneurship in Emerging Economies*, *12*(2), 279–304. doi:10.1108/JEEE-02-2019-0025

Santos, F., Pache, A. C., & Birkholz, C. (2015). Making hybrids work: Aligning business models and organizational design for social enterprises. *California Management Review*, *57*(3), 36–58. doi:10.1525/cmr.2015.57.3.36

Sharma, D., & Kumar, V. (2017). A Framework for Collaborative and Convenient Learning on Cloud Computing Platforms. *International Journal of Web-Based Learning and Teaching Technologies*, *12*(2), 1–20. doi:10.4018/IJWLTT.2017040101

Siegner, M., Pinkse, J., & Panwar, R. (2018). Managing tensions in a social enterprise: The complex balancing act to deliver a multi-faceted but coherent social mission. *Journal of Cleaner Production*, *174*, 1314–1324. doi:10.1016/j.jclepro.2017.11.076

Singh, J., & Kumar, V. (2022). Combating the Pandemic with ICT Based Learning tools and applications: A case of Indian Higher Education. *International Journal of Virtual and Personal Learning Environments Platforms*, *12*(1), 1–21.

Subagyo, K., Kumar, V., & Ernestivita, G. (2020). Entrepreneurial Parameters and Performance of MSMEs in East Java Province of Indonesia. *International Journal of Business Innovation and Research*, *23*(2), 267–282. doi:10.1504/IJBIR.2020.110102

Tedeschi, R. G., & Calhoun, L. G. (2004). Posttraumatic growth: Conceptual foundations and empirical evidence. *Psychological Inquiry*, *15*(1), 1–18. doi:10.120715327965pli1501_01

Torres, A. P., Marshall, M. I., & Sydnor, S. (2019). Does social Capital pay off? The case of small business resilience after hurricane Katrina. *Journal of Contingencies and Crisis Management*, *27*(2), 168–181. doi:10.1111/1468-5973.12248

Williams, T., Gruber, D., Sutcliffe, D., Shepherd, D., & Zhao, E. (2017). Organizational response to adversity: Fusing crisis management and resilience research streams. *The Academy of Management Annals*, *11*(2), 733–769. doi:10.5465/annals.2015.0134

World Health Organization. (2020). *WHO, coronavirus disease (COVID-19) outbreak*. Available at: www.who.int/emergencies/diseases/novel-coronavirus-2019

York, J. G., & Venkataraman, S. (2010). The entrepreneur–environment nexus: Uncertainty, innovation, and allocation. *Journal of Business Venturing*, *25*(5), 449–463. doi:10.1016/j.jbusvent.2009.07.007

KEY TERMS AND DEFINITIONS

Collaboration: Two or more entities working together to achieve a goal.
Communication: The act of sharing or exchanging information, ideas, or feelings.
Immediate Response: Instant action performed without any delay.
Leadership: The state of being in charge.
Learning: The knowledge one gets by studying and doing.
Recovery: Returning to normal state after a difficult period.
Renewal: To revive or to so start something new.

Chapter 9
Surviving Amid Crisis Episodes:
The Case of Women-Owned Small Enterprises in Bangladesh

Saptarshi Dhar
https://orcid.org/0000-0003-0435-1855
Jahangirnagar University, Bangladesh

Tahira Farzana
Jahangirnagar University, Bangladesh

Sabiha Saju Ibne Abedin
Jahangirnagar University, Bangladesh

EXECUTIVE SUMMARY

The chapter examines how women-owned small businesses in Bangladesh responded to crisis episodes such as COVID-19 and discusses their resilience to shocking events. The study involved a qualitative exploration of three women-owned online small businesses conducted using the case study method. The cases included businesses that sold jewelry and fashion accessories, both imported and locally procured, and exclusively operated on social media platforms, including Facebook and Instagram. The findings suggest that the businesses adopted innovative social media strategies to survive the crisis episode, including page boosting and paid promotions, Facebook and Instagram Live coupled with sales and discount promotions, temporary closure, vendor switching, and product basket modification. The enterprises showed an overall moderate level of resilience, with a moderate level of adaptability, agility, and low flexibility with a high vulnerability to crisis events. Recommendations for policymakers and credit institutions are also discussed.

DOI: 10.4018/978-1-6684-3504-5.ch009

INTRODUCTION

Bangladesh is an emerging economy in South Asia with annual GDP growth of 8.2 percent in FY 2019, the highest in Asia and the Pacific (Asian Development Bank, 2021). A significant portion of the economic growth can be attributed to the small business enterprises sector of the country, which contributes 20.25 percent of its GDP (Khalil, 2020). For a developing country like Bangladesh, small businesses act as drivers of employment generation and poverty alleviation (Kumar et al., 2022). They are helping the country graduate from least developed standing to middle-income developing country status (Asian Development Bank, 2020).

The spread and aftermath of the SARS-COV-2 virus and subsequent economic crisis created an exogenous shock for business enterprises worldwide, and the small business enterprises in Bangladesh are no exception to the massive economic and financial pressure resulting from it. The shock of the crisis created unique challenges for survival (Kumar & Gupta, 2022). It posed threats to the sustainability of these businesses, which were already plagued with a myriad of problems such as lack of marketing strategy, inadequate resources, skill scarcity, poor quality of products, lack of quality control, inadequate infrastructural facilities, lack of technological knowledge, high employee turnover rates and poor policy support (Alauddin and Chowdhury, 2015; Mazumder and Alharahsheh, 2019; Rahman et al., 2018; Kumar & Vidhyalakshmi, 2012). Additionally, financial challenges in the form of lack of access to formal credit, high bank interest rates, collateral-based lending contributed to financial constraints (World Bank Group, 2019). OECD (2004, 2006) states that for a developing country like Bangladesh, problems of financial nature are the most prominent for small businesses that threaten their survival (Karadag, 2015; Kaya and Alpkan, 2012).

Crisis episodes such as the COVID-19 pandemic threaten businesses, distort economies, and disrupt the global supply and logistics chain (Kumar & Malhotra, 2022). For small businesses, exogenous shocks can prove fatal compared to their bigger counterparts that get greater attention in national economies and can influence policymakers to implement reactionary measures in their favor (Morgan et al., 2020). In Bangladesh, the crisis impacted the small business entrepreneurs so significantly that they were at risk of shutting down businesses (Youth Business International, 2020). Small enterprises experienced extreme economic distress during the lockdown and post lockdown as they are dependent on short cash cycles, which were, in turn, affected by supply chain disruptions and loss of revenue.

While the COVID-19 crisis and related responses (e.g., lockdown, isolation, stay at home orders, social and physical distancing) disrupted businesses of all sizes in Bangladesh and beyond, women-owned small enterprises (WOSB) are more likely to be significantly impacted that can be attributed to pre-existing business structures and constraints (OECD, 2020). OECD (2020) identifies a number of these factors: First, compared to men, women lean toward sectors that experienced severe fall in customer demand during the pandemic (e.g., retail, hospitality). Second, women-owned businesses tend to be smaller in size and revenue, leading to lower financial resilience in the event of a crisis. Third, women finance their businesses through informal financing routes such as self-funding or funding from family and friends (due to limited access to external finance), resulting in few financial assets to buffer against crisis episodes. Fourth, women entrepreneurs have limited access to professional contacts and professional advisors who could offer essential guidance in a crisis event compared to men. Fifth, access to commercial digital solutions is limited for women small business owners that create obstacles in converting to a digital business model and overall digital adoption. Sixth, women entrepreneurs share highly disproportionate household and childcare responsibilities, which negatively impact the business in terms of time availability and business continuity. And seventh, many women entrepreneurs fail to qualify for relief and stimulus packages due to the structure and nature of their business, lack of access to banking channels – which are generally the usual routes for disbursing financial assistance.

In Bangladesh, women-owned businesses are drivers of employment generation, household income, and economic growth. There are 8 million micro, small and medium enterprises (MSME) in Bangladesh; however, only 7.2 percent of businesses are women-owned (Rahman, n.d.). Women-owned small enterprises in the country experience a range of financial and non-financial challenges that block their growth and profit potential– lack of collateral and financial infrastructure, high loan rates, social and cultural norms and prejudice surrounding women, limited access to business education, and lack of scope for skill development (IFC, 2014). With the pandemic's emergence and its adverse impacts, women-owned small businesses have become exceedingly vulnerable. A study by the Asia Foundation revealed that women entrepreneurs in Bangladesh suffered several difficulties, including government restrictions on mobility, concern for personal safety, increased production, and operation cost (The Asia Foundation, 2021). 17 percent of women-owned businesses permanently closed off business due to lack of customers and lockdown impositions. Those who kept their businesses running did so with reduced activities due to low customer demand, insufficient cash flow, and declining revenue. Several supply chain issues emerged that threatened women-owned small business survival: canceled contracts with suppliers and buyers, difficulties in delivering products, lack of sufficient labor, and restrictions on international trade. In addition, women entrepreneurs were forced to lay off employees to keep the business running, thereby destroying the years of professional goodwill they had built (Sultana, 2021). Furthermore, uneven family responsibilities exacerbated anxiety and stress among women entrepreneurs. The absence of domestic help and support, school closures forced these entrepreneurs to assume greater household and childcare responsibilities, allowing less time and energy to focus on their business. In April of 2020, the Government of Bangladesh announced a stimulus package of BDT 20 billion to support cottage, micro, small and medium enterprises (CMSME), of which 5.7 percent were allotted for women-owned ones but failed to attract potential beneficiaries due to complex procedures and disinterest from banks (Sultana, 2021)

Despite the grim landscape, women small business entrepreneurs remain optimistic about bouncing back and continuing their business beyond the COVID crisis. Since the onset of the pandemic, women entrepreneurs have been flexible and adaptive to the "new normal," pivoting their business model to a digital one among other diverse coping mechanisms such as diversification, discounts, extensive delivery services (Dhar et al., 2021; Rabbani et al., 2020). They are hopeful to grow their existing business and utilize opportunities in the future. The optimism is evident in the economic forecast. Despite the pandemic, Bangladesh is projected to achieve a GDP growth of 5.2 percent in FY 2020 and rebound to 6.8 percent in FY 2021 (Asian Development Bank, 2021). It can be inferred that regardless of the many challenges, it is apparent that women-owned small businesses in Bangladesh have shown resilience to the exogenous shock, as evidenced by the projected GDP growth rate. And yet, not a lot of literature explores how small businesses build resilience, survive crises, and recover afterward (Davidsson & Gordon, 2016; Devece et al., 2016; Subagyo et al., 2020). Therefore, it can be said that while overwhelming adversities exist for women-owned small businesses in Bangladesh from the COVID-19 crisis, many women entrepreneurs adopted timely and appropriate responses to ensure business survival.

This chapter discusses the survival mechanisms and resilience of the women-owned small businesses in Bangladesh. To do that, the adaptability, agility, flexibility, and vulnerability of these businesses concerning the crisis will be discussed through case studies. The organization of the chapter is as follows: first, the chapter explores the state of the women-owned small business sector in Bangladesh. Second, the chapter investigates the challenges and barriers to women-owned small businesses from a global point of view, followed by crisis survival techniques employed by these firms in response to the COVID crisis. Third, cases from women-owned small businesses in Bangladesh are discussed to understand how these businesses survived the crisis episode and developed resilience. Fourth, the conclusion, recommendations, and future research directions are discussed.

METHODOLOGY

The chapter is designed following a qualitative study approach employing the multiple case study method (Eisenhardt, 1989; Eisenhardt & Graebner, 2007). The reasoning for adopting a qualitative approach with case study design was to attain deeper insights (Wellner & Pierce-Friedman, 2019) and reveal discursive aspects of the COVID-19 phenomenon on the women-owned small enterprises in Bangladesh. The qualitative inquiry was carefully designed using semi-structured in-depth interviews (IDIs), key informant interviews (KIIs), and a review of related literature. Three small enterprises were chosen as cases for the chapter using purposive sampling based on the following criteria: a) categorized as a small enterprise per Bangladesh Bank definition, b) owned by a woman entrepreneur, and c) run on online mode. The reason for selecting online businesses is that women-owned small businesses emerging in the country are primarily operated online. Narrative instrument design was followed to structure the cases. Between August and November 2021, interviews were conducted with the women entrepreneurs and were administered online because of the pandemic. The respondents' identities and their respective businesses have been modified to protect their anonymity (Table 1).

Table 1. Summary of case participants

Case	Ellivera	Twinkle BD	Goynar Haat
Main Products	Imported jewelry, purse, handbag, shoes	Imported beauty, skincare, and fashion accessories	Ethnic locally crafted and imported jewelry
Target Market	Upper and upper middle-class urban women	Upper and upper middle-class urban women	Upper and upper middle-class urban women
Founded	2018	2019	2016
Industry	Import trade	Import trade	Import trade
Sales Channel	Facebook and Instagram	Facebook and Instagram	Facebook and Instagram
Follower count	10,000	15,000	200,000
Respondent	Owner-manager	Owner-manager	Owner-manager

Source: Authors' own

WOMEN-OWNED SMALL BUSINESSES IN BANGLADESH: AN OVERVIEW

Female entrepreneurship has grown worldwide, particularly in developing nations in South Asia (Kunze & Miller, 2017). Bangladesh is among the fastest-growing economies in the region, and its economic development, employment opportunities, and knowledge expansion are heavily reliant on small businesses (Abdin, 2014; ADB, 2016; Yunus, 2017). Like other developing countries, Bangladesh has started concentrating on women's entrepreneurship throughout the last few decades. Women-owned small and medium enterprises (SME) comprise 22 percent of businesses in Bangladesh (Eusuf, 2020) and are primarily involved in the trade, manufacturing, and service sectors. Despite the significant participation, women entrepreneurs fall behind men for several reasons broadly categorized into credit-related, sociocultural, and capacity barriers (Table 2).

First, formal financing opportunities for women-led SME businesses are limited in the country. Obstructions such as unfavorable loan interest rates, guarantor and collateral requirements, complex documentation procedures, high service charges, and non-cooperation by banks hinder women from pursuing formal credit. Commercial banks charge high-interest rates and ask for collateral and guarantors from women entrepreneurs. The society is patriarchal; neither husbands nor other relatives are encouraging enough to become the guarantors that banks require for extending credit. Additionally, limited knowledge and information about credit packages and policies of banks and other lending institutions also act as impediments. For instance, the government and the central bank have established dedicated desks and helplines for women SME enthusiasts, but the information is not widely communicated to the target group. Women entrepreneurs lack sufficient experience to engage in innovative businesses, thus limiting their participation within a few types of ventures such as retail clothing and beauty salons. Banks also harbor a negative perception that women-led SMEs have limited customers and profit potential.

Second, sociocultural constraints add further impediments to women entrepreneurs (Afroze et al., 2015; Islam et al., 2019; Sattar et al., 2016). For example, in a deeply patriarchal society such as Bangladesh, many women do not get enough support (financial or otherwise) from their families to start and continue business activities (Ahmed, 2019; Eusuf, 2020; Shoma, 2019). The stigma around women entrepreneurs is prevalent, and women who own businesses are seen negatively, preferring instead to have them stay at home and help with domestic chores (Chowdhury, 2007). Additionally, uneven family responsibilities and expectations limit women from concentrating fully on business operations, which men seldom face. The issue of discrimination also plays a further role in creating hurdles as suppliers, vendors, and other channel partners harass and threaten women owners to compromise with raw material and product price.

Third, capacity constraints such as lack of managerial experience, limited training, and skill development opportunities restrict women in the country from fully capitalizing on their potential (Ahmed & Chowdhury, 2009). Constraints are further exacerbated by the fact that 24 percent of women SME owners have only a secondary school education, and 67 percent do not have any experience with economic activity (Bangladesh Institute of Development Studies, 2017). Although some facilities for entrepreneurial training are available in the urban areas, rural women seldom have access to these programs. In addition, women SME owners do not have equal access to marketing information as men – they have difficulty penetrating the domestic market and do not know how to break into the export market. Lack of knowledge about marketing promotion activities and available marketing channels creates additional difficulties in successfully running a business. Women-only networks can help these entrepreneurs build the necessary system for support and resource sharing. Still often, these networks are controlled and run by men, thereby limiting the access to support networks. Women entrepreneurs mostly use local and traditional technology to compete with imported products in the domestic market as their access to modern technology is limited (Ahammad & Moudud-ul-Huq, 2013). Several studies suggest that initiatives such as financial assistance, political stability, technological assistance, education and training, research and development facilities, government support, and adequate infrastructural facilities can boost the entrepreneurial environment for women in Bangladesh (Chowdhury, 2007; Chowdhury et al., 2013).

Several public and private institutions offer support services and promote small and medium entrepreneurship for women. These include Bangladesh Small & Cottage Industries Corporation (BSCIC), Women Entrepreneurship Development Programme (WEDP), SME Foundation (SMEF), Micro-Industries Development Assistance & Services (MIDAS), Grameen Bank, Women Entrepreneur Association of Bangladesh (WEA), Jatiya Mohila Sangstha (JMS) and Bangladesh Association of Women in SME (BAWSME).

Table 2. Constraints experienced by women small business owners in Bangladesh

Nature of Constraints	
Access to formal credit	High-interest rates
	Arranging personal guarantor
	Arranging collateral
	Complex documentation
	High service charge
	Non-cooperation from banks
	Lack of information and awareness
Sociocultural barriers	Patriarchal attitude towards women
	Stigma surrounding women entrepreneurs
	Disproportionate family responsibilities and unpaid care
	Gender discrimination
Capacity barriers	Lack of managerial and business experience
	Lack of training and skill development opportunity
	Lack of access to support network
	Lack of access to digital technology
	Knowledge gap
	Limited formal education

Source: (Afroze et al., 2015; Ahammad & Moudud-ul-Huq, 2013; Ahmed & Chowdhury, 2009; Ahmed, 2019; Bangladesh Institute of Development Studies, 2017; Eusuf, 2020; Islam et al., 2019; Sattar et al., 2016; Shoma, 2019; Star Business Report, 2018)

In the pandemic and 'new normal' landscape, pre-existing structural and social barriers, coupled with new challenges emerging from COVID, present a considerable survival threat for women-owned small enterprises. There are commonalities among the findings in the series of studies on women-led small businesses in Bangladesh regarding the challenges emerging from the crisis. For example, a survey by the Asia Foundation (2021) shows that 17 percent of women-led small businesses in Bangladesh completely closed operations in the aftermath of government restrictions (i.e., lockdowns and stay in place orders). More than 50 percent of these enterprises shut down premises to customers, and 22 percent ran operations remotely in a limited capacity. Brac Institute of Governance and Development ran a survey on women-owned online small businesses and found that 49 percent continued operations during government restrictions, whereas 24 percent completely shut down all activities. It can be surmised that online businesses fared better than their non-online counterparts owing to better adaptability (Rabbani et al., 2020). Those engaged in clothing and tailoring performed the best among online businesses, while fashion accessories suffered the most during the crisis.

The reasons for complete shutdown and minimized activities are low demand from customers, shortage of cash flow, and insufficient capital to manage operations. This resulted in substantially low revenue, where 75 percent of owners reported losing at least half of revenue, and 20 percent reported that they suffered a 100 percent revenue loss (Rabanni et al., 2020; The Asia Foundation, 2021). In addition, supply chain disruptions put further stress on the survival of these small enterprises. For example, issues such as lack of customers, delivery troubles, production material unavailability, labor shortage, canceled orders from customers, canceled contracts with suppliers, movement restrictions – created significant challenges. In a chain effect, supply chain problems made the cost of business operation increase manifold – high delivery charge and labor cost, increased rent, payables adjustment, high cost of maintaining covid safety protocols increased production cost. More than 50 percent of women-led businesses reported laying off 76-100 percent employees, and about 33 percent of the owners were unwilling to rehire the lost employees, post-pandemic. It can be interpreted that the women owners do not expect that their business will return to its previous capacity in the new normal.

The Government of Bangladesh announced a loan package worth BDT 20 billion with subsidized interest for CMSME, of which 5.7 percent were designed for women-owned businesses (Sultana, 2021). However, the stimulus package failed to create interest among the intended group for various reasons – lack of information about how to make an application, inconvenient location of the lending institutions, discouragement, and non-cooperation from local and bank officials. In addition, to be eligible for the package, banks required women small business entrepreneurs to be registered with BSCIC/district women chambers, present collateral and personal guarantor, all of which made the application process difficult for entrepreneurs inexperienced with loan procedures (The Asia Foundation, 2021).

WOMEN-OWNED SMALL BUSINESSES AROUND THE WORLD: AN OVERVIEW

The role of entrepreneurship in the socioeconomic development of women is evident worldwide, and entrepreneurial activities have significantly aided their economic growth (Acs & Storey, 2004). Women-owned small businesses have proven to be significant drivers of innovation and employment in developed and developing countries. Investing in women-owned small enterprises pays socioeconomic dividends as women reinvest the revenues to improve communities' health, education, and welfare (WeConnect International, 2020). However, the path of entrepreneurship for women is not devoid of challenges. Disproportionate and inadequate access to resources, gender discrimination, and sociocultural attitude impede women's entrepreneurial success (Fischer et al., 1993; Modarresi et al., 2016; Singh et al., 2010).

Forming a business and growing it is directly proportional to the uninterrupted access to and supply of critical resources such as financial capital (Hill et al., 2006). However, access to finance for women-owned small businesses is limited. Heilbrunn (2004) states that women are less likely to seek growth and external financing; thereby, they are more likely to engage in small service-oriented businesses. Inadequate access to resources, lack of long and short-term financial capital, obstacles in getting bank loans, insufficient cash flow, and lack of savings create challenges for women small business owners (Cesaroni & Sentuti, 2016; Islam et al., 2019; Jennings & Brush, 2013; Maden, 2015; Naguib and Jamali, 2015; Shoma, 2019; Ukonu & Tafamel, 2011). With regards to access to capital, women are disproportionately disadvantaged as compared to men; investors and institutional lenders do not show interest in investing in women-owned small enterprises (Della-Giusta & Phillips, 2006; Leitch et al., 2018; Lindvert et al., 2015; Smith-Hunter & Boyd, 2004). Moreover, women entrepreneurs often struggle to raise capital for running businesses as these are perceived as unattractive traditional retail or service-based ventures by lenders; thus, the women rely on personal savings to start and grow their businesses (De Vita et al., 2014). Women-owned small businesses are denied institutional loans not only because lenders consider the enterprises to be unprofitable, but also because of gender discrimination by the institutions despite the women having similar education, socioeconomic background, and motivation as their male counterparts (Carter, 2000; Marlow & Patton, 2005; Sara & Peter, 1998).

A successful small business requires human capital derived from the entrepreneurs' education, training, skills, employment history, and sociocultural capital (Sara & Peter, 1998). In the case of women-owned businesses, however, a vast array of difficulties creates problems for human capital development. The constraints include lack of access to - education, work experience, employable skills, training, management, business, and technical skills, staff management skills, and information technology (Ghosh & Cheruvalath, 2007; Ghouse et al., 2017; Gobagoba & Littrell, 2003; Isaga, 2019; Ramadani et al., 2015; Rey-Martí et al., 2015; Singh et al., 2010). In addition, women are often socially ghettoized and excluded from high-skilled work in the contemporary economy and more vertically segregated to the lower strata of the career pyramid, which creates the lack of employable skills (Marlow & Carter, 2004). Some of the significant limitations of women entrepreneurs stemming from marginalization include lack of access to training on financial management and business operations, capital management, bookkeeping, market engagement, inability to adapt to technological shifts, lack of industry experience and networking, and insufficient knowledge on hiring and retaining human resources (Brush et al.,

2009; Heilbrunn, 2004; Panda, 2018; Singh & Belwal, 2008). Additionally, gender discrimination, societal and domestic discouragement, family responsibilities, inadequate social networks, and uneven work-life balance play a role in restricting women's entrepreneurial pursuit (Afroze et al., 2015; Ahmed & Chowdhury, 2009; Carter, 2000; Chowdhury, 2007; Fischer et al., 1993; Islam et al., 2019; Marlow & Patton, 2005; Modarresi et al., 2016; Sattar et al., 2016; Shoma, 2019; Singh et al., 2010).

In developing countries, women small business owners face constraints stemming from a multitude of factors. For instance, while African women might not experience family discouragement or obstacles, they would face minimal access to global markets and challenges in the labor market (Kuada, 2009). On the other hand, in Saudi Arabia, the UAE, Turkey, and Lebanon, women's entrepreneurial participation are constrained by religious norms and beliefs, lack of business knowledge, political and economic instability, and domestic dissuasion (Itani et al., 2011; Jamali, 2009; Maden, 2015; Yousuf Danish & Lawton Smith, 2012). Factors such as the wage gap, the need for permission from the dominant male family members, reluctance towards women pursuing entrepreneurial activities involving traveling out of the house and interacting with other men constrain women from achieving business growth in conservative societies. Moreover, women business owners experience high levels of stress generated from playing multiple overlapping roles simultaneously, such as mother, wife, household caretaker, and business owner. According to Brush et al. (2009), motherhood impacts women entrepreneurs more than men, while Smallbone & Welter (2001) argue that this phenomenon might differ from the perspective of country and society. Perception against women as being less capable, less committed, and less credible, and patriarchal culture act as significant constraints towards their success (Ghosh et al., 2017; Itani et al., 2011; Jamali, 2009; Lourenço et al., 2014; Naguib & Jamali, 2015; Ramadani et al., 2015).

In addition to sociocultural barriers, legal and regulatory challenges such as unfavorable economic conditions and inadequate knowledge on property rights and commercial law hinder women's growth as entrepreneurs across the developed and developing economies (Ahmed & Chowdhury, 2009; Ghosh & Cheruvalath, 2007; Mordi et al., 2010; Oluyombo & Ogundimu, 2006; Singh et al., 2010). High tax rates, high competition, rigid male-biased regulations, corruption, economic recession, vague legal structure, and bureaucracy are the most common hindrances towards women entrepreneurship across the developing economies (Jamali, 2009; Maden, 2015; O. Ama et al., 2014; Panda, 2018; Yousuf Danish & Lawton Smith, 2012).

Table 3. Summary of constraints for women-owned small businesses

Nature of Constraints Identified in Literature		References
Financial	Credit gap	(Cesaroni & Sentuti, 2016); (De Vita et al., 2014); (Heilbrunn, 2004); (Hill et al., 2006); (Islam et al., 2019); (Jennings & Brush, 2013); (Leitch et al., 2018); (Lindvert et al., 2015); (Maden, 2015); (Naguib and Jamali, 2015); (Shoma, 2019); (Smith-Hunter & Boyd, 2004); (Ukonu & Tafamel, 2011).
	Barriers to institutional lending	
	Liquidity issues	
Structural	Access to education	(Brush et al., 2009); (Carter, 2000); (Ghosh & Cheruvalath, 2007); (Ghouse et al., 2017); (Gobagoba & Littrell, 2003); (Heilbrunn, 2004); (Isaga, 2019); (Marlow & Carter, 2004); (Marlow & Patton, 2005); (Panda, 2018); (Ramadani et al., 2015); (Rey-Martí et al., 2015); (Sara & Peter, 1998); (Singh & Belwal, 2008); (Singh et al., 2010).
	Lack of work experience	
	Lack of employable skills and training opportunities	
	Lack of management and business skills	
	Lack of staff management skills	
	Lack of access to business knowledge	
	Lack of access to information technology and digitalization	
Social	Gender discrimination	(Afroze et al., 2015); (Ahmed & Chowdhury, 2009); (Ghosh et al., 2017); (Islam et al., 2019); (Itani et al., 2011); (Jamali, 2009); (Kuada, 2009); (Lourenço et al., 2014); (Maden, 2015); (Marlow & Patton, 2005); (Modarresi et al., 2016); (Naguib & Jamali, 2015); (Ramadani et al., 2015); (Sattar et al., 2016); (Shoma, 2019); (Singh et al., 2010); (Smallbone & Welter, 2001); (Yousuf Danish & Lawton Smith, 2012).
	Societal and domestic discouragement	
	Religious and cultural norms and beliefs	
	Uneven family responsibilities	
	Limited social and business networks	
	Patriarchy	
	Wage gap	
	Uneven work-life balance	
Legal and Regulatory	Lack of Property Rights	(Ahmed & Chowdhury, 2009); (Ghosh & Cheruvalath, 2007); (Jamali, 2009); (Maden, 2015); (Mordi et al., 2010); (O. Ama et al., 2014); (Oluyombo & Ogundimu, 2006); (Panda, 2018); (Singh et al., 2010); (Yousuf Danish & Lawton Smith, 2012).
	Unfavorable Economic Condition	
	High Tax Rates	
	Rigid Male-Biased Regulations	
	Corruption	
	Bureaucracy	

Source: Authors' compilation from the literature

WOMEN-OWNED SMALL BUSINESSES AND COVID-19

The COVID-19 pandemic has caused widespread socioeconomic problems worldwide, with notably detrimental repercussions on society's most vulnerable members, including female entrepreneurs who are significantly prone to its impacts and have suffered considerably from macroeconomic transitions (Federici, 2018; Martinez Dy & Jayawarna, 2020). While many small businesses may remain temporarily closed to abide by social distancing limitations, policy mandates, health issues, and other preventive factors, many of them may remain closed indefinitely due to the owners' inability to pay the ongoing expenses (Fairlie, 2020). Previous literature has indicated that female entrepreneurs are disadvantaged and more adversely affected in several ways during economic downturns and natural disasters such as the COVID-19 pandemic and are more prone to take a defensive crisis response attitude (Cesaroni et al., 2018). The COVID-19 has highlighted the gender differentials between men and women-owned micro, small and medium enterprises (MSMEs) in terms of disproportionate impact. For example, Goldstein et al. (2020) state that in the Sub-Saharan African countries, 43 percent of women-led MSMEs were temporarily closed during the pandemic compared to only 34 percent male-led MSMEs. Women-owned MSMEs are more likely to be involved in consumer-oriented sectors (retail, service, hospitality) such as education, childcare, and wellness, personal grooming, sports, and fitness services that faced the most significant impact of the demand shock.

According to Manolova et al. (2020), the global pandemic has created three significant challenges for small business owners. First, the industries owned by the majority of female entrepreneurs have been disproportionately affected by the recession. Second, women operate many of the smallest and most vulnerable enterprises. Third, with educational institutes closing and elderly family members under health risk, women are more likely to balance responsibilities and priorities such as homemaking and business survival. With revenues declining during the pandemic, the literature further identifies actions taken by female entrepreneurs such as reducing and delaying pay, reducing employee hours, shutting down the business temporarily/permanently, moving employee status and layoffs, seeking alternative income, and rehiring vendors at a lower rate (Manolova et al., 2020). Studies claim that women are less likely to seek equity capital than men (Rosa & Sylla, 2018). Moreover, financial institutions have become cautious with lending female entrepreneurs questioning their "credibility" regarding funding decisions like mortgage repayment (Grandy et al., 2020).

Female entrepreneurs have adopted several crisis management techniques to survive and thrive through economic efforts and innovation strategies. In their efforts to compensate for the loss, female entrepreneurs often choose digital media to offer new products and services; employ online marketing; apply for soft loans at microfinance institutions; adopt cash management strategies such as reducing utility and inventory costs, removing the extras, reducing wasteful discretionary expenses (Anderson et al., 2014; Francesca et al., 2017; Sultan & Sultan, 2020).

As a part of the preparation for the first few months of surviving the Covid-19 pandemic, women-owned small enterprises focused on the existing inventory and cash-on-hand to cover the running payroll and expenses. Most women owners adopted temporary or permanent business adjustments to survive the crisis by marketing and promoting in unconventional ways, such as showcasing products on Facebook Live and other social media platforms to increase customer engagement and sales (Manolova et al., 2020; Sultan & Sultan, 2020). Although some considered temporary or permanent business closure, most focused on understanding the changing customer needs and reshaping and transforming their traditional business models by shifting online (Afshan et al., 2021; Jaim, 2020). Although the sudden decrease in customers' disposal income led to the permanent closure of many, others relied on their savings to address business expenses (Mustafa et al., 2021).

Most women entrepreneurs sought alternative business ideas that they could run and manage from home. Studies revealed that women entrepreneurs of developing countries like Bangladesh lack adequate skills to operate a business and the Covid-19 pandemic enhanced the pre-existing barriers for these women resulting in a decrease in customers, networks, and recurring financial loss (Brickell et al., 2020; Mishra & Rampal, 2020; Mustafa et al., 2021). Operating a business online means delivering products through a delivery organization, and delivery charges became higher than ever before during the pandemic in developing countries like Bangladesh. Support from the family played a dual role here. For instance, a household that owned a private vehicle would allow the women entrepreneurs to deliver the products by their cars/bikes to help reduce the delivery cost and maintain the profit margin. At the same time, however, women hardly drive a car or ride a motorcycle in Bangladesh, which makes them dependent on their husbands. In these cases, women entrepreneurs faced survival issues with their businesses followed by their skill inadequacy which directly relates to their gender and puts them in a disadvantageous position (Barragan et al., 2018; Constantinidis et al., 2019; Jaim, 2020).

Table 4. Summary of crisis management techniques adopted by women-owned small businesses

Crisis Management Techniques Identified in Literature	References
Temporary/permanent business closure	(Afshan et al., 2021); (Brickell et al., 2020); (Cesaroni et al., 2018); (Constantinidis et al., 2019); (Jaim, 2020); (Manolova et al., 2020); (Mishra & Rampal, 2020); (Mustafa et al., 2021); (Sultan & Sultan, 2020).
Micro-credit loans	
Personal savings	
Delaying accounts payable	
Reducing employee hours	
Temporary employees and layoffs	
Alternate sources of income and substituting vendors	
Digital adoption (social media and e-commerce)	
Reducing utility and inventory costs	
Reducing non-essential costs	
Family support	
Personal Vehicles for making deliveries	

Source: Authors' compilation from the literature

SURVIVING AMID COVID-19 CRISIS EPISODE: CASE STUDIES

This section illustrates cases that were developed using semi-structured in-depth interviews with female small business owners in Bangladesh. Online small enterprises owned by women in the informal sector were purposely selected instead of large e-commerce ones for two reasons. First, online purchasing has become a convenient form of purchase for many buyers, particularly in the COVID-19 environment. Second, small businesses offer greater flexibility to downsize and avoid significant losses in crisis episodes. However, because they operated in the informal sector, these women entrepreneurs had little resilience and no support network to help them recover from the shock.

The cases presented here describe the survival and crisis management of the businesses in response to the impact of the COVID-19 pandemic and their resilience to sustain through crisis periods.

Case 1: Ellivera

Since 2018, Somi has been running a thriving fashion accessory business called "Ellivera" on Facebook and Instagram. Ellivera targets women and sells fashion accessories such as jewelry, purses, and shoes imported from India, Pakistan, China, Malaysia, Thailand, the United States, and the United Kingdom through its Facebook and Instagram pages. Ellivera already had a stable customer base of approximately 50000 followers before the onset of COVID-19.

As lockdowns began, the pandemic's immediate impact on Somi's business became clear. Somi was put under severe duress by a quick fall in sales, import restrictions, and order cancellations. Somi lost around 70% of her sales volume during the pandemic's first seven to eight months. Additionally, because she could not import new items, the number of orders placed decreased, and several customers canceled previous orders. Stocked in preparation for the festival season (Eid Ul Fitr, Bengali New Year), the merchandise remained largely unsold.

All these immediate effects resulted in a cascade of domino effects. For instance, cash flow insufficiency struck severely because Somi's investments were tied up in import orders that she could not fulfill. Additionally, Somi was required to continue paying staff salaries, rent, and utilities. Further, customer engagement on her social media sites plummeted, and she lost around 50% of her followers. She temporarily shut down her business for about five months; no new posts were made, although the page was active. Somi believes that the absence of new items and collections contributed to losing followers, as constantly uploading new products is critical for maintaining customer engagement with the business page.

Since 2021, as people adjusted to the "new normal," Somi reports that her business has improved significantly, to the point where her sales volume has now reached pre-covid levels and is on track to surpass them. She attributes her survival and crisis resolution to a variety of tactics she employed. She began paying for promotions and page boosting on her Facebook and Instagram sites to increase customer reach as soon as the "new normal" became the norm and import restrictions were relaxed. Second, she initiated stock clearing and sales promotion programs to boost customer involvement and recoup lost revenue. Additionally, maintaining frequent contact with customers aided her in preserving the goodwill that eventually culminated in excellent word of mouth.

She began the business with personal savings and supplemented it with loans from relatives when necessary. Somi has not yet sought institutional financing but intends to do so in the future. She is a member of the Facebook group "WE" for female business owners.

Case 2: Twinkle BD

Lamia founded Twinkle BD on Facebook in 2019, offering imported beauty, skincare, and fashion accessories from the UK. The business model follows a pre-order system. She places orders for imported products only after receiving confirmation from her customers. Before the lockdown, Lamia steadily grew her customer and follower base and earned between 80,000 and 100,000 BDT per month. However, due to the lockdowns, cargo flights between the UK and Bangladesh were limited. Lamia was forced to cancel new orders, and her pending shipments were delayed for five months. Lamia, as a result, lost almost 50% of her followers and frequent customers. After lockdowns were eased and cargo flights resumed, Lamia began accepting orders, although freight shipment costs had tripled. Lamia saw that several of her usual customers had stopped placing orders after adjusting for the increased shipping costs.

According to Lamia, all other competitors increased their pricing in response to higher freight expenses. To stay afloat, Lamia prioritized retaining existing customers and page followers above acquiring new ones. She lowered the prices of all her products by keeping a negligible markup and earning a minimal profit. Lamia explains that when customers saw that product prices had increased across the platform and Twinkle BD was the only business offering the lowest pricing, they returned to Twinkle BD, and she garnered new followers. Additionally, she advertised flash sales on popular products to attract customers. She asserts that she is now virtually back to pre-COVID revenue levels and is optimistic about the future regardless of future pandemic waves.

Lamia began her firm with a loan from her husband. For day-to-day working capital financing, she takes loans from her husband and relatives if needed. While she is not a member of any professional organization, she is an active member of several Facebook-based entrepreneurs' groups and attends their fairs regularly.

Case 3: Goynar Haat

Hosna founded Goynar Haat, a Facebook shop selling ethnic and imported fashion jewelry, in 2016. Since then, Goynar Haat has amassed over 200,000 Facebook and Instagram followers and focuses on upper- and upper-middle-class women in Bangladesh's urban districts. Hosna encountered difficulties importing jewelry from India during the lockdown, owing to limitations and the lack of freight flights. Freight rates had skyrocketed, and shipment delays were generating supply chain problems. As a result, Hosna relocated her sourcing to China and expanded her product line with Chinese jewelry. Additionally, Hosna maintained sales during the initial lockdown because she had sufficient imported Indian jewelry in stock and placed new orders for ethnic jewelry with her local designers. At first, sales were slow due to customers' hesitation and uncertainty, but Hosna gained customer confidence by hosting sales sessions on Facebook and Instagram Live.

After the lockdowns were lifted, Hosna focused on selling ethnic jewelry created locally, as she detected a shift in client preference toward traditional local jewelry.

Hosna founded Goynar Haat with her savings and a family loan. When she needs financing, she leans on her family for loans rather than institutional financing. She is an active member of a few Facebook-based entrepreneurs' groups and regularly attends their fairs and training.

Table 5. Summary of survival strategy and resilience

Case	Survival Strategy	Resilience			
		Adaptability	**Agility**	**Flexibility**	**Vulnerability**
Ellivera	• Increase social media visibility • Discount and sales promotion • Temporary closure • Page boosting and paid promotion	Moderate	Moderate	Low	High
Twinkle BD	• Increase social media visibility • Discount and sales promotion • Page boosting and paid promotion	Moderate	Moderate	Low	High
Goynar Haat	• Increase social media visibility • Discount and sales promotion • Alternate sourcing • Product basket change • Facebook and Instagram Live	Moderate	Moderate	Moderate	High

Source: Authors' own

CONCLUSION AND RECOMMENDATION

In the face of a prolonged crisis, small enterprises in the informal sector become the most vulnerable owing to limited access to formal sources of financing, fewer employees, limited risk and insurance management, and limited access to market opportunities (Rabbani et al., 2020). The cases presented in this chapter show that the women-owned small businesses were initially negatively affected; however, they quickly could bounce back from the loss and are almost reaching their pre-pandemic status quo in the "new normal".

Mohan and Rollo (2020) identified four phases that small businesses would travel through during this pandemic either simultaneously or successively: semi or complete shutdown of economic activities, disruptions in the supply chain, a decline in demand, and recovery. From the discussion in this chapter, it is evident that the businesses have already gone through the first three phases and are now in sharp rebound (Case 1, 2, and 3). COVID-19 initially dealt a heavy financial blow to the women-owned small businesses. Given that the early months of COVID-19 and subsequent lockdowns coincided with the peak festival season in Bangladesh (Bengali New Year and Eid) when jewelry and fashion accessories are in the highest demand, the loss of revenue was significant (Case 1, 2, and 3). Simultaneously, knock-on effects included liquidity crisis (Case 1), loss of customers and followers (Case 1 and 2), supply chain interruption (Case 1, 2, and 3), shipment delays (Case 1, 2, and 3), increased freight costs (Case 2 and 3), unsold inventory (Case 1), and order cancellations (Case 1). The severity of the impact on these businesses likely depended on the age of business, size, follower count, owner characteristics and customer trust, and product novelty. For example, Case 3 (Goynar Haat) was least affected by the crisis than the other two presented in the chapter, although the product offerings are similar. Such discrepancy can be attributed to the reason that Case 3 has been in operation for much longer (since 2016) and has developed a large base of loyal and frequent customers in addition to selling locally made ethnic jewelry, which the other two do not have.

To recover from the crisis impacts, the entrepreneurs attempted several response mechanisms. The predominant strategy was to control damage through increasing social media visibility (Case 1, 2, and 3), selling the stock at discounts, running sales promotions (Case 1, 2, and 3), choosing alternate vendors and partners (Case 3), modifying product basket (Case 3), temporary inactivity (Case 1), adopting innovative marketing approaches including Page boosting (Case 1, 2 and 3), Facebook and Instagram Live (Case 3). Although the businesses incurred losses during the Eid and festive seasons in 2020, they quickly adjusted to the "new normal" as they better understood how to respond. By 2021, they have almost reached their pre-pandemic levels of revenue (Case 1, 2, and 3).

The sharp rebound of the businesses is partly due to online existence and urban upper and upper-middle-class customers. Online shopping over social media platforms is now the most favored shopping mode among the urban population in Dhaka. It allows for social distancing and doorstep delivery of products with minimal human contact. Moreover, these online small businesses have low overheads, with zero marketing and sales barrier – therefore can quickly scale down if needed. In addition, as soon as the initial containment measures were eased in the country, the urban customers started placing orders to make up for the lost purchase opportunities combined with lucrative discounts from the sellers.

The entrepreneurs discussed in the chapter belong to the informal sector, with no formal business registration and identity. Such a status makes them ineligible for the stimulus package for CMSMEs by the Government of Bangladesh. During episodes of crisis when the businesses are losing sales, financial support is essential. The entrepreneurs sustained their businesses with informal finance, depending on personal funds (Case 1, 2, and 3) and help from family and relatives (Case 1, 2, and

3). It indicates that women-owned informal online small businesses have weak links to the institutional financing system in the country. Additionally, they do not have access to government or non-government agencies for institutional support; however, they have their own network for non-financial support. The female entrepreneurs are part of several Facebook-based entrepreneur forums and groups (Case 1, 2, and 3) where they seek guidance, advice, and essential business information and know-how from fellow business owners. They attend training programs, webinars to learn business skills and knowledge and participate in fairs and events organized by the forums.

Erol et al. (2020) characterize the resilience of a business to survive crises by adaptability, agility, flexibility, and vulnerability. Rabanni et al. (2020) assess adaptability, agility, and flexibility through survival mechanisms, income status, and changes made in the business, respectively. Vulnerability is appraised by the preparedness of the business to endure a crisis (i.e., nature of business, access to financial and non-financial support). The cases presented here show that the enterprises have moderate levels of adaptability and agility with a low level of flexibility (Table 5). For instance, adopting several immediate response mechanisms to sustain the business through the crisis and recovering the lost revenue through those strategies indicate adaptability and agility. The businesses have not made any significant change in how they operate the business or in the business model in response to the crisis, except for selecting new sourcing vendors (Case 3) – thereby suggesting low flexibility for Case 1 and 2. In terms of vulnerability, the businesses are highly vulnerable as they lack any institutional financial assistance and formal support network due to their informal nature.

Several policy recommendations for policymakers and regulators can be suggested in light of the findings. First, since October 2021, as per a decision by the Government of Bangladesh, all e-commerce businesses must register with the Ministry of Commerce and deposit a security amount in Bangladesh Bank to run their operation as part of robust monitoring and regulation program of online businesses by the government. However, it is unclear if the f-commerce businesses would fall under this program. Therefore, developing an all-inclusive policy that places all online businesses, especially those on social media platforms, would enable small businesses to enter the formal economy and credit system. Second, business network and support platforms such as the E-commerce Association of Bangladesh (e-CAB) can extend its membership to the female small business entrepreneurs engaged in online businesses and assist them in payment gateway, product delivery, e-security, digital marketing, and representing their rights and interests. Third, lending institutions such as banks and non-bank financial institutions can design customized credit and banking solutions for women-led small online businesses as a source of a potentially untapped market. Fourth, making the import and customs process easier and international freight affordable for businesses engaged in import trade would enable the businesses to operate with less paperwork and red tape.

FUTURE RESEARCH DIRECTIONS

The chapter contains crucial information and insight about how the women-led small enterprises have survived the COVID-19 shock and their resilience to the crisis. Yet, some limitations remain that point the way forward for future exploration. The sample size is limited to a few women entrepreneurs, rendering it inadequately representative of the small business sector and limiting the generalization of the conclusions. Thus, future research might include more significant sample size and a panel design to better understand the small enterprises' resilience in a pre-pandemic and pandemic comparison.

REFERENCES

Abdin, M. (2014). Vision-2021: The role of small and medium enterprises in Bangladesh economy. SSRN *Electronic Journal*. doi:10.2139/ssrn.2465763

Acs, Z., & Storey, D. (2004). Introduction: Entrepreneurship and economic development. *Regional Studies, 38*(8), 871–877. doi:10.1080/0034340042000280901

ADB. (2016). *ADB to provide loans to SMEs, women entrepreneurs in rural Bangladesh*. https://www.adb.org/news/adb-provide-loanssmes-women-entrepreneurs-rural-bangladesh

Afroze, T., Alam, M., Akther, E., & Jui, N. (2015). Women entrepreneurs in Bangladesh- challenges and determining factors. *Journal Of Business and Technology, 9*(2), 27–41. doi:10.3329/jbt.v9i2.26194

Afshan, G., Shahid, S., & Tunio, M. (2021). Learning experiences of women entrepreneurs amidst COVID-19. *International Journal of Gender and Entrepreneurship, 13*(2), 162–186. doi:10.1108/IJGE-09-2020-0153

Ahammad, I., & Moudud-Ul-Huq, S. (2013). Women entrepreneurship development in Bangladesh challenges and prospects. *International Journal of Innovative Research and Development, 2*(7), 41–48. https://www.researchgate.net/publication/281115595

Ahmed, K., & Chowdhury, T. (2009). Performance evaluation of SMEs of Bangladesh. *International Journal of Business and Management, 4*(7), 126–133. doi:10.5539/ijbm.v4n7p126

Ahmed, N. (2019). SME: Challenges women entrepreneurs face. *The Financial Express*. https://www.thefinancialexpress.com.bd/views/sme-challenges-women-entrepreneurs-face-1551886089

Alauddin, M., & Chowdhury, M. M. (2015). Small and medium enterprise in Bangladesh – prospects and challenges. *Global Journal of Management and Business Research*, *15*(7), 1–10.

Ama, N., Mangadi, K., & Ama, H. (2014). Exploring the challenges facing women entrepreneurs in informal cross-border trade in Botswana. *Gender in Management*, *29*(8), 505–522. doi:10.1108/GM-02-2014-0018

Anderson, N., Potočnik, K., & Zhou, J. (2014). Innovation and creativity in organizations. *Journal of Management*, *40*(5), 1297–1333. doi:10.1177/0149206314527128

Asian Development Bank. (2020). Asian Development Bank Member Fact Sheet. Metro Manila: Asian Development Bank.

Asian Development Bank. (2021). *Bangladesh and ADB*. Retrieved from Asian Development Bank: https://www.adb.org/countries/bangladesh/economy

Bangladesh Institute of Development Studies. (2017). *Women Entrepreneurs in SMEs: Bangladesh Perspective 2017*. Retrieved from https%3A%2F%2Fthink-asia.org%2Fbitstream%2Fhandle%2F11540%2F9681%2FSummary_SME_women_entrepreneur_nazneen_27-12-18.pdf%3Fsequence%3D1

Barragan, S., Erogul, M., & Essers, C. (2018). 'Strategic (dis)obedience': Female entrepreneurs reflecting on and acting upon patriarchal practices. *Gender, Work and Organization*, *25*(5), 575–592. doi:10.1111/gwao.12258

Brickell, K., Picchioni, F., Natarajan, N., Guermond, V., Parsons, L., Zanello, G., & Bateman, M. (2020). Compounding crises of social reproduction: Microfinance, over-indebtedness and the COVID-19 pandemic. *World Development*, *136*, 105087. doi:10.1016/j.worlddev.2020.105087 PMID:32834384

Brush, C., de Bruin, A., & Welter, F. (2009). A gender-aware framework for women's entrepreneurship. *International Journal of Gender and Entrepreneurship*, *1*(1), 8–24. doi:10.1108/17566260910942318

Carter, S. (2000). Improving the numbers and performance of women-owned businesses: Some implications for training and advisory services. *Education + Training*, *42*(4/5), 326–334. doi:10.1108/00400910010373732

Cesaroni, F., Pediconi, M., & Sentuti, A. (2018). It's always a women's problem! micro-entrepreneurs, work-family balance, and economic crisis. *Administrative Sciences*, *8*(4), 74. doi:10.3390/admsci8040074

Cesaroni, F., & Sentuti, A. (2016). Economic crisis, women entrepreneurs and bank loans: Some empirical evidence from Italy. *Economic Research-Ekonomska Istraživanja*, *29*(1), 1050–1061. doi:10.1080/1331677X.2016.1211953

Chowdhury, M. (2007). Overcoming entrepreneurship development constraints: The case of Bangladesh. *Journal Of Enterprising Communities: People and Places in The Global Economy*, *1*(3), 240–251. doi:10.1108/17506200710779549

Chowdhury, M., Alam, Z., & Arif, M. (2013). Success factors of entrepreneurs of small and medium sized enterprises: Evidence from Bangladesh. *Business and Economic Review*, *3*(2), 38. doi:10.5296/ber.v3i2.4127

Constantinidis, C., Lebègue, T., El Abboubi, M., & Salman, N. (2019). How families shape women's entrepreneurial success in Morocco: An intersectional study. *International Journal of Entrepreneurial Behaviour & Research*, *25*(8), 1786–1808. doi:10.1108/IJEBR-12-2017-0501

Davidsson, P., & Gordon, S. R. (2016). Much ado about nothing? The surprising persistence of nascent entrepreneurs through macroeconomic crisis. *Entrepreneurship Theory and Practice*, *40*(4), 915–941. doi:10.1111/etap.12152

De Vita, L., Mari, M., & Poggesi, S. (2014). Women entrepreneurs in and from developing countries: Evidences from the literature. *European Management Journal*, *32*(3), 451–460. doi:10.1016/j.emj.2013.07.009

Della-Giusta, M., & Phillips, C. (2006). Women entrepreneurs in the Gambia: Challenges and opportunities. *Journal of International Development*, *18*(8), 1051–1064. doi:10.1002/jid.1279

Devece, C., Peris-Ortiz, M., & Rueda-Armengot, C. (2016). Entrepreneurship during economic crisis: Success factors and paths to failure. *Journal of Business Research*, *69*(11), 5366–5370. doi:10.1016/j.jbusres.2016.04.139

Dhar, S., Farzana, T., & Abedin, S. S. (2021). Impact, Reaction, and Learning from Overcoming the COVID-19 Crisis: Cases From Small-Scale Businesses in Bangladesh. In S. Stephens (Ed.), *Cases on Small Business Economics and Development During Economic Crises* (pp. 27–51). IGI Global. doi:10.4018/978-1-7998-7657-1.ch002

Eisenhardt, K. M. (1989). Building Theories from Case Study Research. *Academy of Management Review*, *14*(4), 532–550. doi:10.2307/258557

Eisenhardt, K. M., & Graebner, M. E. (2007). Theory Building from Cases: Opportunities and challenges. *Academy of Management Journal*, *50*(1), 25–32. doi:10.5465/amj.2007.24160888

Erol, O., Sauser, B. J., & Mansouri, M. (2010). A framework for investigation into extended enterprise resilience. *Enterprise Information Systems*, *4*(2), 111–136. doi:10.1080/17517570903474304

Eusuf, M. A. (2020). The challenges faced by women-led SMEs and the way forward. *The Daily Star*. https://www.thedailystar.net/round-tables/news/the-challenges-faced-women-led-smes-and-the-way-forward-1848013

Fairlie, R. (2020). The impact of COVID-19 on small business owners: Evidence from the first three months after widespread social-distancing restrictions. *Journal of Economics & Management Strategy*, *29*(4), 727–740. doi:10.1111/jems.12400 PMID:32904856

Federici, S. (2018). *Witches, witch-hunting, and women*. PM Press.

Fischer, E., Reuber, A., & Dyke, L. (1993). A theoretical overview and extension of research on sex, gender, and entrepreneurship. *Journal of Business Venturing*, *8*(2), 151–168. doi:10.1016/0883-9026(93)90017-Y

Francesca, M., Paola, D., & Paola, P. (2017). Women in business and social media: Implications for female entrepreneurship in emerging countries. *African Journal of Business Management*, *11*(14), 316–326. doi:10.5897/AJBM2017.8281

Ghosh, P., & Cheruvalath, R. (2007). Indian female entrepreneurs as catalysts for economic growth and development. *International Journal of Entrepreneurship and Innovation*, *8*(2), 139–147. doi:10.5367/000000007780808048

Ghosh, P., Ghosh, S., & Chowdhury, S. (2017). Factors hindering women entrepreneurs' access to institutional finance- an empirical study. *Journal of Small Business and Entrepreneurship*, *30*(4), 279–291. doi:10.1080/08276331.2017.1388952

Ghouse, S., McElwee, G., Meaton, J., & Durrah, O. (2017). Barriers to rural women entrepreneurs in Oman. *International Journal of Entrepreneurial Behaviour & Research*, *23*(6), 998–1016. doi:10.1108/IJEBR-02-2017-0070

Gobagoba, M., & Littrell, M. (2003). Profiling micro apparel enterprises in Botswana: Motivations, practices, challenges, and success. *Clothing & Textiles Research Journal*, *21*(3), 130–141. doi:10.1177/0887302X0302100303

Goldstein, M., Martinez, P. G., Papineni, S., & Wimpey, J. (2020). *The global state of small business during COVID-19: Gender inequalities.* World Bank Blogs. https://blogs.worldbank.org/developmenttalk/global-state-small-business-during-covid-19-gender-inequalities

Grandy, G., Cukier, W., & Gagnon, S. (2020). (In)visibility in the margins: COVID-19, women entrepreneurs and the need for inclusive recovery. *Gender in Management, 35*(7/8), 667–675. doi:10.1108/GM-07-2020-0207

Heilbrunn, S. (2004). Impact of gender on difficulties faced by entrepreneurs. *International Journal of Entrepreneurship and Innovation, 5*(3), 159–165. doi:10.5367/0000000041513420

Hill, F., Leitch, C., & Harrison, R. (2006). 'Desperately seeking finance?' The demand for finance by women-owned and led businesses. *Venture Capital, 8*(2), 159-182. doi:10.1080/13691060600555347

IFC. (2014). *Women-owned SMEs: A business opportunity for financial institutions.* https%3A%2F%2Fwww.ifc.org%2Fwps%2Fwcm%2Fconnect%2F44b004b2-ed46-48fc-8ade-aa0f485069a1%2FWomenOwnedSMes%2BReportFinal.pdf%3FMOD%3DAJPERES%26CVID%3DkiiZZDZ

Isaga, N. (2019). Start-up motives and challenges facing female entrepreneurs in Tanzania. *International Journal of Gender and Entrepreneurship, 11*(2), 102–119. doi:10.1108/IJGE-02-2018-0010

Islam, M., Jantan, A., Hunt, A., Rahman, M., & Abdullah, M. (2019). Exploration of barriers faced by female graduate entrepreneurs in Bangladesh. *Entrepreneurship And Sustainability Issues, 7*(2), 1000–1014. doi:10.9770/jesi.2019.7.2(15)

Itani, H., Sidani, Y., & Baalbaki, I. (2011). United Arab Emirates female entrepreneurs: Motivations and frustrations. *Equality, Diversity and Inclusion, 30*(5), 409–424. doi:10.1108/02610151111150654

Jaim, J. (2020). Exist or exit? Women business-owners in Bangladesh during COVID-19. *Gender, Work and Organization, 28*(S1), 209–226. doi:10.1111/gwao.12546

Jamali, D. (2009). Constraints and opportunities facing women entrepreneurs in developing countries. *Gender in Management, 24*(4), 232–251. doi:10.1108/17542410910961532

Jennings, J., & Brush, C. (2013). Research on women entrepreneurs: Challenges to (and from) the broader entrepreneurship literature. *The Academy of Management Annals*, *7*(1), 663–715. doi:10.5465/19416520.2013.782190

Karadag, H. (2015). Financial management challenges in small and medium-sized enterprises: A strategic management approach. *EMAJ: Emerging Markets Journal*, *5*(1), 26–40. doi:10.5195/EMAJ.2015.67

Kaya, S., & Alpkan, L. (2012). Problems and solution proposals for SMEs in Turkey. *Emerging Markets Journal*, *2*(2), 178-196. doi:10.5195/EMAJ.2012.26

Khalil, T. (2020, August 11). The impact of COVID-19 on small businesses. *The Daily Star*. https://www.thedailystar.net/lifestyle/news/the-impact-covid-19-small-businesses-1942713

Kuada, J. (2009). Gender, Social Networks, and Entrepreneurship in Ghana. *Journal of African Business*, *10*(1), 85–103. doi:10.1080/15228910802701445

Kumar, V., & Gupta, G. (Eds.). (2021). *Strategic Management During a Pandemic*. Routledge. doi:10.4324/9781003125648

Kumar, V., & Malhotra, G. (Eds.). (2021). *Stakeholder Strategies for Reducing the Impact of Global Health Crises*. IGI – Global Publications. doi:10.4018/978-1-7998-7495-9

Kumar, V., Nanda, P., & Tawangar, S. (2022). Social Media in Business Decisions of MSMES: Practices and Challenges. *International Journal of Decision Support System Technology*, *14*(1), 1–12. doi:10.4018/IJDSST.286686

Kumar, V., & Vidhyalakshmi, P. (2012). Cloud computing for business sustainability. *Asia-Pacific Journal of Management Research and Innovation*, *8*(4), 461–474. doi:10.1177/2319510X13481905

Kunze, A., & Miller, A. (2017). Women helping women? Evidence from private sector data on workplace hierarchies. *The Review of Economics and Statistics*, *99*(5), 769–775. doi:10.1162/REST_a_00668

Leitch, C., Welter, F., & Henry, C. (2018). Women entrepreneurs' financing revisited: Taking stock and looking forward. *Venture Capital*, *20*(2), 103–114. doi:10.1080/13691066.2018.1418624

Lindvert, M., Yazdanfar, D., & Boter, H. (2015). Perceptions of financial sources among women entrepreneurs in Tanzania. *African Journal of Economic and Management Studies*, *6*(2), 197–218. doi:10.1108/AJEMS-10-2013-0090

Lourenço, F., Sappleton, N., Dardaine-Edwards, A., McElwee, G., Cheng, R., & Taylor, D., & Taylor, A. (2014). Experience of entrepreneurial training for female farmers to stimulate entrepreneurship in Uganda. *Gender in Management, 29*(7), 382–401. doi:10.1108/GM-05-2013-0054

Maden, C. (2015). A gendered lens on entrepreneurship: Women entrepreneurship in Turkey. *Gender in Management, 30*(4), 312–331. doi:10.1108/GM-11-2013-0131

Manolova, T., Brush, C., Edelman, L., & Elam, A. (2020). Pivoting to stay the course: How women entrepreneurs take advantage of opportunities created by the COVID-19 pandemic. *International Small Business Journal: Researching Entrepreneurship, 38*(6), 481–491. doi:10.1177/0266242620949136 PMID:35125599

Marlow, S., & Carter, S. (2004). Accounting for change: Professional status, gender disadvantage and self-employment. *Women in Management Review, 19*(1), 5–17. doi:10.1108/09649420410518395

Marlow, S., & Patton, D. (2005). All credit to men? Entrepreneurship, finance, and gender. *Entrepreneurship Theory and Practice, 29*(6), 717–735. doi:10.1111/j.1540-6520.2005.00105.x

Martinez Dy, A., & Jayawarna, D. (2020). Bios, mythoi and women entrepreneurs: A Wynterian analysis of the intersectional impacts of the COVID-19 pandemic on self-employed women and women-owned businesses. *International Small Business Journal: Researching Entrepreneurship, 38*(5), 391–403. doi:10.1177/0266242620939935

Mazumder, A., & Alharahsheh, H. (2019). Key challenges and barriers facing small and medium enterprises (SMEs) in Bangladesh. *South Asian Journal of Business Management, 1*(3), 118–120. doi:10.36346arjbm.2019.v01i03.005

Mishra, K., & Rampal, J. (2020). The COVID-19 pandemic and food insecurity: A viewpoint on India. *World Development, 135*, 105068. doi:10.1016/j.worlddev.2020.105068

Modarresi, M., Arasti, Z., Talebi, K., & Farasatkhah, M. (2016). Women's entrepreneurship in Iran. *International Journal of Gender and Entrepreneurship, 8*(4), 446–470. doi:10.1108/IJGE-03-2016-0006

Mohan, S., & Rollo, V. (2020). *From shutdown to recovery: Unraveling the impact of COVID-19 on small firms.* International Trade Centre. https://www.intracen.org/covid19/blogs/from-shutdown-to-recovery/

Mordi, C., Simpson, R., Singh, S., & Okafor, C. (2010). The role of cultural values in understanding the challenges faced by female entrepreneurs in Nigeria. *Gender in Management*, *25*(1), 5–21. doi:10.1108/17542411011019904

Morgan, T., Anokhin, S., Ofstein, L., & Friske, W. (2020). SME response to major exogenous shocks: The bright and dark sides of business model pivoting. *International Small Business Journal: Researching Entrepreneurship*, *38*(5), 369–379. doi:10.1177/0266242620936590

Mustafa, F., Khursheed, A., Fatima, M., & Rao, M. (2021). Exploring the impact of COVID-19 pandemic on women entrepreneurs in Pakistan. *International Journal of Gender and Entrepreneurship*, *13*(2), 187–203. doi:10.1108/IJGE-09-2020-0149

Naguib, R., & Jamali, D. (2015). Female entrepreneurship in the UAE: A multi-level integrative lens. *Gender in Management*, *30*(2), 135–161. doi:10.1108/GM-12-2013-0142

OECD. (2004). *Small and Medium-Sized Enterprises in Turkey, Issues and Policies*. Retrieved September 2020, from Organization for Economic Co- operation and Development: http:// www. oecd. org/ industry /smes /3193 2173.pdf

OECD. (2006). *The SME financing gap (Vol. I): Theory and evidence*. Organization for Economic Co- operation and Development.

OECD. (2020). *Women enterprise policy and COVID-19: Towards a gender-sensitive response*. OECD.

Oluyombo, D., & Ogundimu, K. (2006). Microfinance as a strategy for poverty alleviation in Nigeria. SSRN *Electronic Journal*. doi:10.2139/ssrn.2885378

Panda, S. (2018). Constraints faced by women entrepreneurs in developing countries: Review and ranking. *Gender in Management*, *33*(4), 315–331. doi:10.1108/GM-01-2017-0003

Rabbani, M., Zahan, I., & Matin, M. (2020). *How Resilient Are Female Online Entrepreneurs? Findings From the COVID-19 Shock*. Brac Institute of Governance and Development. https://bigd.bracu.ac.bd/study/resilience-of-online-entrepreneur-against-the-covid-19-induced-economic-slow-down/

Rahman, M. (n.d.). *Women Micro-Merchants in Bangladesh: Can digital tech break barriers?* Retrieved August 16, 2021, from https://www.microentrepreneursasia.com/women-micro-merchants-in-mangladesh#:~:text=Of%20the%20almost%208%20million,of%20the%20World%20Bank%20Group

Rahman, M. M., Nesa, M., & Ghose, D. (2018). The prospects and causes of failure of small and medium enterprises (SMEs): A case study of Bangladesh. *Journal of Green Business School, 1*(11), 90–108.

Ramadani, V., Hisrich, R., & Rashiti, S. (2015). Female entrepreneurs in transition economies: Insights from Albania, Macedonia and Kosovo. *World Review of Entrepreneurship, Management and Sustainable Development, 11*(4), 391. doi:10.1504/WREMSD.2015.072066

Report, S. B. (2018). Women entrepreneurship in Bangladesh face less social barriers now: BIDS. *The Daily Star*. https://www.thedailystar.net/business/women-entrepreneurship-in-bangladesh-face-less-social-barriers-now-bids-1659283

Rey-Martí, A., Tur Porcar, A., & Mas-Tur, A. (2015). Linking female entrepreneurs' motivation to business survival. *Journal of Business Research, 68*(4), 810–814. doi:10.1016/j.jbusres.2014.11.033

Rosa, J. M., & Sylla, D. (2018). A comparison of the performance of majority female-owned and majority male-owned small and medium-sized enterprises. *International Journal of Entrepreneurship and Small Business, 35*(3), 282–302. doi:10.1504/IJESB.2018.095901

Sara, C., & Peter, R. (1998). The financing of male– and female–owned businesses. *Entrepreneurship and Regional Development, 10*(3), 225–242. doi:10.1080/08985629800000013

Sattar, A., Dewri, L., & Ananna, S. (2016). Working environment for women entrepreneurs in developing countries: An empirical study of Bangladesh. *International Journal of Business and Management, 11*(12), 197. doi:10.5539/ijbm.v11n12p197

Shoma, C. (2019). Financing female entrepreneurs in cottage, micro, small, and medium enterprises: Evidence from the financial sector in Bangladesh 2010–2018. *Asia & the Pacific Policy Studies, 6*(3), 397–416. doi:10.1002/app5.286

Singh, G., & Belwal, R. (2008). Entrepreneurship and SMEs in Ethiopia. *Gender in Management, 23*(2), 120–136. doi:10.1108/17542410810858321

Singh, S., Mordi, C., Okafor, C., & Simpson, R. (2010). Challenges in female entrepreneurial development— A case analysis of Nigerian entrepreneurs. *Journal of Enterprising Culture, 18*(04), 435–460. doi:10.1142/S0218495810000628

Smallbone, D., & Welter, F. (2001). The distinctiveness of entrepreneurship in transition economies. *Small Business Economics, 16*(4), 249–262. doi:10.1023/A:1011159216578

Smith-Hunter, A., & Boyd, R. (2004). Applying theories of entrepreneurship to a comparative analysis of white and minority women business owners. *Women in Management Review, 19*(1), 18–28. doi:10.1108/09649420410518403

Subagyo, K., Kumar, V., & Ernestivita, G. (2020). Entrepreneurial Parameters and Performance of MSMEs in East Java Province of Indonesia. *International Journal of Business Innovation and Research, 23*(2), 267–282. doi:10.1504/IJBIR.2020.110102

Sultan, S., & Sultan, W. (2020). Women MSMEs in times of crisis: Challenges and opportunities. *Journal of Small Business and Enterprise Development, 27*(7), 1069–1083. doi:10.1108/JSBED-06-2020-0226

Sultana, M. (2021, March 8). Women entrepreneurs get more than target from stimulus package for smaller units. *The Financial Express*. https://www.thefinancialexpress.com.bd/economy/bangladesh/women-entrepreneurs-get-more-than-target-from-stimulus-package-for-smaller-units-1615170323

Sultana, S. A. (2021, May 16). *Barely staying afloat: COVID-19 and women entrepreneurs in Bangladesh.* Development Policy Centre. https://devpolicy.org/barely-staying-afloat-covid-19-and-women-entrepreneurs-in-bangladesh-20210517/

The Asia Foundation. (2021). *COVID-19 & the new normal for women in the economy in South Asia.* https%3A%2F%2Fasiafoundation.org%2Fwp-content%2Fuploads%2F2021%2F03%2FCovid-19-The-New-Normal-for-Women-in-the-Economy-in-South-Asia.pdf

Ukonu, O., & Tafamel, A. (2011). Problems, challenges and prospects of female entrepreneurs in Gwagwalada, Abuja. *African Research Review, 5*(3). Advance online publication. doi:10.4314/afrrev.v5i3.67354

WeConnect International. (2020). *Report urges escalated support to women-owned business during pandemic.* WeConnect International. https://weconnectinternational.org/report-urges-escalated-support-to-women-owned-business-during-pandemic/

Wellner, L., & Pierce-Friedman, K. (2019). The Types of Case Studies in Research and Career-Based Endeavors. In *Case Study Methodology in Higher Education* (pp. 83–108). IGI Global. doi:10.4018/978-1-5225-9429-1.ch005

World Bank Group. (2019). *Financing solutions for micro, small and medium enterprises in Bangladesh.* The World Bank Group.

Yousuf Danish, A., & Lawton Smith, H. (2012). Female entrepreneurship in Saudi Arabia: Opportunities and challenges. *International Journal of Gender and Entrepreneurship*, *4*(3), 216–235. doi:10.1108/17566261211264136

Youth Business International. (2020). *Supporting small businesses to ensure the future of Bangladesh*. Retrieved August 2020, from Youth Business International: https://www.google.com/search?client=firefox-b-d&q=Youth+Business+International

Yunus, M. (2017). *Entrepreneurship: A Global Social Movement*. Sage Publications.

KEY TERMS AND DEFINITIONS

COVID-19 Crisis: Medical, economic, financial, social crisis emerging from the Coronavirus (SARS-COV-2) pandemic.

Crisis Episode: Any specific occurrence or period that will result in, or may result in, an unstable environment that affects a person, group, or the entire society.

Pandemic: Epidemic of an infectious disease that spreads across geographic regions and continents.

Resilience: Capacity to overcome hardship and recover from negative experiences.

Survival Mechanism: Techniques employed to endure through adverse situations.

Women-Owned Small Enterprise: A privately owned business with 25 employees or less and is owned by women.

Chapter 10
Revisiting Employee Engagement in the New Normal:
A Study of a Few Select Organizations

Parul Saxena
Sharda University, India

Reena Kovid
Shobhit Institute of Engineering and Technology (Deemed), India

Asiya Nasreen
Jamia Millia Islamia, India

EXECUTIVE SUMMARY

The chapter provides for developing an understanding of the various aspects of employee engagement, namely the concept, levels, and techniques for measuring employee engagement during and after COVID-19. It explores employee engagement practices and its implications in some selected organizations during and after the pandemic. It highlights the most affected dimensions of employee engagement. Additionally, this chapter maps the practices followed by various industry organizations and presents these practices as a way forward to overcome the hurdle of keeping employees engaged in the new normal. The findings indicate that the organisations appeared to have made considerable changes in their employee engagement strategies and have integrated technology at a large scale to suit the remote work environment and emotional well-being as well.

DOI: 10.4018/978-1-6684-3504-5.ch010

INTRODUCTION

The COVID-19 pandemic's abrupt, fast, and disruptive developments have confronted practitioners and researchers with a completely new working environment (Singh & Kumar, 2022). As a result, it necessitates a thorough examination of its impact on all aspects of work as well as on personnel. The goal of this research is to look into the concept of employee engagement in the new normal. Employee engagement refers to the process of building an environment and culture in which engaged employees can thrive. An engaged employee is one that understands and believes in the direction in which the company is heading, as well as how their job impacts and contributes to the company's purpose, mission, and goals. Engaged employees have a sense of energetic and effective connection to their work activities and believe they are capable of meeting the demands of their employment (Schaufeli & Bakker, 2004). It is frequently confused with the employee experience; however, they are not the same. The employee experience, which comprises important events throughout the employee lifecycle that either encourage or inhibit employee engagement, is linked to engagement. Work engagement is thus the fundamental outcome of improving the employee experience, and it encompasses more than ping pong tables and complimentary lunches.

Kahn (1990) first proposed the concept of employee engagement and observed it, "as the harnessing of organization members' selves to their work roles; self-employment and self-expression of people physically, cognitively, and emotionally in their work lives". He stated that employee engagement shows physiological and physical existence of performing an organizational role. The construct which forms the engagement in an organisation include psychological conditions of safety, meaningfulness, and availability. Employee engagement creates an experience of awareness and increases involvement during a business enterprise in way that employees can carry out their best. Aspects such as performance, goals, recognition, development, and supervisor effectiveness are all inextricably connected to worker engagement. In the corporate settings, employee engagement is frequently used interchangeably with employee satisfaction and loyalty, and that is a mistake, because it is way more than those concepts.

Employee engagement refers to the physical, cognitive, and emotional involvement of employees in the work. Organizational elements (leadership, advanced support, process resources, fairness, etc.), job elements (work environment, job participation, job enrichment, etc.) and individual factors (extraversion, resilience, self-consciousness, etc.). are all influencing elements of employee engagement. The research on consequences of employee engagement mainly focusses on two aspects—the influence of employee engagement on individual performance (enthusiasm, excellence, satisfaction, devotion, etc.) and on organizational performance (productivity, profitability, customer loyalty, etc.) Employee engagement, according to Aon Hewitt Organization (2001), is defined as the number of employees who are willing to live with and work hard for the company, and it is measured in three ways – a) Say -usage of language by employees to explain their colleagues, jobs and organization; b) Stay: when there is a strong desire among employees to be a member of the organization for an extended time, rather than the usage of current jobs as a transient transition and c) Strive: There is inclination among employees to commit greater attempt to contribute to the achievement of the organization. The concept can be well presented diagrammatically to depict the three critical elements of work engagement viz., Organization, team and work. (Refer Figure 1)

Shuck and Wollard (2010) identified engagement as an individual's cognitive, emotional, and behavioural condition that contributes to the fulfilment of organisational goals. While, Andrew and Saudah (2012) said that it can be considered as a mediator to improve employee behaviour, intention, and attitudes toward greater job performance. The executive should aid the manager in providing developmental assistance, career support, and recognition because these aspects effectively promote employee engagement. Identifying definitions and associated measurements of employee engagement, as well as analysing the causes, results, and boundary conditions of employee engagement, has been the main emphasis of human resource research (Basquille, 2013; Lee at el., 2017).

Figure 1. The employee engagement concept
Source: Authors

According to the Society for Human Resource Management (SHRM), the use of the term "employee engagement" seems to be ubiquitous and most organizations use a definition of engagement as something beyond satisfaction describing the discretionary effort of employees. A study conducted by Vander Elst (2016) among home care nurses using the JD-R model that job demands were positively correlated with burnout and job resources positively with commitment. Kumar (2021) provided a list of reference variables ready to improve the level of employee engagement during and after COVID-19 and suggested five main elements of employee engagement in his 5V Model which include value, voice, variety, virtue and vision.

Chapter Objectives

The chapter provides the detailed account of conceptual understanding of employee engagement in context of the corona pandemic and how organisations used it to keep their employees productive and happy as well. It aims to highlight the strategies of employee engagement practiced by organisations during or post covid scenario by means of few cases study analysis.

EMPLOYEE ENGAGEMENT: THEORETICAL FOUNDATIONS

The idea of Employee engagement derives from the Job Demands-Resources Theory (Bakker et al., 2003) which explored the transaction among organisation and employees from a needs-sources perspective). Individual employees automatically juggle Job requirements (e.g., work overload) vis-a-vis process sources (e.g., manager support). The balance or lack thereof, results in various levels of worker engagement or inflicts burnout, as positive or negative results respectively. Engagement happens while Job resources are good enough to satisfy and exceed Job demands (Bakker & Demerouti, 2006). Job demands are the ones that encompass physical, mental, social, and organizational factors of the process which might be obligatory to the process. These require sustained physical and/or mental attempt or talents and are consequently related to positive physiological and/or mental costs. Job sources arise from the physical, mental, social, or organizational factors of the process. Therefore, resources are not only necessary to deal with job demands, but they also are important in their own right. Job resources can be placed at the extent of the business enterprise at large (e.g., pay, profession opportunities, task security), the interpersonal and social relations (e.g., manager and co-employee assist, group climate), the organizations work (e.g., position clarity, participation in selection making), and at the extent of the challenge (e.g., talent variety, challenge identity, challenge significance, autonomy, overall performance comments).

The second aspect of this theory proposed that JD-R version is motivational in nature, wherein it's assumed that Job resources have motivational ability and result in high work engagement, low cynicism, and great overall performance. For instance, right comments foster learning, thereby growing task competence, while social support fulfils the want for autonomy and the sense of belongingness respectively. It is in favour of the organisations to maintain Job Demands low and to offer adequate resources to its personnel for most desirable performances. Bakker (2015) discusses the "loss cycle of Job demands and tiredness" and the "advantage cycle of Job resources and engagement" in his work. Bakker & Demerouti (2017) confirmed that stressed employees wane their position by engaging in self-defeating behaviours, resulting in increased job demands and exhaustion. Motivated employees, on the other hand, work actively to enhance their work condition, resulting in increased resources and motivation.

Elements of Employee Engagement

A commonly agreed definition of employee engagement would be physical, psychological or emotional involvement of the employee while at work. The four critical elements of Employee engagement are given below.

- **Commitment**: The degree to which individuals identify with the job, the obligations, and the organisational goals is referred to as commitment. Employees that are engaged are enthralled by their work and determined to overcome all obstacles in order to achieve their objectives.
- **Motivation:** Achievement drives employees more than anything else, thus if employees put in their all to push their company to the next level, this gained position inspires them more than anything else. Employees are motivated to perform more and more for their company when they are properly rewarded and recognised.
- **Loyalty:** Employees that are actively involved in their work are more loyal to their employer. Managers need less focus and attention to do their tasks since they are held to high standards of accountability in terms of work obligations and results achieved. To avoid such employees from becoming disengaged, organisations should have a well-defined reward structure.
- **Trust:** Employee engagement thrives only when it is mutually recognised as a critical component by both the company and the employees. The company should have faith in its employees' ability and offer them the freedom to complete their responsibilities in their own way.

Stakeholders in Employee Engagement

Personnel across organisation should be involved in planning, administering, and taking action based on the data. It's crucial to include the right stakeholders while measuring employee engagement for the purpose accuracy. The following are the key players in the employee engagement process

- **Executives:** Buy-in and collaboration from the c-suite are critical to the success of any employee engagement program. Executives provide input to the measurement strategy so that it aligns with business priorities. They also become role models of communication, accountability, and feedback, thereby empowering their employees to make change happen.
- **Human Resources:** Human Resources traditionally leads the employee engagement survey process. They should drive the survey design and champion positive change based on results. HR leaders will coach executives to be role models and build managers' capabilities. The HR team can also promote the program across the enterprise to ensure everyone knows what is happening and when.
- **Managers:** Managers take ownership of the process, facilitating ongoing conversations and a two-way approach to improving employee engagement. They see survey results as a catalyst, and not a replacement for ongoing dialogue with their teams. They know their teams well and have a good understanding of what matters to them. Overall, your managers consider employee engagement vital to your organization's performance.
- **Employees:** Employees are at the heart of any engagement program. Their open, honest responses are what will drive real improvements across the organization. Leaders must let employees know that their voices will be heard and acted on, making a positive impact on the organization. This includes encouraging their anonymous feedback, communicating survey results to them in real time, and promptly making improvements in response to their feedback. This approach sets up employees for feeling a shared ownership in making improvements.

Measuring Employee Engagement

The authors discovered that researchers have spent a significant amount of time establishing validated measures of employee engagement based on construct conceptualization and description. The Utrecht Work Involvement Scale (UWES), established by Schaufeli et al. (2006), is the most widely used scale in employee engagement research, but its reliability has been questioned by Byrne, Peters and Weston (2016). Nimon et al. (2011) emphasised the ambiguity of employee engagement conceptualization and suggested an alternative to the Work Cognition Inventory (WCI), offering the idea of work involvement as a multidimensional theory. The scale established by Shuck, Adelson, and Reio (2017), which consists of three sub-constructs, is another acceptable measure of employee engagement (cognitive, emotional, and behavioural). In many firms, however, determining employee engagement can be difficult. Employee engagement is determined by a variety of elements, including connections with managers and co-workers, chances for personal and professional development, and meaningful work. A thorough approach to evaluating employee engagement, according to Rooy David et al. (2011), ensures that a business is successfully meeting difficulties and getting the most out of the process.

Tools for Measuring Employee Engagement

- **Pulse Surveys**: More and more organisations are conducting Pulse surveys to know the sentiments of the employees toward their work and organisations. Pulse surveys are the on-line questionnaires generally encompass small, conceivable units of survey questions and may be scheduled monthly, quarterly, or at a frequency suitable to the organization. These surveys provide almost real-time glimpse into the aptness of the organization. They permit managers to recognize group sentiment and pinpoint problems early, as opposed to months—or maybe a year after situations have worsened. These are considered to be the simplest employee engagement techniques employed by the organisations. These surveys reveal the country of worker engagement throughout the organization, uncover possibilities for improvement and enable short reaction to cope with trouble areas.

Based on employees' level of engagement, they can be categorized based on their level of engagement using four employee engagement profiles (Figure 2).

Figure 2. The four employee engagement profiles
Source: Generated by Authors

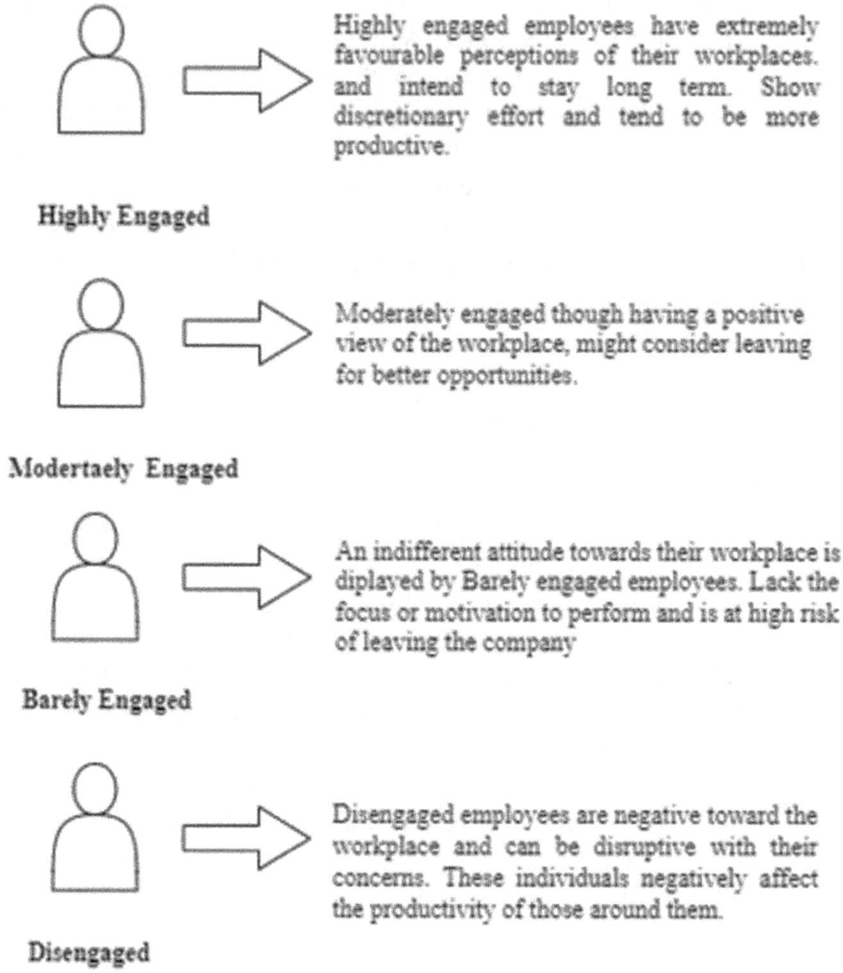

COVID- 19 AND EMPLOYEE ENGAGEMENT

COVID-19 rapidly disrupted lives, economies, and workplaces in 2020 (Kumar & Malhotra, 2021). It wreaked havoc on people's lives, economies, and workplaces. The unprecedented nature of the COVID-19 pandemic meant that everyone, from human resource departments to managers to every employee, all ned to quickly adjust to new ways of working while simultaneously mitigating the changes and stressors that were popping up in their home lives (Kumar & Gupta, 2021). As a result of the spread of the pandemic in early 2020, employers of all shapes, sizes, and sectors hurried to implement remote work which had a significant influence on employee engagement (Bhardwaj & Kumar, 2022).

Human resource departments need to entwine their past experience along with protocols in the 'new normal' to ensure employees continue to be protected and valued. Employee engagement became more important than it ever was in pre-pandemic times. Quantum Workplace's Best Places organised a contest in 2020, and the result showed increased levels of employee engagement across all the sector. The analysis, further revealed an increased levels of employee engagement during the first month and a half of 2020, but as the global pandemic spread, employee engagement took a dip from a 78% in January 2020 to a low 70% by February end

According to ABBYY's COVID-19 Technology and Business Process Report, where the Survey participants were from organizations with 50+ employees and were located in the U.S., UK, France, and Germany, the employee engagement is divided across ages (Refer Box 1).

Box 1. Employee Engagement Post Covid and Generational Divide

• The report found that leaders of all ages face challenges – in the UK, 81 percent of senior decision-makers struggled, with many citing remote collaborations (37 percent), motivation to work (29 percent), and productivity (26 percent) as top challenges – and that there is a clear generational divide in the findings.
• Throughout the crisis, senior executives aged 55 and over have fared better than Millennial (under 35) leaders.
• According to the study, 61 percent of executives aged 18-34 said processes made their work more challenging, compared to 35 percent of decision-makers aged 55 and up.
• It seems that Millennials and Baby Boomers also have different opinions on processes at work, as 60% of younger executives claimed that there is not enough information provided on business processes, however just 26% of older execs agreed.

Source: ABBYY's COVID-19 Technology and Business Process Report 2020

As per the survey conducted on Employee Engagement by Quantum Workplace, the facets of employee engagement impacted most dramatically during the pandemic include (Refer Figure 3):

- Communication and Leadership
- Compensation and Benefits
- Health, Wellbeing, and Balance

Figure 3. Employee engagement areas most-affected during pandemic
Source: Adapted from 'Quantum Workplace Benchmark Report and Analysis (QWBRA ,2020)

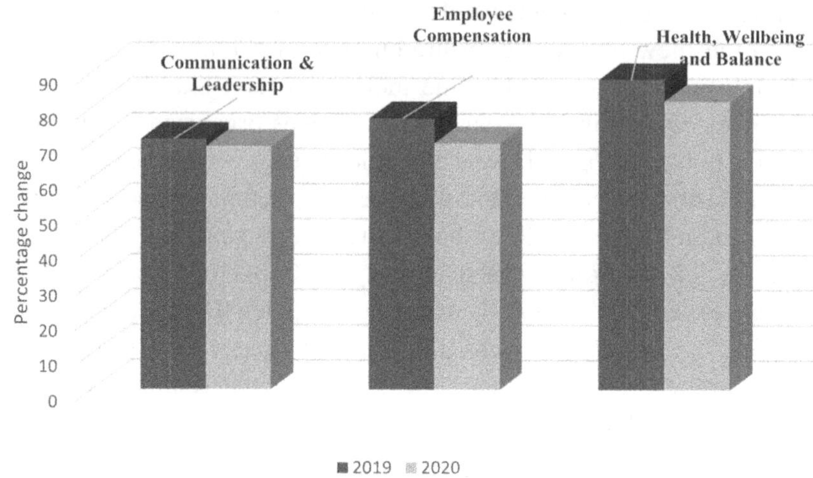

Issues and Challenges of Employee Engagement During COVID-19

This segment highlights the issues and challenges faced by organisations while keeping employees engaged during COVID-19. In terms of learning and development, engagement is already considered to be the most pressing concern as, "it's difficult to catch, hold, and maintain people's attention" during normal times, this issue was further aggravated during Pandemic. Employees and leaders alike were battling with camaraderie, connectedness, and alignment, rather than productivity during COVID- 19.

- **Lack of Alignment, Insights, and Support from the Top:** The first issue faced by most of the organisations during COVID was top management's mindset and priorities setting; top management was more focused on more tangible challenges than maintaining a leadership focus on engagement. While senior leaders agreed that workplace culture and employee engagement are important, many have trouble connecting them to business objectives or figuring out where to start with employee engagement programmes. As, the majority of firms don't have proper mechanisms to measure engagement or other structured methods of gathering feedback, leaving executives to guess (or assume) what matters most to their employees.

- **External Environment Hampered Engagement Efforts:** Getting support from other stakeholders, particularly investors, was difficult during COVID, even when senior executives are united and committed to making culture a part of their bottom-line strategy. Executive teams had to tread with caution whether or not to take steps that would jeopardise investor confidence.
- While boards of directors are close to the company and may be more aware of the need to develop an engaged workforce, striking the correct balance between investing and short-term returns proved to be difficult.
- **Communication Channels were Jeopardised:** Almost all the organisations shifted to remote work during COVID, which jeopardized the normal communication channels as employee felt alienated and isolated from the work environment. This issue was prominently faced by many organisations as it was difficult to cut through the clutter in today's information-overloaded environment. Getting employees' attention was difficult, during remote work.
- **Lack of Trust in Leadership:** Employee engagement is affected by leadership trust. The leadership impressions increased heavily in 2020, to have fallen in the second half of 2021. During the peak of the pandemic, about 9 out of 10 employees trusted their top leaders to lead the company to future success. In May of 2021, that figure had plummeted to 84 percent. There a s dire need to create a workplace atmosphere based on trust by designing processes and channels that prioritise consistent communication.

CASES ON EMPLOYEE ENGAGEMENT DURING PANDEMIC

The term "employee engagement" has been redefined thanks to Covid-19. During COVID, the corporate sector saw a higher number of layoffs and furloughed employees, and as a result, many firms began to de-prioritize employee engagement due to severe business losses caused by the lockdown. As economies progressively recover, it is critical to invest in employee engagement in a more meaningful approach that considers the 'new normal.' This section of the chapter looks at some of the best practises used by a few companies during and after a pandemic to keep their employees engaged.

Employee Engagement at Coca Cola

It is critical for a beverage multinational like Coca-Cola, which employs over 700,000 employees worldwide, to guarantee that staff never feel lost, unappreciated, or bored. Employee engagement was the primary objective for this beverage company, during pandemic Coca-Cola Beverages established a virtual employee engagement initiative aimed at employees' co-workers and family members physical and mental well-being. Protecting employee Health and Well-being of Coca-Cola system employees was the top priority of the company. To ensure the health and safety of employees in offices, production, distribution, and retail sites around the world had rigorously followed guidelines from health authorities. The Coca-Cola Company urged the majority of office-based workers to work remotely, in accordance with recommendations to limit mass gatherings and enhance social distancing. Some other employee engagement measures at Coca- Cola, during pandemic include:

Continuous Feedback and Sharing of Employee Experiences

Its 'Unbottled' blog invited employees to share their positive experiences outside of the workplace. The Coca-Cola team started this practice by sharing these posts internally. These heartfelt tales quickly became popular. The Company ensured that employees' views would be heard, their ideas would be considered for implementation, their accomplishments would be recognised and celebrated, and their efforts would be rewarded. Coca- Cola created five dedicated teams to engage its employees and each of these team focused on certain activities that had an encouraging outcome on the employee engagement (refer figure 4).

Figure 4. Five employee engagement teams at Coca- Cola
Source: Generated by Authors

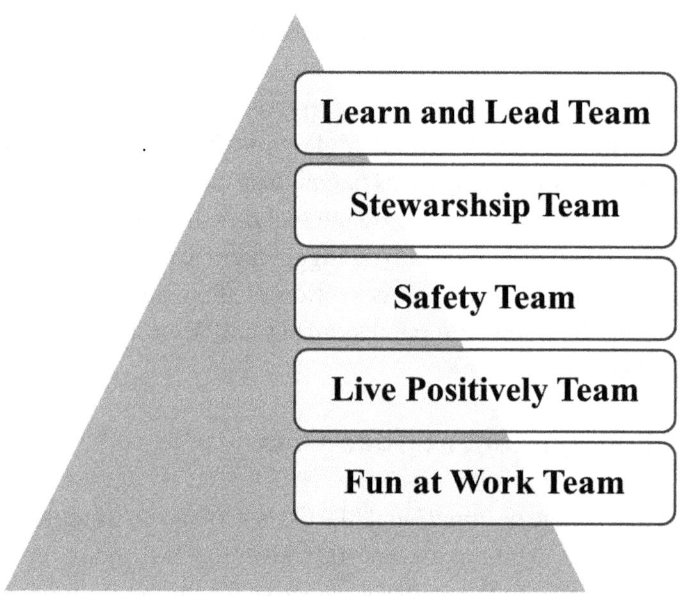

Fun at Work Team focused on the principle of open happiness. Its activities were focused on subjects other than work. *Stewardship Team* was dedicated to giving back and promoting the Coke Cares brand. *Safety Team* educated employees on how to be safe and trains them to respond appropriately in the event of an emergency. *Learn and Lead Team* was devoted to the employees' general growth, providing them with knowledge of duties beyond what they were accustomed to completing on a regular basis. *Live Positively Team* was involved in initiatives that promote employee health and wellness.

Employee Engagement at McDonalds

As per the Corporate Governance report (2020) published on the Company website, The Company had continued to evolve its approach to employee listening and engagement and invented even more ways to give its employees a voice. Love to Listen 2020, an initiative of the company, was adopted in 2020 due to the pandemic for providing employees a platform that is "always on".

Initiatives at McDonalds to Keep Communication Intact During Pandemic

- **Love to Listen 2020:** McDonald's approach to Love to Listen Surveys in 2020 was fluid, and reflected the challenges that restaurant and office teams faced through the COVID 19 pandemic. The survey results showed that 77% really happy or happy with their jobs; and 81% strongly agreed or agreed that their health and wellbeing was a priority for their management teams.
- **Love to Listen Meet Ups:** Love to Listen Meet-Ups started in early 2020. These meetings help the employees give their concerns and suggestions for positive change. The Virtual Love to Listen Meet-Ups were launched, and have been held throughout 2020/21
- **OurLounge:** it was an internal communication channel to help restaurant employees feel closer to the company's brand and to understand their role in achieving company's vision and improving employee engagement. As the main channel of communication from the centre to hourly paid restaurant employees, it played a vital role in communicating key business priorities but also had an important role in raising awareness of Company initiatives, news and messages as well as giving employees access to opportunities such as apprenticeships. Employee opinions and feedback were regularly collated through surveys, Bright Ideas and the Social Feed. Bright Ideas is a platform for sharing ideas, during 2020 internal communication was even more important and OurLounge focused on being the one source of truth for

employees to visit for information on coronavirus, updates from the Company and wellbeing support.

- **Town Halls**: To bring in the transparency in communication, regular town halls were organised to give a monthly business update, presented by the Executive and senior leadership team. Each town hall had a different theme and gave staff the opportunity to hear from other departments about their upcoming plans and initiatives. The key overarching topics covered during town halls for 2020 were the COVID 19 pandemic and company's response to the crisis, employee wellbeing and mental health and diversity and inclusion. The company also had one Global Town Hall in 2020 focused on response to COVID-19, recent earnings and new food promotions.
- **Regular Email Communications:** The company realised that regular communication is the key to engage with employees working in the remote mode. The employees were updated regularly via email, which are tailored to their role and updated them with their goals.
- **Operations Update:** It was a 'to do list' for the week, focusing on operations excellence in order of priority, providing timely information to help restaurants focus on quality service and cleanliness. It included a rolling 5-week operations calendar, and a crew operation update and other necessary attachments. In 2020, The company issued 130 Operations Updates.

Furthermore, according to an article published by HRKatha, involvement at McDonald's occurred on three levels: for frontline restaurant employees, restaurant managers, and corporate office employees. The organization's existing learning management system (LMS) was upgraded to meet the learning and engagement demands of employees at all levels. Many of McDonald's India's classroom training modules have been converted to digital format, and the company created e-learning modules, quizzes, management master classes, and a variety of other creative learning events that employees may access on their phones while at home in quarantine.

- **Virtual Training of the Crew Members:** As per the article published on HRKatha- an online HR platform (HRKatha, 2020), McDonalds made an effort to provide staff, mainly teenagers, with thrilling and valuable learning opportunities. Each crew trainer was in charge of eight members, and the crew's education revolved around the products they sell. For example, if the theme of the day was French fries, the module would cover everything from the type of potatoes used to the farms from where they are sourced, how they were cooked, and how they were served. After each module, the trainer used to call the crew and conducts a series of exams on the topics covered over the day. The quizzes are repeated in case a member fails to score above a certain number.

- **Masterclasses for the Trainers:** The Company organised masterclasses for crew trainers, which are led by the management team. For example, if there is a lesson on hospitality, the customer experience manager will teach it to the crew trainers and then organise a recap session to summarise what they learned. Health, cleanliness, and safety are some of the other themes covered.
- **Engaging Employees at the Corporate Office:** The goal was to provide the appropriate communication tools while also ensuring that IT support was available at all times. The functional heads were required to communicate with their team members every three days, and the leadership team was required to communicate with the respective heads once a week. Furthermore, the company decided to use video calls rather than phone calls. Moreover, the company organised a competition, #hatchallenge in 2020 to engage them. It required employees to create TikTok videos at home and sharing on the Social Feed

Employee Engagement at Mastercard

This international financial services conglomerate rose to the top of its industry's employee engagement firms. The credit card company employs roughly 20,000 individuals worldwide, with a "significant portion" working from home during the Pandemic. The company's headquarters are in New York, with regional offices in Dubai, Singapore, and Brussels. Mastercard's success at engaging its employees can be attributed to a few key employee engagement drivers. Rather, than forcing its employees to return to work, Mastercard gave them the option of returning to work and encouraged to continue work from home. It formed a "future of work" task team to figure out how to effectively deal with employee demands in the wake of the coronavirus outbreak. The company's commitment to an inclusive work environment was firm and backed by extensive employee training in the virtual mode.

- **Continuous Feedback:** Employee engagement and workplace inclusiveness, according to Mastercard, are the most important drivers of innovation and improved company success. Regular employee input was at the heart of this, ensuring that all employees' opinions were heard.
- **Flexible Work:** Mastercard has evolved to adapt to flexible work arrangements since remote work became the norm during the coronavirus epidemic. Many Mastercard employees can now work from home until they are comfortable returning to the office.

- **Developing Coaching Skills**: Coaching for Impact is a customised coach training programme that enables managers and executives to integrate important coaching skills and behaviours into their management style and address each of the issues in the Employee Engagement process.

Employee Engagement at Capgemini India

Capgemini India, headquartered in Pune, is an Indian information technology and consultancy firm. Capgemini introduced a series of employee engagement programmes such as constant communication with employees through video messages, creating and maintaining social networks in virtual communities, creating a sense of belonging, counselling service for employees, conducting webinars on stress management, and implementing best practises of maintaining health and hygiene (The Hindu, 2020). Physical security is also provided by the company. Employees' mental and emotional well-being is improved through meditation and exercise programmes.

- **Creating a Sense of Belonging and Connecting with Employees:** Ashwin Yardi, CEO, Capgemini India in an interview to The Hindu (National Daily) on April 2020, stated that during the Pandemic Employee morale and engagement at Capgemini were boosted by regular communication updates, which include video messages from the company's leadership. The organisation constantly publishes best practises for sustaining health and hygiene during difficult times through its open communication policy, which reiterates that employees' safety and well-being is the first priority.
- **Virtual Leadership Initiatives:** During the pandemic, Capgemini launched a 'Leadership podcast series,' in which every leader discusses working in a virtual environment, with a focus on maintaining client centricity, employee morale and motivation, and employee health and safety. Leaders work together with their teams to develop objectives so that employees are invested in the outcomes, which is crucial for establishing leadership legitimacy in a virtual environment. Leaders must also exhibit empathy for their employees' well-being.
- **Wellness Initiatives:** Capgemini rolled out many wellness initiatives and also arranged counselling service for its employees that needed emotional support provided by firm's empanelled counsellors. The firm hosted webinars for its staff, in collaboration with an external partner, with focus on how to deal with worry and pandemic triggered stress. It also began a Guided Meditation programme involving light pre-exercise, meditation, and post-exercise activities.

- **Team/Family Engagement Initiatives:** During the Pandemic, the company initiated the "Capgemini Big Boss challenge,' in which employees participated in an exciting series of tasks or contests with their family or friends. This included tasks such as show casing creativity, exhibiting a special talent of a family member or friend, an online quiz contest, a fitness challenge, and a themed dressing challenge. Every day the manager reached out to the entire team on anything other than work such as wellbeing, productivity, development, health in order to keep employees engaged and inculcate the team spirit.

DISCUSSION AND WAY FORWARD

Organizations that value their people understand that they are their best bet for corporate success. And, according to 92 percent of bosses, engaged people perform better. This is only one of the several employee engagement statistics that demonstrate the importance of employee involvement in a company. Employee engagement has so arisen as a strategic approach that is beginning to appear in organisations around the world, not simply in HR departments but across the organisation. It's about shifting away from short-term rewards and toward long-term programmes that focus on three factors that every company can influence: culture, technology, and physical space. During this difficult period, organisations developed unique and creative employee engagement initiatives. Even after the pandemic, it is imperative for organisations to keep employees motivated, stimulated, devoted, fulfilled, and joyous. Working from home has become quite popular lately, and it would be impossible to succeed without the use of virtual methods. Organizations should use an online practise strategy to stay competitive during these difficult times and prioritise virtual relationships in order to increase employee engagement. Based on the analysis of the practices followed by the select organisations undertaken during the course of this study, some of the common employee engagement strategies that have emerged are (Refer Table 1):

Table 1. Common employee engagement strategies that have emerged prominently during COVID-19

<table>
<tr><th>Organisation</th><th>Employee Engagement Strategies During COVID</th><th>Common Employee Engagement Strategies That Have Emerged Prominently During COVID-19</th></tr>
<tr><td>Coca- Cola</td><td>• Employee Health and Wellness
• Employee Safety and Security
• Continues Feedback
• Family Engagement Initiatives
• Virtual Learning & Development initiatives
• Virtual Leadership</td><td rowspan="4">• Virtual Learning & Development initiatives
• Employee Wellness & safety
• Robust communication & Continuous Feedback mechanisms
• Family Engagement
• Virtual Leadership</td></tr>
<tr><td>McDonalds</td><td>• Greater emphasis on Virtual Learning & Development
• Robust communication channel to suit remote work
• Strong Feedback mechanisms
• Employee Wellness & safety</td></tr>
<tr><td>Mastercard</td><td>• More focus on Employee training & Coaching in virtual mode
• Continuous feedback</td></tr>
<tr><td>Capgemini India</td><td>• Team/ Family Engagements
• Employee Wellness Initiatives
• Virtual Leadership
• Family Engagement Initiatives</td></tr>
</table>

Source: Authors

Thus, it is evident from the findings that businesses can make remote work equally exciting and stimulating as in-person office work with the appropriate strategies, correct tools and commitment. Finally, remote work necessitates that leader adjust their management style to meet the current scenario. Connecting a remote or hybrid workforce, without a doubt, necessitates a different set of abilities than in-person labour. The payback, however, will be enormous if organisations commit to a constant feedback culture, a process based on solid connections, and some technical support.

Employee Engagement Trends in New Normal

As evident from the few case studies listed above, Engagement is at an all-time high, but rough waters lie ahead as organizations lead through change to the Next Normal. Some of the employee engagement trends that organisations can imbibe:

- **Build Team Confidence:** To increase team trust, employers must create personal and professional relationships within the organisation. The demand for the work required to develop this culture of trust and collaboration will increase as the company grows and move towards hybrid work environment.

- **Leverage Cross-Functional Teams:** Cross-functional teams are a terrific approach to interact and examine different contributions and viewpoints from various functional areas. When forming a cross-functional team or project, make it clear who will be assisting the team.
- **Create a Culture of Psychological Safety:** Psychological security relates to how confident team members are that they can take calculated risks and communicate their thoughts inside their group without facing unwanted consequences. Managers and leaders should be able to weave a psychological safety net for their teams and employees through several initiatives.
- **Building Employer Brand:** Organizations should distinguish themselves as an employer of choice in order to retain the best and most difficult-to-replace personnel. This is especially vital in today's work market, where there is a lot of rivalry for talent. Organizations' incentives, benefits, and culture may not be what employees desire right now. Organizations should rethink their employee value proposition in order to stay competitive by attracting top talent while keeping employees who are already producing outcomes. Employees may have felt compelled to take a less-than-desirable job to support themselves during the epidemic, and may leave the organisation for better prospects as the situation improves.
- **Leveraging Predictive Analytics:** Utilize tools that provide leaders with insight about the likelihood of employee departure. Detect high-risk employees before they leave. With a sophisticated information intelligence platform, organisations can keep top performers and lower turnover rates. Actively mitigate the danger of such individuals leaving and improve their overall performance by providing opportunities for organisational growth to help them succeed.
- **Emphasis on Learning and Development:** To address internal skill shortages and recognise employee growth, organisations must optimise their learning and development activities. It is critical to invest in employee learning and development, to listen to their ideas and thoughts, and to remove impediments to their success. The top companies invest money, time, and other resources in their coaching programmes. This is becoming increasingly vital as leaders require more support than ever before.
- **Promote Flexibility and Mental Wellbeing:** During the pandemic, mental and emotional well-being have become corporate buzzwords. Organizations that prioritise these issues are better able to attract and retain great talent. It is proposed that businesses develop an environment in which these benefits are prioritised as a new priority in the employee experience.

- **Family Engagement:** Many organisations have already started encompassing family engagement as an integral part of employee engagement. Remote work has become the norm and is going to stay, in such circumstances, it becomes imperative for the organisations to include them as part of their engagement initiatives.

Theoretical Implications

As evident from the findings above, the Job Demand resource theory needs to be revisited to incorporate changes brought in by the pandemic on employee engagement. The scope of the definition of Job resources needs to be widened to include family engagement, and employee well-being, which during remote work have become critical elements of employee engagement (Refer Figure 5). Similarly, as remote work becomes more and more prominent during pandemic, the employees have expressed a critical need for upskilling or reskilling to integrate technology in the changing business environment. Thus, the technical demands of the workforce need to be kept in mind by the organisations while designing the learning & development road map. As listed by the majority of the organisations above, family is an integral part of the employee working in a virtual mode. Sarkar (2020) in his recent article in Economic Times (Dated April 9, 2020), has reiterated that family engagement is the new aspect of employee engagement. Many companies such as Genpact, Accenture and Deloitte are providing employee assistance programs such as Kids care to their employees. Further, goal setting and leadership have also emerged as the key job resources to tackle job demands. Job demand aspect of employee engagement need to be upgraded to include element such as "continuous reskilling and upskilling', adoption of technical skills for the job. Talukdar in his article published on Business2community, (Dated April 6, 2020) made five critical propositions for practicing employee engagement during the COVID-19 pandemic that include: robust communication, instant reward and recognition, ensuring flexibility, creation of a strong virtual network of employees, and virtual team building sessions. Bedarkar and Pandita had previously endorsed this (2014), and mentioned in their work that employee engagement is predicted to be based on an integrated model that includes leadership, communication, and work–life balance as major drivers. Some organizations have already implemented new changes that will impact the way their companies operate into the future. Many large companies such as Amazon and Microsoft have changed their views and policies toward remote work.

Figure 5. Proposed additions to job demand and job resources during/post pandemic

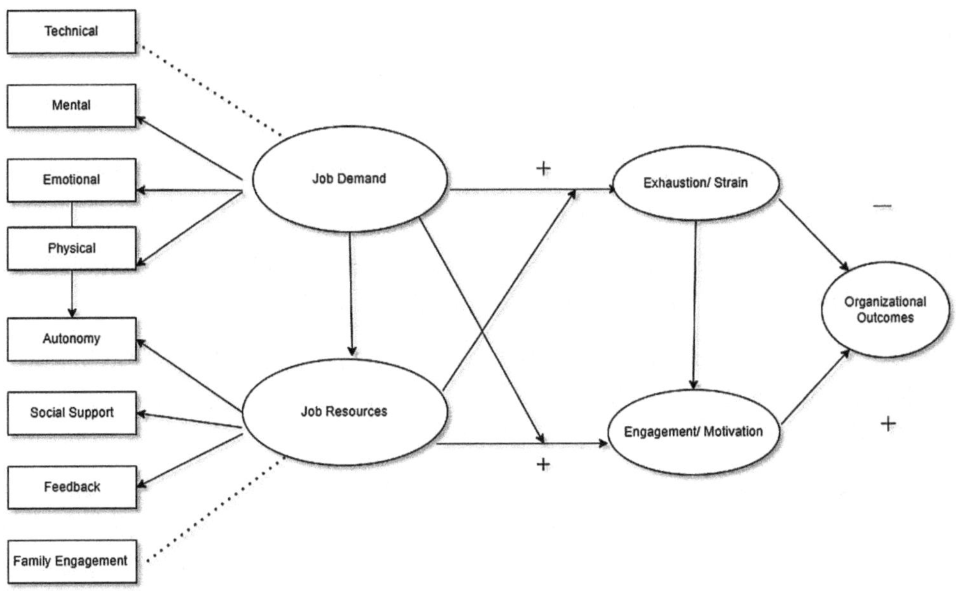

CONCLUSION

In many companies, the 2020 pandemic, resulted in the reversal of organisational plans and the acceleration of change. Employee engagement, on the other hand, became more critical as businesses negotiate this new world of work. Focused, proactive, and evidence-based approaches should be put to use by firms to ensure that people are engaged and can perform at their best. Establishing employee engagement measures that are well integrated with technology is crucial for developing firms in today's environment. Many companies are developing or have already integrated technology at a large scale with employee engagement strategies which can be prominently seen in practises such as virtual team meetings, virtual learning and development, hosting weekly online alignment sessions, webinars with industry experts, and even webinars on anxiety and stress management, creating online team activities, online family engagement practises, online brainstorming, and employee appreciation sessions.

REFERENCES

Andrew, O. C., & Saudah, S. (2012). Individual factors and work outcomes of employee engagement. *Procedia-Social and Behavioural Sciences, 40*, 498–508. doi:10.1016/j.sbspro.2012.03.222

Bakker, A., & Demerouti, E. (2006). The job demands-resources model: State of the art. *Journal of Managerial Psychology, 22*(3), 309–328. doi:10.1108/02683940710733115

Bakker, A. B. (2015). A job demands-resources approach to public service motivation. *Public Administration Review, 75*(5), 723–732. doi:10.1111/puar.12388

Bakker, A. B., & Demerouti, E. (2017). Job demands-resources theory: Taking stock and looking forward. *Journal of Occupational Health Psychology, 22*(3), 273–285. doi:10.1037/ocp0000056 PMID:27732008

Bakker, A. B., Demerouti, E., & Schaufeli, W. B. (2003). Dual processes at work in a call centre: An application of the Job Demands-Resources model. *European Journal of Work and Organizational Psychology, 12*(4), 393–417. doi:10.1080/13594320344000165

Basquille, M. (2013). *In this recession, has engagement remained high? –Research within an Irish financial company* (Unpublished dissertation). National College of Ireland. Retrieved from https://core.ac.uk/download/pdf/45382349.pdf

Bedarkar, M., & Pandita, D. (2014). A study on the drivers of employee engagement impacting employee performance. *Procedia-Social and Behavioural Sciences, 133*, 106-115. doi:10.1016/j.sbspro.2014.04.174

Bhardwaj, A., & Kumar, V. (2022). Privacy and Healthcare during COVID-19. In *Cybersecurity Crisis Management and Lessons Learned From the COVID-19 Pandemic* (pp. 82–96). IGI-Global. doi:10.4018/978-1-7998-9164-2.ch005

Chanana, N., & Sangeeta. (2021). Employee engagement practices during COVID-19 lockdown. *Journal of Public Affairs, 21*(4), e2508. doi:10.1002/pa.2508 PMID:33041656

Demerouti, E., Bakker, A. B., Nachreiner, F., & Schaufeli, W. B. (2001). The job demands-resources model of burnout. *The Journal of Applied Psychology, 86*(3), 499–512. doi:10.1037/0021-9010.86.3.499 PMID:11419809

HRKatha. (2020). https://www.hrkatha.com/employee-engagement/how-mcdonalds-is-keeping-its-crew-engaged-during-lockdown

Josephine & Virginia. (2013). Employee Engagement - An Approach to Organisational Excellence. *International Journal of Social Science & Interdisciplinary Research, 2*(5).

Kahn, W. A. (1990). Psychological conditions of personal engagement and disengagement at work. *Academy of Management Journal, 33*(4), 692–724. doi:10.2307/256287

Kumar, P. (2021). V-5 Model of Employee Engagement During COVID-19 and Post Lockdown. *Vision (Basel), 25*(3), 271–274. doi:10.1177/0972262920980878

Kumar, V., & Gupta, G. (Eds.). (2021). *Strategic Management During a Pandemic*. Routledge. doi:10.4324/9781003125648

Kumar, V., & Malhotra, G. (Eds.). (2021). *Stakeholder Strategies for Reducing the Impact of Global Health Crises*. IGI Global Publications. doi:10.4018/978-1-7998-7495-9

Lee, Y., Shin, H. Y., Park, J., Kim, W., & Cho, D. (2017). An integrative literature review on employee engagement in the field of human resource development: Exploring where we are and where we should go. *Asia Pacific Education Review, 18*(4), 541–557. doi:10.100712564-017-9508-3

McDonalds. (2022). www.mcdonalds.com

Nimon, K., Zigarmi, D., Houson, D., Witt, D., & Diehl, J. (2011). The work cognition inventory: Initial evidence of construct validity. *Human Resource Development Quarterly, 22*(1), 7–35. doi:10.1002/hrdq.20064

QWBRA. (2020). *The Impact of COVID-19 on Employee Engagement, A Quantum Workplace Benchmark Report and Analysis*. https://marketing.quantumworkplace.com/hubfs/Marketing/Website/Resources/PDFs/The-Impact-of-COVID-19-on-Employee-Engagement.pdf

Rooy David, L. V., Whitman, D. S., Hart, D., & Caleo, S. (2011). Measuring Employee Engagement During Financial Downturn: Business Imperative or Nuisance? *Journal of Business and Psychology, 26*(2), 147–152. doi:10.100710869-011-9225-6

Saks, A. M., & Gruman, J. A. (2014). What do we really know about employee engagement? *Human Resource Development Quarterly, 25*(2), 155–182. doi:10.1002/hrdq.21187

Sarkar, B. (2020, April 9). Companies roll out initiatives to keep employees kids engaged at home. *The Economic Times*. https://economictimes.indiatimes.com/news/company/corporate-trends/companies-roll-out-initiatives-to-keep-employees-kids-engaged-at-home/articleshow/75058556.cms

Schaufeli, W. B., & Bakker, A. B. (2004). Job demands, job resources, and their relationship with burnout and engagement: A multi-sample study. *Journal of Organizational Behavior*, *25*(3), 293–437. doi:10.1002/job.248

Schaufeli, W. B., Bakker, A. B., & Salanova, M. (2006). The measurement of work engagement with a short questionnaire: A cross-national study. *Educational and Psychological Measurement*, *66*(4), 701–716. doi:10.1177/0013164405282471

Shrotryia, V. K., & Dhanda, U. (2020). Exploring Employee Engagement Using Grounded Theory: Experiences from the Best Firms in India. *Vision (Basel)*, *24*(2), 171–183. doi:10.1177/0972262920915070

Shuck, B., Adelson, J. L., & Reio, T. G. Jr. (2017). The employee engagement scale: Initial evidence for construct validity and implications for theory and practice. *Human Resource Management*, *56*(6), 953–977. doi:10.1002/hrm.21811

Shuck, B., & Wollard, K. K. (2010). Employee engagement and HRD: A seminal review of the foundations. *Human Resource Development Review*, *9*(1), 89–110. doi:10.1177/1534484309353560

Singh, J., & Kumar, V. (2022). Combating the Pandemic with ICT Based Learning tools and applications: A case of Indian Higher Education. *International Journal of Virtual and Personal Learning Environments Platforms*, *12*(1), 1–21.

Talukdar, A. D. (2020, April 9). *5 tips for practicing employee engagement amidst the covid-19 pandemic*. Business 2 Community. https://www.business2community.com/human-resources/5-tips-for-practicing-employee-engagement-amidst-the-covid-19-pandemic-02300396

The Hindu. (2020). https://www.thehindubusinessline.com/companies/capgemini-launches-employee-engagement-programmes-to-help-beat-coronavirus-stress/article31310564.ece

Vander, E. T. (2016). Job demands-resources predicting burnout and work engagement among Belgian home health care nurses: A cross-sectional study. *Nursing Outlook*, *64*(6), 542–556. doi:10.1016/j.outlook.2016.06.004 PMID:27427405

KEY TERMS AND DEFINITIONS

Employee Engagement: Employee engagement refers to employees' physical, cognitive and emotional input in the work.

Employee Experience: Employee experience is the relationship an organization creates with employees. More specifically, it is the culmination of the various processes, spaces, and channels organizations use to communicate how they prioritize and value their workforces.

Hybrid Teams: A hybrid team is a staff that includes both office-based staff and remote employees. It could also mean that employees split their time between the office and their homes. A hybrid work model can allow employees to choose how and when they work most effectively and open up new kinds of talent to employers.

Pulse Surveys: A pulse survey is a brief and regular set of questions sent to employees. As the term "pulse" suggests, it is carried out to continuously gain employees' views on subjects such as job-related roles, communication and relationships, and the overall work environment.

Chapter 11
Responding to COVID-19:
A Case of Psychological Response Centers

Rajesh Verma
FGM Government College, Adampur, India

EXECUTIVE SUMMARY

To contain the spread of COVID-19, governments across the globe adopted strict mobility limiting measures. In India, 443,497 people died and 351,087 people are still struggling. The governments realising the long-lasting impact redefined their policies to offset the loss. The timely appropriate response of the governments in all sectors including psychological retarded the deadly impact. It was the first time in human history governments and NGOs realized the importance of mental health and responded with building up online mental health infrastructure. Some of the successful post-COVID-19 psychological response centers include the mental health rehabilitation helpline 'KIRAN' by Government of India and iCALL multilingual telephonic and email-based services in India by Tata Institute of Social Sciences.

INTRODUCTION

The global psycho-physical health emergency engendered by the COVID-19 led pandemic not only provided a glimpse of soft vulnerability also reminded humanity about level of preparedness to deal with biomedical catastrophes (Kumar & Malhotra, 2021). It crumbled the socio-economic paradigms and created a window of options to deal with the environmental degradation. And widened the scope of organized institutional responses from mere addressing the physio-medical needs to

DOI: 10.4018/978-1-6684-3504-5.ch011

psychological health (Kumar & Malhotra, 2021). It is nothing less than a delightful opportunity of blessings in disguise for those who suffered more psychologically than physiologically. It hastened the adjustment, quickened the adaptations, pressured for the compliance, inflicted the dread, initiated the manufacturing, engendered the pharma collaborations and opened the doors of new dimensions. All responded within the scope of their limits. It led to the emergence of Digital Infrastructure for Psychological Support (DIPS) for addressing mental health needs. The digital revolution furthered the reach of mental health services, a neglected component of whole health. It provided platform to the psychological health service providers. The response centers became integral part of health and wellbeing. The services are available 24X7 in almost all Indian languages (Singh & Kumar, 2022). The author has attempted to explain the relevancy and efficacy of one of the DIPS [TISS run iCall] through a case study.

The unprecedented situation created by the intentional and unintentional release of corona virus from the confines of Wuhan lab (Chinese) into free floating mode is a tip of devastation biomedical weapons can cause. The spread and survival of pathogens is dependent upon several factors, the quality of environment is one of them. The degradation of the environment as a result of human settlements and increased interaction between animals and humans offers fertile ground and a conducive environment for pathogens to survive and transmit across species (Lata & Gupta 2021). Climate change also facilitates transmission (Piret & Boivin, 2021). Corona virus's survival across climate types and infection patterns raised serious doubts over its genesis.

The history of pandemics suggests that the pandemic-causing pathogens infects areas that are and were highly structured (Piret & Boivin, 2021). Similar pattern was observed during this pandemic. The virus that belongs to Betacoronavirus family (Bhatt et al., 2020a) was designed to wreck undefined destruction in all possible terms including physical, economical (Gaur, & Patel, 2021) and most importantly psychological (Malik et al., 2020; Kaurani et al., 2020, Singh et al., 2021; Singh et al., 2020). The virus directly invaded the human body and impacted the functioning of various internal systems and organs (Ramakrishna et al., 2020) while indirectly created mess (Sudha & Gayatridevi, 2021) of financial and socio-economic systems (Shukla et al., 2021; Srivastava et al., 2021; Raj et al., 2021) and increased the morbidity and mortality (Patel & Singh, 2020). The main feature of coronavirus is that it compromises the human respiratory system (Jindal et al., 2020; Bhatt et al., 2020b) and significantly contributes to comorbidity.

Pandemics demands immediate interventions to mitigate the damage and contain the spread. The infection rate and consequent mortality raised alarm bells across the globe leading to quick institutional response (IR). The IR to contain and control the pandemics was started during the Black death pandemic way back in 14th century.

At the current times to contain the 'spread' governments across the globe adopted strict mobility limiting measures in the form of complete lockdown.

The social sciences mandated strategies are quarantine, isolation, lockdown, social distancing, greeting without handshakes, social distancing acted as effective for containing the spread (Mittal & Singh, 2020; Srivastava et al., 2021). These measures literally induced a comprehensive slow down (Kaila, 2021) and subsequently had deleterious effects on psychological health (Roychowdhury, 2020). The institutional enforced limiting measures brought the social and economic life to grinding halt (Manickam, 2020; Varma et al., 2021). As of 22 Sep 2021, in India 32783743 people recovered and subsequently discharged, 445768 people died and 301989 are still struggling with it (https://www.mygov.in, 2021).

Mental health is another area that more often suffers in the event of absence of credible information about the invader unknown. Undoubtedly, mental health was one of the first casualties of coronavirus (Bagi & Chand, 2020). Ramakrishna et al. (2020) rightly called it 'Covidism' and interestingly Mukherjee et al. (2021) addressed it 'Patriarchal Pandemic' because of excessive adverse impact on women.

At the initial stage when there was no pharmaceutical clue, the behavioural measures acted as first line of defence (Fras-Armenta et al., 2021). The science and specifically medical science were in midnight dark about its features and working. Evidence suggests that in the absence of scientific information there are higher chances of assumption-based decision making by governments which have inherent demerits in the form of various kinds of accidental biases. The biases are biases whether accidental or intentional but escalate the sufferings of sufferers. This pandemic was no exception. To overcome such issues Kapur (2020) suggests that "government advice in the future should as much as possible be based on relevant empirical evidence".

The governments across the globe realizing the gravity of long-lasting impact (Mushtaq et al., 2021) redesigned their policies to offset the loss. The timely appropriate response of the governments of the day in all sectors [including psychological] retarded the spread and limited the deadly impact. And the Indian government's response to contain the spread and manage post COVID-19 outcomes was praiseworthy (Bhardwaj & Kumar, 2022). For the first time in human history various government and non-government agencies realized the importance of mental health and responded quite well with building up mental health infrastructure.

The 'Technology' played a significant role as a 'frontline defender' in implementing the spread containing measures (Pandey, et al., 2021). An unusual spectacle of social pressure for compliance to preventive guidelines was witnessed during and even after easing the impact which demonstrates the intensity of fear people perceived. Saraff et al. (2021) suggested that "Fear of self-protection from an unknown virus changed everything that humans cherished on a social and community frontier".

The earlier unquestionable traditional systems were challenged and the paradigms of psycho-social relations underwent complete transformation. The changes were bidirectional [negative and positive]. The negative change in relationships was expressed through increase in family discord (Anindya et al., 2020; Maji et al., 2020; Poonam et al., 2020; Varma et al., 2021) commonly known as domestic violence. Even the dietary habits (Singh et al., 2020) and consumption pattern were altered during the lockdown period (Prasad & Srivastava, 2021).

The 'risk from unknown' was the major factor that initiated an unprecedented psychological response. The experience and expression of Fear, Panic and Anxiety (FPA) trio was high to an extent that it motivated the people to endure the psycho-socio-economic hardship accrued on the account of mobility restrictions. The virus made humans suspicious of each other because human to human contact was identified as the most common mode of transmission of coronavirus (Woelfert & Kunst, 2020). Everyone around was perceived as a potential 'carrier' and social distancing became a new norm (Manickam, 2020; Maurya & Pandey, 2021). The 'potential carrier' perspective is the genesis of apprehension (Hussain & Pervez, 2020) social stigma and FPA trio. Bhanot et al. (2021) defined stigmatization as a "social process set to exclude those who are perceived to be a potential source of disease and may pose threat to the effective social living in the society". During the peak period one step beyond the threshold of home was portrayed as an open invitation to certain 'death'.

Chapter Objective

The central objective of this chapter is to analyse the post COVID-19 responses of government and non-government organizations to address the behavioural and mental health issues of the general public. It includes a case study. The key take-away from this chapter is the strategy and success rate of the response through DIPS. The objectives of this chapter are:

1. To understand the motivation and purpose of the responses through DIPS.
2. To explore the working pattern of the Psycho-social support helpline.
3. To record and share the success rate.

COVID-19 PANDEMIC: KEY FEATURES

The transmission and proliferation of the virus was rapid (Varma et al., 2021); the first case was detected in Wuhan in China on 31 December 2019 and within 70 days World Health Organization declared it a pandemic (11 March 2020) (https://

covid19.who.int). The global trade and travel (Piret & Boivin, 2021) accelerated the transmission, consequently the virus invaded 213 countries (Ojha et al., 2020) within less than 11 weeks. In this short span of time, it covered almost every piece of human settlement except a few Island nations. Traditionally, during-&-post-pandemic the common organizational response (Fig 1) was limited to medical & pharmaceutical interventions, physical preparedness and economic rebuilding. The medical intervention deals with medical support, containment and extensive preventive communication. For example, Rastogi et al. (2021) in their letter to editor explained their concerns regarding unsupervised use of complementary alternative medicine (CAM) for improving the immune system in order to biologically prepare for impending danger. While the physical preparedness more often deals with equipping the affected population with information and relief material necessary for survival. The economic rebuilding includes financial relief packages, moratorium on taxes and industry stimulants.

Figure 1. Traditional administrative response pattern of government and non-government agencies

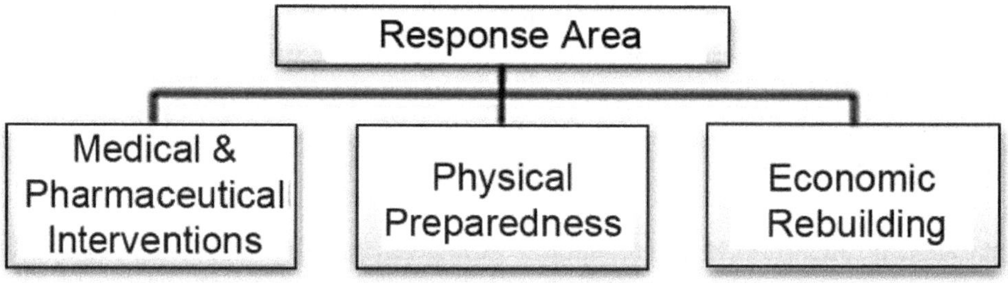

Figure 2. Post COVID-19 administrative response pattern of government and non-government agencies

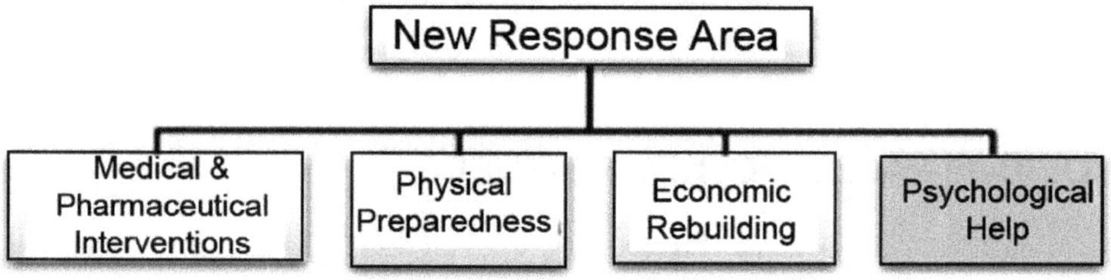

The information feed from media [mainstream and social] was rapid, excessive and at various times contained misleading figures that added fuel to the trio of FPA fires. One of the interesting aspects were reported by one of the main stream English newspapers (ToI, 2021) that 90% patients who were administered with fake remdesivir injection recovered from lung infection. It was nothing more than a placebo. The event indicates the role of psychological variables in physical health. Using the mathematical analogy, the opposite is equally true that vindicates the claim of various findings which suggests that the pandemic deteriorated the mental health of the individuals. The Table 1 explains certain risk factors associated with COVID-19. For the first time in the history of pandemics, it initiated an internal mass human exodus (Padhi, 2020) of the labour force from the cities or place of work which are away from their native place. It led to emergence of additional constructive and adverse (Bapu & Babu 2021) outcomes such as follows:

1. Improved air quality and environment (Balla, 2020),
2. Physical fitness awareness (Kaur, et al., 2020),
3. Excessive work pressure on medical health care workers (Kanthy, 2021; Pant & Mahour, 2020),
4. Enhanced awareness of personal hygiene (Pandey et al., 2021),
5. Disruption of regular learning (Ahuja & Garg, 2021) and use of alternative means of teaching and learning (Jena, 2020; Vaidya et al., 2021; Padhi, 2020a)
6. Engaging in yogic asana (Thakur et al., 2021) & meditation (Sheoran, 2021a) for health management and use of defence mechanism for coping up with unusual circumstances (Fatima & Mahour, 2021).
7. Experimentation in kitchen and preparation of creative dishes,
8. Improved level of digitalization by women entrepreneurs (Kovid et al., 2021)
9. Increase of child sexual abuse cases (Poddar & Mukherjee, 2020),

There were exclusive challenges for parents (Mazumdar & Gupta, 2021) irrespective of their culture, socio-economic status, place of residence, and geographical location. Real & deadly threat but was from unknown (Gairola & Mishra, 2020), unseen and even the inoculated fighting force [health workers] was dreading to face it. There was disturbed the psychological equilibrium (Vahali, 2021) of a sizable population

People resorted to video streaming platforms, writing blogs (Surbhi et al., 2021), accessed, downloaded and created open education resources, access to news, attending, participating, presenting research findings which indicates phenomenal increase in Internet usage (Sheoran, 2021) resulting in increased screen time (Zaman & Sharma, 2021).

Initially students enjoyed the homestay [meta-morphing of weekdays into Sunday, no school uniforms, no school bus, no prayers, no punishments, no home-work, no early getting up and so on…]. The boom of celebratory days was short-lived and changed into doom of monotony and regular parental scolding. The confines of homes and lack of stimulating environment led to the adverse effect on their mental health (Moghe et al., 2021). The unexpected outfits (terrorists) seized this opportunity to ramp up their agenda (radicalization of youth, brainwashing, recruitment, weapon deals and related activities) (daijiworld, 2021).

COVID-19 PANDEMIC: PSYCHOLOGICAL FACTORS

Adjustment in Times of Pandemic

The coping up with the pandemics, epidemics and outbreaks demand psycho-physiological adjustment and preparedness. The ensuing pandemic prompted human beings to adjust at behavioural (Chaudhary and Chandel, 2021) and mental health fronts. Behavioural adjustment is comparatively easier than mental health adjustment. The behavioural adjustment is facilitated by observing others (role model) and even without the active support or intervention of others. In extreme cases experts' help can be sought and scientific literature is the other important source that provides some measures. On the other hand, mental health is a fragile component of the cognitive domain. More often mental health is difficult to manage at the individual level especially during highly unpredictable and risky situations. It is highly sensitive to negativism (Shukla et al., 2021) and pessimism. When the immediate psycho-social environment is flooded by global and local media with sickening perspectives the individual finds it relatively hard to effectively cope-up with life challenges leading to helplessness (Pervez & Hussain, 2020) and hopelessness (see table 1).

Table 1. Psychological risk factors identified by research studies that associates directly or indirectly with COVID-19

Model	Components
Behavioural	Stress Depression Disturbed sleep-wake patterns Excessive mood swing that might culminate into mood disorders
Cognitive	Excessive worry Increased risk of suicide ideation Extreme emotional reactions or expression Self-harm behaviour

Courtesy: Author

Post COVID-19 Cogno-Behavioural Reappraisal

Face has been the center of identity since time immemorial. The wearing of masks, a protective measure, imposed several restrictions and cut down the liberty of verbal expression. The face mask was found to interfere by reducing the identification of emotions leading to misinterpretation (Carbon, 2020). The cognitive system has to evolve and transform itself (Mukund & Dehuri, 2021) to adjust to new paradigms of physical identification in tune with changed facial apparatuses. It has to realign and redesign its neural networks. The system responded well and evolved rapidly for additional job! The facial features that were employed for identification prior to 'mask era' includes eyes, lips, nose, cheeks, eyebrows, smiling style, cheek bones, teeth, presence or absence of moustaches, jaw, hair colour, voice, body language, hand gestures and of course lipsticks shades. However, the face mask masked almost 66% of these facial features. The cognitive system was left perplexed to handle the situation with only 33% available resources. The pandemic induced evolutionary process whetted the observational acuity of the cognitive system for finer observations and information processing ability for coming out with similar output with different ingredients. The idea of identification went for the paradigm shift with new features that includes crowfoots, peculiarity of shape of the outer canthus of the eyes, shape of upper nasal ridge, glabellar lines, eyebrow shape, temples, ear size, hairline pattern, ear locks, ear piercings, shades of periorbital dark circles and black or red mole on the unmasked face. This was nothing less than evolution of new species mandated by the cognitive realignments.

Table 2 shows some of the causal factors that induce the stress (Kaur & Rathee, 2021; Olff et al., 2021, Agashe, et al., 2021), anxiety (Shiva Kumar et al., 2021) and phobic reactions in the individual and families (Sahithya et al., 2020; Lindinger-Sternart et al., 2021).

Table 2. Causal factors of altered psychological states

Causal Factors Categories	Anticipated/Witnessed Situations
Self-Perceived	Comprehensive fear of infection Deterioration in physical state Post infection consequences Socio-economic disruption Poor coping strategies
Medical Infrastructure	Insecurity due to perceived inadequate health services Lack of know-how to deal with the situation Scarce pharmaceutical interventions
Physically Proximity	Loss of trust and increased inter-human suspicion Death of a well-known due to infection
Social	Decreased self-perceived social support Social stigma Quarantine and Isolation (Kaul & Lakhotia, 2021)
Information related	Images of people who died of infection Advertised fear through constant media feed Misinformation through social media
Clinical	Post-Traumatic Stress Disorders Anxiety Clinical depression

Courtesy: Author

DIGITAL INFRASTRUCTURE FOR PSYCHOLOGICAL SUPPORT (DIPS)

DIPS is an umbrella term that includes paid or unpaid digital initiatives such as tele-counselling, email support, application-based support designed by government and non-government bodies to address the mental health concerns. The DIPS is based upon certain assumptions.

Assumptions

1. Client is aware that she/he is suffering from some kind of psychological problem.
2. Client is aware that she/he needs professional help to tide over the problem.
3. Client has voluntarily called up.
4. Client voluntarily agrees to share personal details.
5. The services provided by these helplines have no legal implications.

Government's Contribution in Creating DIPS

Mental health rehabilitation helpline 'KIRAN' was launched by the Government of India. The KIRAN offers psychological services in 13 languages to various stakeholders such as COVID-19 patients and their families, healthcare workers, supporting staff, students, NGO's and others in the language of their choice. It is being managed by 660 clinical and rehabilitation psychologists and 668 psychiatrists through registered associations. The helpline is coordinated by two of the eminent institutes (NIMHR, Sehore and NIEPMD), Chennai) that have vast experience in dealing with psychological issues and disabilities. The usage of word mental rehabilitation by the central government indicates that present day government and administrators are well informed that COVID-19 not only compromised the physical health of infected individuals and their family members but also spoiled their mental health too. Rehabilitation means to put someone on the mainstream track post-recovery from the offtrack time period. It's gratifying to see a methodological response to address the psychological issues emerging from the corridors of power.

Information Technology Tools

The premier mental health institute of India NIMHANS issued comprehensive and useful guidelines for Mental Health in the times of COVID-19 pandemic. UNICEF issued guidelines for parents and caregivers regarding how to provide psychosocial support to children during COVID-19. FGM Government college Adampur, Hisar, Haryana started a Psychometric Assessment and Counselling Cell to address the psychological need of the students and community. Apart from this various universities, colleges, state governments, non-government organizations, hospitals and private institutions responded by setting up mental help centers across India. These were indeed human gestures and recognition of the importance of mental health. One of the important unthought-of benefits accrued from DIPS is that those families that have a mentally challenged or mentally ill person, they also can seek the help from these response centers.

The extensive post COVID-19 DIPS to address the psychological needs was varied, but stands on similar objectives. Some to the common objectives of DIPS are: -

1. offering Psychological First Aid (PFA) (Haleemunnissa et al., 2021),
2. managing distress and crisis,
3. psychological support and counselling,
4. inculcating positivism and optimism,
5. coping-up strategies to deal with pandemic induced psychological problems, and

6. behaviour modification.

Table 3. Governments initiated digital infrastructure for psychological support

State/Union Territory/ Organization	Time	Helpline Name	Helpline Number	Targeted Clients	Remarks
Andhra Pradesh	24x7	No name	104/1902	For all	Professional Mental health Support
Assam	24x7	Sarathi	104	For all	Toll Free, Integrated health related consultation
Chandigarh	24x7	No Name	1800-180-2063	COVID-19 Patients, Caregivers & HCP*	Toll Free
Chhattisgarh	24x7	Arogya Seva	104	For all	Medical and Psychological Advice
Gujarat	24x7	Jeevan Aastha	1800233330	For all	Mental Health Support
Haryana	24x7	Nayi Disha	7419864999	Students	Psychological First Aid Centre
Himachal Pradesh	Consultation at Hospital	No Name	104	For all	eSanjeevni at Hospitals for psychological needs
Jharkhand	Not mentioned	COVID Help Desk	Published list on Website	For all	Tele- Psychological Intervention / Tele-Counselling by SMHA
Karnataka	8 AM to 8 PM	Apthamitra	14410	For all	For Medical Help – COVID-19 Symptoms
Maharashtra	24x7	Mpower 1on1	1800-120-820050	For all	Addressing Mental health concerns
Manipur	24x7	No Name	1800-345-3818	Especially for people who are at quarantined & under depression.	Toll Free
Meghalaya	Issued a Positive Psychology Protocol for individuals who are affected by COVID-19 through Psycho Social Support Units that are operating from each district.				
Puducherry	9 am- 7 pm	TYCL Mental Support Helpline	0413-2262 547 and 96555 07090	For all	Mental Health Support
Rajasthan	24x7	Mann Samvad	1800-180-0018	COVID-19 Patients & others	OPD, IPD and special programs for remote areas.

Continued on following page

Table 3. Continued

State/Union Territory/ Organization	Time	Helpline Name	Helpline Number	Targeted Clients	Remarks
Tamil Nadu	24x7	Crisis Lines	8552747471	For all	Addressing Mental health crisis
Tripura	10 am & 4 pm (Mon-Sat)	No name	0381-241-0053	Students of Class-I to Class XII	Toll Free
Uttar Pradesh	24x7	No Name	1800-180-5145	For all	Toll Free
West Bengal	11 am to 5 pm	No name		For all	Toll Free
NIMHANS	24x7	No name	080 – 4611 0007	For all	Psycho-social support
TISS	10 am & 8 pm (Mon-Sat)	iCall	9152987821 icall@tiss.edu	For all	Psychological Issues
RCI	Published state-wise list of 640 RCI registered professionals along with their contact numbers on their website. Those who wish to seek psychological services can pick-choose-&-call.				

*Health Care Providers. The list is not exhaustive.

Information Courtesy: Various websites of respective states, union territories and organization.

Table Developed by: Author.

The multiple agencies both public and private sector across India stepped-in to offer various kinds of psychological services via offline and online mode. In this chapter the focus will be only on iCALL, a multilingual telephonic and email-based services in India run by Tata Institute of Social Sciences. It is online, toll free, non-profit and operates for the common cause.

DIPS CASE

iCall at TISS

It is an initiative of Tata Institute of Social Sciences, Mumbai and started in 2012. iCall operates on two modes i.e., telephonic and email. According to the iCall website "Since its inception in 2012, the helpline has addressed 45,000 calls and nearly 5000 emails from individuals in 25 out of 29 Indian states and 20 countries across the globe". The idea to start this helpline was to offer psychological services to the people who are facing psychological issues. The objective of iCall is to "information and referral to people in emotional, psychological distress across age groups, gender and sexual identities, geographies and other issues".

Figure 3. Three core values of iCall
(Curtesy: https://icallhelpline.org, 2021)

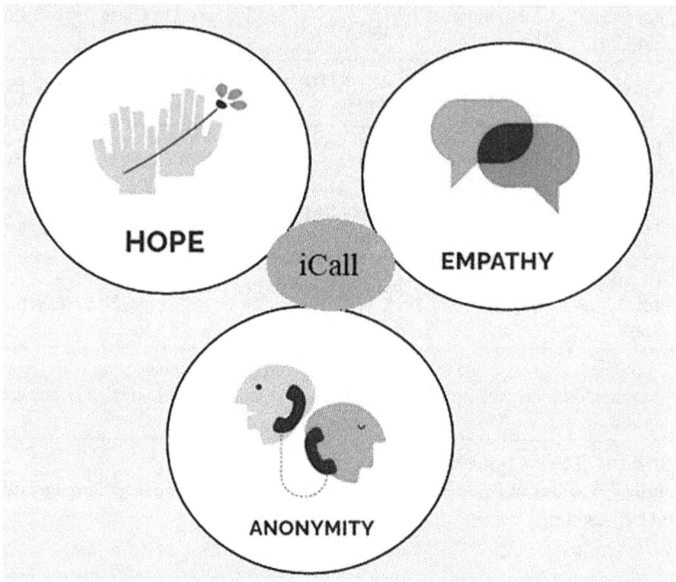

Telephonic Mode

The client can call the helpline number given in Table 3. When the client dials the designated number an automatic response system welcomes on the Psycho-social helpline and informs the caller that the 'your call will be documented and recorded for research and monitoring purposes" in English and Hindi successively for the first 18 seconds. Then the caller will hear a recorded message for almost 12 seconds and thereafter a human voice responds with an identifying message 'hello, iCall helpline'. The iCall helpline does not ask for personal details except for three things, client's contact number, age and geographical location (name of district). The central idea behind this is to ensure that the client does not need to share her/his personal details with the unknown human being and feels safe and secure. Because while detailing the psychological issues the client often hesitates to share personal identification particulars. The hesitation stems from the apprehension of being judged by the counsellor on the basis of stereotypes and prejudices which are the integral part of human behaviour. Clients might assume that she/he may be judged by the counsellor on the basis of his name, surname, place of residence etc. The iCall has circumvented all these issues in one masterstroke by not asking the personal details. It has various communication lines to cater for more than one client simultaneously. One of the demerits is that the caller every time is connected to a different counsellor because the automatic forwarding system allocates the unoccupied line. And there are high chances that she/he might get connected to a different counsellor every time. In such circumstances the client is likely to be irritated and frustrated to repeat the same thing each time he calls. Again, the iCall team has come up with a unique solution. Once the caller identifies himself with age and geographical location the previous recorded discussion will be instantly available with the new counsellor. The counsellor listens to the recorded version and appraises himself with the history of the client. The client is saved from the frustrating phenomenon of repetition of the same thing.

Process

The iCall has a ten steps procedure between call pick up and final good bye. The model procedure starts with assurance of keeping the details and data confidential and terminates at feedback from the client. After initial rapport building, the counselling process begins. During the process the client is encouraged to share the problem in detail from all possible psychological angles. The details are collated and the problem is pinpointed. Post identification of the issue the client is suggested suitable techniques and specific tasks that help in addressing the issue. The session is summarized and feedback is sought. The consent of the client for follow up is sought and the case is followed up accordingly.

Email Based Counselling

Another unique modality of iCall is email based counselling. The clients who feel insecure in talking about their psychological issues can write and share with the iCall team with a dedicated email address (Table 3). Here the only requirement is that the client should have minimal knowledge of the operation of email services. The email-based counselling service has some challenges associated with it. First, the individual in distress more often finds it difficult to transform their psychological problems into words which makes correct identification of key issue/s from the statement of the client a little difficult. Secondly, the counsellor has to have literary as well as conceptual ability. The literary ability helps in understanding the meaning of the words and phrases written by the client while conceptual ability helps in understanding the spirit behind what has been written. The counsellor has to transcend the literary characteristic of the sentence and to understand it in the client's context. She/he is required to collate both these features to arrive at conclusion and later take decisions. Thirdly, it is not possible to grasp and consequently identify the psychological issues just by one email. For that the counsellor has to wait for additional information prior to arriving at a definite conclusion. The information shared by the client remains confidential and none other than the counsellor can have access to them.

Process

The client has to write an email to the iCall team through a dedicated email address. The iCall team responds to the email queries within two to three days. At the first instance the iCall responds with an automatic reply with acknowledgement. They reply through the trail mail and remain in touch with the client continuously. The responses of the client are meticulously studied for clues regarding the psychological problems. Once the problem is identified the client is suggested techniques for behaviour modification. The team remains in contact with the client and provides various resources to deal with issues. When the responses of the client indicate improvement the booster tasks are suggested. And in case of no improvement is perceived the techniques are changed. This process goes on till the client gains. Finally, the feedback is sought and consent for follow up is solicited. If clients agree to the follow up, the team responds accordingly.

Merits and Demerits of Email-Based Counselling

Merits

1. The client feels psychologically safe while sharing his issues because he knows that the other individual is not face to face.
2. It is easy to make references i.e., the client and counsellor need not to remember when and what has been discussed earlier.
3. This modality is culture free and culture fare.

Demerits

1. Higher probability of time delay in interactions.
2. Difficulty in expression of psychological issues and emotional feelings through words.

3. Familiarity with usage of email and requirement of active internet connection.
4. Difficult in writing email in local and vernacular language.
5. Lacks a human touch.
6. Difficult to verify the veracity of the information.

One of the unique features of the iCall is that clients are free to switch between both modalities i.e., Telephonic to Email and vice versa. This switching flexibility offers an opportunity to the clients to express their concerns in either or both modes. It is helpful for the counsellor also because it provides information in dual mode where counselors have liberty to collate and attest the authenticity of the information provided by the client.

The iCall website under Covid-19 tab offers multimedia resources in four languages i.e., Hindi, Marathi, Telugu and English. The resources are designed for various stakeholders such as parents, children & adolescents, frontline health workers and employees. The resources can be accessed in three formats which includes pdf documents, web pages and video links. The pdf documents contain probable psychological problems an individual can encounter along with their standard solutions, suggestions and advice. For example, the document named 'Caring for Carers' is one page that talks about the potential sources of stress and the expert suggestion concerning caring about self during and post working hours. The topic appropriate matching emotion expressing human illustrations make the document attractive. The webpage layouts are well structured and embedded with hyperlinks that offer crucial inputs regarding managing a host of psychological problems. iCall runs a Youtube channel [iCall Helpline] that has animated videos concerning psychological problems in Hindi and English. The iCall partnered with nULTA, an online consultation platform was funded by Mr Roy de Souza, an entrepreneur. This platform connects the client with medical doctors and psychologists depending upon the requirement of the client. The clients can use nULTA to access psychological services through live chat.

The psycho-social support modalities indicate that iCall has played a lead role in optimal utilization of technology for reaching out to the people in distress.

Presence on Social-Media and Collaborations

iCall can be accessed on several social networking websites such as, facebook, LinkedIn, Google+, Yahoo Mail, Twitter and GMail. It has partnered with IIT Bombay, Mariwala Health Initiative (MHI), Aspire, a Kalyan-based educational organisation, Synergy Marine Group, and other several institutes to offer psycho-social support services. Additionally, iCall collaborated with UNFPA, UN Women and World Health Organization to equip mental health service providers from five states (Rajasthan, Odisha, Madhya Pradesh, Bihar and Maharashtra). And partnered with non-government organizations too.

Contribution in Other Areas

iCall regularly conducts customized workshops and training for individuals working in various sectors including public sectors via all possible modes such as face to face, video conferencing, talks, distribution of written material and regular newsletters. These activities garners support from the community and helps in spreading the news about the organization. Additionally, such programs create awareness about the efficacy of mental health in day-to-day living and maintaining the optimal productive capacity of an individual.

Deduced Para

The iCall is a venture of the School of Human Ecology of Tata Institute of Social Sciences. Though it started offering psychological services way back in 2012 but contributed significantly in addressing the post COVID-19 psychological issues. The early start and wide reach with complete professionalism helped in making iCall a significant contributor in the field. Some of the factors that led to the success of iCall are: -

1. The genuine efforts of managing and operating which is nearly equivalent to '*Nishkām Karma*' as explained by Lord Krishna to Arjuna.
2. Continuity of all round efforts.
3. Investing efforts to reach where others hesitate to go.
4. Full exploitation of technology tools for delivery of service and spreading awareness.
5. Complete adherence to the principles of counselling with scientific approach.

CONCLUSION AND SUGGESTIONS

The emergence of pandemics is expected to rise with the rise in comprehensive human aspirations which in turn may have adverse impact upon mental health. The DIPS type initiative tends to further the idea of total health. It has come up on the recognition of idea of mental health as an important component of comprehensive wellbeing (CWb). The pandemic necessitated the existence of DIPS like systems. To further the CWb, government and non-government organizations taken up the lead and significantly contributed. The DIPS in the form of helplines is continuous process and designed to stay for longer time. In fact, some of the helplines mentioned in the Table 3 existed prior to the Covid-19 pandemic. The iCall is one of the such response centers. The collective effort in the form of DIPS has engendered hope and positivism in the minds of the public vis-à-vis psychological wellbeing.

Suggestions

Till now the idea of DIPS seems to have served its purpose yet there is always a window of growth and development. The present model of DIPS serves only for the individual, who have some kind of self-realization of psychological sufferings, have access to information technology and its tools, are conversant with psychological lexicon, are minimally digitally literate, and know the means and processes to reach out to these response systems.

The population who meets these parameters is merely a fraction of the total population. So, to reach the last individual in the queue the DIPS needs to do a lot. The following suggestions might come in handy for those who are already running DIPS or planning to kick-start a new one.

1. The present DIPS caters to the needs of an exclusive class; hence it is required to extend its reach.
2. The DIPS can yield better results if it is integrated with the National Rural Health Mission.
3. The major shortcoming of the current DIPS is ‘Follow up’, a system must be evolved where chances of follow up increases.
4. The short certificate course of Psychological First Aid may be introduced for the health care workers, college students and teachers.
5. The most DIPS must maintain their operations continuously, the break in between defeats the purpose.

ACKNOWLEDGMENT

The contribution of my revered teacher Prof Rajbir Singh for proof reading and providing valuable inputs and my wife Dr Sujit Verma for helping me in designing the structure of this chapter was immense.

REFERENCES

Agashe, S., Kumar, S., & Rai, R. (2021). Exploring the relationship between social ties and resilience from evolutionary framework. *Frontiers of Human Dynamics*, *3*, 683755. doi:10.3389/fhumd.2021.683755

Ahuja, K., & Garg, M. (2021). Stress and well-being among first year and last year college students during COVID-19. *Indian Journal of Mental Health*, *8*(1), 66–69. doi:10.30877/IJMH.8.1.2021.65-69

Anindya, S. N., Debora, M. A., & Manickam, L. S. S. (2020). Refining psychological services and strategies in India in the wake of COVID-19. In L. S. S. Manickam (Ed.), COVID-19 pandemic: Challenges and responses of psychologists from India (pp. 8-22). Thiruvananthapuram: The Editor.

Bagi, P. D., & Sunita Chand, S. (2020). Effect of lockdown on mental health: A study of Haryana. *Mrida: An International Journal of Humanities and Social Sciences*, *1*(1), 1–8.

Balla, D. (2020). Manipulating CORONA VIRUS's adverse effects for the benefit of humanity - A psychologist's perspective. *Tejasvi Astitva*, 1-8. http://www.tejasviastitva.com/manipulating-coronaviruss-adverse-effects-for-the-benefit-of-humanitya-psychologists-perspective-by-dr-deepthi-balla/

Bapu, V. K. G., & Babu, K. N. C. (2021). Impact of COVID-19 on intolerance of uncertainty and safety behaviour. *Ilkogretim Online*, *20*(4).

Bhanot, D., Singh, T., Verma, S. K., & Sharad, S. (2021). Stigma and discrimination during COVID-19 pandemic. *Frontiers in Public Health*, *8*, 577018. doi:10.3389/fpubh.2020.577018 PMID:33585379

Bharat, R., Uzaina, Niranjan, S., Yadav, T., Newman, S., Marriott, J., Smith, G., & Sawlani, G. (2021). Autism spectrum disorder in the COVID 19 era: New challenges – new solutions. *Indian Pediatrics*, *58*(15), 890–892. doi:10.100713312-021-2314-3 PMID:34183470

Bhardwaj, A., & Kumar, V. (2022). Privacy and Healthcare during COVID-19. In *Cybersecurity Crisis Management and Lessons Learned From the COVID-19 Pandemic* (pp. 82–96). IGI-Global. doi:10.4018/978-1-7998-9164-2.ch005

Bhatt, A., Arora, P., & Prajapati, S. K. (2020a). Can algal derived bioactive metabolites serve as potential therapeutics for the treatment of SARS-CoV-2 like viral infection? *Frontiers in Microbiology*, *11*, 596374. doi:10.3389/fmicb.2020.596374 PMID:33262750

Bhatt, A., Arora, P., & Prajapati, S. K. (2020b). Occurrence, fates and potential treatment approaches for removal of viruses from wastewater: A review with emphasis on SARS- CoV-2. *Journal of Environmental Chemical Engineering*, *8*(5), 104429. doi:10.1016/j.jece.2020.104429 PMID:32895629

BS. (2021). https://www.business-standard.com/article/economy-policy/covid-19-lockdown-effect-every-second-indian-now-on-internet-in-cities-120050801805_1.html

Carbon, C.-C. (2020). Wearing face masks strongly confuses counterparts in reading emotions. *Frontiers in Psychology*, *11*, 566886. doi:10.3389/fpsyg.2020.566886 PMID:33101135

Chaudhary, M., & Chandel, P. (2021). Digital education a boon or doom for children of digital India during COVID-19. In N. Gupta & N. Srivastava (Eds.), *Psychosocial impact of digital education during COVID-19* (Vol. 1, pp. 1–18). Insta.

Daijiworld. (2021). https://www.daijiworld.com/news/newsDisplay?newsID=883674

Fatima, H., & Mahour, P. (2021). Manifestation and usefulness of defence mechanisms during COVID-19 pandemic. *International Journal of Indian Psychology*, *9*(1), 1469–1475.

Frias-Armenta, M., Corral-Frias, N. S., Corral-Verdugo, V., & Lucas, M. Y. (2021). Psychological predictors of precautionary behaviours in response to COVID-19: A structural model. *Frontiers in Psychology*, *12*, 559289. doi:10.3389/fpsyg.2021.559289 PMID:33995161

Gairola, V., & Mishra, P. K. (2020). COVID-19 turned upside down: A psychological perspective. *Pedagogy of Learning*, *6*(4), 1–7.

Gaur, A., & Patel, A. K. (2021). Psychosocial intervention among COVID-19 and their care givers: A therapeutic approach. In P. Kansra (Ed.), *Socio economics of COVID-19 in India* (pp. 112–118). Wesser Books.

Haleemunnissa, S., Didel, S., Kumar Swami, M., Singh, K., & Vyas, V. (2021). Children and COVID19: Understanding impact on the growth trajectory of an evolving generation. *Children and Youth Services Review*, *120*, 105754. doi:10.1016/j.childyouth.2020.105754 PMID:33281255

Husain, A., & Pervez, R. (2020). Relationship of positive and negative behaviours with Covid-19. In A. K. Bansal & A. R. Adam (Eds.), *The COVID-19 Pandemic (Fallout & Recovery)* (pp. 31–39). Kripa Drishti Publications.

Icallhelpline. (2021). https://icallhelpline.org/what-is-icall/

Jena, P. K. (2020). Indian education in pandemic COVID-19. In R. Borah, B. Borkakoty, & P. P. Borah (Eds.), *Impact of COVID-19 on Indian Society: Challenges & Opportunities* (pp. 9–18). Balaji Publications.

Jindal, A., Jagdish, R. K., & Gupta, A. (2020). COVID-19 and liver disease. *Acta Scientific Gastrointestinal Disorders*, *3*(10), 20–27.

Kaila, H. L. (2021). Critical questions on COVID-19 and behavioural safety culture: India case study. *Chemical News*, 28-40.

Kanthy, D. U. (2021). COVID-19: The change of face through resilience, sustainability and interdependency. In M. A. Wani, M. K. Verma, B. Rathakrishna, & D. Srivastava (Eds.), *COVID-19 Crises Psychosocial Perspectives* (pp. 100–106). Novel Nuggets.

Kapur, N. (2020). Covid-19 and cognitive bias. *British Medical Journal,* 1-4.

Kaul, A., & Lakhotia, C. (2021). Psychological impact of COVID-19. *International Journal of Indian Psychology*, *9*(1), 2349–3429.

Kaur, H., Singh, T., Arya, Y. K., & Mittal, S. (2020). Physical fitness and exercise during the COVID-19 pandemic: A qualitative enquiry. *Frontiers in Psychology*, *11*, 590172. doi:10.3389/fpsyg.2020.590172 PMID:33250827

Kaur, S., & Rathee, N. (2021). Coping with COVID-19: Cross-cultural comparison across countries. *Wesleyan Journal of Research*, *13*(65), 45–56.

Kaurani, P., Batra, K., & Hooja, H. R. (2020). Psychological impact of COVID-19 lockdown (phase 2) among Indian general population: A cross-sectional survey. *International Journal of Scientific Research*, *9*(8), 2277–8179. doi:10.36106/ijsr/2439876

Kazmi, S. S. H., Hasan, K., Talib, S., & Saxena, S. (2020). COVID-19 and lockdown: A study on the impact on mental health. SSRN *Electronic Journal*. doi:10.2139/ssrn.3577515

Kovid, R. K., Kumari, D., & Pandey, S. (2021). Strategic response to the corona pandemic crisis: A case of Indian women entrepreneurs. In V. Kumar & G. Malhotra (Eds.), *Stakeholder Strategies for Reducing the Impact of Global Health Crises* (pp. 68–84). IGI Global Publishers. doi:10.4018/978-1-7998-7495-9.ch005

Kumar, V., & Gupta, G. (Eds.). (2021). *Strategic Management During a Pandemic*. Routledge. doi:10.4324/9781003125648

Kumar, V., & Malhotra, G. (Eds.). (2021). *Stakeholder Strategies for Reducing the Impact of Global Health Crises*. IGI Global Publications. doi:10.4018/978-1-7998-7495-9

Kurian, A., Farisha, A. T. P., Raseela, K. N., Sabeena, P. K., & Suhana, E. K. (2021). Impact of E-learning in India during COVID-19 and measures to overcome them. In M. A. Wani, M. K. Verma, B. Rathakrishna, & D. Srivastava (Eds.), *COVID-19 Crises Psychosocial Perspectives* (pp. 67–88). Novel Nuggets.

Lata, M., & Gupta, A. (2020). Role of Social Media in Environmental Democracy. In *Examining the Roles of IT and Social Media in Democratic Development and Social Change* (pp. 275–293). IGI Global. doi:10.4018/978-1-7998-1791-8.ch011

Lindinger-Sternart, S., Widyaningsih, Y. S., Kaur, V., & Patel, A. K. (2021). A global pandemic: How different nations coped with COVID-19 phobia. *Journal of Psychiatry & Mental Disorders*, *6*(3), 1–10.

Maji, S., Bansod, S., & Singh, T. (2020). Domestic violence during COVID-19 pandemic: The case for Indian women. *Journal of Community & Applied Social Psychology*, 1–8. PMID:33821118

Malik, V. S., Poonam, & Bahmani, R. K. (2020). Effect of COVID-19 lockdown on mental health and family relationship in north Indian people: Lockdown and you. *Shodh Sarita*, *7*(27), 76–84.

Manickam, L. S. S. (2020). COVID-19 Pandemic: A time for prudent and ethical action. In COVID-19 pandemic: Challenges and responses of psychologists from India (pp. 218-228). Thiruvananthapuram: The Editor.

Manickam, L. S. S., John, A., Debora, M. A., Krishnan, P., & Jasseer, J. (2020). Refining psychological services and strategies in India in the wake of COVID-19. In COVID-19 Pandemic: Challenges and responses of psychologists from India (pp.8-18). Thiruvananthapuram: The Editor.

Maurya, M. K., & Pandey, M. K. (2021). Collective actions, social distancing and belief in science in the age of COVID-19: A correlational study. *Anvesak*, *51*(2), 90–96.

Mazumdar, K., & Gupta, P. (2021). The invisible frontline workers: Narratives of Indian mothers' experiences through the pandemic. In A. O'Reilly & F. Green (Eds.), *Mothers, Mothering, and COVID-19: Dispatches from the pandemic* (pp. 467–478). Demeter Press. doi:10.2307/j.ctv1h45mcj.44

Mittal, S., & Singh, T. (2020). Gender-based violence during COVID-19 pandemic: A mini- review. *Frontiers in Global Women Health*, *1*, 4. doi:10.3389/fgwh.2020.00004 PMID:34816149

Moghe, K., Kotecha, D., & Patil, M. (2021). COVID-19 and mental health: A study of its impact on students in Maharashtra, India. medRxiv.

Mukherjee, T., Chowdhury, S., & Ahmed, T. (2021). A patriarchal pandemic: Looking at COVID 19 through a gendered lens. In A. Dubey & A. Shukla (Eds.), *Mental Health: Psychosocial Perspectives; Volume 6-Women Mental Health* (pp. 16–26). Concept.

Mukund, B., & Dehuri, B. K. (2021). Resilience and coping strategies essentials for thriving successfully. In S. Lata, S. Verma, & S. Joshi (Eds.), *COVID-19 in India-Problems, Challenges and Strategies* (pp. 394–412). Global Vision.

Mushtaq, N. F., Shiva Kumar, B. K., Vinay, H. R., & Honnugudi, B. D. (2021). A comparative study of stress and coping strategies among undergraduate medical students during pre and post COVID-19 pandemic lockdown. *International Journal of Scientific Research*, *10*(10), 1–2. doi:10.36106/ijsr/2903859

Ojha, R., Gupta, N., Naik, B., Singh, S., Verma, V. K., Prusty, D., & Prajapati, V. K. (2020). High throughput and comprehensive approach to develop multiepitope vaccine against minacious COVID-19. *European Journal of Pharmaceutical Sciences*, *151*, 105375. doi:10.1016/j.ejps.2020.105375 PMID:32417398

Olff, M., Primasari, I., Qing, Y., Coimbra, B. M., Hovnanyan, A., Grace, E., Williamson, R. E., Hoeboer, C. M., & Consortium, T. G. C. (2021). Mental health responses to COVID-19 around the world. *European Journal of Psychotraumatology*, *12*(1), 1929754. doi:10.1080/20008198.2021.1929754 PMID:34262666

Padhi, S. (2020). COVID-19 Pandemic and issues of migrant labourers in India. *Ajanta*, *9*(3), 66–72.

Padhi, S. (2020a). Challenges of COVID-19 pandemic and interrupted education system. In S. Mishra, V. Sharma, & S. Prasad (Eds.), *Evolution of New Teaching Practices in COVID-19* (pp. 9–17). Akhand.

Pandey, V., Astha, A., Mishra, N., Greeshma, R., Lakshmana, G., Jeyavel, S., Rajkumar, E., & Prabhu, G. (2021). Do social connections and digital technologies act as social cure during COVID-19? *Frontiers in Psychology*, *12*, 634621. doi:10.3389/fpsyg.2021.634621 PMID:33868099

Pandey, V., Misra, N., Greeshma, R., Astha, A., Jeyavel, S., Lakshmana, G., Rajkumar, E., & Prabhu, G. (2021). Techno trend awareness and its attitude towards social connectedness and mitigating factors of COVID-19. *Frontiers in Psychology*, *12*, 637395. doi:10.3389/fpsyg.2021.637395 PMID:34113286

Pant, A., & Mahour, P. (2020). Perceived threat and psychological impact of COVID-19 on families of health care professionals in India. *International Journal of Indian Psychology*, *8*(2), 961–966.

Patel, A. K., & Singh, J. (2020). Psychological impact of COVID-19 on daily life: A comprehensive understanding. In A. P. Sikarwar & B. C. Yadav (Eds.), *Social and Community Aspects of COVID-19 Pandemic* (pp. 1–12). Shriyanshi Prakashan.

Pervez, R., & Husain, A. (2020). Coping strategies for personal and health-related problems linked with Covid-19. In A. K. Bansal & A. R. Adam (Eds.), *The COVID-19 Pandemic (Fallout & Recovery)* (pp. 23–30). Kripa Drishti Publications.

Piret, J., & Boivin, G. (2021). Pandemics throughout history. *Frontiers in Microbiology*, *11*, 631736. doi:10.3389/fmicb.2020.631736 PMID:33584597

Poddar, S., & Mukherjee, U. (2020). Ascending child sexual abuse statistics in India during COVID-19 lockdown: A darker reality and alarming mental health concerns. *Indian Journal of Psychological Medicine*, *42*(5), 493–494. doi:10.1177/0253717620951391 PMID:33414605

Poonam., S., & Behmani, R. K. (2020). Impact of the COVID-19 pandemic on domestic violence in India. *Journal of Social Sciences, 48*(3), 1769-1779.

Prasad, R. K., & Srivastava, M. K. (2021). Switching behaviour toward online shopping: Coercion or choice during COVID-19 pandemic. *Academy of Marketing Studies Journal*, *1*(25), 1–15.

Raj, S., Ghosh, D., Singh, T., Verma, S. K., & Arya, Y. K. (2021). Theoretical mapping of suicidal risk factors during the COVID-19 pandemic: A mini-review. *Frontiers in Psychiatry*, *11*, 589614. doi:10.3389/fpsyt.2020.589614 PMID:33551864

Ramakrishna, G., Kumar, P., Aggarwal, S., Islam, M., Singh, R., Jagdish, R. K., & Trehanpati, N. (2020). SARS-Cov-2 (human) and COVID-19: Primer 2020. *Hepatology International*, *14*(4), 475–477. doi:10.100712072-020-10049-7 PMID:32333304

Roychowdhury, D. (2020). 2019 Novel coronavirus disease, crisis, and isolation. *Frontiers in Psychology*, *11*, 1958. doi:10.3389/fpsyg.2020.01958 PMID:32849147

Sahithya, B. R., Kashyap, R. S., & Roopesh, B. N. (2020). Perceived stress, parental stress, and parenting during COVID-19 lockdown: A preliminary study. *Journal of Indian Association of Child Adolescent and Mental Health*, *16*(4), 44–63.

Saraff, S., Singh, T., & Biswal, R. (2021). Coronavirus disease 2019: Exploring media portrayals of public sentiment on funerals using linguistic dimensions. *Frontiers in Psychology*, *12*, 626638. doi:10.3389/fpsyg.2021.626638 PMID:33679546

Sheoran, P. (2021). Prevalence of psychological distress among adolescents in relation to internet addiction during COVID-19 times. *IOSR Journal of Humanities and Social Science*, *26*(4), 46–52.

Sheoran, P. (2021a). Meditation as a therapeutic tool for boosting mental health during COVID- 19 times. *SSRG International Journal of Humanities and Social Science*, *8*(2), 37–41.

Shiva Kumar, B. K., Mushtaq, N. F., Vinay, H. R., & Bramaramba, D. H. (2021). Depression, anxiety and stress among undergraduate medical students during COVID-19 pandemic. *International Journal of Scientific Research*, *10*(3), 56–58.

Shukla, M., Pandey, R., Singh, T., Riddleston, L., Hutchinson, T., Kumari, V., & Lau, J. Y. F. (2021). The effect of COVID-19 and related lockdown phases on young peoples' worries and emotions: Novel data from India. *Frontiers in Public Health*, *9*, 645183. doi:10.3389/fpubh.2021.645183 PMID:34095054

Singh, A., Gupta, K., & Yadav, V. K. (2021). Adopting e-learning facilities during COVID-19: Exploring perspectives of teachers working in Indian public-funded elementary schools. *Education 3-13 International Journal of Primary, Elementary and Early Years Education,* 1-15.

Singh, J., & Kumar, V. (2022). Combating the Pandemic with ICT Based Learning tools and applications: A case of Indian Higher Education. *International Journal of Virtual and Personal Learning Environments Platforms*, *12*(1), 1–21.

Singh, V., Poonam, & Behmani, R. K. (2020). Influence of food pattern on life of people during COVID-19 lockdown. *International Journal of Creative Research*, *8*(7), 4922–4941.

Srivastava, A., Arya, Y. K., Joshi, S., Singh, T., Kaur, H., Chauhan, H., & Das, A. (2021). Major stressors and coping strategies of internal migrant workers during the COVID-19 pandemic: A qualitative exploration. *Frontiers in Psychology*, *12*, 648334. doi:10.3389/fpsyg.2021.648334 PMID:34093333

Sudha, R., & Gayatridevi, S. (2021). Building psychological wellbeing through compassion focused therapy among COVID survivors. *Kalyan Bharathi, 24*(8).

Surbhi, K. A., & Yadav, N. (2021). Hidden power of being simple: Learnings during COVID- 19. *Vidyabharati International Interdisciplinary Research Journal*, (Special Issue), 1276–1282.

Surbhi, Yadav, N., & Kumar, A. (2021). An exploratory study to analyze the impact of COVID- 19 on the daily lives of people: A focus group discussion. In *Health Informatics and Technological Solutions for Coronavirus (COVID-19)*. New York: CRC Press.

Thakur, J., Singh, I., & Sethi, S. R. (2021). Role of Yoga and meditation for anxiety among working adults during COVID-19. *International Journal of Indian Psychology, 9*(2), 128–135.

ToI. (2021). https://timesofindia.indiatimes.com/city/bhopal/90-patients-who-got-fake-remedesivir-in-mp-beat-covid/articleshow/82642139.cms?utm_source=twitter.com&utm_medium=social&utm_campaign=TOIDesktop

Vahali, H. O. (2021). Psychosocial challenges in the midst of the coronavirus. In C. R. Reddy (Ed.), *India and the pandemic: The first year* (pp. 275–283). Orient Black Swan.

Vaidya, A., Patil, A., & Vaidya, A. (2021). Perception of online education during the COVID- 19 pandemic in India. *International Journal of Creative Research Thoughts, 9*(7), f8–f17.

Varma, R., Das, S., & Singh, T. (2021). Cyberchondria amidst COVID-19 pandemic: Challenges and management strategies. *Frontiers in Psychiatry, 12*, 618508. doi:10.3389/fpsyt.2021.618508 PMID:33995143

Woelfert, F. S., & Kunst, J. R. (2020). How political and social trust can impact social distancing practices during COVID-19 in unexpected ways. *Frontiers in Psychology, 11*, 572966. doi:10.3389/fpsyg.2020.572966 PMID:33381063

Zaman, T., & Sharma, S. (2021). Screen time, sleep quality and depressive symptoms during lockdown due to COVID-19. In *The new normal - psychological perspectives: Selected papers from Dr. MGR-Janaki College of Arts & Science for Women International E Conference 2021* (pp. 174-182). Academic Press.

Chapter 12
Response of the Ayurvedic Healthcare Sector to COVID-19:
Insights From India

Shagun
Sharda University, India

Manisha Gupta
Sharda University, India

Raj K. Kovid
https://orcid.org/0000-0001-5224-0725
Sharda University, India

Madhu Rani
Sharda University, India

EXECUTIVE SUMMARY

The WHO, in collaboration with national and international health authorities, set the standard for preparing global healthcare systems facing the pandemic which claimed more lives than any other single disease during the corona pandemic. The preparedness and management of the pandemic, being the subject of national priority, witnessed concrete measures taken by the Indian Government to fight the pandemic with executive support of the Ministry of Health and other nationwide Health Services. Ayurveda, an Indian indigenous wholistic healthcare approach, was widely adopted at large. Ayurvedic medicine producing companies saw exponential growth in their revenue during the period of pandemic. This chapter aims at exploring responses of certain constituents of the Ayurvedic treatment system in India—the leading Ayurvedic companies and AYUSH department—to the coronavirus pandemic. The Ayurvedic companies and the AYUSH department responded to the pandemic in a varied way including product diversification, digital marketing, and promotion of yogic exercises and herbal remedies.

DOI: 10.4018/978-1-6684-3504-5.ch012

INTRODUCTION

The COVID-19 situation, accompanied by societal, public health & economic disruptions, was most likely to escalate the conflict (Kumar & Malhotra, 2021). As the number of COVID-19 patients grew exponentially, several nations healthcare systems came to a virtual standstill. The elderly, immunocompromised, those with other comorbidities were more likely to develop the severe acute respiratory syndrome, which had a high fatality rate, despite the fact that most infected persons have a mild to moderate clinical course (Kumar & Gupta, 2021). In order to prevent, contain, and manage the COVID-19 pandemic, governments and the medical community have been forced to make difficult decisions balancing the general good with individual liberties, and the necessity to restrict the spread of the disease against the economic losses makes it difficult to make decisions about treatment. Poor health systems, inadequate government capacity to respond to public health crises, and limited water and associated infrastructure all contributed to Covid-19's vulnerable status. The corona pandemic became a calamity for all businesses, especially those run by women, who lost a great deal of money despite their willingness to use information technology and their desire to take advantage of the pandemic catastrophe (Kovid et al., 2021).

The Indian healthcare system faced several issues as a result of Covid-19. For the first 21 days, the world's longest lockdown was put in place in India, which was later extended to a total of 55 days. Lockdowns to enforce compliance with social and physical distance have resulted in massive economic losses and social, behavioural effects that might unravel in the near future (Bhardwaj & Kumar, 2022). This epidemic might be too big for India's under-resourced healthcare system, which is plagued by constant staffing shortages and equipment shortages. The Indian scenario needed better preventive, early control, and less resource-intensive management (Shaikh, 2020).

For high-risk people, such as asymptomatic frontline health professionals and asymptomatic home contacts of laboratory-confirmed patients, the Indian Council of Medical Research (ICMR) advised the usage of Hydroxychloroquine (HCQ) (MOHFW, 2020). Covid-19's present treatment includes solely symptomatic treatment, supportive care, and avoidance of complications; however, no particular medicine or focused intervention is available yet. As of September 30, 2020, there are 3489 clinical trials listed on the National Institutes of Health Clinical Trials website. The repurposed experimental medications being tried include Hydroxychloroquine, Lopinavir/ Ritonavir, Remdesivir, experimental vaccination, convalescent plasma, altered cells, and occasionally high dosage steroids. All of these medications, save Hydroxychloroquine & steroids, are expensive or need complex manufacturing techniques, and all of them might result in major side effects. The best and most cost-effective method would be to reduce exposure to the virus, restrict its spread, halt development, and enhance individual immunity by employing natural & safer immunomodulating medicines.

Traditional Chinese Medicine had been largely ignored in India's efforts to prevent and treat Covid-19 as Indian's active medical adoption for treatment was the Modern Medicine, but China had effectively incorporated TCM into conventional healthcare (NHCPRC, 2020). Patients in India have always had freedom of choice when it comes to medical care, according to the country's long history of pluralistic Medicine. An autonomous Ministry of AYUSH governs the Indian Government's recognition of traditional systems such as Ayurvedic, Homeopathic, Unani, Naturopathy, Yoga, Siddha. Each system has its own practising strategy, requirements for professional credentials, register of practitioners, and research council. Medicines from the different AYUSH systems were included in the recommendation as preventative measures. According to a study by public health specialists, they were called "myths," "placebos," or/& "pseudoscience" in response to this. March 6 brought an additional advisory from the Ministry to State, and union territory chief secretaries, accompanied by an annexure of 33 studies published that explained the rationale behind the various systems. It seemed that after some initial slip-ups, AYUSH Ministry also was working hard to improve its public communication (PIB,2020). Furthermore, national ethical norms for holistic management (Ayurvedic/ AYUSH) of COVID-19 in research subjects were developed. These guidelines were intended to be used for prevention in healthy subjects, intervention strategies for milder symptoms, strategic planning of severe COVID.19, and therapeutic interventions for severe phases of the infection.

Ayurveda is a timeless and time-tested reservoir of knowledge about the world's healthcare system. This panacea has the potential to open up new frontiers in the fields of health and wellbeing while also offering enormous prospects for entrepreneurship and commercial growth that will benefit the global economy.

The majority of persons who fell unwell as a result of COVID-19 would be able to recuperate at their homes. When you have COVID-19, some of the things that you do to feel better when you have a common cold — getting sufficient rest, keeping hydrated, having a healthy diet and using drugs to reduce fever and muscle aches — also work to make you feel better. Corona Virus is generally treated through the symptomatic way as there is no confirmed medication to be given to the patient; henceforth, the patients suffering from corona are given the medications to relieve the particular symptom seen in the patient. Also, there have been advised by the WHO and Health Ministry of India to have a diet that can help in boosting immunity. The following tips are being floated on how to boost your immune system using Ayurvedic methods during the coronavirus outbreak in India- Warm water, herbal tea (kadha) with tulsi, kalimirch, cinnamon, shunthi, black pepper, dalchini, shunthi, and munnaka, as well as the golden milk of turmeric are among the Ayurvedic therapies that may be used to alleviate symptoms. There is also mention of Chyawanprash, which is becoming more popular in the natural and organic medical field. Practising 30 mins yoga asanas and Pranayama daily may enhance respiratory health. PM Narendra Modi encouraged people to follow the instructions published by the AYUSH ministry to boost their immunity on social media and during an interview on TV. The nasal application of sesame or coconut oil or ghee and the oil pulling therapy along with steam inhalations were advised by the Ministry of Ayush.

AYUSH DEPARTMENT

Ayurveda, yoga, naturopathy, Unani, Siddha, and homoeopathy comprise India's alternative medical system (AYUSH). As of November 9, 2014, the Ministry of Ayush was established in order to revitalise the ancient knowledge of Medicine and ensure the best possible development and spread of the Ayush healthcare systems. Ayurvedic treatment aims at preventing the underlying causes of disease with the use of Panchkarma procedures, drugs, a healthy diet, physical activity, and a programme for strengthening the Body's natural defences in order to prevent or limit disease relapse (Ministry of Ayush, 2020).

AYUSH was included in the 2017 National Health Policy of India. It emphasises the integration of traditional and contemporary Medicine in prevention and treatment in India since independence (MoHFW, 2017). In Kerala and Tamil Nadu, the AYUSH sector has helped control dengue & chikungunya in the last 6–7 years. This pandemic's probable dynamics, virological investigations and vaccine development, as well as clinical therapeutics research, have been promptly addressed by scientists. AYUSH's Ministry of Public Health issued a piece of public advice on the importance of preventing disease as the first case was observed. The Government gave the go-ahead to the AYUSH industry for "scientific evidence-based alternatives treatment from the AYUSH systems," with an encouragement to restrict inaccurate claims in the banner of AYUSH in order to address the problem of COVID.19 (Ministry of AYUSH, 2020). The State of Kerala established Statewide as well as District Ayush COVID-19 Response Cells, Ayur Raksha Clinics for control work and then for implementing Swasthyam therapies with lifestyle, nutritional and medicinal elements for various age groups and risk exposures, and Niramaya, an official virtual platform for proper deployment of AYUSH strategies for COVID-19 patients (The Hindu, 2021).

India's AYUSH and alternative medicine industry is expected to grow much faster during the pandemic period. In the context of COVID-19, the market for complementary and alternative medicines, such as Ayurveda, has been growing due to increased demand for various ayurvedic treatments that promote immunity. According to a survey published in August 2020, demand for honey increased by 45 percent since March, chyawanprash by 85 percent, and turmeric by 40% at ayurvedic stores. The Ministry of AYUSH's instructions to combat COVID-19 fuelled demand for these items (Mordor Intelligence, 2021).

The Modified Extra Mural Research Scheme for SARS CoV-2 infection and COVID-19 disease was launched by the Ministry of Ayush on April 21 and was open to research proposals until May 10, 2020. The programme provided funding for a total of 21 Ayurveda medicine research projects. The rest are government-run institutions, with only eight belonging to the private sector. The Indian Council of Medical Research (ICMR), Department of Biotechnology (DBT), Council of Scientific and Industrial Research (CSIR), All India Institute of Medical Sciences (AIIMS), and Ayush Institutions formed an Inter-disciplinary Ayush R&D Task Force under the Ministry of Ayush (First Post, 2021).

Treatment of COVID-19 patients under various conditions of infection was clearly outlined in the official regulations and self-care measures for Ayurvedic and Unani practitioners. Thus, the Ayush-based responses to the pandemic would be uniform and consistent throughout the country as a result. COVID-19 management activities were aided by this information, which was also provided to state and local governments. As a result of these guidelines and measures, Ayush solutions for managing COVID-19 were becoming more mainstream, which was great news for the public because these solutions were widely available and would help to alleviate the hardships caused by the pandemic.

Ayurveda hospitals were delivering medications to clients in order to enhance their immunity while also taking into consideration any diseases they might be suffering from. According to the Ayurveda department, five programmes were initiated by the Government sector as part of Covid prevention initiatives. Ayurraksha (the programme that provides free Covid preventative treatment to those under the age of 60), Sukhayushyam (the programme that provides preventive Medicine to those over the age of 60), Amritham (the programme that provides treatment for those in isolation), Bheshajam (the programme that provides treatment for Covid patient populations in Category A), and Punarjani were some of the programmes that are available (scheme for patients after Covid health issues). These services were available to the general population at no cost via government-run Ayurveda hospitals (Onmanorama, 2021).

Ayurveda and Unani practitioners were provided with standard guidelines for the management of prophylactic, asymptomatic and mild cases of COVID-19 during home isolation, as well as information on effective home care solutions and recommended Ayush practises to help them build their immunity. According to the Ministry of Ayush, ready-made formulations such as 'AyushKwath,' which is an admixture of four herbal ingredients well-known in India and abroad for their immunomodulatory and antiviral activities, as well as numerous other health benefits, have been encouraged. There have been recommendations that Vasa (Malabar nut), Yashtimdh (liquorice root), and Giloy could be incorporated into the Kwath based on the temperature variation and the patient's constitution. (PIB Delhi,2021).

Former Union health minister of India Dr Harshavardhan launched the Ayush Sanjivani App, developed by the Ministry of Ayush and the Ministry of Information Technology. When it comes to Medicine, people can often find what they need at home thanks to the Ayush Sanjivani App. Using the Ayush Sanjivani mobile app, researchers can track how well Ayush advocacies and measures are accepted and used by the general public, as well as how they affect COVID-19 prevention. Results from this app's cross-sectional analysis show that 85.1% reported using Ayush measures to prevent COVID-19, with 89.8% agreeing that the practice of Ayush advisory has been beneficial for them. Around 79.1% of users said they felt better overall after taking the Ayush measures, while another 63.4% said they felt better physically and mentally as a result of the Ayush measures (First Post, 2021). Also, The Ministry of AYUSH authorised drug authorities to take action under the terms of the Disaster Management Act, 2005, in order to stop the spread of deceptive claims regarding the treatment of Covid-19 by Ayurveda Siddha, Unani, and homoeopathic medications. A manufacturer of alternative medicine treatments who advertises in print, television, or electronic media that their product treats coronavirus infections might be fined or imprisoned for up to a year under this rule (The Print,2020).

CASES ON AYURVEDIC HEALTHCARE COMPANIES

In addition to response of AYUSH department, the chapter also captured responses of some private ayurvedic firms. The details of each case is given below.

Case 1: Patanjali Ayurved Limited

Patanjali Ayurved Limited was founded in 2006 and is one of India's fastest-growing consumer products companies. Patanjali had a clear goal to promote and expand the use of Indian-made products throughout the country. It opened up a wide selection of products to the general public. Its headquarters are in the industrial zones of Haridwar, in the State of Uttarakhand. The Company developed and introduced around 450 personal care & food products, as well as more than 300 Ayurvedic drugs that were used to treat a broad variety of physical ailments (The Economic Times, 2019). In 2018, Ramdev, founder of Patanjali, announced that Patanjali Ayurved would be turned into a not-for-profit charitable foundation, with all revenue and earnings going to charity. He also stated that the firm's reins would be passed on to only a sanyasi after the company's conversion. Balkrishna, head of Patanjali, stated, 'Turnover & profit have never ever been our primary goals, and this has proven to be the secret to our survival,' (Shashidhar, 2018). Patanjali Ayurved reported revenue of Rs 833 million in the fiscal year 2018–2019, despite the fact that the group's overall profits were substantially higher than this. The Company produced sales of 0.35 billion in the 1st half of the fiscal year 2019-20 and expected to generate revenue in excess of 1 billion in the fiscal year 2019–20, according to its financial statements (The Economic Times, 2019).

Coronil was the very 1st clinical-ayurvedic regulated, research-based, scientifically prooved, and trial-based medication for Covid-19 that was developed through clinical trials. The regular practice of yogasans and pranayam, according to Ramdev, was also useful in preventing & treating off the COVID-19 infection in addition to Coronil treatment (India TV, 2020). In accordance with the Ayush Ministry of the Indian Government, the Ayurvedic Division of Uttarakhand province was authorised to issue a licence to Patanjali on Coronil and its subsidiaries. Following the emergence of the dispute in June 2020, the department revealed that it had received a submission from Patanjali in June 2020, which had been approved by an assessment panel on June 2020, shortly following the receipt of the application. It should be noted that this permission was only for the production of two-three drugs used to improve immunity against cough & fever and not for the manufacture of a drug to treat COVID-19. Additionally, the organisation claimed that this was a cure for Covid-19 as well as an immunity booster. To make this treatment even more potent, they combined minerals with herbs (Kumar, 2020a).

OrderMe, a new e-commerce site from Patanjali, would offer the Company's own ayurvedic items as well as link customers with local businesses that sell Indian goods. In addition, orders placed on the planned website would be delivered to customers' homes free of charge after few hours. Furthermore, it will provide individuals with free medical advice from around 1,500 physicians affiliated with Patanjali 24 hours a day, seven days a week, as well as yoga teachings (ET Now Digital,2020).

On June 30, 2020, Ayush Ministry announced that the Coronil formulation was not a treatment for COVID-19 but rather an immunity booster. As a result of this announcement, Ramdev gave numerous interviews to national news outlets, reassuring anyone still sceptical about trying these drugs. He indicated that, in accordance with the directions of the Ayush Ministry, the firm would begin using the phrase COVID-19 control instead of COVID-19 therapy going forward. Following the Ayush Ministry's recognition of Coronil as the only immunity booster available, the Company announced that Patanjali's product- Coronil, would be provided free of charge to those in need but could not possibly afford it (India TV, 2020). He remained steadfast in his belief that this composition was effective for all of his patients, mild to moderately unwell. The Corona Kit, available all over the country (The Hindu, 2020a).

Nevertheless, the division of medical education was unsure of how to proceed with the application. Ayurvedic treatment was not included in drug trials because allopathic drugs were used. Nishant Warwade, the commissioner of medical education, says the board has received the petition and is reviewing it (Mukherjee, 2021). Ayurvedic medications with scientific proof and certification would be introduced by Patanjali following Coronil, according to the Company. S K Tijarawala, a Patanjali spokesperson, claimed that Coronil, created by Patanjali Research Institute, had done business worth Rs 500 crore over the seven months (Business Standard, 2021a).

Case 2: Dabur India Ltd.

Over a number of months post break out of the pandemic, people probably had been told to repeatedly to "Increase the immunity". Being a vaccine not available till that time, this was only defence against the Covid-19 virus. Immunity-related products saw a dramatic increase in sales, despite the lack of conclusive evidence that certain ingredients actually protect against infection. Over the years, Dabur successfully placed Chyawanprash as an immunity booster. Dabur, the 136-year-old manufacturer of Dabur Chyawanprash, honey and juices is one of the companies benefiting from this trend. Despite Dabur India's "great optimism" about the future, the Company nevertheless faces hurdles from the pandemic. Vice Chairman Mohit Burman observed that Dabur was "well-positioned" to tackle the challenges and achieve sustainable long-term growth by applying last year's pandemic learnings to streamline the supply chain (Business Standard, 2021b).

Dabur India recovered well from the lockdown blues in the April-June 2021 quarter. The Company's profit after tax (PAT) increased by 28.4% on a year-over-year basis. During the third quarter, the Company's net profit was Rs 438.3 crore, up from Rs 341.3 crore in the year-ago period. The operational revenue of the Dabur Company increased by 32%, thanks to a significant uptake volume rise of 34.4% in its local market. In April-June 2020, operating revenue was Rs 2,611.5 crore, up from Rs 1,980 crore in the same period previous year. It outperformed the prior quarter's results as well as those from before the implementation of Covid During the first three months of the year 2020 the Ghaziabad-based Company recently introduced 40 new products across various segments, slashing the usual one-to-two-year timeframe. Tulsi Drops, Wheatgrass Juice, Aloe Vera Juice, Haldi Drops and Amla Juice are all included in the product (Business Standard, 2021b).

The coronavirus outbreak shifted consumer attention back to immunity-boosting and wellness brands, resulting in an explosive surge in sales for FMCG giant Dabur India's chyawanprash and honey line. Healthy volunteers participated in a broad, multi-centric research trial to see if Dabur Chyawanprash could serve as a preventive treatment for COVID-19 infection. Researchers found that daily consumption of Dabur Chyawanprash lowered the probability of COVID-19 infection in test subjects by up to 12 times compared to a control group that did not take Dabur Chyawanprash. Subjects who consistently consumed Dabur Chyawanprash had symptoms of COVID 19 virus that were up to six times less severe than those in the control group who did not take Dabur Chyawanprash (Business Standard, 2021b).

The Ministry of AYUSH recommended some of Dabur's Ayurvedic products as a preventive therapy against the pandemic outbreak. To name a few, there is Dabur Chyawanprash (2 Spoons per day, can provide 2x Body's immune system) Imudab Syrup, Agastaya Haritaki Awleha, and Dabur Giloy Ki Ghanvati. Dabur Ayurvedic Centres and online pharmacies both sell these medications (The ministry of AYUSH, 2020). Durga Prasad (marketing head for the ayurvedic ethical business) stated Dabur India saw a major sales increase of stress reduction products during the second wave of the Corona pandemic and the Company has recently decided to enter the pain management segment. In the middle of the epidemic, Mindwave Media held two purpose-driven ads for two Dabur India products in Bihar And uttar Pradesh, respectively.

Thousands of businesses and millions of jobs were lost as a result of the pandemic's unprecedented nature. However, Dabur, which rose 14 spots in the 2020 Fortune India 500 to No. 160, realised early that the pandemic was not just a chaotic event but offered up an opportunity for growth. In order to stay competitive, it aggressively increased new product development, pushed digitisation and automation initiatives, made required changes to HR policies, and bolstered its online sales presence. Dabur's health portfolio became its primary focus. It was not uncommon for Dabur India to have between 50 and 80 new products in its pipeline at any given time. Dabur took advantage of the fast-tracked launch of those new products that addressed many emerging consumer needs thanks to Covid-19 (Business Standard, 2021c). The quick response paid off for everyone involved. The ayurvedic and natural healthcare company made 2,516 crores in revenue in the three months ending September, 2020 (Fortune India, 2021).

Case 3: Himalaya Wellness

Demand for ayurvedic products with therapeutic properties and immunity-building abilities rose across the country. Major corporations including Himalaya Wellness reported an increase in consumption for Ayurvedic products across their entire product line. An increasing number of people made inquiries about immune-boost products like Chyawanprash and Giloy tablets as well as the recently-launched Immunity Kit. According to Philipe Haydon, CEO of The Himalaya Drug Company, all products under the wellness and immunity umbrella saw a significant increase in demand in Himalaya. According to a report, demand for the Company's Pure Herbs range, including Amalaki, Tulasi, Ashvagandha, and Guduchi, has risen significantly. Many top FMCG firms saw a spike in demand for their hand sanitiser, hand wash, disinfecting spray, and germ protection wipe as India deals with the deadly second wave of the COVID-19 pandemic. A hand sanitizer brand PureHands, introduced in 2003, witnessed a significant increase in demand (Business Standard, 2021c).

Herbal balms and anti-stress treatments like Ashwagandha saw a 50-80% year-on-year increase in sales for Himalaya Drug Company and Dabur as people of all ages became more stressed and anxious because of the uncertainty, lack of a daily routine and lack of social interaction according to the business director, pharmaceutical department, Anil M Jiandani, at The Himalaya Drug Co. Many people started using balms for steam inhalation to relieve Covid-19 symptoms, which were widely reported during the ongoing second wave of the pandemic due to its effect on several families, stories of suffering that have gone viral on social media, and many people using balms for steam inhalation to relieve Covid-19 symptoms (The Economic Times, 2021).

A clinical study conducted by the Himalaya Drug Company to examine the role of their own herbal remedies (Tab. Bresol and Tab. Septilin in combined effect) as an adjunctive treatment in moderately symptomatic and asymptomatic COVID-19–patients were published. The study was funded by the Himalaya Drug Company. Immunomodulatory properties of Septilin, an Ayurvedic formulation, as well as the potential of Bresol to downregulate proinflammatory cytokines made it a popular choice for the treatment of respiratory disorders. Administering Septilin and Bresol combined with SOC as an adjuvant therapy boosts the immune system and reduces inflammation in COVID-19–positive individuals (Express Pharma, 2021). When compared to Favipiravir & Lopinavir or Ritonavir, guduchi (Tinospora cordifolia) had "great binding effectiveness" against SARS-CoV-2 sites involved in attachment and reproduction of the virus (The Hindu, 2020b).

The Himalaya Drug Company was actively assisting India's battle against COVID-19 through different community assistance activities as part of its ongoing community engagement efforts. By working with Karnataka State Road Transport Corporation and Bangalore Metropolitan Transport Corporation, the Company provided over 60,000 employees with hand hygiene items in order to safeguard their health and safety (Indiacsr, 2021). Face masks, sanitisers, gloves, hygiene kits, PPE kits, groceries, and critical health supplies were donated by the Himalaya Drug Company to a wide range of people. Himalaya volunteered to give adult diapers to help the elderly in their fight against COVID-19. Himalaya also provided happiness packages with groceries, hygiene products, and activity books to impoverished children as one of its many philanthropic projects.

Others Firms' Response Cases

A lot of other firms introduced herbal and ayurvedic products while highlighting their immunity-boosting properties. For example, Amul advertised turmeric-flavoured milk dubbed Amul "Haldi Doodh," which used to combine the "greatness of milk with the century-old immune-boosting and therapeutic qualities of Haldi". Similar to this, the Baidyanath Group, a very old ayurvedic medicine manufacturing company, formed specialised field research teams that collected data on herb production and shared the findings of their study among farmers in order to improve their outcomes. Furthermore, Baidyanath and other younger firms considered making investments in technology and innovations like blockchain, which would assist in the authentication of herbs and the streamlining of research by safeguarding unalterable data. It was possible to use the data that had been kept on the blockchain in order to motivate farmers to grow high-yielding herbs and to improve the overall quality of the agricultural operation. It also provided customers with more transparency, allowing them to learn more about the items' origins, travel, and influence on the environment.

DISCUSSION

The coronavirus disease made the society globally to realise the necessity of maintaining good health and having strong and robust immune systems to combat diseases. While efficient and curative drugs were required in the battle against such hostile viruses, human bodies can be considered strongest line of defence against such infections. Due to the fact that COVID-19 was a novel condition, there was no precise equivalent in classical Ayurvedic literature. When it came to COVID-19 prevention, the AYUSH Ayurveda guidelines established a justification. The potential degrees and realistic modes of action in Coronavirus preventive, management, and post-infection rehabilitative were identified. No matter how one looks at it, herbal decoctions had been created and eaten by the general population since the virus was first reported in March 2020. The ayurvedic medicines were bought by large size of population in India as indicated by lengthy lines in front of ayurvedic medicine pharmacies and medical clinics. Meditation had been demonstrated to have a favourable impact on stress reduction, and as a result, it might have contributed to a more positive immunological response throughout the Body.

The worldwide demand for herbal supplements has been increasing specifically from an ageing population that is more conscious of the need for good nutrition and preventative healthcare. Consumers are turning to Ayurvedic and natural goods in view of the adverse effects of mainstream therapy of healthcare. This includes

Ayurvedic medications, Ayurvedic nutraceuticals and nutritional supplements for personalised care and health. Individuals are treated as well as provided cure of an illnesses as per ancient healthcare system, which promotes the holistic approach to diagnosis and therapy. Additionally, Ayurvedic prognosis involves substantial herb usage, physical activity and nutrition modifications, as well as adjustments to one's way of life. The traditional foods with therapeutic benefits are just being packaged and marketed in new and creative ways in order to match customer tastes that are shifting away from traditional diets towards more sophisticated and healthier food options. A variety of distribution network interruptions have been used during and after COVID-19 to make it easier for consumers to obtain products. Private actors in the Ayurveda sector may potentially earn high income for the industry, either locally or globally, with the goal of benefiting many more people throughout the globe. Table 1 provides the summary of Healthcare organisations' Responses

Table 1. Summary of healthcare organisations' responses

Basis	Patanjali	Dabur	Himalaya	Other Cases
Product Differentiation	Heterogenous products- FMCG, Food products, Immunity Boosting, Personal care products, Ayurvedic Medicine.	Heterogenous products- FMCG, Herbal Products, Ayurvedic Medicine, Immunity Boosting Products, Health Supplements.	Heterogenous products- FMCG, Health Supplements, Immunity Boosting, Pharmaceutical Products.	Homogenous Products- Immunity Boosting
Marketing Strategy- Promotion	Using e-commerce, using digital media for marketing	Fast-tracked launch of new products, pushed digitisation and automation initiatives for products	Social media and online advertising	Launched herbal/ ayurvedic products citing immunity boosting, also investments in technology and innovations like blockchain
Marketing Strategy- Price	Penetration Pricing strategy	Competitive Pricing strategy	Competitive Pricing strategy	Low-cost pricing strategy
Societal Marketing	Coronil formulation for corona management and promotion of YOGA for mental and physical wellbeing	Across the middle of the epidemic, Mindwave Media planned 2 purpose-driven campaigns for Dabur India brands.	Face masks, sanitisers, gloves, hygiene kits, PPE kits, groceries, and critical health supplies donated by the Himalaya Drug Company	Motivate farmers to grow high-yielding herbs and to improve the overall quality of the agricultural operation

Source: prepared by authors

Companies that have been promoting these goods have taken advantage of the not only linkages between COVID-19 and immunity boosting but also the Government's support of Ayurveda & yoga for mild and moderate illnesses. Also ayurvedic medicines assisted in the healing process after COVID-19 exposure. Patanjali's Coronil formulation was approved by the AYUSH Ministry only as an immune booster, but not as a therapeutic remedy for COVID-19. This issue of Coronil made the headlines and controversy for a long time since the firm promoted it as an effective treatment for coronavirus disease. In the midst of the epidemic, Ayurveda looks to be prospering. Dabur India's Ayurveda business grew by more than 50% in the quarter ending in June 2020. Immunity-related items, such as honey, chawanprash and herbal tea, are expected to expand by 38 percent year-on-year in urban India in fiscal 2021. The Indian Government has played a significant role in supporting the Ayurveda business, which is estimated to be worth 30,000 crores (CII, 2019). Medication manufacturers like Himalaya Drug Company's "Septilin" and "Immusante," which include proprietary formulas, confirmed even during the shutdown, there was a spike in sales for immunity and health products that contain pure herbs

Many people adopted ayurvedic rituals for centuries. In addition to being a medical system, it has applications in agriculture, animal care, nutrition, aesthetics, and rejuvenation. However, practitioners of contemporary Medicine have also questioned the efficacy of herbal remedies in the treatment or prevention of COVID-19 due to unfounded claims made by well-known Ayurvedic medication proprietors. Even the new coronavirus infection is not preventable by any home cure or alternative therapy. The WHO expressly notes out, "To yet, there is no particular drug indicated to prevent or manage the novel coronavirus" (World Health Organisation, 2020) (see Table 1).

CONCLUSION

COVID-19 crisi made the Ministry of Ayurveda, Yoga and Naturopathy made significant efforts to develop a culture of multidisciplinary cooperation while maintaining the fundamental principles of each discipline. It should be emphasised that perhaps the Ministry of Health & Family Welfare is also supporting the use of integrative techniques in healthcare. An important step in this manner has been taken with the creation of an integrative AYUSH Research & Development Taskforce for Covid-19. In the early stages of the epidemic, the Indian Government permitted the use of an Ayurvedic regimen to improve the population's immunity to COVID-19. With the establishment of a government-sponsored multidisciplinary AYUSH task group for COVID-19, the conceivable potential of a system such as Ayurveda can be investigated and extended at the community level. To go hand in hand with the preventative methods established by the Government, such as social distance and physical barriers, these advocacy initiatives that are simple and cost-efficient, realistic and time-proven procedures are feasible for implementation in the public realm.

The private sector, led by companies like Dabur, Himalaya and Patanjali, is promoting Ayurveda and helping the AYUSH to grow in different sectors. Food supplements and immune boosters are becoming more popular throughout the world as people shift from curative treatment to proactive and preventative healthcare. Because of COVID-19, there is an increasing desire for all-natural alternatives to traditional healthcare, which is helping to drive the expansion of the worldwide herbal medicine market. Consumers post-pandemic are increasingly turning to herbal alternatives because of their lower toxic potential and fewer adverse effects, even after long-term usage. The possibility of fraudulent promises about miraculous treatments from many sources exists, but this does not negate the reality that well developed and verified regimens have a critical part to play at the population level. The contributions of AYUSH seem to be in the form of improving general immunity so that a greater percentage of those exposed may stay asymptomatic or have just moderate illness, and a smaller proportion progresses to become serious conditions.

REFERENCES

Bhardwaj, A., & Kumar, V. (2022). Privacy and Healthcare during COVID-19. In *Cybersecurity Crisis Management and Lessons Learned From the COVID-19 Pandemic* (pp. 82–96). IGI-Global. doi:10.4018/978-1-7998-9164-2.ch005

Business Standard. (2021a). *Coronil has got Ayush Ministry certification as per WHO scheme: Patanjali.* https://www.business-standard.com/article/pti-stories/coronil-has-got-ayush-ministry-certification-as-per-who-scheme-patanjali-121021901231_1.html

Business Standard. (2021b). *Dabur India's profit after tax jumps 28.4%, beats pre-Covid levels.* https://www.business-standard.com/article/companies/dabur-india-s-profit-after-tax-jumps-28-4-beats-pre-covid-levels-121080302039_1.html

Business Standard. (2021c). *Well-positioned to handle challenges of another Covid wave: Dabur India.* https://www.business-standard.com/article/companies/well-positioned-to-handle-challenges-of-another-covid-wave-dabur-india-121081900933_1.html

CII. (2019). *Resurgence of the Ayurveda Industry.* https://www.ciiblog.in/resurgence-of-the-ayurveda-industry/

Express Pharma. (2021). *Himalaya study finds herbal immunomodulators effective as adjuvant treatment for COVID-19*. https://www.expresspharma.in/himalaya-study-finds-herbal-immunomodulators-effective-as-adjuvant-treatment-for-covid-19/

Firstpost. (2021). *In India's fight against COVID-19, thrust from Ministry of Ayush has been unrelenting*. https://www.firstpost.com/health/in-indias-fight-against-covid-19-thrust-from-ministry-of-ayush-has-been-unrelenting-9862281.html

Fortune India. (2021). *How Dabur is riding the new normal*. https://www.fortuneindia.com/enterprise/how-dabur-is-riding-the-new-normal/105069

India, T. V. (2020, June 14). *Coronil: Swami Ramdev shares cure for Coronavirus through Ayurvedic Medicine, yogasanas and Pranayama*. https://www.indiatvnews.com/health/know-all-about-coronil-made-from-ashwagandha-giloy-tulsi-ayurvedic-cure-for-coronavirus-by-patanjali-626021

Indiacsr. (2021). *The Himalaya Drug Company Collaborates with BMTC and KSRTC to fight COVID-19*. https://indiacsr.in/the-himalaya-drug-company-collaborates-with-bmtc-and-ksrtc-to-fight-covid-19/

Kovid, R. K., Kumari, D., & Pandey, S. (2021). Strategic Response to the Corona Pandemic Crisis: A Case of Indian Women Entrepreneurs. In V. Kumar & G. Malhotra (Eds.), *Stakeholder Strategies for Reducing the Impact of Global Health Crises* (pp. 68–84). IGI Global. doi:10.4018/978-1-7998-7495-9.ch005

Kumar, R. P. (2020a, June 24). *Coronavirus treatment: Ramdev's Patanjali launches Coronil kit for ₹545*. LiveMint. https://www.livemint.com/news/india/coronavirus-vaccine-coronil-patanjali-baba-ramdev-press-conference-live-updates-11592893304534.html

Kumar, V., & Gupta, G. (Eds.). (2021). *Strategic Management During a Pandemic*. Routledge. doi:10.4324/9781003125648

Kumar, V., & Malhotra, G. (Eds.). (2021). *Stakeholder Strategies for Reducing the Impact of Global Health Crises*. IGI – Global Publications. doi:10.4018/978-1-7998-7495-9

Ministry of AYUSH. (2020). *Notification to be published in the Extraordinary Gazette of India, No. L.11011/8/2020/AS*. New Delhi: Ministry of AYUSH, Government of India. https://main.ayush.gov.in/about-the-systems/ayurveda/treatment

MoHFW. (2017). *National Health Policy*. Ministry of Health and Family Welfare.

MOHFW. (2020). *Indian Council of Medical Research. Recommendation for empiric use of Hydroxychloroquine for prophylaxis of SARS Cov- 2 infection.* New Delhi: ICMR. Available from: https://www.mohfw.gov.in/pdf/AdvisoryontheuseofHydroxychloroquinasprophylasxisforSARSCoV2infection.pdf

Mordor Intelligence. (2021). *Ayush and alternative medicine industry in india - growth, trends, covid-19 impact, and forecasts (2021 - 2026).* https://www.mordorintelligence.com/industry-reports/ayush-and-alternative-medicine-industry-in-india

Mukherjee, J. (2021). Patanjali Ayurveda's Coronil: Marketing Controversy on COVID-19 Cure. *Vision (Basel).*

NHCPRC. (2020). *Protocol on diagnosis and treatment of COVID-19* (6th ed.). Beijing: National Health Commission of the People's Republic of China. Available from: http://en.nhc.gov.cn/2020-03/29/c_78468.htm

Now Digital, E. T. (2020). *Baba Ramdev's Patanjali to launch swadeshi-only ecommerce platform OrderMe, free home delivery of products.* https://www.timesnownews.com/business-economy/companies/article/baba-ramdevs-patanjali-to-launch-swadeshi-only-ecommerce-platform-orderme-free-home-delivery-of-products/592127

Onmanorama. (2021). *Utilise the schemes of Ayurveda dept, says doctor.* https://www.onmanorama.com/lifestyle/health/2021/05/09/ayurveda-against-coronavirus.html

PIB. (2020). *AYUSH Ministry Urges Diligence in COVID.19 Claims and Initiates Work for Scientific and Evidence. Based Solutions to Fight the Corona Virus.* Available at: https://pib.gov.in/PressReleaseIframePage.aspx?PRID=1609523

PIB. (2021). *Ayush Ministry Releases fresh COVID-19 Guidelines Focus on Self-Care and Home Isolation Ayurveda & Unani guidelines released, rest to follow soon.* https://www.pib.gov.in/PressReleasePage.aspx?PRID=1714205

Shaikh, S. (2020). *Corona Virus spread not Just Epidemic, Pseudoscience has Made it a 'Misinfo.demic' Too.* https://theprint.in/opinion/coronavirus.not.just.epidemic.pseudoscience.has.m ade.it.misinfo.demic/357397/

Shashidhar, A. (2018). Decoding the Patanjali phenomenon, will Patanjali Ayurveda be able to sustain its exponential growth? *Business Today (Norwich).*

The Economic Times. (2019). *Patanjali Ayurveda posts Rs 3,562 crore revenue for April–September, November 19.* https://economictimes.indiatimes.com/industry/cons-products/fmcg/patanjali-ayurved-posts-rs-3562-crore-revenue-for-april-september/articleshow/72126682.cms?from=mdr

The Economic Times. (2021). *Surging demand makes Ayurvedic stress busters the star category of second Covid wave.* https://economictimes.indiatimes.com/industry/cons-products/fmcg/demand-for-ayurvedic-stress-busters-surges-amid-second-wave-of-covid-19/articleshow/83492980.cms

The Hindu. (2020a). *Patanjali to sell Coronil as 'immunity booster', not cure for COVID-19.* https://www.thehindu.com/news/national/patanjali-can-sell-its-drug-but-not-ascureto-covid-19-says-union-health-ministry/article31962529.ece

The Hindu. (2020b). *In rush for 'immunity', Ayurveda supplements have an untested run.* https://www.thehindu.com/news/national/coronavirus-ayurveda-supplements-see-sales-boost-despite-thin-research-evidence-on-efficacy/article32886185.ece

The Hindu. (2021). *COVID-19: People throng to buy Siddha drug kabasura kudineer.* https://www.thehindu.com/news/cities/chennai/covid-19-people-throng-to-buy-siddha-drug-kabasura-kudineer/article31225180.ece

The Print. (2020). *Alternate medicine manufacturers claiming Covid-19 cure could face year in jail.* https://theprint.in/india/governance/alternate-medicine-manufacturers-claiming-covid-19-cure-could-face-year-in-jail/393607/

World Health Organisation. (2020). *WHO "Solidarity" Clinical trial for COVID 19 treatments.* https://www.who.int/solidarity-clinical-trial-for-covid-19-treatments

Chapter 13
Pandemic and Sustainability Practices:
A Case of Waste Management at Hospitals

Anu Gupta
https://orcid.org/0000-0002-4704-5172
Guru Jambheshwar University of Science and Technology, India

Minakshi Verma
Guru Jambheshwar University of Science and Technology, India

EXECUTIVE SUMMARY

The whole world was disturbed because of COVID-19. It brought several positive and negative effects on human, environment, and climate. During the lockdown period of COVID-19, all movements and activities slowed. All socio-economic activities, industrial workshops, and production units were completely closed. Due to restriction and slowdown of these activities, some environmental conditions improved including air quality and water pollution. But due to the increasing number of COVID-19 patients, rate of generation of medical waste increased (PPE kit, face mask, and hand gloves). Unplanned discarding and production of medical waste causes ill effects on the environment as well as human beings. These environmental and human consequences have long-lasting effects; therefore, they require proper and well-planned sustainable strategies for a better future and to overcome these consequences. The COVID-19 pandemic has obtained an overall global response to win this COVID-19 battle.

DOI: 10.4018/978-1-6684-3504-5.ch013

INTRODUCTION

Medical waste, also known as hospital waste or health care waste is serious concern to the society. It refers to all type of waste generated from health care activities and health care centers including laboratories, clinic, blood banks, hospitals etc. (Tsai, 2021).WHO estimated that bio-medical waste contains approximately 10% infectious waste, 85% non-hazardous waste and 5% non-infectious waste (Datta et al.,2018).

During COVID-19, hospitals generated more waste as compared to before pandemic conditions (Mekonnen et al., 2021). In Wuhan city of China, daily hospital waste increases from 40tons/day to 240tons/day. In US, generation of hospital waste increases from 2.5 million tones/year to 5 million tones /year (Ilyas et.al,2020). Increase in hospital waste generation causes greater challenges to the world as well as environmental health specially in the lower middle-income countries. Towards the proper management of hospital waste, there is significant difference in management techniques of developed and developing countries (Caniato et al., 2015; Tsai, 2021). It affects most specially in those countries which are not much developed and also not having advanced technologies for their waste disposal and treatment like Bangladesh (Rahman et al., 2020).

It is estimated that across the world approximately 5.2 million people die due to mismanagement of medical waste (Rahman et al., 2020). Because it causes spreading of many infectious diseases some infectious disease like hepatitis, cholera, and typhoid are causing due to improper disposal of single-use biomedical equipment (WHO,2018). The well-developed countries manage their health care waste properly by using appropriate disposal methods like dumped in sanitary landfill and energy recovery. Besides developing countries disposed their health care waste in mismanaged way like dumped in open area that cause serious public health. (Yasmin and Rahman,2017). During COVID-19 period one of the reasons of spreading is lack of proper management of generating medical waste from COVID patients (Kumar & Malhotra, 2021). Sometimes health care waste is mixed with municipal city waste and burnt in open area that can pollute the environment because of emission of harmful pollutants in atmosphere. So appropriate management and disposal of medical waste is necessary for public health and environment health. Generally, in total amount of waste generated from health care units contribute about 85-90% general or non- hazardous waste. Remaining 10-15% waste is considered as hazardous waste that may be infectious or radioactive (WHO,2020).

In normal conditions, no special treatment is required for non- hazardous waste. This is only processed with normal waste treating methods like disinfection, reuse, recycle, landfilling and incineration etc. But during COVID-19 pandemic, all type of waste generated from hospital require special disinfection treatment and disposed with extra care while taking all the precautionary measures. (Liang et.al,

2021). During COVID-19 period quarantine centers, hospitals, isolation wards and large and small health care units generated large amount of hospital waste across the world. Hospital waste, including personal protective equipment like face mask, hand gloves, PPE kits, is generated in huge amount. Generation of this infectious waste during COVID-19 period is area of great concern for public health as well as environmental conditions because waste from these COVID-19 centers cause spreading of COVID-19 infection in human beings and in atmosphere (Kumar & Gupta, 2021). Also, this unmanaged disposal of infectious waste became a serious threat for public and environment. To overcome spreading COVID-19 infection and for healthy and sustainable environment required proper disposal and treatment of hospital waste (Ilyas et al., 2020). As per the Bio-Medical Waste Rules (2016), the waste should be segregated into three categories and corresponding containers of different colors should be used. This has been illustrated in Table 1. The steps to be followed for disposal have been illustrated in Figure 1.

Table 1. Segregation of biomedical waste and its treatment and disposal methods

Type of Medical Waste	Type of Container	Pretreatment	Disposal Method
Soiled waste like item infected with blood PPEs like face mask, gown, cap, plastic, discarded linen, mattresses	Yellow	Not required	Incineration or deep burial
Waste originated from disposable items such as tubing, bottles, intravenous tubes, urine bags, gloves, syringes without needles & gloves	Red	Not required	Autoclave, shredding trailed by recycling
Sharp objects that cause leakage and cuts like needled, syringes with fixed needles, needles tip, cutter, or burner scalpers blades etc.	White translucent (leaked & puncture proof container)	Not required	Autoclave with dry heat sterilization. Final disposal to iron foundries or sanitary landfill
Broken or discarded and infectious glass bottles like medicine vials and ampoules ex	Blue	Not required	Disinfection trailed by recycling

Figure 1. Steps taken in hospital waste treatment and disposal

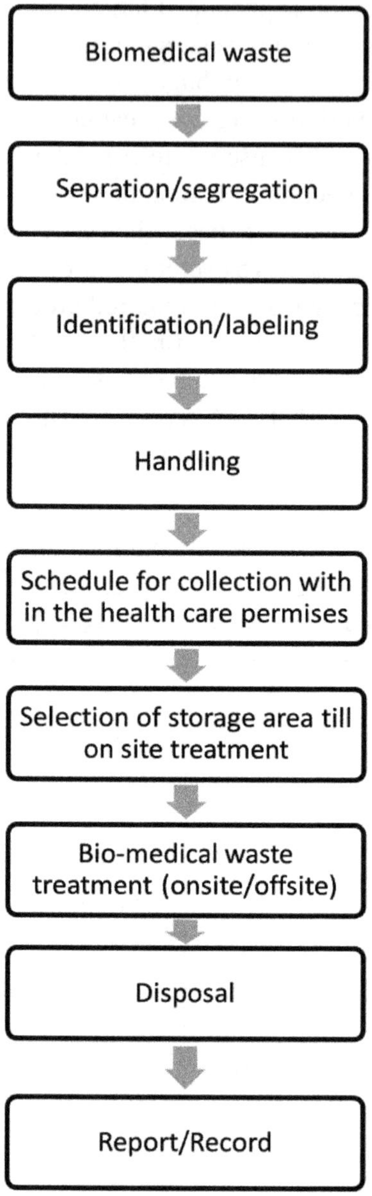

Collection

During the COVID-19 period, waste generated from laboratories and health care centers are considered infectious waste and should be collected with taking precautions

(WHO,2020). This waste is firstly disinfected. According to BMW policy2016, RED containers are specially for hand gloves, aprons, face masks, goggles, plastic covers and PPE kits, etc. (BMW,2019). Non- chlorinated red containers are used for collecting oxygen masks, bottles, tubing, intravenous tubes catheters, etc. The approach has been illustrated in Figure 2.

Figure 2. Segregation of waste

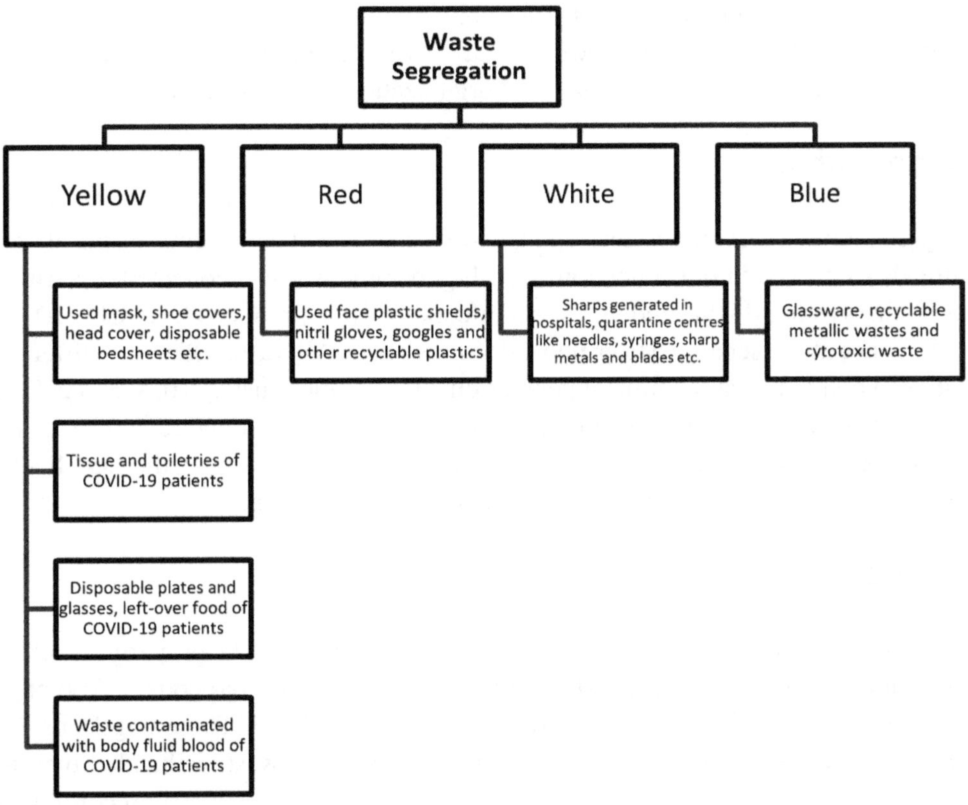

YELLOW non-chlorinated containers are especially for the gathering of bedding material like mattresses infected with body fluid or blood. Some microbial infectious waste like waste from biological culture live attenuated vaccines and other pathogenic material first sterilize by autoclaving under high pressure then collected in yellow containers (BMW, 2016).

TRANSLUCENT WHITE puncture-proof containers are used for sharp materials like syringes with needles, needles, surgical blades, burners, etc. (BMW,2016).

BLUE-coloured puncture-proof containers are specially used for infectious waste and broken glass, slides, etc.

All these wastes are firstly disinfected by chemicals and then packed in suitable containers or discarding bags. 1%Sodium hypochlorite is used as a disinfectant for half an hour. Sodium hypochlorite denatures the cell structure of pathogenic microbes by the oxidation of peptide bonds (Duarte& Santana, 2020; Behera 2020).

According to CPCB guidelines processing of disposal and treatment should be very fast and packed into double-layered leak-proof bags (CPCB guidelines 18 March 2020). Separate containers are used for collecting the COVID-19 infectious waste and ought to not be kept in crowded areas. After all these processing containers should be handed over to an authorized organization for disposal.

Segregation

Segregation is a very important step in waste management before final disposal. We already discussed in the collection step all generated waste is collected in various containers as per BMW guidelines. All infectious waste produced from COVID-19 centres need to be separated from non-infectious waste. All waste is kept into different labelled containers at the time of generation (BMW guidelines 2016, WHO 2020).

Labelled containers or dustbins have different types of waste and cannot be mixed with other types of waste. All containers filled with waste are kept in the COVID-19 storeroom and should be disinfected with a chlorine solution.

Transportation

After segregation of all type of waste infectious waste should be properly sealed in several bags, all bags are properly marked and labeled with bar code. These bags are first transported to storage house with COVID-19 label. These bags must be sanitized by 1% sodium hypochlorite is use. Finally, the waste is handed over to common biomedical waste treatment and disposal facility (CBWTF). According to BMW guidelines 2016, for safe transportation of waste they follow safe route which has less crowded, trained driver and separate close type vehicle. (BMW, 2016).

COVID-19 waste collectors are well trained. During transportation close type of vehicles and close containers are used to devoid no material can come outside in blowing air. All waste collectors and transporters are fully covered with special personal protective equipment (PPEs) (CPCB, guidelines 18 march 2020). After completion of this process transporting vehicle must be sterilized by 1% sodium hypochlorite. The whole journey of hospital waste has been illustrated in Fig 3.

Figure 3. Journey of hospital waste

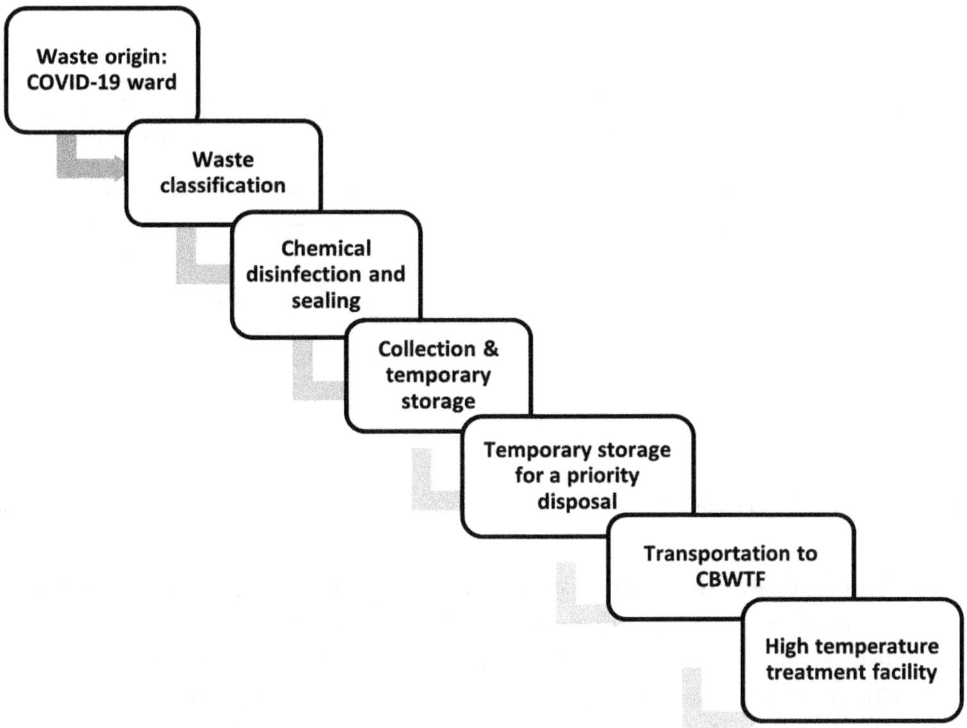

Treatment and Disposal Methods

Best method for treatment of COVID-19 waste are autoclaving, incineration and chemical treatment. When the amount of waste is overloaded then some amount of waste is temporarily stored in designated area but for less than 12 hours (Ministry of ecology and environment of People's Republic of China, 2020). By incineration method, all contaminated waste material and pathogenic viruses are killed under high temperature (Mattielloet.al, 2013). As per BMW guidelines, incineration is best method for disposal of COVID-19 waste.

During incineration some harmful gases are released in environment like furans and dioxins. In some countries like Europe and North America prefer chemical treatment (autoclaving &sterilization) rather than incineration. Because during incineration dioxin and furans are released which causes serious ill effect in human beings. (Zubair&Adrees 2019; Behera 2020). Different methods of treatment have been illustrated in Figure 4.

Figure 4. Methods of waste treatment

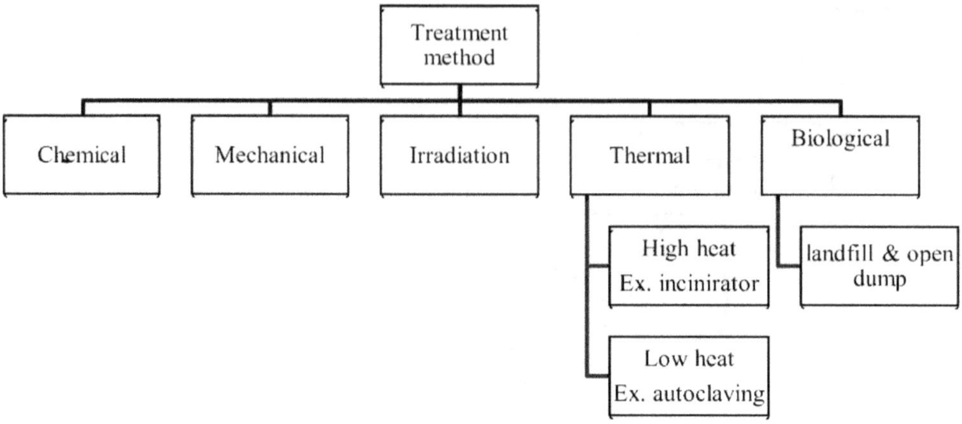

Chemical Treatment

- **Disinfection:** Most common method of waste treatment is disinfection; it means get rid of infectious microbes. Mostly chlorine is used as a disinfectant, it is mixed with liquid waste to kill the pathogenic microbes. Chemical treatment can also be done in case of solid waste when severe contamination has occurred. Common chemicals used as disinfectant are sodium hypochlorite, chlorine dioxide, hydrogen peroxide etc. (Shareefdeen, 2012)

Chemical treatment is only suitable for shredded solid waste. Many times, some chemicals used as a disinfectant themselves act as hazardous, so it is not used for treating other material and infectious waste. (Shareefdeen, 2012)

Mechanical Treatment

Mechanical treatment is used to modify shape, structure, size, and characteristic of generated waste. Two common mechanical treatments are:

- **Compaction:** In compaction process the size and shape of big material is converted into small pieces with the help of machines. Main purpose of compaction is to reduce the volume of waste. Maximum waste is settled in minimum space.

- **Shredding:** This process is used to cut the material into small pieces. Like paper and plastic waste generated from hospitals is shredded after disinfection process.
- **Irradiation Treatment:** In this method, waste is sterilized with the help of ionization radiation to inactive microbes. It is very cost-effective method for sterilizing single use material like syringes, surgical gloves etc.

Several single use life protecting/lifesaving equipment are sterilized by irradiation. Approximately 40% of generated hospital waste is sterilized with the help of gamma radiation (IAEA).

These gamma radiations are emitted from cobalt source. These radiations kill all pathogenic microbes present in single use medical waste.

Thermal Treatment

Based on heat intensity there are two types of thermal treatment-

- High temperature treatment: Pyrolysis & Incineration
- Low temperature treatment: Microwave &Autoclaving

High Heat Treatment

- **Pyrolysis:** Technically pyrolysis is better incineration technique for waste disposal (Ilyas et al., 2020). It is thermo-chemical process because it require high temperature and chemical treatment. In this process disintegration of organic substance takes place under high temperature in deficiency of air and atmospheric inert gases (Czajezynska et al., 2017). It usually working on high temperature range (540-830°c) that includes plasma pyrolysis & oxidation pyrolysis (Ilyas et al., 2020).

In comparison with combustion, incineration pyrolysis has processed at low temperature and less emission of air pollutants like PBDEs (Polybrominated biphenyl ether). Best thing of this process is, it provides transformation of short energy density material into higher energy density biofuels. Pyrolysis occurred in inner zone bed, so this is also called "quasi-pyrolysis". During processing the flammable gaseous vapor combust at very high temperature and complete destruction of dangerous gases such as furans & dioxins took place. Rapid spreading of COVID-19, by using plasma pyrolysis quick decomposition of COVID-19 infectious waste is occurred. (Wang et al., 2020; Ilyas et al.,2020)

- **Incineration:** This process is commonly used for disposal of waste. It is working on high temperature range (800-1200°c) that is helpful in complete destruction of pathogenic microbes and successfully burn it upto ninety percent organic material (Datta et al., 2018; Wang et al., 2020).

Incinerators are of several types and different types have their specific purposes. For example mobile incinerator is used for disposal of pharmaceutical material and this process is called as **"drug termination"**.

Diesel fired medical waste incinerator is specially used for disposal of pathological remains and small infectious waste generated from small scale health care centers. This incinerator is also called **"Medi burn".**These types of incinerators are portable and easy to use and can incinerate everything generated from laboratories including anatomical waste. Best advantage of incineration is reduction in amount of waste up to 50-400 times.

Some disadvantages of incinerator are cost, smoke generation and pollutant emission like dioxin & furans. In small incinerators more harmful gases are emited as compared to incinerators used in municipality.

Low Temperature Treatment

- **Autoclaving:** It is basically used for sterilization. In autoclave, sterilization is done by steam under high temperature upto 140°c and pressure upto 35psi. Autoclave significantly generates less air pollutant as compared to incineration and other high heat thermal processes.

Autoclaving is done prior to discarding of waste in landfill. Bags of collected waste are positioned in autoclave vessel under pressure and temperature for a specified time (approximately 45 minutes). All pathogenic microbes are completely destructed. Approximately 90% of total waste generated from hospitals could be easily sterilized by autoclave particularly microbiological waste, but autoclave is not intended for pathological or anatomical and additional poisonous chemical waste. Autoclave is used especially for reusable equipment or materials.

- **Microwave:** This technique intervenes under low temperature ranges upto 177-540°c. It includes breaking of organic matter under inert atmosphere under high energy microwave. In this microwave technique, vibration is created because of absorption of electromagnetic wave with wavelength of

1mm to 1m the frequency of 3000 MHz that cause increase in internal energy that ultimately causes collision of molecules. This method could attain exponential value for killed hydrophilic microbes. Microwave technique also used with autoclaving in which steam is used for sterilization (WHO, 2020).

- **Gas–Sterilization:** In gas sterilization, hospital waste is placed into a vacuum sealed compartment and treated with disinfection/ sterilizing agent like ethylene oxide/ formaldehyde. When the sterilization gas encounter pathogenic microbes it kills them because of its high toxicity level. In case of those hospital equipment/articles made up of thermo labile material are specially sterilized by gas sterilization technique. For effective sterilization having a volume of 10ltr, humidity 80-100% at room temperature is maintained (Vashkov et al).

Biological Treatment

There are mainly two type of disposal method based on microbial activity.

- **Open Dump:** Open dumps are those landfill sites where unmanaged, uncontrolled, and scattered waste is deposited in an area. Open dumps cause a serious ill effect for everyone humans, animals, and environment also. Open dumps cause acute pollution, fires, and scavenger.

Hospital generated waste should not be placed in open dumps. Risk of spreading various infectious disease increases in human as well as in animals. Open dumps waste cause transmission of various disease directly or indirectly through wound infection, inhalation, ingestion or indirectly through seepage of leachate in ground water and surface water and through mixed with food chain. (WHO, 2020)

- **Sanitary Landfill:** Landfill for disposal of waste is much better then open dumps. Landfill disposal has many advantages like waste has been geologically isolated from environment. Landfills are constructed under the guidance of experienced engineers and well examined before the disposal of waste in it. Municipal workers are done their duty on landfill sites for proper management of waste. Municipal committee follows the guideline given by WHO and CPCB. Sanitary landfills are disposing various type of pharmaceutical & infectious waste and prevent soil and water from contamination.

WASTE DISPOSAL GUIDELINE

To overcome from COVID-19 pandemic various steps are taken by government: like setting-up of quarantine centres, isolation wards, sample collection and testing laboratories. Certain guidelines are issued by CPCB (Central Pollution Control Board) for proper management and treatment of generated waste from isolation wards, quarantine centres, sample collection centres, laboratories during diagnostics and treatment of COVID-19 suspected /confirmed patients, are required to be followed. These guidelines are important to the present situation of pandemic COVID-19 and infectious waste management practices.

Guidelines issued time to time by different organisations and agencies like WHO (World Health Organization), MoH&FW(Ministry of Health and Family Welfare),ICMR (Indian Council of Medical Research), CDC (Centres for Disease Control) are referred for better handling, treatment and disposal of generated infectious waste from health care units, quarantine centres and laboratories.
Some guidelines issued by WHO and CPCB:

1. Isolation wards for COVID-19 patients: During COVID-19 pandemic some temporary isolation wards are arranged like rail coach, COVID care centres etc. COVID positive patients must follow some rules for safe disposal and handling waste generation during treatment:
    a. As per guidelines given by CPCB and BMWM 2016 different colour coded dustbins are kept in isolation wards with feet operated lid and proper segregation of waste following the guidelines by BMWM 2016.
    b. double layered bags are used for collection of waste in COVID-19 isolations wards to prevent from leakage
    c. All bins are used for collecting generated waste from isolations wards should be properly labelled as "COVID-19 Waste"
    d. Record of waste generation from isolations wards should be properly maintained
    e. Collection equipment's like bins, container, trolleys are properly disinfected with 1% hypochlorite solution from both side outer and inner.
    f. PPE (personal protective equipment's) kits like face-shield, goggles, apron, head cover and gloves are collected into red bag
    g. Used face mask like surgical mask and N-95 mask, head cover, shoe cover is collected in yellow bag.
    h. Segregation of generated biomedical waste should be done at the point of generation like isolation ward.
2. Guidelines for laboratories Sample Collection Centres and COVID-19 suspected patients:

   a. COVID-19 sample collection centres testing laboratories are operating according to guidelines provided by CPCB/SPCB.
   b. All guidelines provided in above section (a) should be followed by these centres
   c. Pre-treat viral transport media, plastic vials, vacutainers, Eppendorf tubes, plastic cryovials, pipette tips as per BMWM Rules, 2016 and collect in red bags.
3. Guidelines for those persons which are working and operating Quarantine Centres/Camps:
   a. In Quarantine Camps/centres and quarantine home suspected COVID-19 and confirmed cases are stayed for 14 days directed by authorised hospital for more observation or the contacts of suspected / confirmed cases who have been directed by authorized hospitals or local authorities to stay at home for at least 14 days or more for observation for any symptom of COVID-19.
   b. Biomedical waste at Quarantine Camps / Home-care may also comprise of used syringes, date expired or discarded medicines, used masks/gloves and in case of patients with other chronic diseases may also include drain bags, urine bags, body fluid or blood-soaked tissues/cotton empty ampules etc.
   c. Biomedical waste generated from Quarantine Camps / Quarantine-Home / Home-care would be treated as 'domestic hazardous waste' as defined under Solid Waste Management Rules 2016, and shall be disposed as per provisions under Biomedical Waste Management Rules 2016 and these guidelines.
4. Guidelines for Common Biomedical Waste Treatment Facility (CBWTF):
   a. Report of receiving of waste from COVID-19 isolation wards / Quarantine Quarantined homes / COVID-19 Testing Centres; submit to SPCB/PCC time to time.
   b. workers and operator that are working in common biomedical waste treatment faculty should be properly sanitize
   c. Appropriate PPE kits that include three-layer masks, splash proof aprons/ gowns, nitrile gloves, gum boots and safety goggles; shall be provided
   d. Authorised specific labelled (COVID-19 WASTE) waste transport vehicle should be used that are completely closed.
   e. 1% sodium hypochlorite solution is used to disinfect transport after every trip.
   f. Operator of CBWTF shall maintain separate record for collection, treatment and disposal of COVID-19 waste.

g. Do not allow any worker showing symptoms of COVID-19 infection to work at the CBMWTF. May provide sufficient leave without any deduction in their salary amount

5. Disposal of used PPE
   a. Used masks and gloves from houses and other health care centres should be kept in paper bags for minimum 3 days.
   b. Used PPE kits from health centres, health workers and COVID-19 patients should be treated as infectious BMW and disposed as per guidelines.
   c. Used PPE kits should be collected in separate yellow-coloured bins and hand over to authorised waste picker for disposed by CBWTF

WASTE DISPOSAL PRACTICES

Following the different international norms and the local laws, different countries follow different waste management practices. A comparative summary of five countries have been presented in Table 2 for the Covid 19 waste disposal.

Table 2. Waste disposal practices by different countries

Country	Waste Treatment and Disposal Method
INDIA	• The generated waste is finally handed over to Common biomedical waste treatment facility (CBWTF) for disposal • In case of generation of large volume of yellow colour Coded waste or incinerable COVID-19 waste beyond the capacity of existing CBWTFs and the Bio-medical waste incinerators are allowed to hospital waste incinerators to dispose of waste in nearby industrial incinerators if any exist in the State/Union territory. In such case, proper arrangement is setup for handling and disposing of waste. (WHO,2020)
NEPAL	• Generated waste is disposed through the burning process, dumped backyard municipal landfill, small scale incineration (Nepal Medical council) NMC,2020
JAPAN	• Generated hospital waste is disposed through the high heat treatment like Incineration, and low heat method like steam sterilization (autoclave), microwave etc. after shredding and disinfection steps. (Islam et al, 2021)
INDONESIA	• The generated waste during COVID-19 is disposed through the incineration after disinfection the waste at source and transport through authorised vehicle to the disposal sites. (UNEP, IETC,2020)
SOUTH AFRICA	• Mostly generated waste during COVID-19 is disposed through high heat methods like Incineration, and low heat methods like (autoclave, converter, microwave) (UNEP, IETC,2020)

CHALLENGES TO WASTE DISPOSAL

Due to COVID -19 pandemic amount of BMW increases tremendously due to increasing BMW, waste managing system are disturbed. Approximately 3.4 kg waste generated from a single COVID patient per day (ADB,2020) so BMW increasing with very fast rate that creates a big problem for present waste transport and disposal system. All countries face same problem during this pandemic. Management of this huge amount of waste became challenge all around the world.

Developing countries already lacks sufficient waste management practices because of technical, practical and financial issues. Because of these regions developing countries are always at-risk during pandemic. During pandemic the waste collection activities are also disturbed because of shortage of workers.

In India generated BMW finally hand over to CBWTF (Common Biomedical Waste Treatment Faculty) which prefers incineration method for waste treatment because as it has highest potential for pathogenic microorganism destruction and it also helps in reducing the volume of waste. But the process has some disadvantages for human health and environment health, it emits large number of harmful elements in the atmosphere. In case the wastes are not completely burned during incineration, this can lead to the production of some toxins like dioxin, furans and some other by-products which can be harmful for environmental health (Goswami et al., 2021). Emission of highly toxic gases can be a reason for ill effect for human and nature. In humans it creates a big problem during reproductive and developmental phase of fetus

Dioxins are group of persistent organic pollutant which is carcinogenic in nature and persist for a long time in body that can disrupt endocrine system, nervous system, immune system and other processes inside the body and can be lethal for human beings. Devices that are used in hospitals and health care facilities are generally made up of synthetic fibers like polyvinyl chloride (PVC), polypropylene (PP), polyurethane (PU) polystyrene (PS) (Joseph et al.,2021). Burning of these types of synthetic fibers produce large amount of harmful toxins like dioxins in the atmosphere (Mattiello et al., 2013). The residual ash present after the incineration can contain heavy metals and other toxic substances that can be harmful for the environment if not disposed properly (Vivek et al.,2019).

Patients who have mild symptoms of COVID-19 infectious treated in home isolation and quarantine centers. Waste generated from these centers are also contaminated with SARS-CoV-2 and infectious in nature. and infectious. This contaminated and infectious wastes get mixed with the general wastes and lead to increasing the COVID infection among the peoples. This situation makes the waste management situation even worse as common people don't know how to segregate the waste according to categories. These peoples collect all type of waste even contaminated waste also in a single bin and then collected by the workers, but this can cause spreading of infection among the waste management workers.

In developing countries waste management workers are not properly skilled and worked without proper sanitation that can be a serious problem. In developed countries waste management workers are well trained, and equipped with better technical facilities with high order machines and better precautionary measures are considered. In undeveloped countries, waste management by untrained sanitary personnel can be a major concern. Unsegregated waste created in undeveloped countries can lead to severe problems since untrained employees must segregate the wastes individually without any safety precautions, which not only takes a long time to dispose of but also puts workers at threat of virus transmission. Workers who spend more time in the waste management process are more susceptible to SARS-CoV-2 infection. (Ganguly & Chakraborty, 2021

Recycling process of generated recyclable waste also disturbed during COVID-19 pandemic. Due to shortage of workers, restriction and lockdown in the countries, recycling plants are remained closed during this period. Due to closing of recycling plant the volume of waste kept on increasing (Somani et al., 2020). Recycling of COVID-19 wastes can be a tricky task as it can cause of risk of transmission of the virus in the workers involved in the process. There is no proper management system for recycling of COVID-19 wastes till now.

CASE STUDIES

Indonesia

In 2020, Indonesia's population was estimated to be 269,197,500 people, with Covid-19 patients accounting for 0.27 percent of the total. Medical trash weighing between 873.38 kg and 4,231.60 kg was found in one of Indonesia's intensive care facilities in 2020. The biggest number of Covid-19 patients was discovered in December, when the number of patients in all areas of Indonesia surged dramatically. In Indonesia, medical waste disposal facilities and information, particularly regarding SARS-CoV-2, are scarce. In 2020, Indonesia's population was estimated to be 269,197,500 people, with Covid-19 patients accounting for 0.27 percent of the total. Medical trash weighing between 873.38 kg and 4,231.60 kg was found in one of Indonesia's intensive care facilities in 2020. The biggest number of Covid-19 patients was identified in December, when the number of patients in all areas of Indonesia surged dramatically. In Indonesia, medical waste management facilities and knowledge, particularly those linked to SARS-CoV-2, are limited.

According to Indonesian law waste generated from health care facilities are consider as a part of hazardous waste (UNEP, IETC,2020). EPM (environment protection and management) regulate and manage this type of waste. In terms of segregation, collection, storage, transportation, and disposal, there are numerous standards for infectious waste management in Indonesia that have been changed by WHO, UNEP and the Directorate of Environmental Health (2020). Infectious waste from Covid-19 intensive care facilities is collected and stored for up to 12 hours in a yellow leak-proof plastic bag with a visible biohazard marking. The yellow bags were disinfected for 30 minutes with 0.50 percent chlorine before being placed in hazardous short-term storage for a maximum of 48 hours. These disinfected yellow bags transported through trolleys immediately to licensed hazardous treatment facility for sterilization and incineration. If licensed landfill is not accessible, the residue may be disposed of on-site in a well-designed pit as per WHO, UNEP and the Directorate of Environmental Health guidelines. Infectious waste created in regions lacking incinerator or autoclave facilities may be disposed of on-site if it has been proven that it has been disinfected with chlorine. Furthermore, the Covid-19 critical care facility, which lacks a certified incinerator, should work with a third party to transport and disposal process. Labelled yellow bags through incineration or sterilization, and then dispose of them in a permitted landfill. The description and data of hospital care waste management (HCWM) is submitted to (MEF) Ministry of Environment and forestry. In Indonesia management and coordination of COVID-19 is under "COVID-19 Taskforce". This taskforce is help in accelerating handling COVID-19, under the National Disaster Control Agency. MEF (Ministry of Environment and Forestry) provide guidelines for management of generated waste from health care facilities during pandemic. It regulates according to waste description how to reduce, sort, store, transport, treat, bury, and dispose of this waste. It can be done by two types on site treatment (autoclave and incineration) by health care facility and by private organization (only incineration) by transportation and treatment.
Some practices followed by waste disposal facility on site and off -site locations:

- Generated collected waste is carry out in sealed packages for transport.
- Transport and shred after disinfection.
- Incinerate the generated health care waste with combustion temperature at least of 800 °C
- Combustion residue like ash is properly labelled.
- Transport the residue of hazardous and toxic waste for further treatment

India (AIIMS Hospital)

Some specific guidelines are used for proper disinfection disposal in COVID-19 designated area:
Three types of bins are used for collection and segregation of PPE

RED BIN 1: In this bin only googles and plastic face shields are collected
RED BIN 2: In this bin N-95 mask and all types of cover like shoe cover, head cover etc.
RED BIN 3: In this bin disposable PPEs are collected

BMW disposal:
As per guidelines color coded double layered bins are used to prevent from leakage
Dedicated collection bins are used which are properly labelled as "COVID-19"
Bag bins and trolleys are also properly labelled as "COVID-19 WASTE" for transporting wards to disposal sites.
Maintain proper record of generated waste, segregation and disposal record also.

China

The outburst of COVID-19 has been started in December, 2019 from eatable seafood market in the city of China (Rume&Islam, 2020). This pandemic spread very fast all over the world and was declared as pandemic by (WHO, 2020). Because of increasing COVID patients biomedical waste increased sharply by 40 tons per day to 247 tons. The pressure of disposal this increased waste is increasing, when this waste not properly managed this virus spreads in environment.

In China for management of biomedical waste is regulated by "Measures for the administration of hazardous waste business license"(Yufeng et al.,2020). Infectious hazardous waste generating during COVID-19 should be disposed by authorized license centralized disposal units. In China the "Work Plan for Comprehensive Treatment of Waste in Medical Institutions" is regulated by National Health Commission of the People's Republic of China, National Development and Reform Commission, Ministry of Ecology and Environment of China and ten other ministries and commissions. Of the People's Republic of China and ten other ministries and commissions. In "Work Plan for Comprehensive Treatment of Waste in Medical Institution" manage and dispose health care waste guidelines issued by centralized disposal of medical waste. By following these guidelines prevent from mismanagement of entire process collection, storage, transfer, transportation, and disposal. During COVID-19 outburst generation rate of health care waste increasing abruptly. So, Ministry of Ecology and Environment of the People's Republic of China issued

"COVID-19 Infected Medical Waste Emergency Disposal Management Technical Guide" by using hazardous waste incinerators, municipal and solid waste incinerators, industrial furnaces, and other facilities to meet pandemic prevention needs.

During an epidemic, medical waste disposal is primarily concerned with the following four aspects:

First, a medical waste disposal emergency strategy should be implemented. Units involved The local environmental authority shall apply in the centralized disposal of medical wastes. They must apply to the Department of Environmental Protection for a hazardous waste business license if they do not already have one. Participate in efforts relating to centralized medical waste disposal. During emergency disposal health care units prefer centralized medical waste disposal units with in their administrative region. When the city's current disposal capacity is depleted. The emergency plan should be implemented as soon as possible if the area cannot satisfy the demands of emergency disposal, the emergency disposal facilities were included in the emergency disposal according to the resource list. In case the conditions are not fulfill by centralized disposal facilities, the generated healthcare waste is incinerated onsite according to the rules of local government.

Second, medical waste disposal facilities should be employed in the event of an emergency. When medical institutions use mobile medical waste disposal facilities for emergency medical waste disposal, they may save time and money. Environmental impact assessments, medical waste company licenses, and other requirements have been waived. Different methods are adopted by medical institutions in reasonable manner, avoid environmentally sensitive locations, such as those protecting drinking water sources.

Third, infected and non-infectious medical waste should be handled separately. Medical facilities should make every effort to categories and manage infectious medical waste as well as other medical waste created during COVID infection prevention and treatment. Medical waste disposal facilities, both centralized and mobile, are available. Priority will be given to treating infectious medical waste created during the event.

Fourth, because COVID-19 generated medical waste is highly contagious, so high-temperature burning of medical waste is a top priority. Depending on the scenario and local variables, each location might pick an emergency treatment strategy for medical waste during COVID period. Medical waste containing COVID virus should be incinerated at a high temperature. On the other hand, no incineration techniques, such as high-temperature steam sterilizing facilities are available. Chemical sterilization and microwave sterilization are further options. In other ways, disposal of medical waste infected with COVID virus should pay attention to protect the safety of the environment.

Bangladesh

In Bangladesh during pandemic period health care waste disposed of inappropriately and haphazardly. (Behnam et al. 2020). Due to using inappropriate methods of disposal like disposal in open areas, in open wastebins, open lands, drains, rivers and roadsides etc. the situation is even worse in many cities. The condition became even worse during pandemic, 76,653 pieces of aprons and gowns; 1,123,457 pieces of examination and surgical gloves; 1,201,127 pieces of shields; 6,787,300 pieces of masks; 1,104,674 pieces of PPE kits; and 189,232 pieces of sanitizers are provided by the DGHS (Directorate General of Health Services) in health care units all over Bangladesh (Shammi and Tareq 2020). The final destination this health care equipment will be wastebin. Before pandemic the process of waste management includes collection, washing, re-marketing and recycling of used masks, PPE, hand gloves, and empty plastic bottles from various hospitals and dumping sites (Hassan et al.2008; Syed et al. 2012). Besides during COVID-19 outburst demand of health care equipment increases and regulatory & monitoring process like recycling reselling are restricted that's why increases amount of infectious hazardous waste.

Environmental Protection Agency (EPA) and World Health Organization (WHO) issued guidelines for safe disposal of health care waste because of its hazardous and infectious nature. The situation became more worse when disposed waste in open areas is collected by slum peoples for earning their livelihood by selling them. The Medical Waste act 2008 for (management and processing) of medical waste does not support mixing of infectious hazardous waste and general house hold waste (MOHFW 2008). During pandemic period generated household waste also not properly disposed according to WHO guidelines. Inappropriate disposal of used PPE kit that includes (face-mask, gloves, head cover, shoe cover apron etc.) will cause ill effect for both environment as well as humans.

In Dhaka city of Bangladesh during COVID-19 only one NGO (Non-Government Organization) PRISM is actively working for collection and disposal of COVID-19 waste from health care units and designated COVID centers (Yeasmin and Tasnime,2020). Modern facilities for disposal of waste are not available in Dhaka city and other cities are also not having such minimum setup yet (Faisal et al. 2021).

CONCLUSION

Bio-medical waste is a serious issue for human health as well as environmental health. Unmanaged treatment of bio-medical waste can cause serious health issues for human health and give birth to no. of pathogenic microbes. By following the guidelines of BMW 2016 and CPCB biomedical waste became easy to handle and safer to the environment and community. During COVID-19 pandemic some national and international regulations and guidelines are issued for management of health care waste. These guidelines provide good basis for handling and management of health care waste during pandemic. According to some medical council reports the SARS Cov-2 virus is viable for 72 hours. Proper handling methods that include segregation, storage and transportation are followed to prevent from viral infection. Proper PPE kits are used during handling healthcare waste and healthcare activities and many other precautionary activities are carried out.

In developing countries which lacks technologies to treat BMW before disposal, it creates big problems for humans as well as environment. According to CPCB and BMW 2016 guidelines disposal of waste in landfill and open dumping is not allowed. These methods are not appropriate for disposal of BMW, because open dumping causes contamination of environment and can cause spreading of many infectious diseases. During pandemic period proper guidelines and disposal methods are followed by the disposal organization that helps in prevention of spreading COVID-19 infection and many other infectious diseases. These guidelines and regulations are further followed in future to prevent spreading of pathogenic and infectious disease and for clean and healthy environment also.

REFERENCES

Aung, T. S., Luan, S., & Xu, Q. (2019). Application of multi-criteria-decision approach for the analysis of medical waste management systems in Myanmar. *Journal of Cleaner Production*, *222*, 733–745. doi:10.1016/j.jclepro.2019.03.049

Behera, B. C. (2021). Challenges in handling COVID-19 contaminated waste material and its sustainable management mechanism. *Environmental Nanotechnology, Monitoring & Management*, 100432. doi:10.1016/j.enmm.2021.100432 PMID:33614423

Birchall, J., & Ketilson, L. (2009). *Resilience of the Cooperative Business Model in Times of Crisis*. International Labor Organization.

Borzaga, C., & Tortia, E. (2007). *Social Economy Organization in the Theory of the Firm*. OECD.

Chand, S., Shastry, C. S., Hiremath, S., Joel, J. J., Krishnabhat, C. H., & Mateti, U. V. (2021). Updates on biomedical waste management during COVID-19: The Indian scenario. *Clinical Epidemiology and Global Health*, *11*, 100715. doi:10.1016/j.cegh.2021.100715

Czajczyńska, D., Anguilano, L., Ghazal, H., Krzyżyńska, R., Reynolds, A. J., Spencer, N., & Jouhara, H. (2017). Potential of pyrolysis processes in the waste management sector. *Thermal Science and Engineering Progress*, *3*, 171–197. doi:10.1016/j.tsep.2017.06.003

Datta, P., Mohi, G. K., & Chander, J. (2018). Biomedical waste management in India: Critical appraisal. *Journal of Laboratory Physicians*, *10*(1), 6. doi:10.4103/JLP.JLP_89_17 PMID:29403196

Duarte, P., & Santana, V. T. (2020). Disinfection measures and control of SARS-COV-2 transmission. *Global Biosecurity, 1*(3).

EASPD (European Association of Service Providers with Persons with Disabilities). (2020). *COVID-19: How social enterprises are fighting back.* Author.

Elavarasan, R. M., & Pugazhendhi, R. (2020). Restructured society and environment: A review on potential technological strategies to control the COVID-19 pandemic. *The Science of the Total Environment*, *725*, 138858. doi:10.1016/j.scitotenv.2020.138858 PMID:32336562

Ganguly, R. K., & Chakraborty, S. K. (2021). Integrated approach in municipal solid waste management in COVID-19 pandemic: Perspectives of a developing country like India in a global scenario. *Case Studies in Chemical and Environmental Engineering*, *3*, 100087. doi:10.1016/j.cscee.2021.100087

Guerci, M., Radaelli, G., Siletti, E., Cirella, S., & Shani, A. R. (2015). The impact of human resource management practices and corporate sustainability on organizational ethical climates: An employee perspective. *Journal of Business Ethics*, *126*(2), 325–342. doi:10.100710551-013-1946-1

Guerriero, C., Haines, A., & Pagano, M. (2020). Health and sustainability in post-pandemic economic policies. *Nature Sustainability*, *3*(7), 494–496. doi:10.103841893-020-0563-0 PMID:32845942

Hadi, M. I., Widiyanti, M., Kumalasari, M. L. F., Alamudi, M. Y., & Suprayogi, D. (2020). Management of SARS-COV-2 medical waste against a COVID19 pandemic in Indonesia: A literature review. *Jurnal Kesehatan Lingkungan*, *12*(4), 244–253. doi:10.20473/jkl.v12i4.2020.244-253

Hysa, E., Kruja, A., Rehman, N. U., & Laurenti, R. (2020). Circular economy innovation and environmental sustainability impact on economic growth: An integrated model for sustainable development. *Sustainability*, *12*(12), 4831. doi:10.3390u12124831

Ilyas, S., Srivastava, R. R., & Kim, H. (2020). Disinfection technology and strategies for COVID-19 hospital and bio-medical waste management. *The Science of the Total Environment, 749*, 141652. doi:10.1016/j.scitotenv.2020.141652 PMID:32822917

Islam, A., Kalam, M., Sayeed, M., Shano, S., Rahman, M., Islam, S., Ferdous, J., Choudhury, S. D., & Hassan, M. M. (2021). Escalating SARS-CoV-2 circulation in environment and tracking waste management in South Asia. *Environmental Science and Pollution Research International, 28*(44), 61951–61968. doi:10.100711356-021-16396-8 PMID:34558044

Joseph, B., James, J., Kalarikkal, N., & Thomas, S. (2021). Recycling of medical plastics. *Advanced Industrial and Engineering Polymer Research, 4*(3), 199–208. doi:10.1016/j.aiepr.2021.06.003

Kalantary, R. R., Jamshidi, A., Mofrad, M. M. G., Jafari, A. J., Heidari, N., Fallahizadeh, S., Hesami Arani, M., & Torkashvand, J. (2021). Effect of COVID-19 pandemic on medical waste management: A case study. *Journal of Environmental Health Science & Engineering, 19*(1), 1–6. doi:10.100740201-021-00650-9 PMID:33758671

Kumar, V., & Gupta, G. (Eds.). (2021). *Strategic Management During a Pandemic*. Routledge. doi:10.4324/9781003125648

Kumar, V., & Malhotra, G. (Eds.). (2021). *Stakeholder Strategies for Reducing the Impact of Global Health Crises*. IGI Global Publications. doi:10.4018/978-1-7998-7495-9

Ma, Y., Lin, X., Wu, A., Huang, Q., Li, X., & Yan, J. (2020). Suggested guidelines for emergency treatment of medical waste during COVID-19: Chinese experience. *Waste Disposal & Sustainable Energy, 2*(2), 81–84. doi:10.100742768-020-00039-8 PMID:32838200

Ma, Y., Lin, X., Wu, A., Huang, Q., Li, X., & Yan, J. (2020). Suggested guidelines for emergency treatment of medical waste during COVID-19: Chinese experience. *Waste Disposal & Sustainable Energy, 2*(2), 81–84. doi:10.100742768-020-00039-8 PMID:32838200

Natarajan, G. S., & Wyrick, D. A. (2011, July). Framework for implementing sustainable practices in SMEs in the United States. In *Proceedings of the world congress on engineering* (*Vol. 1*, No. 1, pp. 6-8). Academic Press.

Pan, J. (2016). *China's environmental governing and ecological civilization*. Springer Berlin Heidelberg.

Ramteke, S., & Sahu, B. L. (2020). Novel coronavirus disease 2019 (COVID-19) pandemic: Considerations for the biomedical waste sector in India. *Case Studies in Chemical and Environmental Engineering*, *2*, 100029. doi:10.1016/j.cscee.2020.100029

Sari, G. L., Hilmi, I. L., Nurdiana, A., Azizah, A. N., & Kasasiah, A. (2021). Infectious waste management as the effects of Covid-19 pandemic in Indonesia. *Asian J Soc Sci Manage Technol*, *3*, 62.

Sarkis, J. (2020). Supply chain sustainability: Learning from the COVID-19 pandemic. *International Journal of Operations & Production Management*, *41*(1), 63–73. doi:10.1108/IJOPM-08-2020-0568

Shammi, M., Behal, A., & Tareq, S. M. (2021). The escalating biomedical waste management to control the environmental transmission of COVID-19 pandemic: A perspective from two south Asian countries. *Environmental Science & Technology*, *55*(7), 4087–4093. doi:10.1021/acs.est.0c05117 PMID:33434001

Shareefdeen, Z. M. (2012). Medical waste management and control. *Journal of Environmental Protection*, *3*(12), 1625–1628. doi:10.4236/jep.2012.312179

Singh, N., Tang, Y., & Ogunseitan, O. A. (2020). Environmentally sustainable management of used personal protective equipment. *Environmental Science & Technology*, *54*(14), 8500–8502. doi:10.1021/acs.est.0c03022 PMID:32597663

Su, M., Wang, Q., & Li, R. (2021). How to Dispose of Medical Waste Caused by COVID-19? A Case Study of China. *International Journal of Environmental Research and Public Health, 18*(22), 12127.

Tsai, P. P. (2020). *Information and FAQs on the Performance*. Protection, and Sterilization of Face Mask Materials.

Vashkov, V. I., Kareev, N. V., Ramkova, N. V., & Chudnova, L. B. (1974). A gaseous method for sterilizing medical instruments. *Biomedical Engineering*, *8*(6), 341–343. doi:10.1007/BF00566462

Vivek, J. M., Singh, R., Sutar, R. S., & Asolekar, S. R. (2019). Characterization and disposal of ashes from biomedical waste incinerator. In *Advances in Waste Management* (pp. 421–435). Springer. doi:10.1007/978-981-13-0215-2_30

Wang, J., Shen, J., Ye, D., Yan, X., Zhang, Y., Yang, W., Li, X., Wang, J., Zhang, L., & Pan, L. (2020). Disinfection technology of hospital wastes and wastewater: Suggestions for disinfection strategy during coronavirus Disease 2019 (COVID-19) pandemic in China. *Environmental Pollution*, *262*, 114665. doi:10.1016/j.envpol.2020.114665 PMID:32443202

Waste, B.-M. (Management and Handling) Rules of 2016. The Gazette of India, Extraordinary, Part II, Section 3(i). Central Pollution Control Board, India. Ministry of Environment, Forest and Climate Change, Notification. (2016). https://cpcb.nic.in/uploads/ Projects/Bio-Medical-Waste/Bio-medical_Waste_Management_Rules_2016.pdf

Yeasmin, F., & Tasnime, Z. (n.d.). *Impact of Healthcare Related Plastic Waste Towards Sustainable Environment During Covid*. Academic Press.

Yong, Z., Gang, X., Guanxing, W., Tao, Z., & Dawei, J. (2009). Medical waste management in China: A case study of Nanjing. *Waste Management (New York, N.Y.)*, *29*(4), 1376–1382. doi:10.1016/j.wasman.2008.10.023 PMID:19157838

Compilation of References

Abdin, M. (2014). Vision-2021: The role of small and medium enterprises in Bangladesh economy. SSRN *Electronic Journal*. doi:10.2139/ssrn.2465763

ACI. (2021). *The impact of COVID-19 on the airport business and the path to recovery*. Airports Council International. https://aci.aero/2021/03/25/the-impact-of-Covid-19-on-the-airport-business-and-the-path-to-recovery/

Acs, Z., & Storey, D. (2004). Introduction: Entrepreneurship and economic development. *Regional Studies*, *38*(8), 871–877. doi:10.1080/0034340042000280901

ADB. (2016). *ADB to provide loans to SMEs, women entrepreneurs in rural Bangladesh*. https://www.adb.org/news/adb-provide-loanssmes-women-entrepreneurs-rural-bangladesh

Afroze, T., Alam, M., Akther, E., & Jui, N. (2015). Women entrepreneurs in Bangladesh- challenges and determining factors. *Journal Of Business and Technology*, *9*(2), 27–41. doi:10.3329/jbt.v9i2.26194

Afshan, G., Shahid, S., & Tunio, M. (2021). Learning experiences of women entrepreneurs amidst COVID-19. *International Journal of Gender and Entrepreneurship*, *13*(2), 162–186. doi:10.1108/IJGE-09-2020-0153

Agashe, S., Kumar, S., & Rai, R. (2021). Exploring the relationship between social ties and resilience from evolutionary framework. *Frontiers of Human Dynamics*, *3*, 683755. doi:10.3389/fhumd.2021.683755

Ahammad, I., & Moudud-Ul-Huq, S. (2013). Women entrepreneurship development in Bangladesh challenges and prospects. *International Journal of Innovative Research and Development*, *2*(7), 41–48. https://www.researchgate.net/publication/281115595

Ahmed, N. (2019). SME: Challenges women entrepreneurs face. *The Financial Express*. https://www.thefinancialexpress.com.bd/views/sme-challenges-women-entrepreneurs-face-1551886089

Ahmed, K., & Chowdhury, T. (2009). Performance evaluation of SMEs of Bangladesh. *International Journal of Business and Management*, *4*(7), 126–133. doi:10.5539/ijbm.v4n7p126

Ahuja, K., & Garg, M. (2021). Stress and well-being among first year and last year college students during COVID-19. *Indian Journal of Mental Health, 8*(1), 66–69. doi:10.30877/IJMH.8.1.2021.65-69

Alauddin, M., & Chowdhury, M. M. (2015). Small and medium enterprise in Bangladesh – prospects and challenges. *Global Journal of Management and Business Research, 15*(7), 1–10.

Aldin, N., & Stahre, F. (2003). Electronic commerce, marketing channels and logistics platforms—a wholesaler perspective. *European Journal of Operational Research, 144*(2), 270–279. doi:10.1016/S0377-2217(02)00393-4

Ama, N., Mangadi, K., & Ama, H. (2014). Exploring the challenges facing women entrepreneurs in informal cross-border trade in Botswana. *Gender in Management, 29*(8), 505–522. doi:10.1108/GM-02-2014-0018

Ameen, A. (2020, April 20). *TnlSalutes: This Is How Lemon Tree Hotels Is Helping In The Fight Against COVID-19.* Retrieved on November on 6, 2021, from https://www.travelandleisureindia.in/featured/lemon-tree-hotels-covid-19

Anderson, K., & Wittwer, G. (2021). *Projecting Global Beverage Markets to 2025.* The International Wine Marketing & Wine Tourism Database.

Anderson, N., Potočnik, K., & Zhou, J. (2014). Innovation and creativity in organizations. *Journal of Management, 40*(5), 1297–1333. doi:10.1177/0149206314527128

Andrew, O. C., & Saudah, S. (2012). Individual factors and work outcomes of employee engagement. *Procedia-Social and Behavioural Sciences, 40*, 498–508. doi:10.1016/j.sbspro.2012.03.222

Anindya, S. N., Debora, M. A., & Manickam, L. S. S. (2020). Refining psychological services and strategies in India in the wake of COVID-19. In L. S. S. Manickam (Ed.), COVID-19 pandemic: Challenges and responses of psychologists from India (pp. 8-22). Thiruvananthapuram: The Editor.

Ardito, L., Coccia, M., & Messeni Petruzzelli, A. (2021). Technological exaptation and crisis management: Evidence from COVID-19 outbreaks. *R & D Management, 51*(4), 381–392. doi:10.1111/radm.12455

Asian Development Bank. (2020). Asian Development Bank Member Fact Sheet. Metro Manila: Asian Development Bank.

Asian Development Bank. (2021). *Bangladesh and ADB.* Retrieved from Asian Development Bank: https://www.adb.org/countries/bangladesh/economy

Asquith, J. (2020). Coronavirus travel update—Over 90% of people live under travel restrictions. *Forbes.*

Aung, T. S., Luan, S., & Xu, Q. (2019). Application of multi-criteria-decision approach for the analysis of medical waste management systems in Myanmar. *Journal of Cleaner Production, 222*, 733–745. doi:10.1016/j.jclepro.2019.03.049

Ayala, J.-C., & Manzano, G. (2014). The resilience of the entrepreneur. Influence on the success of the business: A longitudinal analysis. *Journal of Economic Psychology*, *42*, 126–135. doi:10.1016/j.joep.2014.02.004

Backer, E., & Ritchie, B. W. (2017). VFR travel: A viable market for tourism crisis and disaster recovery? *International Journal of Tourism Research*, *19*(4), 400–411. doi:10.1002/jtr.2102

Bagi, P. D., & Sunita Chand, S. (2020). Effect of lockdown on mental health: A study of Haryana. *Mrida: An International Journal of Humanities and Social Sciences*, *1*(1), 1–8.

Bakker, A. B. (2015). A job demands-resources approach to public service motivation. *Public Administration Review*, *75*(5), 723–732. doi:10.1111/puar.12388

Bakker, A. B., & Demerouti, E. (2017). Job demands-resources theory: Taking stock and looking forward. *Journal of Occupational Health Psychology*, *22*(3), 273–285. doi:10.1037/ocp0000056 PMID:27732008

Bakker, A. B., Demerouti, E., & Schaufeli, W. B. (2003). Dual processes at work in a call centre: An application of the Job Demands-Resources model. *European Journal of Work and Organizational Psychology*, *12*(4), 393–417. doi:10.1080/13594320344000165

Bakker, A., & Demerouti, E. (2006). The job demands-resources model: State of the art. *Journal of Managerial Psychology*, *22*(3), 309–328. doi:10.1108/02683940710733115

Balla, D. (2020). Manipulating CORONA VIRUS's adverse effects for the benefit of humanity - A psychologist's perspective. *Tejasvi Astitva*, 1-8. http://www.tejasviastitva.com/manipulating-coronaviruss-adverse-effects-for-the-benefit-of-humanitya-psychologists-perspective-by-dr-deepthi-balla/

Bangladesh Institute of Development Studies. (2017). *Women Entrepreneurs in SMEs: Bangladesh Perspective 2017*. Retrieved from https%3A%2F%2Fthink-asia.org%2Fbitstream%2Fhandle%2F11540%2F9681%2FSummary_SME_women_entrepreneur_nazneen_27-12-18.pdf%3Fsequence%3D1

Bapu, V. K. G., & Babu, K. N. C. (2021). Impact of COVID-19 on intolerance of uncertainty and safety behaviour. *Ilkogretim Online*, *20*(4).

Barragan, S., Erogul, M., & Essers, C. (2018). 'Strategic (dis)obedience': Female entrepreneurs reflecting on and acting upon patriarchal practices. *Gender, Work and Organization*, *25*(5), 575–592. doi:10.1111/gwao.12258

Bartik, A. W., Bertrand, M., Cullen, Z. B., Glaeser, E. L., Luca, M., & Stanton, C. T. (2020). *How are small businesses adjusting to COVID-19? Early evidence from a survey (No. w26989)*. National Bureau of Economic Research. doi:10.3386/w26989

Basquille, M. (2013). *In this recession, has engagement remained high? –Research within an Irish financial company* (Unpublished dissertation). National College of Ireland. Retrieved from https://core.ac.uk/download/pdf/45382349.pdf

Battilana, J. (2018). Cracking the organizational challenge of pursuing joint social and financial goals: social enterprise as a laboratory to understand hybrid organizing. *M@n@gement, 21*(4), 1278-1305.

Bedarkar, M., & Pandita, D. (2014). A study on the drivers of employee engagement impacting employee performance. *Procedia-Social and Behavioural Sciences, 133*, 106-115. doi:10.1016/j.sbspro.2014.04.174

Behera, B. C. (2021). Challenges in handling COVID-19 contaminated waste material and its sustainable management mechanism. *Environmental Nanotechnology, Monitoring & Management*, 100432. doi:10.1016/j.enmm.2021.100432 PMID:33614423

Benaben, F., Lauras, M., Trupil, S., & Salatage, N. (2016, January). *A metamodel for Knowledge Management in Crisis Management* [Paper presentation]. The 49th Hawaii International Conference De on System Sciences (HICSS 2016), Koloa, HI.

Bhanot, D., Singh, T., Verma, S. K., & Sharad, S. (2021). Stigma and discrimination during COVID-19 pandemic. *Frontiers in Public Health, 8*, 577018. doi:10.3389/fpubh.2020.577018 PMID:33585379

Bharat, R., Uzaina, Niranjan, S., Yadav, T., Newman, S., Marriott, J., Smith, G., & Sawlani, G. (2021). Autism spectrum disorder in the COVID 19 era: New challenges – new solutions. *Indian Pediatrics, 58*(15), 890–892. doi:10.100713312-021-2314-3 PMID:34183470

Bhardwaj, A., & Kumar, V. (2022). Privacy and Healthcare during COVID-19. In *Cybersecurity Crisis Management and Lessons Learned From the COVID-19 Pandemic* (pp. 82–96). IGI-Global. doi:10.4018/978-1-7998-9164-2.ch005

Bhatt, A., Arora, P., & Prajapati, S. K. (2020a). Can algal derived bioactive metabolites serve as potential therapeutics for the treatment of SARS-CoV-2 like viral infection? *Frontiers in Microbiology, 11*, 596374. doi:10.3389/fmicb.2020.596374 PMID:33262750

Bhatt, A., Arora, P., & Prajapati, S. K. (2020b). Occurrence, fates and potential treatment approaches for removal of viruses from wastewater: A review with emphasis on SARS- CoV-2. *Journal of Environmental Chemical Engineering, 8*(5), 104429. doi:10.1016/j.jece.2020.104429 PMID:32895629

Biospectrumindia. (n.d.). *Medical device manufacturers are facing a lot of challenges.* Retrieved March 10, 2021, from https://www.biospectrumindia.com/features/17/11062/medical-device-manufacturers-are-facing-a-lot-of-challenges.html

Birchall, J., & Ketilson, L. (2009). *Resilience of the Cooperative Business Model in Times of Crisis*. International Labor Organization.

Borzaga, C., & Tortia, E. (2007). *Social Economy Organization in the Theory of the Firm.* OECD.

Branicki, L. J., Sullivan-Taylor, B., & Livschitz, S. R. (2018). How entrepreneurial resilience generates resilient SMEs. *International Journal of Entrepreneurial Behaviour & Research, 24*(7), 1244–1263. doi:10.1108/IJEBR-11-2016-0396

Breier, M., Kallmuenzer, A., Clauss, T., Gast, J., Kraus, S., & Tiberius, V. (2021). The role of business model innovation in the hospitality industry during the COVID-19 crisis. *International Journal of Hospitality Management, 92*, 102723. doi:10.1016/j.ijhm.2020.102723

Brickell, K., Picchioni, F., Natarajan, N., Guermond, V., Parsons, L., Zanello, G., & Bateman, M. (2020). Compounding crises of social reproduction: Microfinance, over-indebtedness and the COVID-19 pandemic. *World Development, 136*, 105087. doi:10.1016/j.worlddev.2020.105087 PMID:32834384

Brush, C., de Bruin, A., & Welter, F. (2009). A gender-aware framework for women's entrepreneurship. *International Journal of Gender and Entrepreneurship, 1*(1), 8–24. doi:10.1108/17566260910942318

Bruwer, J. (2003). South African wine routes: Some perspectives on the wine tourism industry's structural dimensions and wine tourism product. *Tourism Management, 24*(4), 423–435. doi:10.1016/S0261-5177(02)00105-X

BS. (2021). https://www.business-standard.com/article/economy-policy/covid-19-lockdown-effect-every-second-indian-now-on-internet-in-cities-120050801805_1.html

Bucklin, L. P., Ramaswamy, V., & Majumdar, S. K. (1996). Analyzing channel structures of business markets via the structure-output paradigm. *International Journal of Research in Marketing, 13*(1), 73–87. doi:10.1016/0167-8116(95)00035-6

Business Standard. (2021a). *Coronil has got Ayush Ministry certification as per WHO scheme: Patanjali.* https://www.business-standard.com/article/pti-stories/coronil-has-got-ayush-ministry-certification-as-per-who-scheme-patanjali-121021901231_1.html

Business Standard. (2021b). *Dabur India's profit after tax jumps 28.4%, beats pre-Covid levels.* https://www.business-standard.com/article/companies/dabur-india-s-profit-after-tax-jumps-28-4-beats-pre-covid-levels-121080302039_1.html

Business Standard. (2021c). *Well-positioned to handle challenges of another Covid wave: Dabur India.* https://www.business-standard.com/article/companies/well-positioned-to-handle-challenges-of-another-covid-wave-dabur-india-121081900933_1.html

Business Today. (2020). Coronavirus impact: Oyo allots ESOPs worth Rs 130 crore to furloughed employees. *Business Today*. Retrieved from https://www.businesstoday.in/latest/corporate /story/oyo-allots-esops-worth-rs-130-crore-to-former-existing-staff-impacted-by-covid-19-259837-2020-06-01

Business World. (2021). *Lemon Tree Hotels introduces various initiatives amidst the COVID-19 pandemic.* Retrieved on November 4, 2021, from http://bwhotelier.businessworld.in/article/Lemon-Tree-Hotels-introduces-various-initiatives-amidst-the-COVID-19-pandemic-/05-06-2021-392063/

Byrd, E., Canziani, B., Hsieh, Y. C., Debbage, K., & Sonmez, S. (2016). Wine tourism: Motivating visitors through core and supplementary services. *Tourism Management*, *52*, 19–29. doi:10.1016/j.tourman.2015.06.009

CAAC. (2020). *CAAC to Further Intensify and Refine Prevention and Control Measures to Win the Battle against the Novel Coronavirus Epidemic.* Civil Aviation Administration of China. http://www.caac.gov.cn/en/XWZX/202002/t20200221_201090.html

CAAC. (2021). *Group Standard of China Air Transport Association Promoted in International Aviation Industry for the First Time.* http://www.caac.gov.cn/XWZX/MHYW/202103/t20210324_206897.html

CAAC. (2021a). *2020 Statistical bulletin on the development of the civil aviation industry in 2020.* Civil Aviation Administration of China. http://www.caac.gov.cn/XXGK/XXGK/TJSJ/202106/P020210610582600192012.pdf

CAPA. (2021). *Domestic advantages boost China Southern's post-COVID prospects.* https://centreforaviation.com/analysis/reports/domestic-advantages-boost-china-southerns-post-covid-prospects-558104

Carbon, C.-C. (2020). Wearing face masks strongly confuses counterparts in reading emotions. *Frontiers in Psychology*, *11*, 566886. doi:10.3389/fpsyg.2020.566886 PMID:33101135

CARNC. (2020). *The most beautiful retrograde: Several civil aviation-chartered planes pick up hundreds of overseas stranded passengers in Hubei.* Civil Aviation Resource Net of China. http://news.carnoc.com/newsList/index.html?date=2020-02-01

Carter, S. (2000). Improving the numbers and performance of women-owned businesses: Some implications for training and advisory services. *Education + Training*, *42*(4/5), 326–334. doi:10.1108/00400910010373732

Castro, M.P., & Zermeño, M.G.G. (2020). Being an entrepreneur post-COVID-19–resilience in times of crisis: a systematic literature review. *Journal of Entrepreneurship in Emerging Economies.*

CCAA. (2020). *Guideline for regular epidemic prevention and control of COVID-19 for civil airports in China.* China Civil Airport Association. https://www.aci-asiapac.aero/f/blog/1798/4468/CCAA%20Guideline%20for%20regular%20epidemic%20prevention%20and%20control%20of%20COVID-19%20for%20civil%20airports%20in%20China%2020200828.pdf

Cesaroni, F., Pediconi, M., & Sentuti, A. (2018). It's always a women's problem! micro-entrepreneurs, work-family balance, and economic crisis. *Administrative Sciences*, *8*(4), 74. doi:10.3390/admsci8040074

Cesaroni, F., & Sentuti, A. (2016). Economic crisis, women entrepreneurs and bank loans: Some empirical evidence from Italy. *Economic Research-Ekonomska Istraživanja*, *29*(1), 1050–1061. doi:10.1080/1331677X.2016.1211953

Chadee, D., Ren, S., & Tang, G. (2021). Is digital technology the magic bullet for performing work at home? Lessons learned for post COVID-19 recovery in hospitality management. *International Journal of Hospitality Management, 92*, 102718. doi:10.1016/j.ijhm.2020.102718 PMID:33071425

Chadha, A. (2015). Hotel Taj in The Context Of CRM and Customer Retention. *Arabian Journal of Business and Management Review, 4*(7). Retrieved on October 24, 2021, from https://www.arabianjbmr.com/pdfs/KD_VOL_4_7/1.pdf

Chanana, N., & Sangeeta. (2021). Employee engagement practices during COVID-19 lockdown. *Journal of Public Affairs, 21*(4), e2508. doi:10.1002/pa.2508 PMID:33041656

Chand, S., Shastry, C. S., Hiremath, S., Joel, J. J., Krishnabhat, C. H., & Mateti, U. V. (2021). Updates on biomedical waste management during COVID-19: The Indian scenario. *Clinical Epidemiology and Global Health, 11*, 100715. doi:10.1016/j.cegh.2021.100715

Chaturvedi, A. (2020, April 8). *COVID-19: Lemon Tree Hotels undertakes pay cuts for senior leadership*. Retrieved on December 2, 2021, from https://economictimes.indiatimes.com/industry/services/hotels-/-restaurants/covid-19-lemon-tree-hotels-undertakes-pay-cuts-for-senior-leadership/articleshow/75050051.cms

Chaudhary, M., & Chandel, P. (2021). Digital education a boon or doom for children of digital India during COVID-19. In N. Gupta & N. Srivastava (Eds.), *Psychosocial impact of digital education during COVID-19* (Vol. 1, pp. 1–18). Insta.

Chenarides, L., Manfredo, M., & Richards, T. J. (2021). Covid-19 and food supply chains. *Applied Economic Perspectives and Policy, 43*(1), 270–279. doi:10.1002/aepp.13085

Chen, C. (2006). CiteSpace II: Detecting and Visualizing Emerging Trends and Transient Patterns in Scientific Literature. *JASIST, 57*(3), 359–377. doi:10.1002/asi.20317

Chen, C., Ibekwe-Sanjuan, F., & Hou, J. (2010). The Structure and Dynamics of Cocitation Clusters: A Multiple-Perspective Cocitation Analysis. *JASIST, 61*(7), 1386–1409. doi:10.1002/asi.21309

Chesbrough, H. W. (2003). *Open innovation: The new imperative for creating and profiting from technology*. Harvard Business Press.

China Daily. (2021). *China world's largest domestic air travel market in 2020*. https://www.chinadaily.com.cn/a/202108/10/WS6112254aa310efa1bd667ebd.html

China, A. (n.d.). *Information on Response to the COVID-19 Epidemic*. Retrieved August 19, 2021. https://www.airchina.us/US/GB/promotion/epidemicp?pid=TP_epidemicp:20200909:KV:KYQF:US:EN

Chinairport. (2021). *Operational status of domestic airlines' wide-body aircrafts*. Chinairport. https://www.chinairport.net/news/2630.html

Chowdhury, M. (2007). Overcoming entrepreneurship development constraints: The case of Bangladesh. *Journal Of Enterprising Communities: People and Places in The Global Economy, 1*(3), 240–251. doi:10.1108/17506200710779549

Chowdhury, M., Alam, Z., & Arif, M. (2013). Success factors of entrepreneurs of small and medium sized enterprises: Evidence from Bangladesh. *Business and Economic Review*, *3*(2), 38. doi:10.5296/ber.v3i2.4127

Chowdhury, P., Paul, S. K., Kaisar, S., & Moktadir, M. A. (2021). COVID-19 pandemic related supply chain studies: A systematic review. *Transportation Research Part E, Logistics and Transportation Review*, *148*, 102271. doi:10.1016/j.tre.2021.102271 PMID:33613082

CII. (2019). *Resurgence of the Ayurveda Industry*. https://www.ciiblog.in/resurgence-of-the-ayurveda-industry/

CIRIUM. (2020). *Cirium weekly Covid-19 update – A golden week for Chinese operators*. https://www.cirium.com/thoughtcloud/cirium-weekly-Covid-19-update-a-golden-week-for-chinese-operators/

CIRIUM. (2021). *Impact of COVID-19 on China*. https://discover.cirium.com/discover/ideas/Covid-19-impact?intcmp=discover-idea-impact-china

Constantinidis, C., Lebègue, T., El Abboubi, M., & Salman, N. (2019). How families shape women's entrepreneurial success in Morocco: An intersectional study. *International Journal of Entrepreneurial Behaviour & Research*, *25*(8), 1786–1808. doi:10.1108/IJEBR-12-2017-0501

Crane, A., & Matten, D. (2020). COVID-19 and the future of CSR research. *Journal of Management Studies*, *58*(1), 280–284. https://doi.org/10.1111/joms.12642

Crick, J. M., Crick, D., & Tebbett, N. (2020). Competitor orientation and value co-creation in sustaining rural New Zealand wine producers. *Journal of Rural Studies*, *73*, 122–134. doi:10.1016/j.jrurstud.2019.10.019

CSAIR. (2020). *Deploying the "cabin cargo" market, China Southern Airlines helps the world "carrying cargo"*. https://www.csair.com/cn/about/news/news/2020/1edqrf7pgjv24.shtml

CSR-CSAIR. (2021). *2020 Corporate Social Responsibility Report of China Southern Airlines Company Limited*. https://www.csair.com/au/en/about/shehuizerenbaogao/resource/f9d8ea27e25f5a475282e461d1067a57.pdf

Cuomo, M. T., Tortora, D., Foroudi, P., Giordano, A., Festa, G., & Metallo, G. (2021). Digital transformation and tourist experience co-design: Big social data for planning cultural tourism. *Technological Forecasting and Social Change*, *162*, 120345. doi:10.1016/j.techfore.2020.120345

Cusin, J., & Passebois-Ducros, J. (2015). Appropriate persistence in a project: The case of the Wine Culture and Tourism Centre in Bordeaux. *European Management Journal*, *33*(5), 341–353. doi:10.1016/j.emj.2015.04.001

Czajczyńska, D., Anguilano, L., Ghazal, H., Krzyżyńska, R., Reynolds, A. J., Spencer, N., & Jouhara, H. (2017). Potential of pyrolysis processes in the waste management sector. *Thermal Science and Engineering Progress*, *3*, 171–197. doi:10.1016/j.tsep.2017.06.003

Czerny, A. I., Fu, X., Lei, Z., & Oum, T. H. (2021). Post pandemic aviation market recovery: Experience and lessons from China. *Journal of Air Transport Management*, *90*, 101971. https://doi.org/10.1016/j.jairtraman.2020.101971

Dahles, H., & Susilowati, T. P. (2015). Business resilience in times of growth and crisis. *Annals of Tourism Research*, *51*, 34–50. doi:10.1016/j.annals.2015.01.002

Daijiworld. (2021). https://www.daijiworld.com/news/newsDisplay?newsID=883674

Datta, P., Mohi, G. K., & Chander, J. (2018). Biomedical waste management in India: Critical appraisal. *Journal of Laboratory Physicians*, *10*(1), 6. doi:10.4103/JLP.JLP_89_17 PMID:29403196

Davidsson, P., Achtenhagen, L., & Naldi, L. (2007). What Do We Know about Small Firm Growth? *Springer*.

Davidsson, P., & Gordon, S. R. (2016). Much ado about nothing? The surprising persistence of nascent entrepreneurs through macroeconomic crisis. *Entrepreneurship Theory and Practice*, *40*(4), 915–941. doi:10.1111/etap.12152

De Mestral, A. L., Fitzgerald, P. P., & Ahmad, M. T. (Eds.). (2018). *Sustainable Development, International Aviation, and Treaty Implementation* (1st ed.). Cambridge University Press.

De Vita, L., Mari, M., & Poggesi, S. (2014). Women entrepreneurs in and from developing countries: Evidences from the literature. *European Management Journal*, *32*(3), 451–460. doi:10.1016/j.emj.2013.07.009

Del Mar Alonso-Almeida, M., & Bremser, K. (2013). Strategic responses of the Spanish hospitality sector to the financial crisis. *International Journal of Hospitality Management*, *32*(1), 141–148. doi:10.1016/j.ijhm.2012.05.004

Della-Giusta, M., & Phillips, C. (2006). Women entrepreneurs in the Gambia: Challenges and opportunities. *Journal of International Development*, *18*(8), 1051–1064. doi:10.1002/jid.1279

Demerouti, E., Bakker, A. B., Nachreiner, F., & Schaufeli, W. B. (2001). The job demands-resources model of burnout. *The Journal of Applied Psychology*, *86*(3), 499–512. doi:10.1037/0021-9010.86.3.499 PMID:11419809

Deshpande, R., & Sinha, M. (2011). *Taj Hotels, Resorts and Palaces*. Retrieved November 18, 2021, from www.researchgate.net

DesJardine, M., Bansal, P., & Yang, Y. (2019). Bouncing back: Building resilience through social and environmental practices in the context of the 2008 global financial crisis. *Journal of Management*, *45*(4), 1434–1460. doi:10.1177/0149206317708854

Devece, C., Peris-Ortiz, M., & Rueda-Armengot, C. (2016). Entrepreneurship during economic crisis: Success factors and paths to failure. *Journal of Business Research*, *69*(11), 5366–5370. doi:10.1016/j.jbusres.2016.04.139

Dhanani, S. (2019, April 24). *Making India a hub for product innovation*. Retrieved March 10, 2021, from https://bloncampus.thehindubusinessline.com/entrepreneurship/making-india-a-hub-for-product-innovation/article26933987.ece

Dhar, S., Farzana, T., & Abedin, S. S. (2021). Impact, Reaction, and Learning from Overcoming the COVID-19 Crisis: Cases From Small-Scale Businesses in Bangladesh. In S. Stephens (Ed.), *Cases on Small Business Economics and Development During Economic Crises* (pp. 27–51). IGI Global. doi:10.4018/978-1-7998-7657-1.ch002

Doern, R., Williams, N., & Vorley, T. (2019). Special issue on entrepreneurship and crises: Business as usual? An introduction and review of the literature. *Entrepreneurship and Regional Development*, *31*(5/6), 400–412. doi:10.1080/08985626.2018.1541590

Duan, B., Arcodia, C., Ma, E., & Hsiao, A. (2018). Understanding wine tourism in China using an integrated product-level and experience economy framework. *Asia Pacific Journal of Tourism Research*, *23*(10), 949–960. doi:10.1080/10941665.2018.1512506

Duarte, P., & Santana, V. T. (2020). Disinfection measures and control of SARS-COV-2 transmission. *Global Biosecurity, 1*(3).

Dutton, J., & Normand-Marconnet, N. (2019). *Visual codes on French wine labels for cross-cultural marketing in China and Australia*. Academy of Wine Business Research.

EASPD (European Association of Service Providers with Persons with Disabilities). (2020). *COVID-19: How social enterprises are fighting back*. Author.

Eisenhardt, K. M. (1989). Building Theories from Case Study Research. *Academy of Management Review*, *14*(4), 532–550. doi:10.2307/258557

Eisenhardt, K. M., & Graebner, M. E. (2007). Theory Building from Cases: Opportunities and challenges. *Academy of Management Journal*, *50*(1), 25–32. doi:10.5465/amj.2007.24160888

Elavarasan, R. M., & Pugazhendhi, R. (2020). Restructured society and environment: A review on potential technological strategies to control the COVID-19 pandemic. *The Science of the Total Environment*, *725*, 138858. doi:10.1016/j.scitotenv.2020.138858 PMID:32336562

Erol, O., Sauser, B. J., & Mansouri, M. (2010). A framework for investigation into extended enterprise resilience. *Enterprise Information Systems*, *4*(2), 111–136. doi:10.1080/17517570903474304

Eusuf, M. A. (2020). The challenges faced by women-led SMEs and the way forward. *The Daily Star*. https://www.thedailystar.net/round-tables/news/the-challenges-faced-women-led-smes-and-the-way-forward-1848013

Express Pharma. (2021). *Himalaya study finds herbal immunomodulators effective as adjuvant treatment for COVID-19*. https://www.expresspharma.in/himalaya-study-finds-herbal-immunomodulators-effective-as-adjuvant-treatment-for-covid-19/

Fabeil, N. F., Pazim, K. H., & Langgat, J. (2020). The impact of Covid-19 pandemic crisis on micro-enterprises: Entrepreneurs' perspective on business continuity and recovery strategy. *Journal of Economics and Business*, *3*(2). Available at SSRN: https://ssrn.com/abstract=3612830

Fairlie, R. (2020). The impact of COVID-19 on small business owners: Evidence from the first three months after widespread social-distancing restrictions. *Journal of Economics & Management Strategy*, *29*(4), 727–740. doi:10.1111/jems.12400 PMID:32904856

Fatima, H., & Mahour, P. (2021). Manifestation and usefulness of defence mechanisms during COVID-19 pandemic. *International Journal of Indian Psychology*, *9*(1), 1469–1475.

Federici, S. (2018). *Witches, witch-hunting, and women*. PM Press.

Festa, G., Riad Shams, S. M., Metallo, G., & Cuomo, M. T. (2020). Opportunities and challenges in the contribution of wine routes to wine tourism in Italy – A stakeholders' perspective of development. *Tourism Management Perspectives*, *33*, 100585. doi:10.1016/j.tmp.2019.100585

Financialexpress. (2019). *InnAccel: The Medtech startup that is innovating to save lives*. Retrieved from https://www.financialexpress.com/industry/sme/innaccel-the-medtech-startup-that-is-innovating-to-save-lives/1651781/

Firstpost. (2021). *In India's fight against COVID-19, thrust from Ministry of Ayush has been unrelenting*. https://www.firstpost.com/health/in-indias-fight-against-covid-19-thrust-from-ministry-of-ayush-has-been-unrelenting-9862281.html

Fischer, E., Reuber, A., & Dyke, L. (1993). A theoretical overview and extension of research on sex, gender, and entrepreneurship. *Journal of Business Venturing*, *8*(2), 151–168. doi:10.1016/0883-9026(93)90017-Y

Fortune India. (2021). *How Dabur is riding the new normal*. https://www.fortuneindia.com/enterprise/how-dabur-is-riding-the-new-normal/105069

Francesca, M., Paola, D., & Paola, P. (2017). Women in business and social media: Implications for female entrepreneurship in emerging countries. *African Journal of Business Management*, *11*(14), 316–326. doi:10.5897/AJBM2017.8281

Frias-Armenta, M., Corral-Frias, N. S., Corral-Verdugo, V., & Lucas, M. Y. (2021). Psychological predictors of precautionary behaviours in response to COVID-19: A structural model. *Frontiers in Psychology*, *12*, 559289. doi:10.3389/fpsyg.2021.559289 PMID:33995161

Frost, W., Frost, J., Strickland, P., & Maguire, J. S. (2020). Seeking a competitive advantage in wine tourism: Heritage and storytelling at the cellar-door. *International Journal of Hospitality Management*, *87*, 102460. doi:10.1016/j.ijhm.2020.102460

Gairola, V., & Mishra, P. K. (2020). COVID-19 turned upside down: A psychological perspective. *Pedagogy of Learning*, *6*(4), 1–7.

Ganguly, R. K., & Chakraborty, S. K. (2021). Integrated approach in municipal solid waste management in COVID-19 pandemic: Perspectives of a developing country like India in a global scenario. *Case Studies in Chemical and Environmental Engineering*, *3*, 100087. doi:10.1016/j.cscee.2021.100087

Garibaldi, R., Stone, M. J., Wolf, E., & Pozzi, A. (2017). Wine travel in the United States: A profile of wine travellers and wine tours. *Tourism Management Perspectives*, *23*, 53–57. doi:10.1016/j.tmp.2017.04.004

Gaur, A., & Patel, A. K. (2021). Psychosocial intervention among COVID-19 and their care givers: A therapeutic approach. In P. Kansra (Ed.), *Socio economics of COVID-19 in India* (pp. 112–118). Wesser Books.

Gengatharen, D. E., & Standing, C. (2005). A framework to assess the factors affecting success or failure of the implementation of government-supported regional e-marketplaces for SMEs. *European Journal of Information Systems*, *14*(4), 417–433. doi:10.1057/palgrave.ejis.3000551

Getz, D., & Brown, G. (2006). Critical success factors for wine tourism regions: A demand analysis. *Tourism Management*, *27*(1), 146–158. doi:10.1016/j.tourman.2004.08.002

Ghosh, A. T. (2020, April). A host of troubles for OYO. *Fortune India*. Retrieved from https://www.fortuneindia.com/enterprise/a-host-of-troubles-for-oyo/104512

Ghosh, P., & Cheruvalath, R. (2007). Indian female entrepreneurs as catalysts for economic growth and development. *International Journal of Entrepreneurship and Innovation*, *8*(2), 139–147. doi:10.5367/000000007780808048

Ghosh, P., Ghosh, S., & Chowdhury, S. (2017). Factors hindering women entrepreneurs' access to institutional finance- an empirical study. *Journal of Small Business and Entrepreneurship*, *30*(4), 279–291. doi:10.1080/08276331.2017.1388952

Ghouse, S., McElwee, G., Meaton, J., & Durrah, O. (2017). Barriers to rural women entrepreneurs in Oman. *International Journal of Entrepreneurial Behaviour & Research*, *23*(6), 998–1016. doi:10.1108/IJEBR-02-2017-0070

Global Times. (2021). *Grounded by Covid-19, Chinese airlines search for new opportunities.* https://www.globaltimes.cn/page/202108/1230665.shtml

Gobagoba, M., & Littrell, M. (2003). Profiling micro apparel enterprises in Botswana: Motivations, practices, challenges, and success. *Clothing & Textiles Research Journal*, *21*(3), 130–141. doi:10.1177/0887302X0302100303

Goldstein, M., Martinez, P. G., Papineni, S., & Wimpey, J. (2020). *The global state of small business during COVID-19: Gender inequalities.* World Bank Blogs. https://blogs.worldbank.org/developmenttalk/global-state-small-business-during-covid-19-gender-inequalities

Gómez, M., González-Díaz, M., & Molina, A. (2015). Priority maps at wine tourism destinations: An empirical approach in five Spanish wine regions. *Journal of Destination Marketing & Management*, *4*(4), 258–267. doi:10.1016/j.jdmm.2015.09.003

Gomez, M., Lopez, C., & Molina, A. (2015). A model of tourism destination brand equity: The case of wine tourism destinations in Spain. *Tourism Management*, *51*, 210–222. doi:10.1016/j.tourman.2015.05.019

Gössling, S., Scott, D., & Hall, C. M. (2020). Pandemics, tourism and global change: A rapid assessment of COVID-19. *Journal of Sustainable Tourism*, *29*(1), 1–20. doi:10.1080/09669582.2020.1758708

Grandy, G., Cukier, W., & Gagnon, S. (2020). (In)visibility in the margins: COVID-19, women entrepreneurs and the need for inclusive recovery. *Gender in Management*, *35*(7/8), 667–675. doi:10.1108/GM-07-2020-0207

Guan, W., & Rehme, J. (2012). Vertical integration in supply chains: Driving forces and consequences for a manufacturer's downstream integration. *Supply Chain Management*, *2*(17), 187–201. doi:10.1108/13598541211212915

Guerci, M., Radaelli, G., Siletti, E., Cirella, S., & Shani, A. R. (2015). The impact of human resource management practices and corporate sustainability on organizational ethical climates: An employee perspective. *Journal of Business Ethics*, *126*(2), 325–342. doi:10.100710551-013-1946-1

Guerriero, C., Haines, A., & Pagano, M. (2020). Health and sustainability in post-pandemic economic policies. *Nature Sustainability*, *3*(7), 494–496. doi:10.103841893-020-0563-0 PMID:32845942

Guha, D. (2021). The great promise and dangers of being OYO. *Fortune India*. Retrieved from https://www.fortuneindia.com/enterprise/the-great-promise-and-dangers-of-being-oyo/106035

Guo, C. S. (2021, January 12). *The impact of Covid-19 on the macro economy, civil aviation and aircraft manufacturing industry*. CCAonline. http://www.ccaonline.cn/yunshu/629516.html

Gu, Q. S., & Huang, S. S. (2019). Profiling Chinese wine tourists by wine tourism constraints: A comparison of Chinese Australians and long-haul Chinese tourists in Australia. *International Journal of Tourism Research*, *21*(2), 206–220. doi:10.1002/jtr.2255

Gu, Q. S., Zhang, H., Huang, S., Zheng, F., & Chen, C. (2021). Tourists' spatiotemporal behaviors in an emerging wine region: A time-geography perspective. *Journal of Destination Marketing & Management*, *19*, 100513. doi:10.1016/j.jdmm.2020.100513

Gursoy, D., Chi, C. G., & Chi, O. H. (2020). *COVID-19 Study 2 Report: Restaurant and Hotel Industry: Restaurant and hotel customers' sentiment analysis. Would they come back? If they would, WHEN?* (Report No. 2), Carson College of Business, Washington State University.

Gutiérrez-Leefmans, M., & Holland, C. P. (2019). SME Platforms as Business Models: A User-Centric Activity-System Approach. *Cuadernos Americanos*, *35*(64), 51–76. doi:10.25100/cdea.v35i64.7248

Güzel, O., Ehtiyar, R., & Ryan, C. (2021). The Success Factors of wine tourism entrepreneurship for rural area: A thematic biographical narrative analysis in Turkey. *Journal of Rural Studies*, *84*, 230–239. doi:10.1016/j.jrurstud.2021.04.021

Hadi, M. I., Widiyanti, M., Kumalasari, M. L. F., Alamudi, M. Y., & Suprayogi, D. (2020). Management of SARS-COV-2 medical waste against a COVID19 pandemic in Indonesia: A literature review. *Jurnal Kesehatan Lingkungan*, *12*(4), 244–253. doi:10.20473/jkl.v12i4.2020.244-253

Haleemunnissa, S., Didel, S., Kumar Swami, M., Singh, K., & Vyas, V. (2021). Children and COVID19: Understanding impact on the growth trajectory of an evolving generation. *Children and Youth Services Review*, *120*, 105754. doi:10.1016/j.childyouth.2020.105754 PMID:33281255

Hall, C. M., Johnson, G., Cambourne, B., Macionis, N., Mitchell, R., & Sharples, L. (2000). Wine tourism: An introduction. In C. M. Hall, L. Sharples, B. Cambourne, & N. Macionis (Eds.), *Wine tourism around the world: Development, management and markets* (pp. 1–24). Butterworth-Heinemann.

Hauck, K., Fleuchaus, R., & Szolnoki, G. (2021). *Instagram & Wine – A Quantitative Analysis of the Usage Behaviour of Wine Consumers and Wineries on Instagram*. Academy of Wine Business Research.

Heilbrunn, S. (2004). Impact of gender on difficulties faced by entrepreneurs. *International Journal of Entrepreneurship and Innovation*, *5*(3), 159–165. doi:10.5367/0000000041513420

Hernández, M. (2020). El coronavirus acelerará hasta dos años la adopción del e-commerce en México. *Forbes*. Available at:https://www.forbes.com.mx/tecnologia-ecommerce-coronavirus-adopcion-mexico/

Hill, F., Leitch, C., & Harrison, R. (2006). 'Desperately seeking finance?' The demand for finance by women-owned and led businesses. *Venture Capital*, *8*(2), 159-182. doi:10.1080/13691060600555347

Hilliard, T. W., Scott-Halsell, S., & Palakurthi, R. (2011). Core crisis preparedness measures implemented by meeting planners. *Journal of Hospitality Marketing & Management*, *20*(6), 638–660. doi:10.1080/19368623.2011.536077

Hindu Businessline Bureau. (2020, April 15). *InnAccel Technologies rolls out non-invasive ventilator*. Retrieved March 10, 2021, from https://www.thehindubusinessline.com/companies/innaccel-technologies-rolls-out-non-invasive-ventilator/article31348281.ece

HNN. (2020). *Coronavirus effects color Hilton's 2020 outlook*. Hotel News Now. Available at: www. hotelnewsnow.com/Articles/300258/Coronavirus-effects-color-Hiltons-2020-outlook

Holling, C. S. (1973). Resilience and stability of ecological systems. *Annual Review of Ecology and Systematics*, *4*(1), 1–23. doi:10.1146/annurev.es.04.110173.000245

HRKatha. (2020). https://www.hrkatha.com/employee-engagement/how-mcdonalds-is-keeping-its-crew-engaged-during-lockdown

Hua, X. (2021). *Lax Management Leads to COVID-19 Infections at Nanjing Airport*. XinHua Net. http://www.xinhuanet.com/english/2021-08/03/c_1310105566.htm

Husain, A., & Pervez, R. (2020). Relationship of positive and negative behaviours with Covid-19. In A. K. Bansal & A. R. Adam (Eds.), *The COVID-19 Pandemic (Fallout & Recovery)* (pp. 31–39). Kripa Drishti Publications.

Hysa, E., Kruja, A., Rehman, N. U., & Laurenti, R. (2020). Circular economy innovation and environmental sustainability impact on economic growth: An integrated model for sustainable development. *Sustainability*, *12*(12), 4831. doi:10.3390u12124831

IAB. (2020). *Estudio de consumo de medios y dispositivos entre internautas mexicanos*. Available at: https://www.iabmexico.com/estudios/estudio-de-consumo-de-medios-y-dispositivos-entre-internautas-mexicanos-2020/

IATA. (2021). *Airline Industry Statistics Confirm 2020 Was Worst Year on Record*. https://www.iata.org/en/pressroom/pr/2021-08-03-01/

Icallhelpline. (2021). https://icallhelpline.org/what-is-icall/

IFC. (2014). *Women-owned SMEs: A business opportunity for financial institutions*. https%3A%2F%2Fwww.ifc.org%2Fwps%2Fwcm%2Fconnect%2F44b004b2-ed46-48fc-8ade-aa0f485069a1%2FWomenOwnedSMes%2BReportFinal.pdf%3FMOD%3DAJPERES%26CVID%3DkiiZZDZ

Ilyas, S., Srivastava, R. R., & Kim, H. (2020). Disinfection technology and strategies for COVID-19 hospital and bio-medical waste management. *The Science of the Total Environment*, *749*, 141652. doi:10.1016/j.scitotenv.2020.141652 PMID:32822917

India, T. V. (2020, June 14). *Coronil: Swami Ramdev shares cure for Coronavirus through Ayurvedic Medicine, yogasanas and Pranayama*. https://www.indiatvnews.com/health/know-all-about-coronil-made-from-ashwagandha-giloy-tulsi-ayurvedic-cure-for-coronavirus-by-patanjali-626021

Indiacsr. (2021). *The Himalaya Drug Company Collaborates with BMTC and KSRTC to fight COVID-19*. https://indiacsr.in/the-himalaya-drug-company-collaborates-with-bmtc-and-ksrtc-to-fight-covid-19/

INEGI. (2020, June 25). *Estadísticas a propósito del día de las Micros, Pequeñas y Medianas Empresas Comunicado de Prensa*. Available at https://www.inegi.org.mx/contenidos/saladeprensa/aproposito/2020/MYPIMES20.pdf

Isaga, N. (2019). Start-up motives and challenges facing female entrepreneurs in Tanzania. *International Journal of Gender and Entrepreneurship*, *11*(2), 102–119. doi:10.1108/IJGE-02-2018-0010

Islam, A., Kalam, M., Sayeed, M., Shano, S., Rahman, M., Islam, S., Ferdous, J., Choudhury, S. D., & Hassan, M. M. (2021). Escalating SARS-CoV-2 circulation in environment and tracking waste management in South Asia. *Environmental Science and Pollution Research International*, *28*(44), 61951–61968. doi:10.100711356-021-16396-8 PMID:34558044

Islam, M., Jantan, A., Hunt, A., Rahman, M., & Abdullah, M. (2019). Exploration of barriers faced by female graduate entrepreneurs in Bangladesh. *Entrepreneurship And Sustainability Issues*, *7*(2), 1000–1014. doi:10.9770/jesi.2019.7.2(15)

Israeli, A. A. (2007). Crisis-management practices in the restaurant industry. *International Journal of Hospitality Management*, *26*(4), 807–823. doi:10.1016/j.ijhm.2006.07.005

Israeli, A. A., Mohsin, A., & Kumar, B. (2011). Hospitality crisis management practices: The case of Indian luxury hotels. *International Journal of Hospitality Management*, *30*(2), 367–374. doi:10.1016/j.ijhm.2010.06.009

Israeli, A. A., & Reichel, A. (2003). Hospitality crisis management practices: The Israeli case. *International Journal of Hospitality Management*, *22*(4), 353–372. doi:10.1016/S0278-4319(03)00070-7

Itani, H., Sidani, Y., & Baalbaki, I. (2011). United Arab Emirates female entrepreneurs: Motivations and frustrations. *Equality, Diversity and Inclusion*, *30*(5), 409–424. doi:10.1108/02610151111150654

Jaim, J. (2020). Exist or exit? Women business-owners in Bangladesh during COVID-19. *Gender, Work and Organization*, *28*(S1), 209–226. doi:10.1111/gwao.12546

Jamali, D. (2009). Constraints and opportunities facing women entrepreneurs in developing countries. *Gender in Management*, *24*(4), 232–251. doi:10.1108/17542410910961532

Jarosławski, S., & Saberwal, G. (2013). Case studies of innovative medical device companies from India: Barriers and enablers to development. *BMC Health Services Research*, *13*(1), 1–8. doi:10.1186/1472-6963-13-199 PMID:23721110

Jena, P. K. (2020). Indian education in pandemic COVID-19. In R. Borah, B. Borkakoty, & P. P. Borah (Eds.), *Impact of COVID-19 on Indian Society: Challenges & Opportunities* (pp. 9–18). Balaji Publications.

Jennings, J., & Brush, C. (2013). Research on women entrepreneurs: Challenges to (and from) the broader entrepreneurship literature. *The Academy of Management Annals*, *7*(1), 663–715. do i:10.5465/19416520.2013.782190

Jindal, A., Jagdish, R. K., & Gupta, A. (2020). COVID-19 and liver disease. *Acta Scientific Gastrointestinal Disorders*, *3*(10), 20–27.

Jin, G., Zhu, Y., & Xu, Y. (2017). Mystery behind Chinese liquor fermentation. *Trends in Food Science & Technology*, *63*, 18–28. doi:10.1016/j.tifs.2017.02.016

Joseph, B., James, J., Kalarikkal, N., & Thomas, S. (2021). Recycling of medical plastics. *Advanced Industrial and Engineering Polymer Research*, *4*(3), 199–208. doi:10.1016/j.aiepr.2021.06.003

Josephine & Virginia. (2013). Employee Engagement - An Approach to Organisational Excellence. *International Journal of Social Science & Interdisciplinary Research, 2*(5).

Kahn, W. A. (1990). Psychological conditions of personal engagement and disengagement at work. *Academy of Management Journal*, *33*(4), 692–724. doi:10.2307/256287

Kaila, H. L. (2021). Critical questions on COVID-19 and behavioural safety culture: India case study. *Chemical News*, 28-40.

Kalantary, R. R., Jamshidi, A., Mofrad, M. M. G., Jafari, A. J., Heidari, N., Fallahizadeh, S., Hesami Arani, M., & Torkashvand, J. (2021). Effect of COVID-19 pandemic on medical waste management: A case study. *Journal of Environmental Health Science & Engineering*, *19*(1), 1–6. doi:10.100740201-021-00650-9 PMID:33758671

Kanthy, D. U. (2021). COVID-19: The change of face through resilience, sustainability and interdependency. In M. A. Wani, M. K. Verma, B. Rathakrishna, & D. Srivastava (Eds.), *COVID-19 Crises Psychosocial Perspectives* (pp. 100–106). Novel Nuggets.

Kapur, N. (2020). Covid-19 and cognitive bias. *British Medical Journal,* 1-4.

Karadag, H. (2015). Financial management challenges in small and medium-sized enterprises: A strategic management approach. *EMAJ: Emerging Markets Journal*, *5*(1), 26–40. doi:10.5195/EMAJ.2015.67

Kaul, A., & Lakhotia, C. (2021). Psychological impact of COVID-19. *International Journal of Indian Psychology*, *9*(1), 2349–3429.

Kaurani, P., Batra, K., & Hooja, H. R. (2020). Psychological impact of COVID-19 lockdown (phase 2) among Indian general population: A cross-sectional survey. *International Journal of Scientific Research*, *9*(8), 2277–8179. doi:10.36106/ijsr/2439876

Kaur, H., Singh, T., Arya, Y. K., & Mittal, S. (2020). Physical fitness and exercise during the COVID-19 pandemic: A qualitative enquiry. *Frontiers in Psychology*, *11*, 590172. doi:10.3389/fpsyg.2020.590172 PMID:33250827

Kaur, S., & Rathee, N. (2021). Coping with COVID-19: Cross-cultural comparison across countries. *Wesleyan Journal of Research*, *13*(65), 45–56.

Kaya, S., & Alpkan, L. (2012). Problems and solution proposals for SMEs in Turkey. *Emerging Markets Journal*, *2*(2), 178-196. doi:10.5195/EMAJ.2012.26

Kazmi, S. S. H., Hasan, K., Talib, S., & Saxena, S. (2020). COVID-19 and lockdown: A study on the impact on mental health. SSRN *Electronic Journal*. doi:10.2139/ssrn.3577515

Ketchen, D. J. Jr, & Craighead, C. W. (2020). Research at the intersection of entrepreneurship, supply chain management, and strategic management: Opportunities highlighted by COVID-19. *Journal of Management*, *46*(8), 1330–1341. doi:10.1177/0149206320945028

Khalil, T. (2020, August 11). The impact of COVID-19 on small businesses. *The Daily Star*. https://www.thedailystar.net/lifestyle/news/the-impact-covid-19-small-businesses-1942713

Khanna, T., & Palepu, K. G. (2011). Winning in emerging markets: Spotting and responding to institutional voids. *World Financial Review*, 18–20.

Khosla, V. (2022, January 18). *Hotel industry would bounce back by Oct*. Retrieved on January 31, 2022, from https://www.livemint.com/companies/news/indians-have-got-used-to-the-idea-of-taking-holidays-lemon-tree-s-keswani-11642403374673.html

Kim, S. S., Chun, H., & Lee, H. (2005). The effects of SARS on the Korean hotel industry and measures to overcome the crisis: A case study of six Korean five-star hotels. *Asia Pacific Journal of Tourism Research*, *10*(4), 369–377. doi:10.1080/10941660500363694

Kitsos, A., & Bishop, P. (2018). Economic resilience in Great Britain: The crisis impact and its determining factors for local authority districts. *The Annals of Regional Science*, *60*(2), 329–347. doi:10.100700168-016-0797-y

Korber, S., & McNaughton, R. B. (2018). Resilience and entrepreneurship: A systematic literature review. *International Journal of Entrepreneurial Behaviour & Research*, *24*(7), 1129–1154. doi:10.1108/IJEBR-10-2016-0356

Kovid, R. K., Bhati, B., & Sharma, G. M. (2021). Entrepreneurial competencies, institutional voids and performance of small and medium enterprises: Evidence from an emerging economy. *Vision: Journal of Business Perspective.* Advance online publication.

Kovid, R. K., Kumari, D., & Pandey, S. (2021). Strategic Response to the Corona Pandemic Crisis: A Case of Indian Women Entrepreneurs. In V. Kumar & G. Malhotra (Eds.), *Stakeholder Strategies for Reducing the Impact of Global Health Crises* (pp. 68–84). IGI. doi:10.4018/978-1-7998-7495-9.ch005

Krishna, V. (2019, April 22). *Watch: How incubator-turned-medtech company InnAccel is innovating for Indias needs*. Retrieved March 10, 2021, from https://yourstory.com/2019/04/innaccel-innovates-healthcare-india-emerging-markets

Krishnan, R. (2015, December 14). *Seven charts that show why India's healthcare system needs an overhaul*. Retrieved March 10, 2021, from https://www.livemint.com/Opinion/qXD81719wXXDQVpGyyARrO/Seven-charts-that-show-why-Indias-healthcare-system-needs-a.html

Kuada, J. (2009). Gender, Social Networks, and Entrepreneurship in Ghana. *Journal of African Business*, *10*(1), 85–103. doi:10.1080/15228910802701445

Kumar, A. (2021, June 15). *Hotel Chains Collaborates With Governments To Fight Second Wave*. Retrieved on December 22, 2021, from https://www.traveltrendstoday.in/news/ hotel-and-resorts/item/9789-hotel-chains-collaborates-with-governments-to-fight-second-wave

Kumar, R. P. (2020a, June 24). *Coronavirus treatment: Ramdev's Patanjali launches Coronil kit for ₹545*. LiveMint. https://www.livemint.com/news/india/coronavirus-vaccine-coronil-patanjali-baba-ramdev-press-conference-live-updates-11592893304534.html

Kumar, P. (2021). V-5 Model of Employee Engagement During COVID-19 and Post Lockdown. *Vision (Basel), 25*(3), 271–274. doi:10.1177/0972262920980878

Kumar, V., & Ayodeji, O. G. (2021). E-retail Factors for Customer Activation and Retention: An Empirical Study from Indian e-Commerce Customers. *Journal of Retailing and Consumer Services, 59C*, 102399. doi:10.1016/j.jretconser.2020.102399

Kumar, V., & Ayodeji, O. G. (2021a). Determinants of the Success of Online Retail in India. *International Journal of Business Information Systems, 37*(2), 246–262. doi:10.1504/IJBIS.2021.115373

Kumar, V., Ayodeji, O. G., & Kumar, S. (2020). Online Retail in India: A Comparative Analysis of top Business Players. *Int. J. Indian Culture and Business Management, 20*(3), 359–384. doi:10.1504/IJICBM.2020.107672

Kumar, V., & Bhardwaj, A. (2020). Deploying Cloud Based Healthcare Solutions: A Holistic Approach. *International Journal of Service Science, Management, Engineering, and Technology, 11*(4), 87–100. doi:10.4018/IJSSMET.2020100106

Kumar, V., & Gupta, G. (Eds.). (2021). *Strategic Management During a Pandemic*. Routledge. doi:10.4324/9781003125648

Kumar, V., & Malhotra, G. (Eds.). (2021). *Stakeholder Strategies for Reducing the Impact of Global Health Crises*. IGI Global Publications. doi:10.4018/978-1-7998-7495-9

Kumar, V., Nanda, P., & Tawangar, S. (2022). Social Media in Business Decisions of MSMES: Practices and Challenges. *International Journal of Decision Support System Technology, 14*(1), 1–12. doi:10.4018/IJDSST.286686

Kumar, V., & Pradhan, P. (2015). Trust Management Issues in Social-Media Marketing. *International Journal of Online Marketing, 5*(3), 47–64. doi:10.4018/IJOM.2015070104

Kumar, V., & Vidhyalakshmi, P. (2012). Cloud computing for business sustainability. *Asia-Pacific Journal of Management Research and Innovation, 8*(4), 461–474. doi:10.1177/2319510X13481905

Kunze, A., & Miller, A. (2017). Women helping women? Evidence from private sector data on workplace hierarchies. *The Review of Economics and Statistics, 99*(5), 769–775. doi:10.1162/REST_a_00668

Kurian, A., Farisha, A. T. P., Raseela, K. N., Sabeena, P. K., & Suhana, E. K. (2021). Impact of E-learning in India during COVID-19 and measures to overcome them. In M. A. Wani, M. K. Verma, B. Rathakrishna, & D. Srivastava (Eds.), *COVID-19 Crises Psychosocial Perspectives* (pp. 67–88). Novel Nuggets.

Kuswantoro, F., Rosli, M. M., Abdul, R., & Ghorbani, H. (2012). Impact of distribution channel innovation on the performance of small and medium enterprises. *International Business Management, 5*(1), 52–61.

Kwong, C. C. Y., Cheung, C. W. M., Manzoor, H., & Rashid, M. U. (2019). Entrepreneurship through bricolage: A study of displaced entrepreneurs at times of war and conflict. *Entrepreneurship and Regional Development*, *31*(5/6), 435–455. doi:10.1080/08985626.2018.1541592

Laskovaia, A., Marino, L., Shirokova, G., & Wales, W. (2019). Expect the unexpected: Examining the shaping role of entrepreneurial orientation on causal and effectual decision-making logic during economic crisis. *Entrepreneurship and Regional Development*, *31*(5/6), 456–475. doi:10.1080/08985626.2018.1541593

Lata, M., & Gupta, A. (2020). Role of Social Media in Environmental Democracy. In *Examining the Roles of IT and Social Media in Democratic Development and Social Change* (pp. 275–293). IGI Global. doi:10.4018/978-1-7998-1791-8.ch011

Lease, T., & Conover, T. (2021). *Characteristics of Successful Virtual Wine Tastings: The Participants' Perspective*. Academy of Wine Business Research.

Lee, A. V., Vargo, J., & Seville, E. (2013). Developing a tool to measure and compare organizations' resilience. *Natural Hazards Review*, *14*(1), 29–41. doi:10.1061/(ASCE)NH.1527-6996.0000075

Lee, K. (2009). How the Hong Kong Government lost the public trust in SARS: Insights for government communication in a health crisis. *Public Relations Review*, *35*(1), 74–76. doi:10.1016/j.pubrev.2008.06.003 PMID:32288049

Leenders, M. A., & Chandra, Y. (2013). Antecedents and consequences of green innovation in the wine industry: The role of channel structure. *Technology Analysis and Strategic Management*, *25*(2), 203–218. doi:10.1080/09537325.2012.759203

Lee, Y., Shin, H. Y., Park, J., Kim, W., & Cho, D. (2017). An integrative literature review on employee engagement in the field of human resource development: Exploring where we are and where we should go. *Asia Pacific Education Review*, *18*(4), 541–557. doi:10.100712564-017-9508-3

Leitch, C., Welter, F., & Henry, C. (2018). Women entrepreneurs' financing revisited: Taking stock and looking forward. *Venture Capital*, *20*(2), 103–114. doi:10.1080/13691066.2018.1418624

Liguori, E., & Winkler, C. (2020). *From Offline to Online: Challenges and Opportunities for Entrepreneurship Education Following the COVID-19 Pandemic*. Academic Press.

Lindinger-Sternart, S., Widyaningsih, Y. S., Kaur, V., & Patel, A. K. (2021). A global pandemic: How different nations coped with COVID-19 phobia. *Journal of Psychiatry & Mental Disorders*, *6*(3), 1–10.

Lindvert, M., Yazdanfar, D., & Boter, H. (2015). Perceptions of financial sources among women entrepreneurs in Tanzania. *African Journal of Economic and Management Studies*, *6*(2), 197–218. doi:10.1108/AJEMS-10-2013-0090

Li, T. (2020). A SWOT analysis of China's air cargo sector in the context of COVID-19 pandemic. *Journal of Air Transport Management*, *88*, 101875. https://doi.org/10.1016/j.jairtraman.2020.101875

Li, W., & Chen, J. (2020). Manufacturer's vertical integration strategies in a three-tier supply chain. *Transportation Research Part E, Logistics and Transportation Review*, *135*, 101884. doi:10.1016/j.tre.2020.101884

Li, Y., Liu, H., Lim, E. T. K., Goh, J. M., Yang, F., & Lee, M. K. O. (2018). Customer's reaction to cross-channel integration in omnichannel retailing: The mediating roles of retailer uncertainty, identity attractiveness, and switching costs. *Decision Support Systems*, *109*, 50–60. doi:10.1016/j.dss.2017.12.010

Loose, S. M., Strub, L., & Kurth, A. (2021). *Economic Sustainability of Wine Estates: First Insights and a Roadmap for Future Research*. Academy of Wine Business Research.

Lourenço, F., Sappleton, N., Dardaine-Edwards, A., McElwee, G., Cheng, R., & Taylor, D., & Taylor, A. (2014). Experience of entrepreneurial training for female farmers to stimulate entrepreneurship in Uganda. *Gender in Management*, *29*(7), 382–401. doi:10.1108/GM-05-2013-0054

Lunardo, R., Corsi, A. M., & Jaud, D. A. (2021). *Look at Me and My Glass of Wine! A Moderated Mediation Analysis of the Effect of Narcissism on (Over) Consumption of Wine*. Academy of Wine Business Research.

Luthar, S. S., Cicchetti, D., & Becker, B. (2000). The construct of resilience: A critical evaluation and guidelines for future work. *Child Development*, *71*(3), 543–562. doi:10.1111/1467-8624.00164 PMID:10953923

Maden, C. (2015). A gendered lens on entrepreneurship: Women entrepreneurship in Turkey. *Gender in Management*, *30*(4), 312–331. doi:10.1108/GM-11-2013-0131

Maji, S., Bansod, S., & Singh, T. (2020). Domestic violence during COVID-19 pandemic: The case for Indian women. *Journal of Community & Applied Social Psychology*, 1–8. PMID:33821118

Majumdar, S. (2021). Care, cash, evolution: How OYO navigated Covid-19. *Fortune India*. Retrieved from https://www.fortuneindia.com/people/care-cash-evolution-how-oyo-navigated-covid-19/105593

Malik, V. S., Poonam, & Bahmani, R. K. (2020). Effect of COVID-19 lockdown on mental health and family relationship in north Indian people: Lockdown and you. *Shodh Sarita*, *7*(27), 76–84.

Mandelbaum, R. (2017). *How hotel managers are coping with rising wages*. Available at: https://www.hotelmanagement.net/operate/how-increases-compensation-labor-costs-are-leading-to-cost-savings

Manickam, L. S. S. (2020). COVID-19 Pandemic: A time for prudent and ethical action. In COVID-19 pandemic: Challenges and responses of psychologists from India (pp. 218-228). Thiruvananthapuram: The Editor.

Manickam, L. S. S., John, A., Debora, M. A., Krishnan, P., & Jasseer, J. (2020). Refining psychological services and strategies in India in the wake of COVID-19. In COVID-19 Pandemic: Challenges and responses of psychologists from India (pp.8-18). Thiruvananthapuram: The Editor.

Manolova, T., Brush, C., Edelman, L., & Elam, A. (2020). Pivoting to stay the course: How women entrepreneurs take advantage of opportunities created by the COVID-19 pandemic. *International Small Business Journal: Researching Entrepreneurship, 38*(6), 481–491. doi:10.1177/0266242620949136 PMID:35125599

Marker, A. (2020). *Models and Theories to Improve Crisis Management*. Retrieved on February 24, 2022, from https://www.smartsheet.com/content/crisis-management-model-theories

Marlow, S., & Carter, S. (2004). Accounting for change: Professional status, gender disadvantage and self-employment. *Women in Management Review, 19*(1), 5–17. doi:10.1108/09649420410518395

Marlow, S., & Patton, D. (2005). All credit to men? Entrepreneurship, finance, and gender. *Entrepreneurship Theory and Practice, 29*(6), 717–735. doi:10.1111/j.1540-6520.2005.00105.x

Martinez Dy, A., & Jayawarna, D. (2020). Bios, mythoi and women entrepreneurs: A Wynterian analysis of the intersectional impacts of the COVID-19 pandemic on self-employed women and women-owned businesses. *International Small Business Journal: Researching Entrepreneurship, 38*(5), 391–403. doi:10.1177/0266242620939935

Martin, R. (2011). Regional economic resilience, hysteresis and recessionary shocks. *Journal of Economic Geography, 12*(1), 1–32. doi:10.1093/jeg/lbr019

Martins, J., Gonçalves, R., Branco, F., Barbosa, L., Melo, M., & Bessa, M. (2017). A multisensory virtual experience model for thematic tourism: A Port wine tourism application proposal. *Journal of Destination Marketing & Management, 6*(2), 103–109. doi:10.1016/j.jdmm.2017.02.002

Maurya, M. K., & Pandey, M. K. (2021). Collective actions, social distancing and belief in science in the age of COVID-19: A correlational study. *Anvesak, 51*(2), 90–96.

Ma, Y., Lin, X., Wu, A., Huang, Q., Li, X., & Yan, J. (2020). Suggested guidelines for emergency treatment of medical waste during COVID-19: Chinese experience. *Waste Disposal & Sustainable Energy, 2*(2), 81–84. doi:10.100742768-020-00039-8 PMID:32838200

Mazumdar, K., & Gupta, P. (2021). The invisible frontline workers: Narratives of Indian mothers' experiences through the pandemic. In A. O'Reilly & F. Green (Eds.), *Mothers, Mothering, and COVID-19: Dispatches from the pandemic* (pp. 467–478). Demeter Press. doi:10.2307/j.ctv1h45mcj.44

Mazumder, A., & Alharahsheh, H. (2019). Key challenges and barriers facing small and medium enterprises (SMEs) in Bangladesh. *South Asian Journal of Business Management, 1*(3), 118–120. doi:10.36346arjbm.2019.v01i03.005

McDonalds. (2022). www.mcdonalds.com

McMullen, J. S., & Shepherd, D. A. (2006). Entrepreneurial action and the role of uncertainty in the theory of the entrepreneur. *Academy of Management Review, 31*(1), 132–152. doi:10.5465/amr.2006.19379628

Meristö, T. (2020). Scenarios will help SMEs out of corona crisis and beyond. In *Proceedings of the 2020 ISPIM Innovation Conference (Virtual) Event" Innovating in Times of Crisis" held on 7 to 10 June 2020.* LUT Scientific and Expertise Publications.

MFA. (2020). *CAAC Adjusts Rules on International Passenger Flights Introduces Incentives and Circuit Breaker*. Ministry of Foreign Affairs of the People's Republic of China. https://www.fmprc.gov.cn/mfa_eng/topics_665678/kjgzbdfyyq/t1786310.shtml

Mhalla, M. (2020). The impact of novel coronavirus (COVID-19) on the global oil and aviation markets. *Journal of Asian Scientific Research, 10*(2), 96. https://doi.org/10.18488/journal.2.2020.102.96.104

Ministry of AYUSH. (2020). *Notification to be published in the Extraordinary Gazette of India, No. L.11011/8/2020/AS.* New Delhi: Ministry of AYUSH, Government of India. https://main.ayush.gov.in/about-the-systems/ayurveda/treatment

Mishra, K., & Rampal, J. (2020). The COVID-19 pandemic and food insecurity: A viewpoint on India. *World Development, 135*, 105068. doi:10.1016/j.worlddev.2020.105068

Mishra, O. (2021). Principles of frugal innovation and its application by social entrepreneurs in times of adversity : An inductive single-case approach. *Journal of Entrepreneurship in Emerging Economies., 13*(4), 547–574. doi:10.1108/JEEE-07-2020-0247

Mishra, O., Sharma, R., & Agrawal, B. (2020). Facilitating Women Prosperity with Higher Purpose at Vyomini. *South Asian Journal of Business and Management Cases, 9*(2), 198–207. doi:10.1177/2277977920905820

Mittal, S., & Kumar, V. (2019). Study of knowledge management models and their relevance in organisations. *Int. J. Knowledge Management Studies, 10*(3), 322–335.

Mittal, S., & Singh, T. (2020). Gender-based violence during COVID-19 pandemic: A mini-review. *Frontiers in Global Women Health, 1*, 4. doi:10.3389/fgwh.2020.00004 PMID:34816149

Modarresi, M., Arasti, Z., Talebi, K., & Farasatkhah, M. (2016). Women's entrepreneurship in Iran. *International Journal of Gender and Entrepreneurship, 8*(4), 446–470. doi:10.1108/IJGE-03-2016-0006

Moghe, K., Kotecha, D., & Patil, M. (2021). COVID-19 and mental health: A study of its impact on students in Maharashtra, India. medRxiv.

Mohan, S., & Rollo, V. (2020). *From shutdown to recovery: Unraveling the impact of COVID-19 on small firms.* International Trade Centre. https://www.intracen.org/covid19/blogs/from-shutdown-to-recovery/

MoHFW. (2017). *National Health Policy*. Ministry of Health and Family Welfare.

MOHFW. (2020). *Indian Council of Medical Research. Recommendation for empiric use of Hydroxychloroquine for prophylaxis of SARS Cov- 2 infection.* New Delhi: ICMR. Available from: https://www.mohfw.gov.in/pdf/AdvisoryontheuseofHydroxychloroquinasprophylasxisforSARSCoV2infection.pdf

Money Control. (n.d.). Oyo shedding loss-making assets and ventures: Report. *MoneyControl News*. Retrieved from https://www.moneycontrol.com/news/business/oyo-shedding-loss-making-assets-and-ventures-report-6641581.html Accessed on February 8, 2022

Montréal. (2021, Jan 15). *2020 passenger totals drop 60 percent as COVID-19 assault on international mobility continues.* International Civil Aviation Organization (ICAO). https://www.icao.int/Newsroom/Pages/2020-passenger-totals-drop-60-percent-as-COVID19-assault-on-international-mobility-continues.aspx

Mordi, C., Simpson, R., Singh, S., & Okafor, C. (2010). The role of cultural values in understanding the challenges faced by female entrepreneurs in Nigeria. *Gender in Management, 25*(1), 5–21. doi:10.1108/17542411011019904

Mordor Intelligence. (2021). *Ayush and alternative medicine industry in india - growth, trends, covid-19 impact, and forecasts (2021 - 2026).* https://www.mordorintelligence.com/industry-reports/ayush-and-alternative-medicine-industry-in-india

Morgan, T., Anokhin, S., Ofstein, L., & Friske, W. (2020). SME response to major exogenous shocks: The bright and dark sides of business model pivoting. *International Small Business Journal: Researching Entrepreneurship, 38*(5), 369–379. doi:10.1177/0266242620936590

Mukherjee, A. (2021, June 13). *Why Has It Become Necessary For Hotels To Invest In Technology In A Post-COVID Era.* Retrieved on January 2, 2022, from https://www.travelbizmonitor.com/why-has-it-become-necessary-for-hotels-to-invest-in-technology-in-a-post-covid-era/

Mukherjee, J. (2021). Patanjali Ayurveda's Coronil: Marketing Controversy on COVID-19 Cure. *Vision (Basel).*

Mukherjee, T., Chowdhury, S., & Ahmed, T. (2021). A patriarchal pandemic: Looking at COVID 19 through a gendered lens. In A. Dubey & A. Shukla (Eds.), *Mental Health: Psychosocial Perspectives; Volume 6-Women Mental Health* (pp. 16–26). Concept.

Mukund, B., & Dehuri, B. K. (2021). Resilience and coping strategies essentials for thriving successfully. In S. Lata, S. Verma, & S. Joshi (Eds.), *COVID-19 in India- Problems, Challenges and Strategies* (pp. 394–412). Global Vision.

Mullafiroze, R., & Cha, J. (2020). *Evaluating the impact of COVID-19on multi sectoral humanitarian needs.* https://www.elrha.org/project/evaluating-the-impact-of-covid-19-on-multi-sectoral-humanitarian-needs/

Mushtaq, N. F., Shiva Kumar, B. K., Vinay, H. R., & Honnugudi, B. D. (2021). A comparative study of stress and coping strategies among undergraduate medical students during pre and post COVID-19 pandemic lockdown. *International Journal of Scientific Research, 10*(10), 1–2. doi:10.36106/ijsr/2903859

Musso, F. (2010). Innovation in marketing channels: Relationships, technology, channel structure. *Symphonya: Emerging Issues in Management*, (1), 23-42.

Mustafa, F., Khursheed, A., Fatima, M., & Rao, M. (2021). Exploring the impact of COVID-19 pandemic on women entrepreneurs in Pakistan. *International Journal of Gender and Entrepreneurship, 13*(2), 187–203. doi:10.1108/IJGE-09-2020-0149

Naguib, R., & Jamali, D. (2015). Female entrepreneurship in the UAE: A multi-level integrative lens. *Gender in Management, 30*(2), 135–161. doi:10.1108/GM-12-2013-0142

Nanda, P., & Kumar, V. (2022). Information Processing and Data Analytics for Decision Making: A Journey from Traditional to Modern Approaches. *Information Resources Management Journal, 35*(2), 1–14.

Natarajan, G. S., & Wyrick, D. A. (2011, July). Framework for implementing sustainable practices in SMEs in the United States. In *Proceedings of the world congress on engineering* (*Vol. 1*, No. 1, pp. 6-8). Academic Press.

Nave, A., Laurett, R., & Paco, A. (2021). Relation between antecedents, barriers and consequences of sustainable practices in the wine tourism sector. *Journal of Destination Marketing & Management, 20*, 100584. doi:10.1016/j.jdmm.2021.100584

Ng, A. (2020). *Over 40 airlines have failed so far this year- and more are set to come.* CNBC. https://www.cnbc.com/2020/10/08/over-40-airlines-have-failed-in-2020-so-far-and-more-are-set-to-come.html

NHCPRC. (2020). *Protocol on diagnosis and treatment of COVID-19* (6th ed.). Beijing: National Health Commission of the People's Republic of China. Available from: http://en.nhc.gov.cn/2020-03/29/c_78468.htm

Nicolosi, A., Cortese, L., Nesci, F. S., & Privitera, D. (2016). Combing Wine production and Tourism. The Aeolian Islands. *Social and Behavioral Sciences, 223*, 662–667.

Nimon, K., Zigarmi, D., Houson, D., Witt, D., & Diehl, J. (2011). The work cognition inventory: Initial evidence of construct validity. *Human Resource Development Quarterly, 22*(1), 7–35. doi:10.1002/hrdq.20064

Nižetić, S. (2020). Impact of coronavirus (COVID-19) pandemic on air transport mobility, energy, and environment: A case study. *International Journal of Energy Research, 44*(13), 10953–10961. https://doi.org/10.1002/er.5706

Novelli, M., Burgess, L. G., Jones, A., & Ritchie, B. W. (2018). 'No Ebola... still doomed' – the Ebolainduced tourism crisis. *Annals of Tourism Research, 70*, 76–87. doi:10.1016/j.annals.2018.03.006 PMID:32572288

Now Digital, E. T. (2020). *Baba Ramdev's Patanjali to launch swadeshi-only ecommerce platform OrderMe, free home delivery of products*. https://www.timesnownews.com/business-economy/companies/article/baba-ramdevs-patanjali-to-launch-swadeshi-only-ecommerce-platform-orderme-free-home-delivery-of-products/592127

Obermayer, N., Kovari, E., Leinonen, J., Bak, G., & Valeri, M. (2021). How social media practices shape family business performance: The wine industry case study. *European Management Journal*. Advance online publication. doi:10.1016/j.emj.2021.08.003

OECD. (2004). *Small and Medium-Sized Enterprises in Turkey, Issues and Policies*. Retrieved September 2020, from Organization for Economic Co- operation and Development: http:// www.oecd. org/ industry /smes /3193 2173.pdf

OECD. (2006). *The SME financing gap (Vol. I): Theory and evidence*. Organization for Economic Co- operation and Development.

OECD. (2020). *Women enterprise policy and COVID-19: Towards a gender-sensitive response*. OECD.

Ojha, R., Gupta, N., Naik, B., Singh, S., Verma, V. K., Prusty, D., & Prajapati, V. K. (2020). High throughput and comprehensive approach to develop multiepitope vaccine against minacious COVID-19. *European Journal of Pharmaceutical Sciences*, *151*, 105375. doi:10.1016/j.ejps.2020.105375 PMID:32417398

Olff, M., Primasari, I., Qing, Y., Coimbra, B. M., Hovnanyan, A., Grace, E., Williamson, R. E., Hoeboer, C. M., & Consortium, T. G. C. (2021). Mental health responses to COVID-19 around the world. *European Journal of Psychotraumatology*, *12*(1), 1929754. doi:10.1080/20008198.2021.1929754 PMID:34262666

Oluyombo, D., & Ogundimu, K. (2006). Microfinance as a strategy for poverty alleviation in Nigeria. SSRN *Electronic Journal*. doi:10.2139/ssrn.2885378

Onmanorama. (2021). *Utilise the schemes of Ayurveda dept, says doctor*. https://www.onmanorama.com/lifestyle/health/2021/05/09/ayurveda-against-coronavirus.html

Padhi, S. (2020). COVID-19 Pandemic and issues of migrant labourers in India. *Ajanta*, *9*(3), 66–72.

Padhi, S. (2020a). Challenges of COVID-19 pandemic and interrupted education system. In S. Mishra, V. Sharma, & S. Prasad (Eds.), *Evolution of New Teaching Practices in COVID-19* (pp. 9–17). Akhand.

Panda, S. (2018). Constraints faced by women entrepreneurs in developing countries: Review and ranking. *Gender in Management*, *33*(4), 315–331. doi:10.1108/GM-01-2017-0003

Pandey, V., Astha, A., Mishra, N., Greeshma, R., Lakshmana, G., Jeyavel, S., Rajkumar, E., & Prabhu, G. (2021). Do social connections and digital technologies act as social cure during COVID-19? *Frontiers in Psychology*, *12*, 634621. doi:10.3389/fpsyg.2021.634621 PMID:33868099

Pandey, V., Misra, N., Greeshma, R., Astha, A., Jeyavel, S., Lakshmana, G., Rajkumar, E., & Prabhu, G. (2021). Techno trend awareness and its attitude towards social connectedness and mitigating factors of COVID-19. *Frontiers in Psychology, 12*, 637395. doi:10.3389/fpsyg.2021.637395 PMID:34113286

Pan, J. (2016). *China's environmental governing and ecological civilization.* Springer Berlin Heidelberg.

Pant, A., & Mahour, P. (2020). Perceived threat and psychological impact of COVID-19 on families of health care professionals in India. *International Journal of Indian Psychology, 8*(2), 961–966.

Pappas, N., & Glyptou, K. (2021). Risk-induced Competitive Productivity in Times of Recession: a Chaordic Tourism Decision-making Perspective. *International Journal of Contemporary Hospitality Management.*

Pardeep, R., & Clark, H. (2009). A framework for knowledge-based crisis management in hospitality and tourism industry. *Cornell Hospitality Quarterly, 50*(4), 561–577. doi:10.1177/1938965509341633

Patel, A. K., & Singh, J. (2020). Psychological impact of COVID-19 on daily life: A comprehensive understanding. In A. P. Sikarwar & B. C. Yadav (Eds.), *Social and Community Aspects of COVID-19 Pandemic* (pp. 1–12). Shriyanshi Prakashan.

Pavlatos, O., & Paggios, I. (2009b). Activity-based costing in the hospitality industry: Evidence from Greece. *Journal of Hospitality & Tourism Research (Washington, D.C.), 33*(4), 511–527. doi:10.1177/1096348009344221

Penrose, E. (2009). *The Theory of the Growth of the Firm* (4th ed.). Oxford University Press.

Pervez, R., & Husain, A. (2020). Coping strategies for personal and health-related problems linked with Covid-19. In A. K. Bansal & A. R. Adam (Eds.), *The COVID-19 Pandemic (Fallout & Recovery)* (pp. 23–30). Kripa Drishti Publications.

PIB. (2020). *AYUSH Ministry Urges Diligence in COVID.19 Claims and Initiates Work for Scientific and Evidence. Based Solutions to Fight the Corona Virus.* Available at: https://pib.gov.in/PressReleaseIframePage.aspx?PRID=1609523

PIB. (2021). *Ayush Ministry Releases fresh COVID-19 Guidelines Focus on Self-Care and Home Isolation Ayurveda & Unani guidelines released, rest to follow soon.* https://www.pib.gov.in/PressReleasePage.aspx?PRID=1714205

Pillay, R. (2015). *The changing nature of corporate social responsibility: CSR and development–the case of Mauritius* (1st ed.). Routledge.

Piret, J., & Boivin, G. (2021). Pandemics throughout history. *Frontiers in Microbiology, 11*, 631736. doi:10.3389/fmicb.2020.631736 PMID:33584597

Poddar, S., & Mukherjee, U. (2020). Ascending child sexual abuse statistics in India during COVID-19 lockdown: A darker reality and alarming mental health concerns. *Indian Journal of Psychological Medicine*, *42*(5), 493–494. doi:10.1177/0253717620951391 PMID:33414605

Poonam., S., & Behmani, R. K. (2020). Impact of the COVID-19 pandemic on domestic violence in India. *Journal of Social Sciences, 48*(3), 1769-1779.

Prasad, R. K., & Srivastava, M. K. (2021). Switching behaviour toward online shopping: Coercion or choice during COVID-19 pandemic. *Academy of Marketing Studies Journal*, *1*(25), 1–15.

Priyono, A., Moin, A., & Putri, V. N. A. O. (2020). Identifying digital transformation paths in the business model of SMEs during the COVID-19 pandemic. *Journal of Open Innovation*, *6*(4), 104.

Qin, H., Huo, D., Zhang, L., Yang, L., Zhang, S., Yang, M., Shen, C., & Hou, C. (2012). Colorimetric artificial nose for identification of Chinese liquor with different geographic origins. *Food Research International*, *45*(1), 45–51. doi:10.1016/j.foodres.2011.09.008

QWBRA. (2020). *The Impact of COVID-19 on Employee Engagement, A Quantum Workplace Benchmark Report and Analysis*. https://marketing.quantumworkplace.com/hubfs/Marketing/Website/Resources/PDFs/The-Impact-of-COVID-19-on-Employee-Engagement.pdf

Rabbani, M., Zahan, I., & Matin, M. (2020). *How Resilient Are Female Online Entrepreneurs? Findings From the COVID-19 Shock*. Brac Institute of Governance and Development. https://bigd.bracu.ac.bd/study/resilience-of-online-entrepreneur-against-the-covid-19-induced-economic-slow-down/

Rachao, S. A. S., Breda, Z. J., Fernandes, C. O., & Joukes, V. N. P. M. (2021). Drivers of experience co-creation in food-and-wine tourism: An exploratory quantitative analysis. *Tourism Management Perspectives*, *37*, 100783. doi:10.1016/j.tmp.2020.100783

Rahman, M. (n.d.). *Women Micro-Merchants in Bangladesh: Can digital tech break barriers?* Retrieved August 16, 2021, from https://www.microentrepreneursasia.com/women-micro-merchants-in-mangladesh#:~:text=Of%20the%20almost%208%20million,of%20the%20World%20Bank%20Group

Rahman, N. A. A., Rahim, S. A., Ahmad, M. F., & Hafizuddin-Syah, B. A. M. (2020). Exploring COVID-19 pandemic: Its impact to global aviation industry and the key strategy. *International Journal of Advanced Science and Technology*, 1829-1836. http://sersc.org/journals/index.php/IJAST/article/view/9344

Rahman, M. M., Nesa, M., & Ghose, D. (2018). The prospects and causes of failure of small and medium enterprises (SMEs): A case study of Bangladesh. *Journal of Green Business School*, *1*(11), 90–108.

Rainer, G. (2016). Constructing globalized spaces of tourism and leisure: Political ecologies of the Salta Wine Route (NW-Argentina). *Journal of Rural Studies*, *43*, 104–117. doi:10.1016/j.jrurstud.2015.11.007

Raj, S., Ghosh, D., Singh, T., Verma, S. K., & Arya, Y. K. (2021). Theoretical mapping of suicidal risk factors during the COVID-19 pandemic: A mini-review. *Frontiers in Psychiatry, 11*, 589614. doi:10.3389/fpsyt.2020.589614 PMID:33551864

Ramadani, V., Hisrich, R., & Rashiti, S. (2015). Female entrepreneurs in transition economies: Insights from Albania, Macedonia and Kosovo. *World Review of Entrepreneurship, Management and Sustainable Development, 11*(4), 391. doi:10.1504/WREMSD.2015.072066

Ramakrishna, G., Kumar, P., Aggarwal, S., Islam, M., Singh, R., Jagdish, R. K., & Trehanpati, N. (2020). SARS-Cov-2 (human) and COVID-19: Primer 2020. *Hepatology International, 14*(4), 475–477. doi:10.100712072-020-10049-7 PMID:32333304

Ramteke, S., & Sahu, B. L. (2020). Novel coronavirus disease 2019 (COVID-19) pandemic: Considerations for the biomedical waste sector in India. *Case Studies in Chemical and Environmental Engineering, 2*, 100029. doi:10.1016/j.cscee.2020.100029

Ratten, V. (2020). Coronavirus disease (COVID-19) and sport entrepreneurship. *International Journal of Entrepreneurial Behaviour & Research, 26*(6), 1379–1388. doi:10.1108/IJEBR-06-2020-0387

Report, S. B. (2018). Women entrepreneurship in Bangladesh face less social barriers now: BIDS. *The Daily Star*. https://www.thedailystar.net/business/women-entrepreneurship-in-bangladesh-face-less-social-barriers-now-bids-1659283

Reuters. (2020). *In China, airlines plug 'all you can fly' deals to pierce coronavirus clouds*. https://www.reuters.com/article/us-health-coronavirus-china-airlines-idUSKCN24T0H9

Rey-Martí, A., Tur Porcar, A., & Mas-Tur, A. (2015). Linking female entrepreneurs' motivation to business survival. *Journal of Business Research, 68*(4), 810–814. doi:10.1016/j.jbusres.2014.11.033

Rial, A., Rial, J., Varela, J., & Real, E. (2008). An application of importance-performance analysis (IPA) to the management of sport centres. *Managing Leisure, 13*(3/4), 179–188. doi:10.1080/13606710802200878

Ritchie, B. W., & Jiang, Y. (2019). A review of research on tourism risk, crisis and disaster management: Launching the annals of tourism research curated collection on tourism risk, crisis and disaster management. *Annals of Tourism Research, 79*, 1–15. doi:10.1016/j.annals.2019.102812

Rohm, A. J. (2001). *Channel strategy transformation within an Internet-enabled channels environment: Findings and implications across five firms*. University of Massachusetts Amherst.

Rooy David, L. V., Whitman, D. S., Hart, D., & Caleo, S. (2011). Measuring Employee Engagement During Financial Downturn: Business Imperative or Nuisance? *Journal of Business and Psychology, 26*(2), 147–152. doi:10.100710869-011-9225-6

Rosa, J. M., & Sylla, D. (2018). A comparison of the performance of majority female-owned and majority male-owned small and medium-sized enterprises. *International Journal of Entrepreneurship and Small Business, 35*(3), 282–302. doi:10.1504/IJESB.2018.095901

Rosenbloom, B. (2007). The wholesaler's role in the marketing channel: Disintermediation vs. reintermediation. *International Review of Retail, Distribution and Consumer Research, 17*(4), 327–339.

Rosenbloom, B. (2013). Functions and institutions: The roots and the future of marketing channels. *Journal of Marketing Channels, 20*(3-4), 191–203.

Roundy, P. T., Holzhauer, H., & Dai, Y. (2017). Finance or philanthropy? Understanding the motivations and criteria of impact investors. *Social Responsibility Journal, 13*(3), 419–512. doi:10.1108/SRJ-08-2016-0135

Roychowdhury, D. (2020). 2019 Novel coronavirus disease, crisis, and isolation. *Frontiers in Psychology, 11*, 1958. doi:10.3389/fpsyg.2020.01958 PMID:32849147

Sabatino, M. (2016). Economic crisis and resilience: Resilient capacity and competitiveness of the enterprises. *Journal of Business Research, 69*(5), 1924–1927. doi:10.1016/j.jbusres.2015.10.081

Sahithya, B. R., Kashyap, R. S., & Roopesh, B. N. (2020). Perceived stress, parental stress, and parenting during COVID-19 lockdown: A preliminary study. *Journal of Indian Association of Child Adolescent and Mental Health, 16*(4), 44–63.

Saks, A. M., & Gruman, J. A. (2014). What do we really know about employee engagement? *Human Resource Development Quarterly, 25*(2), 155–182. doi:10.1002/hrdq.21187

Salisu, I., Hashim, N., Mashi, M. S., & Aliyu, H. G. (2020). Perseverance of effort and consistency of interest for entrepreneurial career success: Does resilience matter? *Journal of Entrepreneurship in Emerging Economies, 12*(2), 279–304. doi:10.1108/JEEE-02-2019-0025

Sangwan, S. (2020, October 20). *Medtech startup InnAccel raises $1.5M in pre-Series A round led by Mount Judi Ventures*. Retrieved March 10, 2021, from https://yourstory.com/2020/10/funding-alert-medtech-startup-innaccel-mount-judi-ventures?utm_pageloadtype=scroll

Santeramo, F. G., Seccia, A., & Nardone, G. (2017). The synergies of the Italian wine and tourism sectors. *Wine Economics and Policy, 6*(1), 71–74. doi:10.1016/j.wep.2016.11.004

Santos, F., Pache, A. C., & Birkholz, C. (2015). Making hybrids work: Aligning business models and organizational design for social enterprises. *California Management Review, 57*(3), 36–58. doi:10.1525/cmr.2015.57.3.36

Sara, C., & Peter, R. (1998). The financing of male– and female–owned businesses. *Entrepreneurship and Regional Development, 10*(3), 225–242. doi:10.1080/08985629800000013

Saraff, S., Singh, T., & Biswal, R. (2021). Coronavirus disease 2019: Exploring media portrayals of public sentiment on funerals using linguistic dimensions. *Frontiers in Psychology, 12*, 626638. doi:10.3389/fpsyg.2021.626638 PMID:33679546

Sari, G. L., Hilmi, I. L., Nurdiana, A., Azizah, A. N., & Kasasiah, A. (2021). Infectious waste management as the effects of Covid-19 pandemic in Indonesia. *Asian J Soc Sci Manage Technol, 3*, 62.

Sarkar, B. (2020, April 9). Companies roll out initiatives to keep employees kids engaged at home. *The Economic Times*. https://economictimes.indiatimes.com/news/company/corporate-trends/companies-roll-out-initiatives-to-keep-employees-kids-engaged-at-home/articleshow/75058556.cms

Sarkis, J. (2020). Supply chain sustainability: Learning from the COVID-19 pandemic. *International Journal of Operations & Production Management*, *41*(1), 63–73. doi:10.1108/IJOPM-08-2020-0568

Sattar, A., Dewri, L., & Ananna, S. (2016). Working environment for women entrepreneurs in developing countries: An empirical study of Bangladesh. *International Journal of Business and Management*, *11*(12), 197. doi:10.5539/ijbm.v11n12p197

SBCB. (n.d.). *Timeline & History, Stanford Byers Center for Biodesign*. Retrieved March 10, 2021, from https://biodesign.stanford.edu/about-us/timeline.html

Schaufeli, W. B., & Bakker, A. B. (2004). Job demands, job resources, and their relationship with burnout and engagement: A multi-sample study. *Journal of Organizational Behavior*, *25*(3), 293–437. doi:10.1002/job.248

Schaufeli, W. B., Bakker, A. B., & Salanova, M. (2006). The measurement of work engagement with a short questionnaire: A cross-national study. *Educational and Psychological Measurement*, *66*(4), 701–716. doi:10.1177/0013164405282471

Shaikh, S. (2020). *Corona Virus spread not Just Epidemic, Pseudoscience has Made it a 'Misinfo. demic' Too*. https://theprint.in/opinion/coronavirus.not.just.epidemic.pseudoscience.has.m ade.it.misinfo.demic/357397/

Shammi, M., Behal, A., & Tareq, S. M. (2021). The escalating biomedical waste management to control the environmental transmission of COVID-19 pandemic: A perspective from two south Asian countries. *Environmental Science & Technology*, *55*(7), 4087–4093. doi:10.1021/acs.est.0c05117 PMID:33434001

Shareefdeen, Z. M. (2012). Medical waste management and control. *Journal of Environmental Protection*, *3*(12), 1625–1628. doi:10.4236/jep.2012.312179

Sharma, A., & Kochher, P. (2018). Taj hotels, Palaces and Resorts: The Road Ahead. *Emerald Emerging Markets Case Studies, 8*(3), 1-21. Retrieved on October 28, 2021, from https://www.emerald.com/insight/content/doi/10.1108/EEMCS-01-2018-0001/full/html

Sharma, M. (2021, January 23). *MindRush 2021: How companies 'rebuilt' businesses amid Covid-19 crisis*. Retrieved on December 5, 2021, from https://www.businesstoday.in /mindrush/mindrush-2021/story/mindrush-2021-how-companies-rebuilt-businesses-amid-covid-19-crisis-285284-2021-01-23

Sharma, D., & Kumar, V. (2017). A Framework for Collaborative and Convenient Learning on Cloud Computing Platforms. *International Journal of Web-Based Learning and Teaching Technologies*, *12*(2), 1–20. doi:10.4018/IJWLTT.2017040101

Shashidhar, A. (2018). Decoding the Patanjali phenomenon, will Patanjali Ayurveda be able to sustain its exponential growth? *Business Today (Norwich).*

Shenoy, S., Upadhyay, S., & Nair, P. (2021, October 18). *Lemon Tree Hotels expects pre-COVID level occupancies by Q4; says consumers preferring branded hotels*. Retrieved on October 31, 2021, from https://www.cnbctv18.com/hospitality/lemon-tree-hotels-expects-pre-covid-level-occupancies-by-q4-says-consumers-preferring-branded-hotels-11136032.htm

Sheoran, P. (2021). Prevalence of psychological distress among adolescents in relation to internet addiction during COVID-19 times. *IOSR Journal of Humanities and Social Science*, *26*(4), 46–52.

Sheoran, P. (2021a). Meditation as a therapeutic tool for boosting mental health during COVID-19 times. *SSRG International Journal of Humanities and Social Science*, *8*(2), 37–41.

Shiva Kumar, B. K., Mushtaq, N. F., Vinay, H. R., & Bramaramba, D. H. (2021). Depression, anxiety and stress among undergraduate medical students during COVID-19 pandemic. *International Journal of Scientific Research*, *10*(3), 56–58.

Shoma, C. (2019). Financing female entrepreneurs in cottage, micro, small, and medium enterprises: Evidence from the financial sector in Bangladesh 2010–2018. *Asia & the Pacific Policy Studies*, *6*(3), 397–416. doi:10.1002/app5.286

Shrotryia, V. K., & Dhanda, U. (2020). Exploring Employee Engagement Using Grounded Theory: Experiences from the Best Firms in India. *Vision (Basel)*, *24*(2), 171–183. doi:10.1177/0972262920915070

Shuck, B., Adelson, J. L., & Reio, T. G. Jr. (2017). The employee engagement scale: Initial evidence for construct validity and implications for theory and practice. *Human Resource Management*, *56*(6), 953–977. doi:10.1002/hrm.21811

Shuck, B., & Wollard, K. K. (2010). Employee engagement and HRD: A seminal review of the foundations. *Human Resource Development Review*, *9*(1), 89–110. doi:10.1177/1534484309353560

Shukla, M., Pandey, R., Singh, T., Riddleston, L., Hutchinson, T., Kumari, V., & Lau, J. Y. F. (2021). The effect of COVID-19 and related lockdown phases on young peoples' worries and emotions: Novel data from India. *Frontiers in Public Health*, *9*, 645183. doi:10.3389/fpubh.2021.645183 PMID:34095054

Siegner, M., Pinkse, J., & Panwar, R. (2018). Managing tensions in a social enterprise: The complex balancing act to deliver a multi-faceted but coherent social mission. *Journal of Cleaner Production*, *174*, 1314–1324. doi:10.1016/j.jclepro.2017.11.076

Sigala, M. (2020). Tourism and COVID-19: Impacts and implications for advancing and resetting industry and research. *Journal of Business Research*, *117*, 312–321. doi:10.1016/j.jbusres.2020.06.015 PMID:32546875

Singh, A., Gupta, K., & Yadav, V. K. (2021). Adopting e-learning facilities during COVID-19: Exploring perspectives of teachers working in Indian public-funded elementary schools. *Education 3-13 International Journal of Primary, Elementary and Early Years Education,* 1-15.

Singh, G., & Belwal, R. (2008). Entrepreneurship and SMEs in Ethiopia. *Gender in Management*, *23*(2), 120–136. doi:10.1108/17542410810858321

Singh, J., & Kumar, V. (2022). Combating the Pandemic with ICT Based Learning tools and applications: A case of Indian Higher Education. *International Journal of Virtual and Personal Learning Environments Platforms*, *12*(1), 1–21.

Singh, N., Tang, Y., & Ogunseitan, O. A. (2020). Environmentally sustainable management of used personal protective equipment. *Environmental Science & Technology*, *54*(14), 8500–8502. doi:10.1021/acs.est.0c03022 PMID:32597663

Singh, S., Mordi, C., Okafor, C., & Simpson, R. (2010). Challenges in female entrepreneurial development— A case analysis of Nigerian entrepreneurs. *Journal of Enterprising Culture*, *18*(04), 435–460. doi:10.1142/S0218495810000628

Singh, V., Poonam, & Behmani, R. K. (2020). Influence of food pattern on life of people during COVID-19 lockdown. *International Journal of Creative Research*, *8*(7), 4922–4941.

Skytrax. (2021). *Guangzhou BaiYun International Airport Receives the Highest 5-Star COVID-19 Airport Safety Rating*. https://skytraxratings.com/guangzhou-baiyun-international-airport-receives-the-highest-5-star-Covid-19-airport-safety-rating

Smallbone, D., & Welter, F. (2001). The distinctiveness of entrepreneurship in transition economies. *Small Business Economics*, *16*(4), 249–262. doi:10.1023/A:1011159216578

Smith-Hunter, A., & Boyd, R. (2004). Applying theories of entrepreneurship to a comparative analysis of white and minority women business owners. *Women in Management Review*, *19*(1), 18–28. doi:10.1108/09649420410518403

Sobaih, A. E., Hasanein, A. M., Elshaer, I. A., & Abdelaziz, A. S. (2021). Responses to COVID-19: The role of performance in the relationship between small hospitality enterprises' resilience and sustainable tourism development. *International Journal of Hospitality Management*, *94*(1), 102824. doi:10.1016/j.ijhm.2020.102824 PMID:34785841

Song, H., Livat, F., & Ye, H. (2019). Effects of terrorist attacks on tourist flows to France: Is wine tourism a substitute for urban tourism? *Journal of Destination Marketing & Management*, *14*, 100385. doi:10.1016/j.jdmm.2019.100385

Song, P., Wang, Q., Liu, H., & Li, Q. (2020). The value of buy-online-and-pickup-in-store in omni-channel: Evidence from customer usage data. *Production and Operations Management*, *29*(4), 995–1010.

Srivastava, A., Arya, Y. K., Joshi, S., Singh, T., Kaur, H., Chauhan, H., & Das, A. (2021). Major stressors and coping strategies of internal migrant workers during the COVID-19 pandemic: A qualitative exploration. *Frontiers in Psychology*, *12*, 648334. doi:10.3389/fpsyg.2021.648334 PMID:34093333

Stephen, A. T., & Toubia, O. (2010). Deriving value from social commerce networks. *JMR, Journal of Marketing Research*, (47), 215–228.

Su, M., Wang, Q., & Li, R. (2021). How to Dispose of Medical Waste Caused by COVID-19? A Case Study of China. *International Journal of Environmental Research and Public Health, 18*(22), 12127.

Suau-Sanchez, P., Voltes-Dorta, A., & Cugueró-Escofet, N. (2020). An early assessment of the impact of COVID-19 on air transport: Just another crisis or the end of aviation as we know it? *Journal of Transport Geography*, *86*, 102749. https://doi.org/10.1016/j.jtrangeo.2020.102749

Subagyo, K. V., & Ernestivita, G. (2020). Entrepreneurial Parameters and Performance of MSMEs in East Java Province of Indonesia. *International Journal of Business Innovation and Research*, *23*(2), 267–282.

Sudha, R., & Gayatridevi, S. (2021). Building psychological wellbeing through compassion focused therapy among COVID survivors. *Kalyan Bharathi, 24*(8).

Sultana, M. (2021, March 8). Women entrepreneurs get more than target from stimulus package for smaller units. *The Financial Express*. https://www.thefinancialexpress.com.bd/economy/bangladesh/women-entrepreneurs-get-more-than-target-from-stimulus-package-for-smaller-units-1615170323

Sultana, S. A. (2021, May 16). *Barely staying afloat: COVID-19 and women entrepreneurs in Bangladesh.* Development Policy Centre. https://devpolicy.org/barely-staying-afloat-covid-19-and-women-entrepreneurs-in-bangladesh-20210517/

Sultan, S., & Sultan, W. (2020). Women MSMEs in times of crisis: Challenges and opportunities. *Journal of Small Business and Enterprise Development*, *27*(7), 1069–1083. doi:10.1108/JSBED-06-2020-0226

Sun, Y. Y., & Drakeman, D. (2020). Measuring the carbon footprint of wine tourism and cellar door sales. *Journal of Cleaner Production*, *266*, 121937. doi:10.1016/j.jclepro.2020.121937

Surbhi, Yadav, N., & Kumar, A. (2021). An exploratory study to analyze the impact of COVID- 19 on the daily lives of people: A focus group discussion. In *Health Informatics and Technological Solutions for Coronavirus (COVID-19)*. New York: CRC Press.

Surbhi, K. A., & Yadav, N. (2021). Hidden power of being simple: Learnings during COVID-19. *Vidyabharati International Interdisciplinary Research Journal*, (Special Issue), 1276–1282.

Tafel, M., & Szolnoki, G. (2020). Estimating the economic impact of tourism in German wine regions. *International Journal of Tourism Research*, *22*(6), 788–799. doi:10.1002/jtr.2380

Talukdar, A. D. (2020, April 9). *5 tips for practicing employee engagement amidst the covid-19 pandemic.* Business 2 Community. https://www.business2community.com/human-resources/5-tips-for-practicing-employee-engagement-amidst-the-covid-19-pandemic-02300396

Tedeschi, R. G., & Calhoun, L. G. (2004). Posttraumatic growth: Conceptual foundations and empirical evidence. *Psychological Inquiry*, *15*(1), 1–18. doi:10.120715327965pli1501_01

Thakur, J., Singh, I., & Sethi, S. R. (2021). Role of Yoga and meditation for anxiety among working adults during COVID-19. *International Journal of Indian Psychology*, *9*(2), 128–135.

The Asia Foundation. (2021). *COVID-19 & the new normal for women in the economy in South Asia*. https%3A%2F%2Fasiafoundation.org%2Fwp-content%2Fuploads%2F2021%2F03%2FCovid-19-The-New-Normal-for-Women-in-the-Economy-in-South-Asia.pdf

The Economic Times. (2019). *Patanjali Ayurveda posts Rs 3,562 crore revenue for April–September, November 19*. https://economictimes.indiatimes.com/industry/cons-products/fmcg/patanjali-ayurved-posts-rs-3562-crore-revenue-for-april-september/articleshow/72126682.cms?from=mdr

The Economic Times. (2021). *Surging demand makes Ayurvedic stress busters the star category of second Covid wave*. https://economictimes.indiatimes.com/industry/cons-products/fmcg/demand-for-ayurvedic-stress-busters-surges-amid-second-wave-of-covid-19/articleshow/83492980.cms

The Economist. (n.d.). Biotechnology Saving Lives & Transforming Healthcare in the 21st Century. *The Economist Magazine*. Retrieved March 10, 2021, from https://archive.bio.org/TransformingHealthcare

The Hindu. (2020). https://www.thehindubusinessline.com/companies/capgemini-launches-employee-engagement-programmes-to-help-beat-coronavirus-stress/article31310564.ece

The Hindu. (2020a). *Patanjali to sell Coronil as 'immunity booster', not cure for COVID-19*. https://www.thehindu.com/news/national/patanjali-can-sell-its-drug-but-not-ascureto-covid-19-says-union-health-ministry/article31962529.ece

The Hindu. (2020b). *In rush for 'immunity', Ayurveda supplements have an untested run*. https://www.thehindu.com/news/national/coronavirus-ayurveda-supplements-see-sales-boost-despite-thin-research-evidence-on-efficacy/article32886185.ece

The Hindu. (2021). *COVID-19: People throng to buy Siddha drug kabasura kudineer*. https://www.thehindu.com/news/cities/chennai/covid-19-people-throng-to-buy-siddha-drug-kabasura-kudineer/article31225180.ece

The Print. (2020). *Alternate medicine manufacturers claiming Covid-19 cure could face year in jail*. https://theprint.in/india/governance/alternate-medicine-manufacturers-claiming-covid-19-cure-could-face-year-in-jail/393607/

ToI. (2021). https://timesofindia.indiatimes.com/city/bhopal/90-patients-who-got-fake-remedesivir-in-mp-beat-covid/articleshow/82642139.cms?utm_source=twitter.com&utm_medium=social&utm_campaign=TOIDesktop

Torres, A. P., Marshall, M. I., & Sydnor, S. (2019). Does social Capital pay off? The case of small business resilience after hurricane Katrina. *Journal of Contingencies and Crisis Management*, *27*(2), 168–181. doi:10.1111/1468-5973.12248

Torres, J. P., Barrera, J. I., Kunc, M., & Charters, S. (2021). The dynamics of wine tourism adoption in Chile. *Journal of Business Research*, *127*, 474–485. doi:10.1016/j.jbusres.2020.06.043

Tsai, P. P. (2020). *Information and FAQs on the Performance*. Protection, and Sterilization of Face Mask Materials.

Tse, A. C. B., So, S., & Sin, L. (2006). Crisis management and recovery: How restaurants in Hong Kong responded to SARS. *International Journal of Hospitality Management*, *25*(1), 3–11. doi:10.1016/j.ijhm.2004.12.001 PMID:32287848

Tyagi, G. (2021). How Oyo's revenue contracted from $1.8 Bn in FY20 to $850 Mn in FY21. *Fintrackr*. Retrieved from https://entrackr.com/2021/10/how-oyos-revenue-contracted-from-1-8-bn-in-fy20-to-850-mn-in-fy21/

Ukonu, O., & Tafamel, A. (2011). Problems, challenges and prospects of female entrepreneurs in Gwagwalada, Abuja. *African Research Review*, *5*(3). Advance online publication. doi:10.4314/afrrev.v5i3.67354

UNWTO. (2020). *UNWTO world tourism barometer*. UNWTO.

U, S.-C., & So, Y.-C. (2020). The impacts of financial and non-financial crises on tourism: Evidence from Macao and Hong Kong. *Tourism Management Perspectives*, *33*, 100628. Advance online publication. doi:10.1016/j.tmp.2019.100628

Vahali, H. O. (2021). Psychosocial challenges in the midst of the coronavirus. In C. R. Reddy (Ed.), *India and the pandemic: The first year* (pp. 275–283). Orient Black Swan.

Vaidya, A., Patil, A., & Vaidya, A. (2021). Perception of online education during the COVID- 19 pandemic in India. *International Journal of Creative Research Thoughts*, *9*(7), f8–f17.

Vander, E. T. (2016). Job demands-resources predicting burnout and work engagement among Belgian home health care nurses: A cross-sectional study. *Nursing Outlook*, *64*(6), 542–556. doi:10.1016/j.outlook.2016.06.004 PMID:27427405

Varma, R., Das, S., & Singh, T. (2021). Cyberchondria amidst COVID-19 pandemic: Challenges and management strategies. *Frontiers in Psychiatry*, *12*, 618508. doi:10.3389/fpsyt.2021.618508 PMID:33995143

Vashkov, V. I., Kareev, N. V., Ramkova, N. V., & Chudnova, L. B. (1974). A gaseous method for sterilizing medical instruments. *Biomedical Engineering*, *8*(6), 341–343. doi:10.1007/BF00566462

Velikova, N., Ghvanidze, S., & Mamardashvili, P. (2021). *Exploring the Role of Nostalgia in Wine Consumption: The Very Best of Georgia*. Academy of Wine Business Research.

Vivek, J. M., Singh, R., Sutar, R. S., & Asolekar, S. R. (2019). Characterization and disposal of ashes from biomedical waste incinerator. In *Advances in Waste Management* (pp. 421–435). Springer. doi:10.1007/978-981-13-0215-2_30

Walters, G., Wallin, A., & Hartley, N. (2019). The threat of terrorism and tourist choice behavior. *Journal of Travel Research*, *58*(3), 370–382. doi:10.1177/0047287518755503

Wang, J., Shen, J., Ye, D., Yan, X., Zhang, Y., Yang, W., Li, X., Wang, J., Zhang, L., & Pan, L. (2020). Disinfection technology of hospital wastes and wastewater: Suggestions for disinfection strategy during coronavirus Disease 2019 (COVID-19) pandemic in China. *Environmental Pollution*, *262*, 114665. doi:10.1016/j.envpol.2020.114665 PMID:32443202

Wan, Y. K. P. (2013). A comparison of the governance of tourism planning in the two special administrative regions (SARs) of China–Hong Kong and Macao. *Tourism Management*, *36*, 164–177. doi:10.1016/j.tourman.2012.12.005 PMID:32287740

Waste, B.-M. (Management and Handling) Rules of 2016. The Gazette of India, Extraordinary, Part II, Section 3(i). Central Pollution Control Board, India. Ministry of Environment, Forest and Climate Change, Notification. (2016). https://cpcb.nic.in/uploads/ Projects/Bio-Medical-Waste/ Bio-medical_Waste_Management_ Rules_2016.pdf

Weatherbee, T., Sears, D., & MacNeil, R. (2019). *Mapping wine business studies: Part 1. International Journal of Wine Business Research*. Academy of Wine Business Research.

WeConnect International. (2020). *Report urges escalated support to women-owned business during pandemic*. WeConnect International. https://weconnectinternational.org/report-urges-escalated-support-to-women-owned-business-during-pandemic/

Wellner, L., & Pierce-Friedman, K. (2019). The Types of Case Studies in Research and Career-Based Endeavors. In *Case Study Methodology in Higher Education* (pp. 83–108). IGI Global. doi:10.4018/978-1-5225-9429-1.ch005

Wen, J., Kozak, M., Yang, S., & Liu, F. (2021). COVID-19: Potential effects on Chinese citizens' lifestyle and travel. *Tourism Review*, *76*(1), 74–87. https://doi.org/10.1108/TR-03-2020-0110

WHO. (2020a). *Novel coronavirus (2019-nCoV) situation report – 1*. Available at: www.who.int/docs/defaultsource/coronaviruse/situation-reports/20200121-sitrep-1-2019-ncov.pdf?sfvrsn=20a99c10_4

WHO. (2020b). *Novel coronavirus (2019-nCoV) situation report – 11*. Available at: www.who.int/docs/ default-source/coronaviruse/situation-reports/20200131-sitrep-11-ncov.pdf?sfvrsn=de7c0f7_4

WHO. (2020c). *WHO characterizes COVID-19 as a pandemic*. WHO.

Williams, T., Gruber, D., Sutcliffe, D., Shepherd, D., & Zhao, E. (2017). Organizational response to adversity: Fusing crisis management and resilience research streams. *The Academy of Management Annals*, *11*(2), 733–769. doi:10.5465/annals.2015.0134

Wilson, D. (2021). *Navigating the Wine Involvement Continuum*. Academy of Wine Business Research.

Woelfert, F. S., & Kunst, J. R. (2020). How political and social trust can impact social distancing practices during COVID-19 in unexpected ways. *Frontiers in Psychology*, *11*, 572966. doi:10.3389/fpsyg.2020.572966 PMID:33381063

World Bank Group. (2019). *Financing solutions for micro, small and medium enterprises in Bangladesh*. The World Bank Group.

World Health Organisation. (2020). *WHO "Solidarity" Clinical trial for COVID 19 treatments*. https://www.who.int/solidarity-clinical-trial-for-covid-19-treatments

World Health Organization. (2020). *WHO, coronavirus disease (COVID-19) outbreak*. Available at: www.who.int/emergencies/diseases/novel-coronavirus-2019

Worldometers. (2021). https://www.worldometers.info/

Wut, T. M., Xu, J. B., & Wong, S. M. (2021). Crisis management research (1985–2020) in the hospitality and tourism industry: A review and research agenda. *Tourism Management*, *85*, 104307. doi:10.1016/j.tourman.2021.104307

Yadavar, S. (2018, September 6). *More Indians Die Of Poor Quality Care Than Due To Lack Of Access To Healthcare: 1.6 Million*. Retrieved March 10, 2021, from https://www.indiaspend.com/more-indians-die-of-poor-quality-care-than-due-to-lack-of-access-to-healthcare-1-6-million-64432/

Yang, Y., Ruan, Q., Huang, S., Lan, T., & Wang, Y. (2021). Impact of the COVID-19 outbreak on tourists' real-time on-site emotional experience in reopened tourism destinations. *Journal of Hospitality and Tourism Management*, *48*, 390–394. doi:10.1016/j.jhtm.2021.07.014

Yang, Y., Zhang, C. X., & Rickly, J. M. (2021). A review of early COVID-19 research in tourism: Launching the Annals of Tourism Research's Curated Collection on coronavirus and tourism. *Annals of Tourism Research*, *91*, 103313. Advance online publication. doi:10.1016/j.annals.2021.103313 PMID:34611371

Yeasmin, F., & Tasnime, Z. (n.d.). *Impact of Healthcare Related Plastic Waste Towards Sustainable Environment During Covid*. Academic Press.

Yin, R. K. (2009). *Case study research: Design and methods* (4th ed.). Sage.

Yin, R. K. (2011). Applications of case study research. *Sage (Atlanta, Ga.)*.

Yong, Z., Gang, X., Guanxing, W., Tao, Z., & Dawei, J. (2009). Medical waste management in China: A case study of Nanjing. *Waste Management (New York, N.Y.)*, *29*(4), 1376–1382. doi:10.1016/j.wasman.2008.10.023 PMID:19157838

York, J. G., & Venkataraman, S. (2010). The entrepreneur–environment nexus: Uncertainty, innovation, and allocation. *Journal of Business Venturing*, *25*(5), 449–463. doi:10.1016/j.jbusvent.2009.07.007

Yousuf Danish, A., & Lawton Smith, H. (2012). Female entrepreneurship in Saudi Arabia: Opportunities and challenges. *International Journal of Gender and Entrepreneurship*, *4*(3), 216–235. doi:10.1108/17566261211264136

Youth Business International. (2020). *Supporting small businesses to ensure the future of Bangladesh*. Retrieved August 2020, from Youth Business International: https://www.google.com/search?client=firefox-b-d&q=Youth+Business+International

Yunus, M. (2017). *Entrepreneurship: A Global Social Movement*. Sage Publications.

Zaman, T., & Sharma, S. (2021). Screen time, sleep quality and depressive symptoms during lockdown due to COVID-19. In *The new normal - psychological perspectives: Selected papers from Dr. MGR-Janaki College of Arts & Science for Women International E Conference 2021* (pp. 174-182). Academic Press.

Zhang. (2020, August 18). *Five strategies - A Perspective on China's civil aviation industry relief policy and proposed measures from airlines during COVID-19*. Aviation Think Tank. http://att.caacnews.com.cn/zkzj/Z/zy/202008/t20200818_56229.html

Zhao, Y., & Xu, H. (2020). *Chinese public attention to COVID-19 pandemic: based on social media*. doi:10.1101/2020.03.18.20038026

About the Contributors

Raj K. Kovid is Professor and Head of Department (General Management) in School of Business Studies at Sharda University, Greater Noida. He brings with him a rich working experience of over 25 years in teaching, research and industry. He has earned his PhD degree in the field of Mergers and Acquisitions and Masters in Business Management and Commerce. His teaching and research area includes Corporate Strategy, M&A, Global Strategy, Strategy for Platform Business, Entrepreneurship & Innovation, Corporate Governance & CSR. He has consulted firms with respect to their growth strategies. He has keen interest in the Case Method of teaching and research. He has published research papers and book chapters in journals of repute at national and international level. His cases are available in Harvard Business Publishing and has also conducted case method workshops. Dr. Kovid is regularly invited as an expert in various conferences and workshops.

Vikas Kumar received his MSc in Electronics from Kurukshetra University, Haryana, India. This was followed by M Sc in Computer Science and further PhD from the same university. He is a life member of Indian Science Congress Association, Computer Society of India, IETE, ICEIE, IPA, VEDA, IVS, and Magnetic Society of India. Along with 13 books, He has more than 100 research papers to his credit in various national and international conferences and journals. Presently, he is serving at Central University of Haryana, India and is a Visiting Professor at the Indian Institute of Management, Indore and University of Northern Iowa, USA.

* * *

Sabiha Abedin is a graduate student currently pursuing her MBA degree from the Institute of Business Administration, Jahanginagar University. With immense interest in social inclusion, development, and entrepreneurship, she aspires to facilitate learning through qualitative research.

Shivani Agarwal is an Assistant Professor, KIET School of Management at KIET Group of Institutions, Ghaziabad, India. She has earned her PhD from Indian Institute of Technology (IIT, Roorkee) in Management. She holds an MBA degree in HRM and IT from Guru Gobind Singh University, India and B.Sc. degree from Charan Singh University (formerly Meerut University), India. She is a recipient of prestigious UGC Junior Research Fellowship and has several years of experience as a faculty in management institutes.

Ameer Asra Ahmed hails from a family of educationists and holds an MBA degree specialising in the field of HR. She is currently working as an Assistant Professor in Dayananda Sagar College and also pursuing her PhD from Jain University, Bangalore. Her area of interest is in Organizational Behaviour and Human Resource Management. She has authored several original research papers in National & International journals and she is interested in Academics and Research and holds more than 10 best paper awards to her credit. She strongly believes that business schools should focus on inculcating a research culture among management students as most of the business problems in the current scenario can be overcome only through research.

Renu Bala is Assistant Professor in Mukhtiar Singh Memorial Degree College, Haryana. She has done MBA and PhD and has published various research paper in indexed journals as well as book chapters by reputed publications.

Sanjeev Bansal is Dean FMS & Director of Amity Business School, Amity University Uttar Pradesh. He is an admired academician with a Ph.D. and D. Litt degree. He has more than 211 research papers in prestigious journals to his credit and authored 44 books. He has successfully guided 27 research scholars to produce works of immense educational impact so far and eight scholars are working with him. He is on board of many National and International journal. He has been awarded Lifetime Achievement Award by GBIT and SIBF. He has also won Dr. Sarvepalli Radhakrishnan Lifetime Achievement National Award and Rashtra Ratan National Award by IRDP.

Ankur Budhiraja is working as a full-time faculty at JIMS, Greater Noida and has a total experience of 15 years in teaching students at the under graduate and post graduate levels. He has to his credit several research papers and articles published in different journals of repute. He completed his Ph.D. in the area of Experiential Marketing from IGNOU, New Delhi.

Saptarshi Dhar is an Assistant Professor at the Institute of Business Administration (IBA-JU), Jahangirnagar University, Bangladesh. Prior to joining Jahangirnagar University, she served as a faculty member at United International University. Her research interests include entrepreneurship and small business development, focusing on qualitative research. She is recognized for her work on entrepreneurs with disabilities in Bangladesh and for publishing research on entrepreneurship for persons with disabilities in national and international journals.

Tahira Farzana obtained her MBA degree from Institute of Business Administration, Jahangirnagar University, Bangladesh. Currently, she is working as Assistant Professor at Institute of Business Administration, Jahangirnagar University, Bangladesh. She has experience of 12 years in market and social research. Her major area of interest include social entrepreneurship, entrepreneurship development for physically challenged people, innovation and marketing. She has affiliation with physically development foundation (PDF) and social welfare club of Institute of Business Administration, Jahangirnagar University, Bangladesh.

Anu Gupta is working as Assistant Professor in Department of Environment Science and Engg. in Guru Jambheswar University of Science and Technology, Hisar. She received B Tech in Chemical Engineering from Punjab Technical University, Jalandhar, India and then M Tech in Polymers from the Panjab University, Chandigarh, India. She has worked in the area of sustainable composite materials for her doctoral thesis at Indira Gandhi National Open University, New Delhi, India. She has been a recipient of the prestigious NFP and DAAD fellowships. She has got Early Career Award in International Chemical Congress of Pacific Basin Societies (Pacifichem 2015), by the American Chemical Society. Dr. Gupta has been an active member of the International Union of Pure and Applied Chemistry, Indian Society For Technical Education, Society For Education & Research Development, Electrochemical Society (USA) and the International Association of Engineers. She has a number of research papers to her credit in the journals and has been serving on the editorial board of numerous international journals. Her areas of interest include the Sustainable Composite Materials, Sustainable building structures, Waste Management and Climate Change.

Manisha Gupta has over 12.5 years of experience in Academics and Teaching subjects like Marketing Management, Sales Management, Digital Marketing, Organizational Behaviour, Principles of Management, and Business Environment with Educational Qualification of B.Sc. and MBA (Marketing) from Dr. B.R. Ambedkar University Agra. Ph.D. from Sharda University Greater Noida and UGC (NET) Qualified. She is a recipient of the gold shield (International award for research 2020) from the Institute of Chartered Accountant of India ICAI. She had Published research Paper in various National and International Journals of repute, Chapters in

Books, and Presented Papers at various Conferences. She had completed a minor Project under the National Human Rights Commission (NHRC) on the topic "Vulnerability, legal protection and work conditions of Domestic Workers".

Rahul Gupta is an Associate Professor in the area of Marketing at Amity Business School, Amity University Uttar Pradesh. He is an MBA with a specialization in Marketing and a Ph.D. in Retail Management. He has also completed FDPM from IIM Ahmedabad. He carries over two decades of experience out of which 11 years were in corporate particularly in the area of Industrial Marketing & Sales covering organizations such as Magna Industrial Co. Ltd, Ador Fontech Ltd, and Sahara India Commercial Corporation Ltd.

Manuela Gutierrez-Leefmans is an Associate Professor at the Marketing Department of the Universidad de las Américas Puebla, México. Funded by CONACYT, she obtained her Ph.D. in Business and Management and MSc in Information Systems from the University of Manchester, UK. She worked for ten years in multinational companies in the food, shipbuilding, and pharmaceutical industries. She has held management roles in international business, supply chain, and marketing. Manuela was also involved in project management for information systems implementation, acting as E-Sourcing Manager for Latin America for a large multinational company. She has presented her work in diverse international conferences and published in international academic journals. Her main research interests are information systems, digital platforms, Internet strategy, business models, and innovation. She won the EFMD Case Writing Competition 2017 for her work in collaboration on continuous improvement. She is a member of the National System of Researchers of Mexico (Level 1).

Emanuela Hanes is an independent researcher. Her cooperations include the Vienna University FH BFI Campus Wien. Her research interests include China-EU business strategies, RegTech, FinTech, Cryptocurrencies, Geopolitics, Chinese Strategic Planning and Development Policies.

Reena Kovid is masters in human resources management and pursuing her doctorate program from Shobhit Institute of Engineering & Technology (deemed-to-be University), Meerut. Her area of interest includes organisation behavour, employee engagement, work engagement and leadership.

Eko Liao graduated from The University of Hong Kong with a PhD degree in Management. Her research interests include optimizing employees' personal thriving and work experiences at workplace, and how leaders and organizations facilitate building a contemporary work environment to enhance such experiences. Dr. Eko Liao teaches management related subjects in undergraduate & postgraduate levels (e.g., MBA, MSc, PhD), and for executive training programs.

Oly Mishra received the BBM degree from Andhra University and MBA (International Business) degree from GITAM University. She completed her Ph.D. in marketing from Andhra University in 2017. She was a Teaching Assistant at Andhra University from 2014 to 2017. Since 2017, she has been an Assistant Professor in Gayatri Vidya Parishad, followed by IILM Institute for Higher Education. She is presently working at GITAM University as an Assistant Professor in the Department of Marketing. She has published research papers in ABDC, and Scopus indexed journals. Her research interests include consumer behavior, online retail, frugal innovations, bottom-of-the-pyramid, sustainability, circular economy. Dr. Mishra was a recipient of the TEQIP Scholarship during 2014 – 17, while pursuing her doctoral studies.

Asiya Nasreen is associated with the Department of Social Work, Jamia Millia Islamia as Assistant Professor. She is PhD in Social Works from Jamia Millia Islamia. She has also done PG Diploma in Industrial Relations and Personnel Management from Bhartiya Vidya Bhawan, Delhi. Her area of interest is human resources management. She has written articles on areas touching HRM practice in journals of national and international repute as well as developed SLM and E-content.

Amit Kumar Pandey is an Associate Professor in the area of Marketing at Amity Business School, Amity University Noida, India. He is Ph.D. from Mahatma Gandhi Kashi Vidyapith Varanasi having profound experience of 19 years in Research, Corporate, Academics, Training and Development. Dr. Pandey has more than 65 research papers in referred National and International journals and 40 research paper presented by him in National and International conferences. Dr. Pandey is the author of 09 books. Apart from that he is regular contributor in various Hindi and English newspapers and magazines.

Harold Andrew Patrick is a qualified Industrial and organizational Psychologist with over three decades of Postgraduate teaching, corporate training and research experience. Presently Professor and Dean -Academics, CMS Business School, Jain (Deemed-to-be University). Former Senior Manager – Leadership and Organization Development, Infosys Leadership Institute, Infosys Limited. Professor and Head - Organizational Behaviour and Human Resource Management area, Institute of Management, Christ (Deemed-to-be University) for close to two decades. He is a member of the Academic Council of ISBR Business School, Bangalore, Member of the advisory board of IREU Tech education private limited, Bangalore and member of the Academic Council of Ramaiah Institute of Management, Bangalore. He has published extensively with over 80 plus articles in refereed and peer reviewed national and international journals with an h-index of 11 and i10-index 11. He has won more than a dozen best paper awards at International conferences. He is a resource person for many training programs for corporate and facilitated individual training modules for HAL, ABB, GMR, BPCL, HP, Infosys, and many small and medium scale organizations for entry level, junior level and middle level managers. He has trained for entry level, junior level and middle level managers on Personal effectiveness, interpersonal effectiveness, leadership, team building, mentoring, conflict management, motivation and commitment, communication skills, Effective presentation skills, Self-awareness, and other tailor made modules for both corporate clients and academic institutions. His facilitation process is based on research, using diagnostic tools and psychometric instruments, videos, cases studies, and introspective learning. His interest lies in Human Behaviour and its application at the work place and has trained extensively in these areas with working managers, faculty members, Christian leaders, educational leaders, business graduate and working students. Elected member of the Society for Industrial and Organizational Psychology (SIOP), USA.

Madhu Rani is an MBA with focus on marketing area. She is pursuing her doctorate program in management, from Sharda University, Greater Noida, India. Her focus area include marketing, digital marketing and market research.

Puja Roshani is an Assistant Professor in the KIET School of Management at KIET Group of institutions, Delhi-NCR, Ghaziabad and She is M.com, M.Phil. & PhD. She is engaged in teaching, research and consultancy assignments. She has around ten years of teaching experience and in handling various administrative as well as academic positions.

Parul Saxena, as an accomplished professional and academician, brings in 19 years of total experience out of which 8 years working for IT and IT Services companies based out of US/India, and over 10 years into academics. Presently working as Head of HR & OB Department, School of Business Studies, and also holding an additional charge of Vice- chairperson Career Counselling & Development Centre, Sharda University Greater Noida . Along with teaching HR specialization subjects, Dr. Saxena, also been actively involved in designing and conducting Personality Development and Orientation Programs for post graduate and graduate level students and guided numerous research students at Post Graduate level. As a prolific writer, Dr Saxena has presented several research papers at National and International conferences with special focus on issues such as Work- Life Balance, Gender Diversity, and Employee engagement and various other HR issues. An IIM Raipur Alumnus, she has also been part of the organizing committee of the national and international conferences and member of academic council at present and previous assignments. Dr Saxena is a Certified Assessor-PPA (Person Profile Analysis) a Certified Assessor in TeIQ Thomas International, UK. As a trainer, she has clocked in more than 1500 Hours of training in the last 2 years with ratings of 4.5/5 or above for National and International participants from countries such as Nigeria, Nepal, Burkina Faso, Cameroon, Ljubljana. She has also conducted and organised Faculty Development Program/ MDPs on soft skills, emotional intelligence and case study methods etc. for national and international clientele. She has several copyrights to her credit and 3 has got 3 patents published.

Shagun, an MBA in marketing, is pursuing her doctorate program in management on consumers' perception about do-it-yourself concept, from Sharda University, Greater Noida, India. Her focus area include marketing, healthcare sector.

Bhavna Sharma is an Assistant Professor in Department of Commerce, JIMS Engineering Management Technical Campus, Greater Noida. She is PhD in Finance with 11 years of teaching experience. She is a Member of the Editorial Board of 'The Journal of Business, Tourism, Public and Legal Management' published by Isabela State University, Philippines. She has to her credit two chapters, one article and nine papers in Scopus indexed and other reputed journals. She has presented 22 papers in various national and international conferences of repute at leading institutes like IIM Ahmedabad, University of Mumbai, University of Delhi, etc. She has organized and participated in many workshops, training programs, and conferences.

Shalini Singh, Assistant Professor in School of Commerce, Finance, and Accountancy, Christ University, is doctorate in Finance from Banaras Hindu University. She has work experience of around 10 years in the area of Finance and Accountancy. She has published good papers in Scopus Indexed & ABDC category Journals.

Rajesh Verma is Assistant Professor at FGM Government College Adampur, Haryana, India. He is masters and doctorate in psychology. His areas of academic interest include Cognitive Psychology, Statistical Analysis, and Psychometrics. He has published number of papers and chapters in journals and books at international level. He is a member of professional bodies such as Indian Science Congress Association and Haryana Psychological Association.

Minakshi Verma is a PhD student in the Department of Environmental Science & Engg. at Guru Jambheshwar University of Science & Technology, Hisar, Haryana (India). She did her master in Environmental Science from Central University of Haryana, Mahendragarh, Haryana. Present area of her research includes the hospital waste management and development of sustainable materials.

Amy (Yamei) Wang obtained her PhD in Management and Masters of Economics from the University of Hong Kong. She also holds a Bachelor of Commerce (Marketing) from the University of British Columbia. She has taught previously at the University of Hong Kong and the Community College of City University. In addition to teaching, Dr Wang's research interests include social exclusion, prosocial behaviours, group dynamics and social information processing. Her teaching interests include management related subjects at both the undergraduate and graduate level such as Business Policy and Strategy, International Business, Asian Family Business, China Business and Principles of Management.

YuHan Wang is an independent researcher. Her research interests include FinTech, Chinese economy and business analytics.

Poshan (Sam) Yu is a Lecturer in Accounting and Finance in the International Cooperative Education Program of Soochow University (China). He is also an External Professor of FinTech and Finance at SKEMA Business School (China), a Visiting Professor at Krirk University (Thailand) and a Visiting Researcher at the Australian Studies Centre of Shanghai University (China). Sam leads FasterCapital (Dubai, UAE) as a Regional Partner (China) and serves as a Startup Mentor for AIC RAISE (Coimbatore, India). His research interests include financial technology, regulatory technology, public-private partnerships, mergers and acquisitions, private equity, venture capital, start-ups, intellectual property, art finance, and China's "One Belt One Road" policy.

Cheryl Qianru Zhang is currently an Assistant Professor at the School of Business in Macau University of Science and Technology, located in Macau SAR China. She has earned a Ph.D. in Law from Macau University of Science and Technology. She gets the Legal Professional Qualification Certificate in the People's Republic of China. Cheryl's teaching areas include commercial law, corporate governance, and the legal environment of business.

Index

H

I

L

M

O

P

R

S

T

V

W

www.ingramcontent.com/pod-product-compliance
Lightning Source LLC
LaVergne TN
LVHW080333021026
849160LV00028B/1239
9781668435052